I0533280

PRAISE FOR A CHRISTIAN THEOLOGY OF BUSINESS OWNERSHIP

Bill English has written an important and unusual book. Instead of settling for business to be made "Christian" simply through personal witness and charitable giving, he has infused scriptural teaching and guidance into all areas of business ownership. Note to readers: Please don't miss two critical sections — one on Covenants and the other on Leadership. Both are worth the price of the book!

Rick Mattson serves an Evangelist/Apologist for InterVarsity's Graduate-Faculty Ministries on college campuses.

In this book, Bill English offers a comprehensive guidebook for Christian business owners that provides a Biblical perspective on many of the common issues business owners face. Readers will be challenged to increase their knowledge and application of Scripture as is relates to being a faithful steward of what God has entrusted to them. This book will remain on the shelf being frequently referred to as a trusted resource for purposeful and faithful business ownership.

Andy Schwandt, MBA, Broker, Sunbelt Business Advisors and True North M&A

A Christian Theology of Business Ownership is a must-read for Christian entrepreneurs seeking to integrate faith with business. With wisdom from experience and Scripture, the author challenges conventional thinking, offering a theologically grounded approach to leadership and stewardship. This book is about transformation, calling, and faithfulness to God's purpose, a powerful guide for business owners and leaders alike."

Dr. Paul D. Miantona, MBA, MAFM, DBA, Christian Business Owner,
PNM Foundation Executive Director & Adjunct Professor, Saint Mary's University

A lot of books claim to mix Christian faith with business, but most just slap a few Bible verses onto regular business advice. Bill takes a completely different approach—he starts with our relationship with God and builds a real, thoughtful theology that makes business owners think about faith first, before business. He challenges us to put God's kingdom ahead of personal gain, even when it's tough. Bill also takes common business ideas and runs them through the filter of Biblical wisdom, helping Christian business owners understand what God expects from us. Is this book long? Yes. Is it a careful read? Definitely. It's not about feel-good stories—it's about deep, meaningful growth. If you're serious about honoring God in your business, take your time with this book over the next few months. You won't regret it.

Jon McTaggert, Christian, Business Owner, CEO, and Strategic Advisor

A CHRISTIAN THEOLOGY OF BUSINESS OWNERSHIP

AN INTRODUCTION FOR CHRISTIAN ENTREPRENEURS ON WHAT THE BIBLE SAYS ABOUT OWNING A BUSINESS

Bill English

Bible & Business
Own with purpose. Live with faith.

A Christian Theology of Business Ownership
An Introduction for Christian Entrepreneurs on What the Bible Says About Owning a Business

Print Version Paperback ISBN 9798218627898
Print Version Hardback ISBN 9798218627881
Cover and interior design by Kingdom Covers.

BIBLE AND BUSINESS

Clarity where there is confusion.
Direction where there is aimlessness.
Purpose where there is triviality.
Confidence where there is hesitation.
Hope where there is discouragement.

Clarity. Direction. Purpose. Confidence. Hope.

Own Purposefully. Live Faithfully.

CONTENTS

DEDICATION

To Kathy
Many women do noble things, but you surpass them all.
(Proverbs 30:29 NIV)

A LEGACY FOR MY CHILDREN

David and Anna
I love you more than life itself.

Every word of God is flawless.
(Proverbs 30:5 NIV)

COMMONLY USED UNCITED ABBREVIATIONS

ANE	Ancient Near East
CBO	Christian business owner
CEO	Chief Executive Officer
CFO	Chief Financial Officer
COO	Chief Operating Officer
cf	Latin: confer, conferature; English: compare
EBITDA	Earnings before interest, taxes, depreciation, and amortization
e.g.	Latin: exempli gratia; English: for example
et al.	Latin: et alia; English: and others
ff	Latin: flavia felix; English: and the following pages, paragraphs, etc.
GRC	Governance, Risk, and Compliance
Ibid	Latin: ibidem; English: in the same place
i.e.	Latin: id est; English: that is (used to clarify the statement before it.
ND or n.d.	No date
NP or n.p.	No page number(s)
NT	New Testament
OT	Old Testament
SA	Latin: sin auctore; English: no author
SD	Latin: sine data; English: no date
USD	United States Dollars
VP	Vice President
vs/vss	verse/verses

LIST OF TABLES

LIST OF FIGURES

COMMONLY USED CITED ABBREVIATIONS

Scripture quotations marked ASV are from the Authorized Standard Version. This Bible is in the public domain in the United States.

References marked BDAG are from Arndt, William, Frederick W. Danker, Walter Bauer, and F. Wilbur Gingrich. *A Greek–English Lexicon of the New Testament and Other Early Christian Literature*. Chicago: University of Chicago Press, 2000.

References marked BDB are from Brown, Francis, Samuel Rolles Driver, and Charles Augustus Briggs. *Enhanced Brown–Driver–Briggs Hebrew and English Lexicon*. Oxford: Clarendon Press, 1977.

References marked CSB are from the Christian Standard Bible®, Copyright © 2017 by Holman Bible Publishers. Used by permission. Christian Standard Bible® and CSB® are federally registered trademarks of Holman Bible Publishers.

References marked DBL are from Swanson, James. *Dictionary of Biblical Languages with Semantic Domains: Greek (New Testament)*. Logos Research Systems, Inc., 1997.

References marked EDNT are from v Balz, Horst Robert, and Gerhard Schneider. *Exegetical Dictionary of the New Testament*. (Eerdmans, 1990).

CORE PRINCIPLES

Biblical wisdom expresses the whole of Scriptural teaching on a given topic and informs the steward of the beliefs, thoughts, actions, and attitudes God expects from the steward.

Success is defined as faithfulness to God and perseverance in obedience because that is how success is defined in the Bible. Success is never defined in monetary terms in the Scriptures.

Christian business owners have a unique stewardship responsibility to steward well a business God has entrusted to them. Corollary: Ministry and church leaders have a nearly identical responsibility to steward their ministries and churches well because God has entrusted those organizations to them.

Christian business owners willingly disadvantage themselves to advantage the Kingdom of God.

You cannot have the best of God and the best of this world. Eventually, God will force you to choose one or the other. Corollary: You cannot serve God and money.

Christian business owners live with an eternal perspective derived from the owner's covenant with God and lived out through Biblical stewardship.

The dysfunction of an owner's personality will be imprinted onto his business, but the results will often be viewed as a business problem to solve instead of a personal problem the owner needs to address.

Even the best management teams can only do so much to compensate for the owner's dysfunctions. If the owner doesn't "shore up" deficits in his personality, the business will be permanently injured and constrained in growth, profits, and mission fulfillment.

WHY?

SOMEONE ONCE WROTE, "Start with Why."[1] So, here's my 'why'.

When I was the majority owner of a rapidly growing software training business, I increasingly wondered why God was giving me a business generating more cash than I had ever seen before. Why would God provide a former psychologist with an advanced theology degree a highly profitable software training business? How did psychology, theology, and business integrate? I knew the dots connected, but I did not know how.

So, I began a quest to learn and understand what the Bible said to me, a business owner, about my role as a *Christian* business owner (CBO). Since I am a writer, I decided to codify what I was learning, first in blog posts and then later in a publishable book format.

I read several books but could find no one who had written what I was after: a coherent theology on what the Bible said about my role as a business owner. To my surprise, no one had delved into this topic. There was growing content on integrating faith and business, but no one focused on faith and business *ownership*. This reality remains surprising since *profitable businesses ultimately support all churches and nonprofit organizations*. But alas, no such book existed.

Roughly twenty years ago, I was given two days at *Forge Ministries*[2] to have an evaluation done of my person and work. The focus was to understand God's call on my life. The result helped set the trajectory for my life. My call was "to deliver a transformational message to business." I had a murky idea of what this meant but little insight into how it would be accomplished. Looking back, I realize this book is part of living out God's call on my life.

From start to finish, it has taken me ten years to write this content after spending ten to twelve years in the "school of hard knocks." I was an inexperienced business owner filled

---

1   Simon Sinek, *Start with Why: How Great Leaders Inspire Everyone to Take Action.* (Penguin Books, 2009).

2   https://www.forgeforward.org/

with pride. God took me through very deep waters to get my attention. I wrote this book out of experience as much as the study of the Bible.

After making more mistakes than a guy should be allowed to make, I self–published *A Christian Theology of Business Ownership* under the Bible and Business imprint. Soon after that publication, I realized the book's organization was not logical. It was poorly edited, not well researched, and I was too "chatty." Much of the book didn't make sense and didn't flow well. It had some bright spots, but it was not the serious book I had hoped it would be.When the opportunity to do more research on Christian business ownership in a PhD program became available, I applied and was accepted.[3] The program allowed me to rework much of the content in the first version of my book and learn more about what the Bible says about the role of a business owner. At my professor's suggestion, my dissertation was titled the same as my first book, *A Christian Theology of Business Ownership*.[4] The book you are holding is a compilation of my first book, my dissertation, and more content I have written to "round out" this book's scope of content.

Over the years, I have owned a counseling practice, a software training business, a software implementation consulting business, and a business advisory business. At the time of this writing, I own a coaching business just getting off the ground (onpathcoaching. com). I have also served as interim CEO for a warehouse/distribution business, a retail firearm business, and a healthcare company. I have managed businesses with as little as $100K and two employees and as large as $25M with 550 employees.

No mistake can be made as a business owner or a leader that I have not already made. I know what it is like to be swimming in so much cash that knowing what to do with it all is difficult. I also know what it is like to wake up in a panic at 3 am on a Thursday, knowing there will not be enough money for Friday's payroll. I know what it's like to lead a business when key employees dislike you. I know the highs of success and the lows of failure. I have experienced a depression that didn't lift for several months, yet I still had to put on a happy, confident face. I have been knocked down more than several times. The only reason I am here today is because, by the grace of God, I got up one more time. Persistence can be a blessing and a curse.

I know what it is to cry out to God in despair because that is the only thing left to do. I know what it is to feel the loneliness of ownership, the insecurity of silent staff, and the pressure of choosing which vendors to pay and which ones to stretch. I know the joy of having a great partner(s) and the unending agony of an abusive partner who engages in inappropriate and unprofessional behavior while others look the other way. I've had to go

---

3　This program was offered through the International Business Relations Network, a partner with Kairos University. You can learn more at https://ibr–network.com/ and https://kairos.edu. For those who want a fully accredited degree that is a research-only, dissertation-only degree in business, I highly recommend IBR.

4　Read my dissertation at Academia.edu: https://www.academia.edu/122417108/Bill_English_Dissertation_A_Christian_Theology_of_Business_Ownership

to God again and again to find the strength and love to forgive those who have abused and betrayed me. Forgiveness is not reconciliation. Some relationships should end.[5]

I also understand what it means to have God convict you of sin in your darkest moments and the freedom that comes from confession and repentance. I know what it is to feel the comforting presence of God in the quiet of an early morning and gain strength from a deeply nested peace that makes no sense. I understand the strength of knowing that God will not let me go. He will not let me down. He *will* provide what I *need*. Fear melts in the promise of God's provision.

I've developed life-giving, close friendships through business. These friendships have taught me more than I can ever repay. Some fantastic, wonderful Christians work in business, and I love them dearly.

My story is not finished. And I am far from perfect. I have not arrived. But I have learned from God and his word. I hope that through appropriate transparency with you, the reader, you can look at snippets of my life and learn from them. You will find those snippets on the pages of this book.

I hope others use my work here to expand, modify, deprecate, or extend the discussions and conclusions about integrating business ownership and Christian theology. Even if there grows a broad consensus that my thinking or methodology is off-base, at least the debate will have been engaged, and others will be weighing in on this vitally important topic.

---

5   Henry Cloud, *Necessary Endings: The Employees, Businesses, and Relationships That all of Us Have to Give Up in Order to Move Forward.* (HarperCollins, 2010).

PREFACE

THE PURPOSE OF this book is to demonstrate two claims. First, I want to establish that Biblical theology[6] has unique applications for a business owner. Second, I want to demonstrate that much of what is taught in the current business literature needs to be filtered through Biblical theology before a Christian business owner can adopt modern advice without hesitation.

I am firmly convinced that God intended to guide us in every area of life and every role we would assume through his written word. This guidance includes the role of business ownership in for-profit businesses.

As I write this text, I have many books on my shelves written by Christians for Christian business owners (CBO). In nearly all of them, the starting point for their discussions has been American business principles. After discussing the business principle(s), the authors "Christianized" their discussions by referencing a few Biblical passages. The result is an American view of integration covered in a patina of Christian jargon.

---

6   In academic circles, the phrase "Biblical theology" means different things to different scholars. For example, Hamilton suggests that Biblical theology is the interpretive perspective of the Biblical writer (James M. Hamilton Jr., *What Is Biblical Theology?: A Guide to the Bible's Story, Symbolism, and Patterns.* (Crossway. Kindle Edition), 16.). For Osborne, Biblical Theology is about tracing themes to develop a unifying theme across the Bible (Grant R. Osborne, "Biblical Theology," in Baker Encyclopedia of the Bible (Baker Books, 1988), 339.). Carson readily admits there is no common definition of Biblical theology and suggests that "in one sense, wherever there has been disciplined theological reflection on the Bible, there has been a *de facto* Biblical theology." (D.A. Carson, "Systematic Theology and Biblical Theology." In *New Dictionary of Biblical Theology*, edited by T. Desmond Alexander and Brian S. Rosner, Electronic ed. (InterVarsity Press, 2000), 90ff.). For purposes of this book, the phrase "Biblical theology" will refer to the fruit of the exegesis of various Biblical texts that speak to a common theme or category.

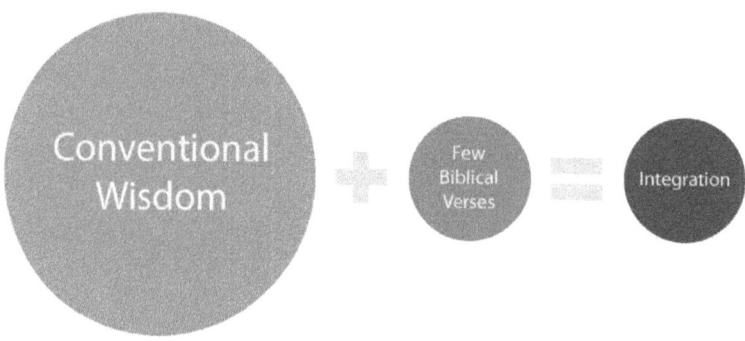

Figure A: Outsized use of Conventional Wisdom to achieve integration with Christian theology.

It isn't that the starting point (starting with American business principles) is wrong. Instead, I contend that these well-meaning authors have reversed the filtering process. They have emphasized the wrong corpus. Yes, they should understand what the current business literature—what I will call *conventional wisdom*—teaches about a given topic. However, conventional wisdom should be filtered through a careful study of what the Bible says—what I will call *Biblical wisdom*—to inform the CBO about what to do or think. The essence of Biblical wisdom can be stated as follows:

> *Biblical wisdom expresses the whole of Scriptural teaching on a given topic and informs the steward of the beliefs, thoughts, actions, and attitudes God expects from the steward.*

Biblical wisdom is authoritative for the CBO because it derives from Scripture, our final authority for life and practices. Biblical wisdom gives the CBO practical skills and understanding to live a life pleasing to God.[7] At best, conventional wisdom is suggestive and can be ignored or embraced from an integration perspective because man, as a source of truth, can be deceived in what truth is. Moreover, as often as not, men's opinions can be as harmful as they might be helpful in a given situation.

In many chapters, I will briefly enumerate a high-level review of conventional wisdom on the chapter's topic. Then, I will pay more attention to what the Bible says about that

---

7   Shields, Martin A. "Wisdom." In *The Lexham Bible Dictionary*, edited by John D. Barry, David Bomar, Derek R. Brown, Rachel Klippenstein, Douglas Mangum, Carrie Sinclair Wolcott, Lazarus Wentz, Elliot Ritzema, and Wendy Widder. (Lexham Press, 2016), [Wisdom].

topic and apply what we learn to the CBO's role as an owner. This book will demonstrate that *today's conventional wisdom for business is usually godless, meaning that conventional wisdom does not account for the existence and impact of one's covenant with God. However, the godless aspect of conventional wisdom does not automatically render conventional wisdom useless or necessarily opposed to God.* Instead, conventional wisdom is usually incomplete for the CBO who wishes to please God in the owner's stewardship and covenant roles.

Hence, a critical task in this book will be to contrast Biblical wisdom with conventional wisdom and surface how conventional wisdom should be adopted when filtered through Biblical wisdom. In filtering conventional wisdom, a Biblical view may sometimes modify, deprecate, or add to what conventional wisdom suggests. A Biblical view may radically conflict with conventional wisdom or merely embrace and extend it. Figure B illustrates how conventional wisdom is filtered through Biblical Wisdom.

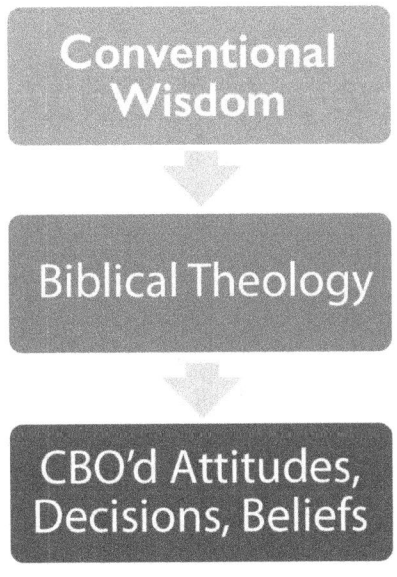

Figure B: Conventional Wisdom Filtered Through Biblical Wisdom

Conventional wisdom is not to be jettisoned simply because it is godless.[8] In many situations, much good can be gleaned from conventional wisdom. However, a CBO must subordinate conventional wisdom to Biblical wisdom due to the absolute authority of the Scriptures in the believer's life.

My claims are not new insights about Biblical theology. But I do offer, perhaps, fresh integrations with Scripture for business owners. I have approached this endeavor asking God

---

8   In the context above, *godless* is not a value or moral assessment, it is merely descriptive.

for the humility necessary to offer these integrations to academic and retail communities. To the extent these integrations draw you closer to Jesus Christ and help you better image his character and persona to a lost and dying world, then I am grateful to God for using this material positively in your life.

Who we are as business owners, what we believe, and the decisions we make *matter*. In writing this book, the vision I have for Christian business owners is:

- Transformation, not only education
- Think theologically first, professionally second

This book is only one tool in a larger discipleship effort. If a CBO reads this book and it is helpful toward

- allowing the Holy Spirit to transform his or her actions, attitudes, affections, and decisions into healthy obedience to the commands of God, and
- learning to filter all of life through Biblical wisdom,

then I will consider that outcome "success." Learning without transformation is dry academics. Thinking professionally before one thinks theologically results in a business–first, Christ–second mentality. We have enough academics in this country. We have enough conventional wisdom that encourages us to put our work and business ahead of all else. We have too many Christians with a rationalistic, Western view of Christianity that gives lip service to the transforming power of Christ while living like skeptics.[9]

Transformation will result in a CBO carefully following God's commands without becoming legalistic. He will understand that the physical reality of what is in front of him pales when compared to the unseen spiritual reality that impacts his daily business and life. And if a critical mass of CBOs are transformed, then that reality will help set the table for revival in this country.

This book is not about how to get rich, how to unlock "secrets of success,"[10] or how to have all of God and all the world offers simultaneously. Becoming wealthy should not be a goal in your life or mine. I have met countless business owners who sincerely want to walk closely with God *and* earn millions in wealth. The insidious corruption of our motivations when a desire for wealth is present is so subtle and destructive that I feel it is better not to desire wealth in the first place.

In addition, I am not convinced that from a motivational viewpoint, both can be pursued without eventually having to choose one or the other (Matthew 6:19–24). We

---

9   Michael Heiser, The Unseen Realm: Recovering the Supernatural Worldview of the Bible. (Lexham Press, 2015), 16.

10   The idea of secrets in the Bible contradicts the Clarity of Scripture, which is discussed in Chapter 7, *The Six Characteristics of Scripture.*

are to seek the kingdom of God first (Matthew 6:33), without equivocations, caveats, or additions.

In this book, success is defined as faithfulness to God and perseverance in obedience because that is how success is defined in the Bible. In this book, success is never defined in monetary terms.

This definition of success is one of many examples of how a CBO needs to think theologically before thinking professionally. Having our minds transformed (Romans 12:2) to the point where we think theologically first means that we have spent quality time studying the Bible. Hence, it is important that I outline the relationship I will assume exists between the CBO and the Bible.

WHO IS THE AUDIENCE FOR THIS BOOK?

I wrote this book primarily for the Christian business owner who owns a for-profit business. The business size (either in revenue or number of employees) does not matter since the topics presented are size-agnostic.

However, there are several secondary audiences. For example, Christian colleges and universities with business degree programs may find adding this book to their content helpful. The book can certainly be used to help prepare Christians whom God has called to the marketplace.

In addition, a business owner's skills and problems are sometimes very similar to those encountered by a ministry leader. Hence, a secondary audience for this book is ministry leaders, executive pastors, and those called by God to enter full–time vocational ministry. Christian colleges and seminaries may find adding this book to their content helpful. This book can certainly be used to help prepare those whom God has called to ministry environments.

THE OPPORTUNITY

What is the estimated reach of Christian business owners in the United States marketplace? Happily, the Census Bureau[11] publishes numbers that help us quantify our opportunity.

---

11   Census Bureau, "2021 SUSB Annual Data Tables by Establishment Industry." Accessed 05/04/2024. https://www.census.gov/data/tables/2021/econ/susb/2021–susb–annual.html.

At this time, the latest figures from the Census Bureau come from 2021. These figures are depicted in Table A, *2021 Summary Numbers of Businesses.*

Table A: 2021 Summary Numbers of Businesses

Enterprise Size	Firms	Establishments	Employment	Annual Payroll ($1,000)
Total	6,294,604	8,148,606	128,346,299	8,278,573,947
<5 employees	4,009,508	4,019,061	6,178,498	344,920,532
5–9 employees	1,021,829	1,036,956	6,726,092	301,779,028
10–19 employees	636,541	671,679	8,559,070	400,743,270
<20 employees	5,667,878	5,727,696	21,463,660	1,047,442,830
20–99 employees	519,015	689,604	20,219,046	1,077,643,283
100–499 employees	88,023	365,365	17,268,572	1,103,595,973
<500 employees	6,274,916	6,782,665	58,951,278	3,228,682,086
500+ employees	19,688	1,365,941	69,395,021	5,049,891,861

Taking the numbers at face value, we have approximately 4 million business owners managing just under 6 million employees in businesses with four or fewer employees. Enlarging our scope, if we merge all the businesses with fewer than one hundred employees, we have approximately 6.2 million businesses that employ 41.6 million people and supply an annual payroll of nearly $2.1 trillion.

Suppose we assume a Christian business ownership rate of 35 percent (roughly one–third) for all businesses with 500 or fewer employees. This supposition means there are ~2.2 million CBOs in the United States. Divide 2.2M by 3,300 counties (roughly the number of counties in the United States), and there are, on average, 668 businesses owned by Christians in each county. This figure represents a significant entrustment by God to CBOs who operate daily in the marketplace.

If this country is going to experience revival toward God, business owners will need to be included as one of several key demographics because of our reach into the marketplace.[12] CBOs

---

12   By contrast, there are only ~400,000 churches in the United States (and that figure is generous), or ~121 churches per county. (Rebecca Randall. "How Many Churches Does American Have? More Than Expected." September 14, 2017. Christianitytoday.com, https://www.christianitytoday.com/news/2017/september/how–many–churches–in–america–us–nones–nondenominational.html.) There are ~5x the number of for–profit businesses owned by Christians than churches in the United States.

who obey God's commands (outlined in this book) will have a better platform to give the Spirit permission and a foothold to introduce the unsaved to Christ.

USE OF THE MALE PRONOUN

In American society, the use of pronouns has become a divisive and toxic topic that can create all sorts of unwarranted assumptions about others that only lead to misunderstandings and conflicts. Writing a book requires the use of pronouns. In the first draft, I used both genders and alternated when I felt it was warranted. But then I began to think that some might be offended by a particular use of one gender or the other in a given part of the book.

I want to draw people in, not push them away. But toss in the over 70 different genders some communities espouse,[13] and the entire situation becomes unworkable. We have created an unwinnable situation for ourselves.

So, I decided to mirror what God did: Jesus was a male, presented as a male, and lived as a male. Why God chose Christ to incarnate as a male instead of a female is a question you all can ask him when you get to heaven. Because I am a Christ–follower, I will use the male pronoun throughout this book because Christ is a man and lived as a man.

The use of the male pronoun is *only* a grammatical decision, it is *not a value or political* decision. The use of the male pronoun in no way suggests *any* bias or misogyny in my beliefs, attitudes, or emotions toward women. I just need a way to talk about a Christian business owner using a pronoun. That is all. Please do not read anything more into using the male pronoun than what I have stated here. I understand and support women owning businesses. Women are no more and no less capable than men to start, grow, lead, and operate businesses. There is nothing in Scripture to preclude women from owning and running businesses, and contra some evangelicals,[14] Christians should whole heartedly support women in business ownership.

HOW TO BECOME A CHRISTIAN

If you are unsure whether you are a Christian, I invite you to read through Bill Graham's *Steps to Peace with God*. These simple steps will help you know God and enter a covenant relationship with him. This book will not make much sense to you until you enter a covenant relationship with God and are transformed by the power of his spirit.[15]

---

13   Shaziya Allarakha, "What are the 72 Other Genders?" February 9, 2024. Medicinenet.com. https://www.medicinenet.com/what_are_the_72_other_genders/article.htm

14   Jessica Eturralde, "John Piper's Position that Women Should Not Lead Parachurch Organizations Sparks Controversy." June 30, 2023, julieroys.com. https://julieroys.com/john-pipers-position-women-should-not-lead-parachurch-organizations-sparks-controversy/

15   Billy Graham, "Steps to Peace with God." Accessed 07/04/2024. Billygraham.org. https://memorial.billygraham.org/steps–to–peace/

TENANTS OF FAITH

I am serving as an Elder in an Evangelical Free Church at the time of this writing. The Evangelical Free Church of America (EFCA) is an association of ~1,600 congregations united around a Statement of Faith[16] and committed to certain distinctives.[17] The church in which I serve is located in Minnesota. I personally align with the EFCA statement of faith (SOF) and our distinctives. These core beliefs, while not directly discussed in this book, are foundational to the theology discussions I engage in this book. For example, concerning the Holy Spirit, the EFCA believes that

> The Holy Spirit, in all that He does, glorifies the Lord Jesus Christ. He convicts the world of its guilt. He regenerates sinners, and in Him they are baptized into union with Christ and adopted as heirs in the family of God. He also indwells, illuminates, guides, equips and empowers believers for Christ–like living and service.

I believe what the EFCA has written, not because the EFCA wrote it, but because this is all taught in the Bible. I will *assume* these and other truths but not discuss them directly.

There is a lack of discussion about these and other core theologies because this book is not intended to be a systematic theology but rather a Biblical theology concerning business ownership, written by a Christian business owner for Christian business owners.

---

16   Evangelical Free Church of America, "EFCA Statement of Faith." Accessed 07/04/2024. Efca.org. https://www.efca.org/sof

17   Evangelical Free Church of America, "Distinctives of the Evangelical Free Church of America." Accessed 07/05/2024. https://www.efca.org/distinctives/

INTRODUCTION TO THE CHRISTIAN BUSINESS REFERENCE ARCHITECTURE

THE CHRISTIAN BUSINESS Reference Architecture (CBRA) has informed my thinking about integrating business and theology for nearly twenty years. However, I admit this bridge was built from the business side of the river. I have modified this model several times. What is presented here is a working model that is subject to being updated as I learn more and have new insights.

Trying to organize discussions that apply Biblical doctrine to a CBO's role using traditional systematic theology categories makes little sense. For example, how would one discuss the Biblical commands to not exploit one's employees by unfairly withholding compensation using traditional systematic theology categories? This example is one of the numerous examples I could give to show that how we think about business—the categorical and hierarchial structures we use today—do not align neatly with standard ways of thinking about theology. Perhaps one can appreciate the problem of how to organize discussions designed to apply Biblical theology to the role of a business owner and the daily decisions a business owner faces.

In dedicating my life to integrating Christian theology and business ownership, I have found it is generally best to use a business-oriented epistemology to organize integrative discussions that apply Biblical theology to business ownership. This book is my attempt to diffuse Biblical theology across business ownership topics while subordinating ownership activities and decisions to the commands of God.

WHAT IS A REFERENCE ARCHITECTURE?

A reference architecture is a document or set of documents an interested party can refer to as a blueprint for developing a new hypostasis based on the architecture.[18] An 'architecture' is "The fundamental organization of a system embodied in its components, their relationships to each other and to the environment and the principles guiding its design and evolution."[19]

WHAT A REFERENCE ARCHITECTURE IS NOT

A reference architecture differs from capabilities, standards, and business architectures and is neither a 'capability' nor a 'standard.' These concepts are expanded upon below:

A reference architecture is not a capability. A capability is an ability or a capacity to achieve a specific purpose or outcome.[20] A reference architecture surfaces that which implementers should consider as they develop their capabilities to further the organization's goals. A reference architecture does not assume any particular capabilities by the implementer. It merely informs the implementer of *what* needs to be considered as the implementer implements a new technology or process.

A reference architecture is not a standard. Similarly, a reference architecture is not a matrix of standards. A standard is a clear definition of a level of quality to attain. Standards can exist within each component of the architecture to inform the implementer of the desired quality level that should be achieved as the implementer is implementing each part of the reference architecture. However, the standards do not originate within the reference architecture; they are layered on top of it.

A reference architecture is not a business architecture, though it is similar. When a reference architecture is applied to creating a business model, it may be confused with a business architecture. A business architecture describes how "an organization uses its essential competencies for realizing its strategic intent and objective."[21] The reference architecture utilized in this book does not inherently assume that the elements presented within it represent essential competencies that every business must possess. Instead, the reference architecture in this research paper merely alerts the business owner that these elements must be considered as the owner constructs an optimal business model and core processes for achieving the aims of the proposed enterprise.

---

18   Muller, G. 2020. *A Reference Architecture Primer.* University of South-Eastern Norway-NISE (Version 0.6)

19   Hilliard, R. 2000. *Recommended Practice for Architectural Description of Software-Intensive Systems.* 04/07/2023, Ieee.org. http://standards.ieee.org, 2000–pdfs.semanticscholar.org.

20   The Open Group. 2016. Open Business Architecture (O-BA) – Part I. Reading, United Kingdom.

21   Ibid, 5.

A reference architecture is not a process. A process usually has inputs, outputs, tasks, and decisions that must be executed in order. Processes can be layered on top of a reference architecture, but a reference architecture is not a process.

A reference architecture is not a business operating system. A business operating system is merely a collection of processes that form a well-run organization.[22] It is a collection of tools and methods that are used throughout the organization as a way to standardize how tasks are completed. For example, many business owners enjoy using the Entrepreneurial Operating System (EOS).[23] EOS and other operating systems can be layered on top of a business reference architecture, but the architecture itself is not an operating system.

I have used this CBRA to operate several different businesses, including:

A software training business.

A business that sourced products out of Asia, warehoused those products in Minneapolis and distributed those products across the United States.

A firearm range with retail sales.

A home care business that provides medical and non-medical care to over 600 patients.

THE CBRA EXPLAINED

The CBRA has three essential layers to it. Figure C illustrates the conceptual layers of the CBRA using a minimalistic view. Figure D offers a more detailed view of the CBRA. One can discern how the three conceptual layers in Figure C are expanded in Figure D. Even though the bottom layer comprises half of the architecture, both in complexity and visually, it is the least important layer when considering the purpose of integrating Christian theology and business ownership.

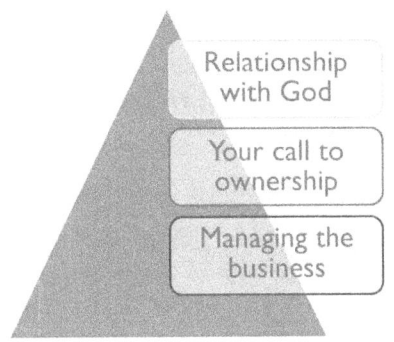

Figure C: Conceptual Layers of the CBRA

---

22   O'Donnell, M. 2018. *What is a Business Operating System and Why Do You Need One?* 04/28/2024, linkedin.com. https://www.linkedin.com/pulse/what-business-operating-system-why-do-you-need-one-mark-o-donnell/

23   Information about EOS is available from https://www.eosworldwide.com/. Accessed 04/28/2024.

Christian Business Reference Architecture

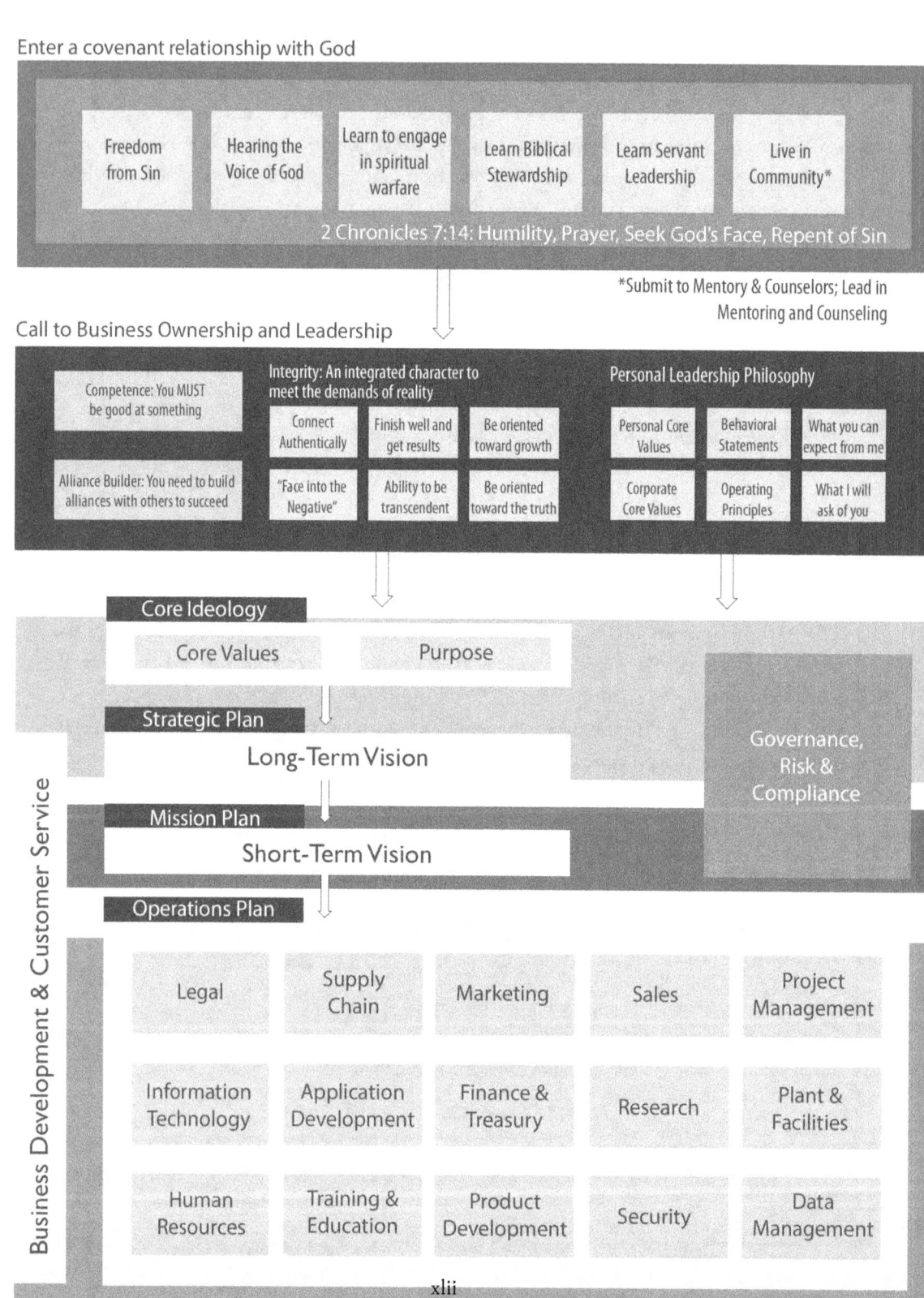

Enter a covenant relationship with God

Freedom from Sin	Hearing the Voice of God	Learn to engage in spiritual warfare	Learn Biblical Stewardship	Learn Servant Leadership	Live in Community*

2 Chronicles 7:14: Humility, Prayer, Seek God's Face, Repent of Sin

*Submit to Mentory & Counselors; Lead in Mentoring and Counseling

Call to Business Ownership and Leadership

Competence: You MUST be good at something

Alliance Builder: You need to build alliances with others to succeed

Integrity: An integrated character to meet the demands of reality

| Connect Authentically | Finish well and get results | Be oriented toward growth |
| "Face into the Negative" | Ability to be transcendent | Be oriented toward the truth |

Personal Leadership Philosophy

| Personal Core Values | Behavioral Statements | What you can expect from me |
| Corporate Core Values | Operating Principles | What I will ask of you |

Core Ideology

Core Values   Purpose

Strategic Plan

Long-Term Vision

Mission Plan

Short-Term Vision

Governance, Risk & Compliance

Operations Plan

Business Development & Customer Service

Legal	Supply Chain	Marketing	Sales	Project Management
Information Technology	Application Development	Finance & Treasury	Research	Plant & Facilities
Human Resources	Training & Education	Product Development	Security	Data Management

xlii

God's Purposes for Business:

1. Enable community flourshing products (productivity)
2. Enable creative work (innovation)
3. Subdue the earth (management)
4. Provide dignity through work (purpose)
5. Create profit and wealth (giving and rest)

Purposes in Balance
- Profits are created for transcendent purposes
- Wisdom is to be desired more than wealth
- If you pursue righteousness, you will be satisfied
- Save your soul, not your wallet
- Flourishing products are righteous products
- Creative work aligns with passions and talents
- Subduing the earth is to steward the earth
- Purpose is given when ddirectives allow for creativity and productivity
- Profits are necessary and goodd
- Profits myst be balanced with other purposes

Business Ownership is outgrowth of Persona and Calling

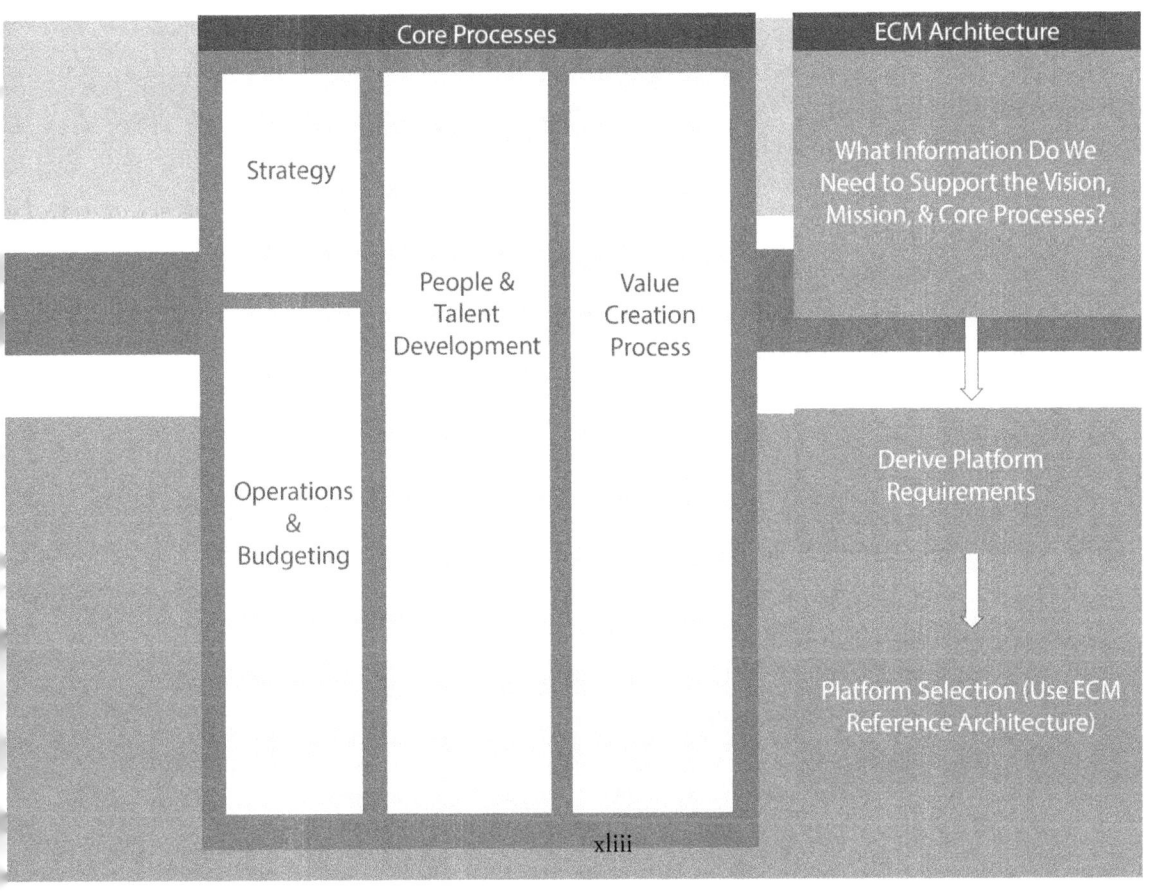

xliii

Previous two pages:
Figure D: Christian Business Reference Architecture[24]

Christian business owners have a *unique stewardship responsibility that no one else has to steward well a business God has entrusted to the owner.* The uniqueness of responsibility is derived from ownership.

Any owner of any item or entity has a stewardship responsibility to the Lord to steward and manage that entity or item well. For example, when one owns a house, a car, or a business, God has granted ownership to that individual for that house, car, or business. When ownership is given, a unique stewardship responsibility is created. If my neighbor owns a house, I'm not responsible to God for the stewardship of that house. If my friend owns a second home on the beach, I'm not accountable to God for how my friend stewards that home. But if God gives me a business to own, then I—and no one else—am responsible to God for how my business is run.

Business owners have an immense responsibility to produce wealth for God's kingdom on this earth. Individually, business owners are responsible for stewarding the health of their employees, customers, partners, vendors, and stakeholders well. Integrating Biblical wisdom is foundational to stewarding well God's entrustment of a business to you. If you don't know the Bible, you'll not have the knowledge to integrate, even if you want to. The CBRA assists the CBO in understanding all of the areas that should be considered when building a new business and integrating Christian theology into one's role as an owner. The CBRA does not describe the integrating theology but points out the areas in which the owner needs integration.

CBRA layer one discussion

From the CBRA itself, layer one (Relationship with God) is depicted in Figure C. You will notice that the first layer, which is the upper layer in this architecture, is focused on the owner's relationship with God, freedom from sin, and, more generally, who the owner is as a person.

The core topics of layer one include:
- Entering a covenant relationship with Christ
- Finding freedom from sin
- Hearing the voice of God
- Learning to engage in spiritual warfare
- Learning the basics of Biblical stewardship
- Learning servant leadership

24   Contact Bill English at bill@bibleandbusiness if you want a poster-sized print out of the CBRA. Note that this is a working document, so future versions may change without notice.

Having worked with numerous business owners over the years, I have observed that some have significant dysfunction in their personalities and yet build successful businesses despite themselves. Their dysfunction becomes imprinted on their businesses through process and culture compensations, which create secondary problems that the owner and top-level managers must manage.

When I refer to "compensations," I do not mean monetary compensation. Instead, I am referring to actions employees must engage in to counteract, neutralize, correct, or offset the dysfunction or abnormalities in the owner's personality. Another way to state this compensating activity is that a counterbalance must be applied in the culture and processes to minimize the harmful effects of the owner's personality deficiencies.

Others in the company bring their dysfunctions into the organization, but they lack the position and power to affect the organization system-wide with their dysfunction.[25] Only the owner(s) have company-wide influence.

The owner's lack of accountability to anyone allows their dysfunction(s) to worsen and harden as the years go by. In family businesses, their dysfunction(s) sometimes drives away their children, who would rather go and do "their own thing" than work for their father or mother. When the business is finally sold or passed to the second generation, the culture is so hardened in its dysfunction that the new leaders and owners often need 2-4 years to "re-do" the company's processes and culture. The company must unlearn and undo what has been baked into the culture and processes to become healthier and more profitable.

The results of the owner's dysfunction are usually viewed as a business problem to solve rather than a personal problem the owner needs to shore up. However, those owners who are secure enough to look at themselves and hear constructive criticism about their personalities have unique opportunities to build outstanding businesses that honor God and further God's kingdom.

CBRA layer two discussion

This layer calls out the CBO's call to ownership and considers the owner's leadership capabilities. Following the general outline of Henry Cloud's book,[26] this layer suggests the following must be true for a CBO to be successful in fulfilling God's purposes for business:

- Competence: you must be good at *something*
- Alliance builder: you must be able to build alliances inside and outside your business
- Character: you must have the skills to resolve conflict, get results, and focus on the truth

25 Yet it must be recognized that the 'higher' a person resides in an organization, the more likely it is that this individual's dysfunction will be imprinted onto a wider scope of the business.

26 Henry Cloud. *Integrity: The Courage to Meet the Demands of Reality.* (HarperCollins, 2006).

- Leadership: you must understand your strengths and challenges as a leader, and you must be able to articulate your leadership philosophy to your employees and stakeholders

CBOs who cannot build alliances usually have businesses that stagnate under $10M in revenue (the vast majority under $5M). Building alliances with key employees means diffusing decision-making authority for hire/fire, contracting, compensation, or spending decisions. Owners who cannot build internal alliances lack trust in other's abilities and usually hold grandiose evaluations of their abilities. If you are a CBO and most of the decisions in your company route through you, then you are *the* problem in your organization's growth. You need to get out of your own way.

Top talent is rarely found in companies whose owners cannot build alliances. Top talent will leave for opportunities where they can exercise the full range of their skills and abilities. They want challenging work that makes a difference and keeps them informed, with purpose and values aligned, and they do not want to be micromanaged.[27] If top talent is given a job with a fancy title but without the commensurate authority and resources to do the job they were hired to do, they will leave for a better employer.

For example, I know of a $400M privately held company whose sole owner will not let his President, CFO, or VP of Sales make compensation changes or hire/fire decisions for anyone in the company. All compensation and hire/fire changes route through this owner, no matter how small. As a result, some employees skilled in negotiating for themselves have made side deals with the owner that undermine the authority and effectiveness of the President, CFO, and VP of Sales. Their authority and effectiveness are diminished because they cannot hold accountable key employees who have made individual compensation deals with the owner, yet the owner holds these three accountable for the productivity and financial performance of these key employees.

This owner has watched top talent leave the President, CFO, or VP of Sales positions *repeatedly* to work for his competitors, yet this owner does not connect his inability to create internal alliances with the revolving door in these leadership positions. This owner does not understand the conflicts that are created by his side deals. He does not have a clear leadership philosophy on which his employees can rely. He lacks emotional intelligence regarding his employees but is highly gifted at numbers, finding profit in deals that most others miss, and charming customers.

---

27   Heidi Lynne Kurter, "4 Things Top Talent Looks for in a Company When Interviewing." August 31, 2021. Forbes.com. https://www.forbes.com/sites/heidilynnekurter/2021/08/31/4-things-top-talent-l ooks-for-in-a-company-when-interviewing/. See also Patty Silbert, "What Top Talent Wants from Their Employer," January 25, 2024. Aspirant.com. https://www.aspirant.com/blog/what-top-talent-wants. Finally, take a look at Ben Wigert, "The Top 6 Things Employees Want in Their Next Job," February 21, 2022. Gallup. com. https://www.gallup.com/workplace/389807/top-things-employees-next-job.aspx.

Layers one and two focus entirely on your work and persona, the CBO. If you are out of balance, your business will be too. What you do, say, and believe *will be* imprinted onto your business. ***The problems you have in your business are often a mirror of your mental and emotional dysfunctions.*** If you commit to allowing God to heal your dysfunctions through counseling or coaching,[28] you will find that over time, your business will function better, be healthier, and have employees and customers who want to stay with your business for years.

James encourages us to look at ourselves.

Christian business owners need to become the most emotionally and psychologically healthy group of business owners worldwide. Why? Because we can allow the Holy Spirit to transform us from the inside out (Romans 12:1-2). Consider how James states this truth:

> [22] But be doers of the word, and not hearers only, deceiving yourselves. [23] For if anyone is a hearer of the word and not a doer, he is like a man who looks intently at his natural face in a mirror. [24] For he looks at himself and goes away and at once forgets what he was like. [25] But the one who looks into the perfect law, the law of liberty, and perseveres, being no hearer who forgets but a doer who acts, he will be blessed in his doing. (James 1:22-25 ESV)

To "hear" the word means to "do" the word: "It is not listening to the word that James opposes or diminishes, but *merely* listening."[29]

Obedience is the practice of following rules or commands.[30] Interestingly, the primary Hebrew word (שָׁמַע, šāma, "to hear") for those living in Semitic times would have included the concept of obedience. While Western thinking stresses the exercise of the intellect and tends to bifurcate hearing and doing, Hebrew thinking emphasizes that a person has not truly taken what was heard into one's heart until what was heard is placed into

---

28 I coach faith-based business owners. You can reach me at onpathcoaching.com.

29 Douglas J. Moo. *The letter of James*. The Pillar New Testament Commentary. (Eerdmans; Apollos, 2000), 88.

30 Faithlife, "Obedience," *Logos Bible Study Factbook*. (Faithlife, 02/24/2024.) https://ref.ly/logos4/Factbook?ref=bk.%25obedience.

verifiable practice.[31] Stewards are expected to hear and put into practice the commands of God.

Christian business owners who do not take time to look at themselves and be accountable to others in business and life are not living out well this James 1:22-25 passage.

CBRA layer three discussion

Layer 3 is focused on the business itself. This layer is where most MBA[32] programs will focus. This layer focuses on core ideology, mission, vision, strategy, GRC,[33] core processes, ECM[34] architecture, business development, customer service, and all the facets of operations.

Parts of layer three are discussed directly in the Scriptures, but most will rely on the application of Scripture to the business context. For example, the Bible does not speak to the topic of marketing, but it does have much to say about truthfulness in speech and deception of one's fellowman. So, a good portion of integration occurs when traditional Scripture commands are applied in an untraditional business context, which can create interesting outcomes.

In this book, I will only scratch the surface of what could be researched and applied. Some topics will get copious page space. Others will not be addressed due to any number of reasons. But I hope that more thought leaders who traffic at the intersection of Christian theology and business ownership will take what I have done here and extend it with their work.

THE POSITIVE USES OF THE BRA

It is not assumed that every business will implement every part of the CBRA at the same intensity or a similar quality level. For example, a business that delivers health care to seniors will have very different complexities in finance and treasury than a business that teaches grade-school children how to play basketball. Both will need a measure of accounting, but the capabilities needed for healthcare accounting will far exceed those required for the basketball training business. The CBRA can be helpful to both businesses, but how much attention is paid to each part of the architecture will be different across different businesses.

---

31   Lois A. Tverberg. *Listening to the Language of the Bible: Hearing it Through Jesus Ears.* (En-Gedi Resource Center, 2006), 3-4.

32   Master of Business Administration.

33   Governance, Risk, and Compliance.

34   Enterprise Content Management

The reference architecture surfaces the natural ebb and flow of undercurrents inherent within business model changes because a change in one area will affect another. More art than science, the CBRA can help surface those cause-effect relationships at a business model level simply by asking, "If a change is made in this area, how will that change affect other areas of the business?" Like a mobile hanging over a baby's crib, when a change is made in one part of a business, the CBRA will help the owner understand how that change will affect other parts of the business.

There are several reasons to engage a business reference architecture by a business owner. The following explains the positive use of a business reference architecture.

Using a reference architecture as a diagnostic tool: The BRA surfaces the natural ebb and flow of undercurrents inherent within business model changes because a change in one area will affect a change in other areas. More art than science, the BRA can help surface those cause-effect relationships at a business model level simply by asking, 'If a change is made in this area, how will that change affect other areas of the business?' Like a mobile hanging over a baby's crib, when a change is made in one part of a business, the BRA will help the owner understand how that change will affect other parts of the business.

An owner can layer specific management models on top of the architecture. The BRA leaves it to the owner to decide which strategy and tactics to employ as the owner manages the business. The BRA is agnostic when developing management strategies or tactics. For example, the owner could use the Entrepreneurial Operating System (EOS) to implement management practices or use a different system, such as the OGSM model[35] to achieve similar ends. The BRA will support the EOS, OGSM, and other strategies and operational models. Selection of a model for managing a business's operations, developing the business's long-term and short-term goals, and mitigating risk are all left to the business owner's discretion.

The BRA can form the organization of integrative research efforts in academia. The BRA can be used as a research organization tool for integration research efforts. For example, the BRA could be used by psychologists to ask the question, "What does the current psychological literature say about human resources, finance, or the purpose in business?" A Christian theologian could use the BRA to organize theological discussions about different parts of a business. For example, a Christian theologian may ask, "What does the Bible say about Governance, Risk, or Compliance?"

CBRA APPLICATION

Christian education programs could use the CBRA to inform themselves about how small and medium-sized businesses operate while maintaining a strong focus on developing the character and persona of the business student. Because the CBRA connects the student's

---

35   Objectives, Goals, Strategies, and Measurements. https://en.wikipedia.org/wiki/OGSM

faith and business operations, more effective Bachelor's and Master's programs that integrate business and Christian theology could be developed that offer a more holistic approach to higher education. These programs would be well-positioned to incorporate the character and spirituality of the business student with the development of business knowledge and skills.

Figure E illustrates the potential integration a Christian education program could achieve even with minimal use of the CBRA. But the effort expended by faculty and researchers focused on integration would need to be increased in order to realize the vision of better integration. I hope God calls me to lead the founding of Bible and Business as a 'think tank' that focuses on this kind of research and then demonstrates through education the transforming power of his word, integrated with one's profession, on the lives of CBOs and the markets they serve. But as of yet, God has not released me to do this work. I have the vision, but not the call. So I'll wait until he moves me. You never want to get ahead of God's timing. Read the sections on selfish vs. Godly ambition. Then you'll know what I'm talking about.

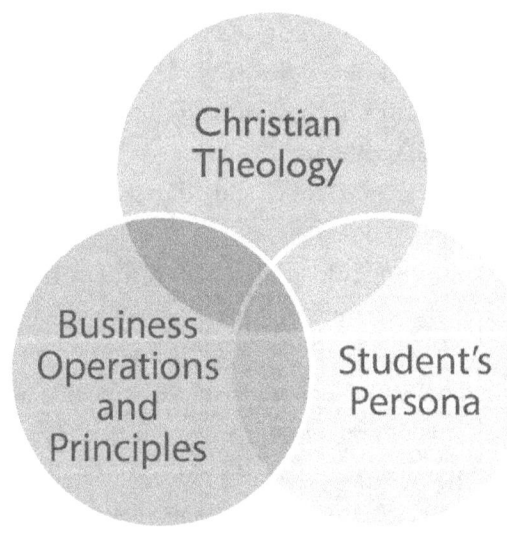

Figure E: Integration of Christian Education Programs using the CBRA

BOOK ORGANIZATION AND FLOW

Recall that the purpose of this book is to demonstrate two claims:
- To establish that there is a theology of business ownership that has many applications to the role of a business owner.

1

- To demonstrate that much of what is taught in the current business literature is incomplete from a Christian worldview and needs to be filtered through Biblical theology

Hence, this book is divided into two parts. The first part will outline the theological foundation for Christian business ownership. The second part will apply theology derived from exegesis to everyday decisions that owners face regularly.

From the CBRA's viewpoint, the book's first part discusses the owners' stewardship and persona, which is a combination of the first and second layers of the CBRA. Then, this book discusses selected parts of layer three in the second part.

Integrated throughout this book are considerations that will briefly discuss one or more the four areas below. After over thirty–five years of starting, growing, and leading businesses, I have concluded these four areas are important to a business owner's success. An owner must "get it right" in each area if the owner will successfully steward a business as God intends.

Character. Character refers to the moral and ethical features we possess.[36] We can grow into mature characters by drawing close to God or stagnate in our character by harboring sin or being lukewarm toward God.

Beliefs. Belief is an acceptance that something is true or exists.[37] What we believe is lived out every day. You may not tell me your thoughts, but I can discern your beliefs by watching what you do.

Decisions. Decisions are a deliberate act of one's will.[38] Decisions constantly emit from our beliefs. In the context of this book, most decisions discussed will have to do with issues of morality or sanctification.[39]

Finishing well. Finishing well brings fulfillment to your work and closes that business owner chapter in your life.[40] How a business owner finishes is the greatest challenge that owner will face. It is also the owner's greatest opportunity to craft his legacy and set a precedence on how future generations will pass the torch in a family business. Finishing well is about getting important decisions right and is usually the culmination of many decisions over many years.

---

36   Faithlife, "Character." In *Logos Bible Study Factbook*. (Faithlife, October 10, 2024.) https://ref.ly/logos4/Factbook?id=ref%3abk.%25character.

37   Faithlife, "Belief." In *Logos Bible Study Factbook*. (Faithlife, October 10, 2024.) https://ref.ly/logos4/Factbook?id=ref%3abk.%25belief.

38   Faithlife, "Decision." In *Logos Bible Study Factbook*. (Faithlife, October 10, 2024.) https://ref.ly/logos4/Factbook?id=ref%3abk.%25decision.

39   "Sanctification is the ongoing supernatural work of God to rescue justified sinners from the disease of sin and to conform them to the image of his Son." (Faithlife, "Sanctification." In *Logos Bible Study Factbook*. (Faithlife, October 10, 2024.) https://ref.ly/logos4/Factbook?id=ref%3abk.%25sanctification.)

40   Faithlife, "Finish." In *Logos Bible Study Factbook*. (Faithlife, October 10, 2024.) https://ref.ly/logos4/Factbook?id=ref%3abk.%25finish.

PART I

THE THEOLOGICAL FOUNDATION TO BUSINESS OWNERSHIP

THIS SECTION DIVES into the tangent planes between Biblical theology and the role of a business owner. The results of these discussions will demand certain attitudes, beliefs, and actions from a business owner if that owner will honor God professionally and personally.

Chapter 1, *The Six Characteristics of Scripture*, outlines what the Bible and what it claims about itself. Because the Scriptures are so visceral to the theses of this book, it is best to have an introduction to the characteristics of Scripture and why the Bible is so important to our Christian faith.

Chapter 2, *Covenants and Business Ownership*, argues for a Biblical center for business ownership, Biblical Stewardship, and Biblical wisdom. I will stress the importance of Biblical covenants to business ownership and differentiate between covenants and modern-day contracts.

In Chapter 3, *Stewardship and Entrustments,* I will discuss the two core elements of stewardship and entrustments within our covenant with God and then highlight associated aspects of covenant, including love, presence, faithfulness, and perseverance.

In Chapter 4, *Contentment and Ambition,* I focus on the fundamental elements of contentment and Godly ambition. It might appear that ambition is the antithesis of

3

contentment, but this is not so. I discuss the temptation of selfish ambition and define what Godly ambition looks like in the real world.

In Chapter 5, *Preparation for Eternity*, I discuss the truth that our lives can be preparatory for reigning with Christ in eternity. Nothing is wasted in God's economy, including our experiences of learning to live in covenant with God while living on this earth.

In Chapter 6, *Our Identity in Christ*, I discuss our need to view ourselves first as God views us. Our identity should be wrapped up in Christ first and only. Our role as business owners is an entrustment and while a small portion of our identity is connected to that role, our primary identity is shaped by God's transformation of us into a new creation.

In Chapter 7, *Listening to God*, I discuss the ways God communicates with us, which forms the channels through which we listen. If we do not hear from God, it is not because he isn't communicating with us.

The topics discussed in these six chapters form the theological foundation for Christian business ownership. Figure F illustrates this foundation.

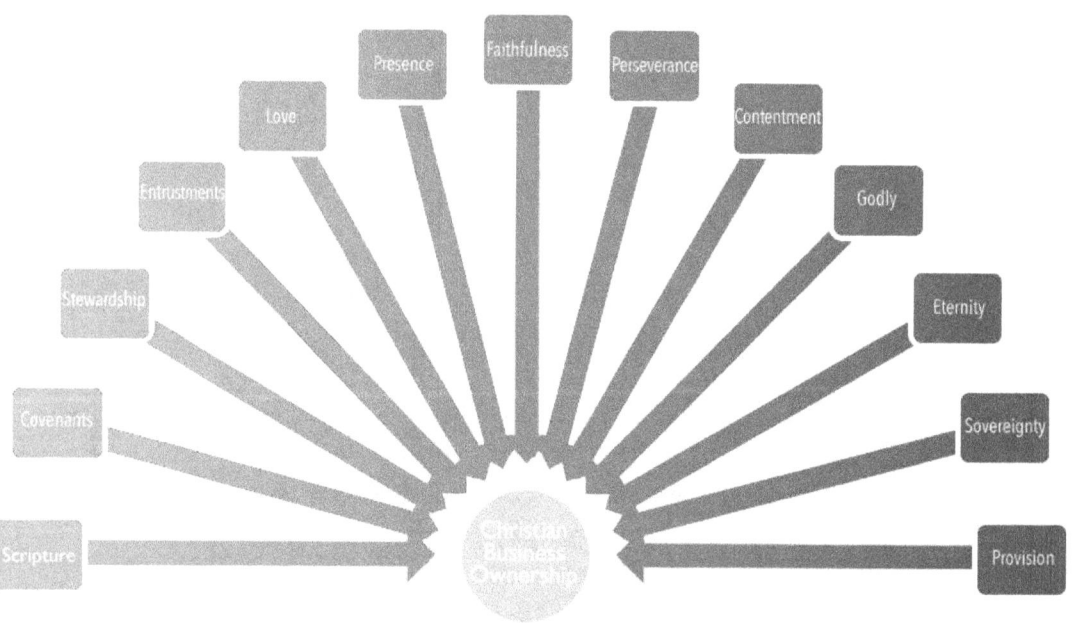

Figure F: Theological Foundation for Christian Business Ownership

CHAPTER 1

THE SIX CHARACTERISTICS OF SCRIPTURE

A Christian business owner is a disciple of Jesus Christ who cares deeply about learning and following God's teachings as presented in the Bible.[41] Hence, understanding the characteristics of Scripture is foundational to interpreting and applying the Scriptures to the life of the CBO personally and professionally.

In this first chapter, I will outline the characteristics of Scripture commonly taught in conservative seminaries. This content is not a mere academic exercise. Instead, understanding the nature of Scripture will be an ambient aid as we work through the content in this book, which is intimately tethered to the Scriptures.

I will also claim that Christian business owners should be more proficient with God's word than their professional skills and industry vertical literature.

---

41   The first characteristic of what is means to be a man defined by the BetterMan ministries is "A real man courageously follows God's Word." Session 5, "Defining Manhood." betterman.com. https://betterman.com/betterman–defined.

FOR MOST WHO pick up this book, this chapter—placed as the first chapter—will seem odd and out of place. But it is not. Because this entire book filters our role as business owners through the Scriptures, we must understand the Bible for what it is and what it claims about itself.

Most pastors will never cover the content of this chapter. I doubt you will ever hear a series of sermons on the characteristics of Scripture and why they matter. So, please take time to read and understand this chapter. Doing so will increase your appreciation for the Bible and indirectly explain why it is emphasized so much in our faith.

THE CHRISTIAN BUSINESS OWNER'S RELATIONSHIP TO SCRIPTURE

Christian business owners should be students of the word of God. A core goal of Bible and Business is to disciple Christian business owners to think theologically first and professionally second. To become a person who thinks theologically first means that an individual studies the Bible instead of merely reading it. Reading the Bible is not studying the Bible.[42] Christian business owners should know God's word better than their industry particulars. Knowing God's Word is critical – it shapes character, integrity, and purpose. Also, knowing one's industry is also important to fulfill one's calling, serve others, and achieve excellence. Christian business owners should prioritize knowing and applying God's Word so that it informs how they excel in their industry. This focus aligns faith with practical diligence, allowing one to honor God both spiritually and professionally.

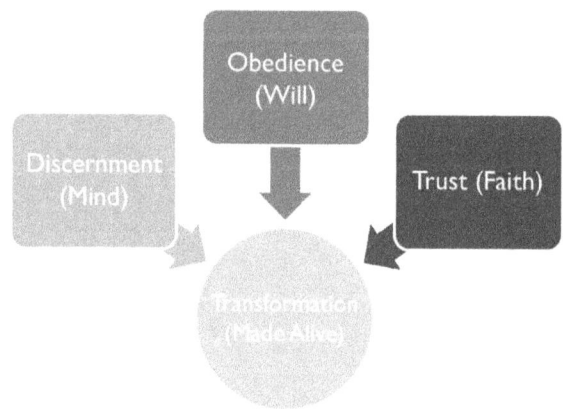

Figure 1–1: Interdependence of Mind, Will, and Faith

42   Michael Heiser, "Naked Bible 016: Heiser's Laws for Bible Study: Learning to Study the Bible, Part 1." *Naked Bible Podcast*, nakedbiblepodcast.com. 2012. 00:40/16:54. Accessed 07/26/2024. https://nakedbiblepodcast.com/wp–content/uploads/2017/08/NB–16–Transcript.pdf.

KNOWING GOD'S WORD SHOULD TRANSFORM OUR PERSONAS

The CBO allows the Scripture to radically transform him into the person God intends him to be. As we are transformed, three aspects of our persona will come into view: discernment (mind) (Romans 12:2), obedience (will) (Matthew 28:20), and trust (faith) (Ephesians 2:8–9) (Figure 1–1). Combined, these three elements will help us understand the true meaning of a text. God's transforming work in the believer's life results in a dynamic interaction between these three areas. All three areas represent qualities that are essential to correctly interpreting the Bible.

Being transformed by God is a change process full of mixed experiences "including discomfort and joy as we ride the roller coaster of repentance and faith, of mortification and vivification, of being humbled and lifted up, of being disciplined and commended, until that day when we are like Christ, and see him as he is.[43] Coming to Christ in faith includes signing up for a Romans 7 life of being transformed by God into the likeness of Christ. Sometimes, we'll feel like we are getting worse, not better, but the more we persevere,

> We will not lose heart. Though our outer self is wasting away, our inner self is being renewed day by day. [17] For our light and momentary troubles are achieving for us an eternal glory that far outweighs them all. [18] So we fix our eyes not on what is seen, but on what is unseen, since what is seen is temporary, but what is unseen is eternal. (2 Corinthians 4:16–18 NIV)

To be transformed by God is to be "made alive."[44] 1 Corinthians 15:22 (ESV) says, "For as in Adam all die, so also in Christ shall all be made alive."[45] Colossians 2:13 (ESV) says:

---

43   J. Gary Millar, *Changed into His Likeness: A Biblical Theology of Personal Transformation*, ed. D. A. Carson, vol. 55, New Studies in Biblical Theology (Apollos; IVP Academic: An Imprint of InterVarsity Press, 2021), 242.

44   "made alive": συζωοποιέω, *make alive together with someone* (BDAG); *raised to life with* (DBL). The sense is both figurative (Johannes P. Louw, and Eugene Albert Nida. *Greek–English Lexicon of the New Testament: Based on Semantic Domains*. (United Bible Societies, 1996), 262.) and supernatural (Faithlife. "To Make Alive Together (supernaturally)." In *Logos Bible Study Bible Sense Lexicon*. Accessed June 22, 2024. https://ref.ly/logos4/Senses?KeyId=ws.make+alive+together+supernaturally.v.01.).

45   Based in part on this passage, some assert a salvific universalism in which there is an eventual salvation for all humans. Utley rightly asserts that universalism wrongly interprets Scripture: "In Adam all die; in Jesus all will be raised (some to reward, some to judgment). It seems obvious to me that Paul's writings, taken in context, demand a repentant faith response by believers." (Robert J. Utley. *Paul's Letters to a Troubled Church: I and II Corinthians*. Vol. 6. Study Guide Commentary Series. (Bible Lessons International, 2002), 177.) To learn more about universalism and why it is a false theology, see Stanley J. Grenz, *Theology for the Community of God*. (Eerdmans Publishing, 2000), 634–37 or G.C. Berkouwer, *Divine Election*. Studies in Dogmatics. (Eerdmans, 1960), 228–41.

[13] And you, who were dead in your trespasses and the uncircumcision of your flesh, God made alive together with him, having forgiven us all our trespasses, [14] by canceling the record of debt that stood against us with its legal demands. This he set aside, nailing it to the cross."

Being made alive is not mainly a physical, mental, or emotional phenomenon. Being made alive is a spiritual phenomenon that holistically affects our personas' physical, mental, and emotional parts. The Scriptures use the phrase "born again" (John 3) to help describe the transforming power of God's work in the life of one who believes. The story of Nicodemus in John 3:1–7 teaches us that when a person's dead spirit is made alive, that is a type of second birth. Being made alive is a spiritual birth, not a physical re–birth.

God's transforming power is "worked out" as a person grows and matures in faith in God. "Work out" is an idiom[46] for "live out." Applying God's transforming power is not a one–time event but a continuous action throughout the believer's life while living on this earth (Philippians 2:12).

Discernment

Once a believer is made alive in Christ, the believer's mind is transformed. He can choose to think the way God thinks instead of how this world thinks. The CBO accepts what is taught in Scripture and learns to think like God. The Holy Spirit's continual activity in our minds is a visceral part of us learning to think like God.

Acceptance of God's truth is the thrust of 1 Corinthians 2:6–16 (please take a moment to read this passage in your Bible.) The natural man has not received the Holy Spirit. He is not in any ordinary sense a 'bad man' or a 'foolish man.' But lacking the Spirit of God, he cannot apprehend spiritual truths, for to him they are foolishness, and he cannot know them because they are discerned only through the Spirit. Barrett notes: "The wisdom taught by the Spirit is the word of the cross (1:18), and to the natural man this is foolishness, for it inverts the values by which he lives."[47]

The teaching of this passage suggests that 'understanding' is not achieved until there is an acceptance and adherence to what is taught. Klein et al. help illuminate the essence of a transformed mind:

---

46   An idiom is a group of words established by usage as having a meaning not deducible from those of the individual words. (Merriam–Webster.com. *Idiom*. Accessed 06/22/2024. https://www.merriam–webster.com/dictionary/idiom.)

47   C. K. Barrett, *The First Epistle to the Corinthians*, Black's New Testament Commentary (Continuum, 1968), 77.

Do not misunderstand. We do not arrogantly assert that one who is not a believer cannot understand anything about the Bible. Unbelievers, even skeptics, can grasp much of its meaning. They may discover what it asserts or claims, even when their own beliefs or value systems lead them to deny those claims. Thus, a competent, unbelieving scholar may produce an outstanding technical commentary on a biblical book—perhaps even better on some details of the text than many believing Christian scholars could write. But that unbelieving scholar cannot understand and portray the true significance of the Bible's message, for he or she is not ultimately committed to the Bible as divine revelation. On the other hand, we do not assert that a believing interpreter will always be right in an interpretation. The believer must be able to defend his or her specific interpretation and demonstrate its validity to believer and non–believer alike." The willingness to believe the Scriptures are God's divine revelation to humanity, by faith, changes how one interprets Scripture.[48]

Transformed minds can judge the right course of action (Proverbs 15:21, Philippians 1:9–10), distinguish good from evil (2 Samuel 14:17, Isaiah 7:15), holy from evil (Leviticus 10:10, 11:47), and understand the significance of current events (Matthew 16:1–4).[49] In addition, a mind transformed by God is able to distinguish between spirits (Hebrews 5:14), and true vs. false teaching (Deuteronomy 13:1–3, 18:21–22; 1 Corinthians 14:29).

Characteristics of a mind that God has transformed are that a person grows in wisdom (Proverbs 1:5), accepts rebuke (Proverbs 17:10, 19:25), and is careful to follow God's law (1 Chronicles 22:12, Psalm 119:34, Proverbs 28:7). Discernment is given by God (Daniel 2:21) through God's word (Hebrews 5:14) and is a quality the transformed person can ask to have more of from God (Psalm 119:66, 119:27, and James 1:5).[50]

Faith

Faith in God's communication via the Holy Spirit (John 16:12–15) to the believer as he reads Scripture is essential to correctly interpreting Scripture. Without faith, it is impossible to please God (Hebrews 11:6 ESV):

---

48   William Klein, Craig Blomberg, and Robert Hubbard, *Introduction to Biblical Interpretation*. Third Edition. (Grand Rapids, MI: Zondervan Academic, 2017), 203.

49   "signs of the times" is in focus in this reference. A sign connotes a visible event intended to convey meaning beyond that which is normally perceived in the event itself. See Walter A. Elwell and Barry J. Beitzel, "Sign." In *Baker Encyclopedia of the Bible*, 2:1961–62. (Baker Books, 1988), 1961–62.

50   Millar posits that God's transforming work can be summed up in five areas: a transformed relationship with God, desire for God, likeness to God, knowledge of God, and life with God. Millar, *Changed into His Likeness*, 225. I recommend Millar's book for further consideration on this topic of transformation.

And without faith, it is impossible to please him, for whoever would draw near to God must believe that he exists and that he rewards those who seek him."

If the Bible is God's revelation to his people, then the believer needs to approach the Bible presupposing that God speaks through his word and is relevant for today.[51] The believing CBO must come to the text to learn from it and better understand what God has for him in that text. The Scriptures were written for all believer's instruction (Romans 15:4). The CBO must come to the Bible with faith, believing that the text means what it says and that God illuminates its significance and meaning through the work of the Holy Spirit (John 16:7–15).

Obedience

Obedience is the practice of following the rules or commands of another.[52] Obedience is learned (Hebrews 5:8), is a result of being disciplined by God (Hebrews 12:3–11), and is a hallmark of one who is righteous before God (Romans 2:13). Obedience expresses covenantal faithfulness to God (Deuteronomy 10:12–22) and incurs God's blessings (Deuteronomy 7:12–26; 28:1–14).[53]

The CBO who wishes to integrate the teachings of the Scriptures into his daily routines must have a heart submitted to God[54] to find the Scriptures to be wise instead of foolish. The CBO understands that God's commands are not intended to guide the owner in a sinless world; instead, God's commands instruct the believer to function in a world that is in rebellion against God and yet be faithful to God in the midst of other's rebellion.[55]

---

51   Klein, *Biblical Interpretation*, 202.

52   Faithlife, "Obedience." In *Logos Bible Study Factbook*. Accessed June 22, 2024. https://ref.ly/logos4/Factbook?id=ref%3abk.%25obedience.

53   Timothy A. Gabrielson, "Obedience." In *Lexham Theological Wordbook*, edited by Douglas Mangum, Derek R. Brown, Rachel Klippenstein, and Rebekah Hurst. Lexham Bible Reference Series. (Lexham Press, 2014.)

54   No one is ever fully submitted to God, except for Christ. Having a "heart submitted to God" is not an either/or statement. It is progressive work of the Spirit in which we grow in maturation through greater submission to the light and the revelations about ourselves which God gives us. God's discipline is a significant part of this growth process. As we seek his face, we are brought into greater maturities (or levels, if you will) of submission to God. At the point of salvation, we are made alive. That is binary. That is justification by faith. But having a heart increasingly submitted to God is analog, not digital; it is growth, not position; it is increasing maturing, but never arriving. Consider Philippians 3:12.

55   Kenneth Kantzer, "God Intends his Precepts to Transform Society." In *Biblical Principles & Business: The Foundations*. Chewning, R.C. (Ed.) (NavPress, 1989), 28.

THE CANON

Different segments of Christianity consider different books or letters written by the ancients as authoritative for faith and practice today. For example, Catholic, Coptic, and Eastern Orthodox churches consider the Old Testament Apocrypha—"hidden things"[56]—which is a collection of writings included in older versions of the Old Testament that were not included in the Masoretic Text of the Hebrew Bible, part of the current Old Testament.[57] Protestant Christians do not consider the Apocrypha part of the canon.[58] In addition, writings by the Apostolic Fathers were not included in the canon developed by Protestant Christians, even though their historical value is thought to be higher than any other Christian literature outside the New Testament.[59]

In both cases—the Old Testament Apocrypha[60] and the writings by the Apostolic Fathers—Protestant contemporaries lacked consensus that these writings were on par with other writings that were eventually included in the current Protestant canon. The contemporaries' lack of initial acceptance of individual writings as canonical at the time of their writing is a core reason many Apocryphal writings are not part of the Protestant Bible today.[61]

The Canon—"measuring rod"[62]—is a collection of authoritative religious writings and is differentiated from Scripture in that a canon "signifies a definitive and closed list of religiously authoritative writings and thus explicitly addresses the question of their scope and limits."[63] The term "Scripture" designates religiously authoritative literature without indicating whether the writing is part of a canon. Hence, the formation of the canon presupposes the availability of Scriptures, but the existence of various Scriptures does not

---

56   Faithlife, "Apocrypha." In *Logos Bible Study Factbook*. Accessed June 7, 2024. https://ref.ly/logos4/Factbook?id=ref%3abk.%25Apocrypha_Writing.

57   Douglas Estes, "Apocrypha, Old Testament." In *The Lexham Bible Dictionary*, Logos edition, edited by John D. Barry, David Bomar, Derek R. Brown, Rachel Klippenstein, Douglas Mangum, Carrie Sinclair Wolcott, Lazarus Wentz, Elliot Ritzema, and Wendy Widder. (Lexham Press, 2016), [Apocrypha, Old Testament], np.

58   David A. DeSilva, "Apocrypha and Pseudepigrapha." In *The Dictionary of New Testament Background: a Compendium of Contemporary Biblical Scholarship*. Porter, S. and Evans, C. (Eds.) (Intervarsity Press, 2000), 58–64.

59   G.F. Zoella, Why Are These Books in the Bible and Not Others? Apostolic Fathers and the New Testament Apocrypha. (Self–Published, 2016), v3, 27.

60   There exists a New Testament Apocrypha in addition to the Old Testament Apocrypha that is not included in today's canon by Protestants.

61   Klein, Biblical Interpretation, 165–172.

62   Faithlife, "Canon." In *Logos Bible Study Factbook*. June 7, 2024. https://ref.ly/logos4/Factbook?id=ref%3abk.%25canon.

63   Albert A. Sundberg, "Canon Muratori: A Fourth–Century List." *Harvard Theological Review*. 1973, 66(1):1–41.

require a strict canonical list.[64] I will adopt the Westminster Confession of Faith canon in this book, published in 1647.[65]

Which Translation Should We Use?

The best translation for any Christian to use is the one he will read and study. Having said this, it should be noted that some translations focus more on *dynamic* equivalence and others more on *formal* equivalence. With dynamic equivalence, the meaning of the text in the original language is stated as clearly and accurately as possible in the receptor language. It is a thought–for–thought translation, hoping to produce the same or similar response in the modern reader as would have been obtained in the original reader.[66]

Formal equivalence attempts to use a word or phrase in the receptor language that exists in the original language. When the translators need to supply a word or phrase to make the receptor language readable, they indicate such insertions in some way, often using *italics* for those inserted words. Formal equivalence should not be considered a literal word–for–word translation. While formal equivalence retains the problematic readings, ambiguities, and odd phraseology as much as possible in the receptor language, there are idioms in the original language that, if translated literally, would obscure the original meaning, not clarify it. Where exact literalness is impossible, the translators supply the best equivalent text possible. Combining these two methods is sometimes referred to as *complete* equivalence.[67]

Examples of formal equivalence include the Authorized Version and the English Standard Version. An example of the dynamic equivalence method is the New International Version.

64   Harry Y. Gamble, "Canonical Formation of the New Testament." In *The Dictionary of New Testament Background: A Compendium of Contemporary Biblical Scholarship.* (InterVarsity Press, 2000), 183–95.

65   Chad Van Dixhoorn, *Creeds, Confessions, and Catechisms: A Reader's Edition.* (Crossway, 2022), 183–85.

66   Alan Cairns, *Dictionary of Theological Terms.* (Ambassador Emerald International, 2002), 140.

67   Carnes, *Theological Terms*, 182–83.

Note: The following six characteristics of Scripture apply only to the written word of God and do not apply to other forms of communication from God, such as visions, dreams, his voice, etc. Even more certainly, they do not apply to any communication from man, such as teaching, preaching, prophecy, or someone 'hearing from God' for you or having a 'word from the Lord' for you.

THE AUTHORITY OF SCRIPTURE

"The authority of Scripture means that all the words in Scripture are God's words such that to disbelieve or disobey any word of Scripture is to disbelieve or disobey God."[68] "Authority" means the right or power to command action or compliance, to determine beliefs or customs, and to expect obedience from those under authority.[69]

The authority of Scripture depends on the authority of God over all that is. If God is not fully authoritative over all that is, then God's words cannot be authoritative.[70] In addition, it is essential to state that if God is fully authoritative over all that is, then there is no authority higher than God. There is no reference point to which God can refer other than himself. Throughout the Scriptures, God claims he is the ultimate authority over all humanity and all that exists. No other can make this claim and make it stick.[71]

In the Scriptures, God reveals he is the complete and final authority over the universe and humanity (Jude 25 ESV):

> To the only God, our Savior, through Jesus Christ our Lord, be glory, majesty, dominion, and authority before all time and now and forever.

In the future, the full authority of Christ will be on display for all of humanity to see (Revelation 12:10 ESV):

> And I heard a loud voice in heaven, saying, "Now the salvation and the power and the kingdom of our God and the authority of his Christ have come, for the accuser of our brothers has been thrown down, who accuses them day and night before our God.

---

68 Wayne Grudem, *Systematic Theology: An Introduction to Biblical Doctrine.* (Inter–Varsity Press; Zondervan Publishing, 2004), 73.

69 Bernard L. Ramm, *The Pattern of Religious Authority.* (Eerdmans, 1959), 10.

70 Sinclair B. Ferguson and J.I. Packer. *New Dictionary of Theology.* (InterVarsity Press, 2000), 627–28.

71 Jeremy D. Myers. "The Gospel is More than "Faith Alone in Christ Alone." *Journal of the Grace Evangelical Society,* 2006. 19(37):32–56.

Immediately before Christ ascended to heaven after the crucifixion and resurrection, Christ claimed all authority on earth and heaven:

> All authority in heaven and on earth has been given to me. (Matthew 28:18 ESV).

"The whole universe is embraced in the authority delegated to him."[72] Christ could not have "all authority" given to him if God did not first possess "all authority."

Hence, if God is fully authoritative over all that is, then so is God's word, as expressed to humanity in Scripture.[73] The Scriptures are authoritative for life and practice because they are the very words of God, and the Scriptures' authority is derived from God's authority as God. An obvious application at this point for a CBO is that God has full authority over the owner's business, money, position, and authority. We will return to this truth again in the coming chapters.

Those who deny the authority of the Bible unavoidably deny the authority of God. Moreover, when deniers exist inside the church, the church's ministry suffers: "Evasion of the authority of Scripture is the sign of a wavering church."[74] I believe the same can be said of a Christian business owner: when an owner evades the authority of Scripture, we will find an owner wavering in submission to the authority of God.

THE CLARITY OF SCRIPTURE

The clarity of Scripture means that "the Bible is written in such a way that all things necessary for our salvation and for our Christian life and growth are very clearly set forth in Scripture."[75] The clarity of Scripture does not assert that everything is clearly written or easily understood in Scripture, but only that which is necessary for humanity to come to God, to know God, and to obey God perfectly.[76]

The Westminster Confession of Faith of 1647 affirms this characteristic of Scripture:

> All things in Scripture are not alike plain in themselves, nor alike clear until all: yet those things which are necessary to be known, believed, and observed for salvation, are so clearly propounded, and opened in some place

---

72   Craig Blomberg, *Matthew*, vol. 22, The New American Commentary (Broadman & Holman Publishers, 1992), 431.

73   Richard L. Mayhue. "The Authority of Scripture." *The Master's Seminary Journal.* 2004, 15(2):227–236.

74   Carl F. Henry. *God, Revelation, and Authority.* (Wheaton, IL: Crossway Books, 1999), 41.

75   Grudem, *Systematic Theology*, 108.

76   Kory D. Maas. "On the Sufficiency and Clarity of Scripture." *Concordia Theological Quarterly.* 2021. 85(1):48.

of Scripture or other, that not only the learned but the unlearned, in a due use of the ordinary means, may attain unto a sufficient understanding of them."[77]

This confession says that something unclear in one part of Scripture will be restated or illustrated more clearly in another part of Scripture if it is necessary for salvation and living a holy life before God.

The clarity of Scripture is attested in Scripture. Deuteronomy 30:11 tells the Christian that God's commands are not too hard to understand. Psalm 119:130 reminds us that understanding is imparted to the one who reads Scripture, and Psalm 19:7 indicates that the simple are made wise when they accept the plain reading of Scripture.

I like how Heiser approaches the clarity of Scripture. Though Heiser does not use the phrase "clarity of Scripture," Heiser suggests that we "let the Bible be what it is."[78] Heiser writes:

> The path to real biblical understanding requires that we do not make the Bible conform to our traditions, our prejudices, our personal crises, or our culture's intellectual battles … letting the Bible be what it is not only helps us interpret Scripture accurately, but it has unexpected apologetic value. Taking Scripture on its own terms helps our focus and fends off distractions. When Scripture is rightly understood, its relevance will also be clear.[79]

Two questions emerge in this discussion. First, what about the weird passages? What about the passages that teach or illustrate weird or unusual concepts or events? Well, two thoughts may help. First, understanding Scripture is not about making it palatable or comfortable for the modern reader. Instead, "It is about discerning what the biblical writer believed and was seeking to communicate to readers who thought the same way."[80] The clarity of Scripture calls a disciple of Jesus Christ to accept what is taught, even if what is taught appears to the interpreter's modern mind as weird or highly unusual.

Most "weird" passages concern a supernatural or cultural world foreign to a modern scientific mind. Some modern theologians have explained away the supernatural parts of Scripture because they are uncomfortable with one or more aspects of how the Scriptures present the unseen realm. Some cannot (will not?) accept the biblical worldview where divine

---

77 Van Dixhoorn, *Creeds, Confessions, and Catechisms*, 186.
78 Michael Heiser, *The Bible Unfiltered: Approaching Scripture on Its Own Terms*. (Lexham Press, 2017), 19.
79 Heiser, *Unfiltered*, 19–22.
80 Ibid, 17.

beings can eat, drink, fight, or produce off–spring with humans (Genesis 6:1–4; 18:1–8; 19:1–11; 32:22–32; Numbers 13:32–33; 2 Peter 2:4–10; Jude 6–7).[81] It is foolishness to some theologians to believe that Jesus Christ was fully God and fully human or that Christ was dead for three days and then came back to life.

In addition, some cannot wrap their minds around highly different cultures from our Western, modern culture. These ANE cultures form the context for large portions of Scripture. Comparative studies help us better understand polytheistic cultures that cared more about maintaining order than living out a moral code, assumed the king was god–like, or never differentiated between the natural and spiritual world.[82]

Passages that appear to us to be weird or odd deserve *greater* attention and study rather than dismissal with a cavalier attitude. The more odd or weird a passage is, *the more likely it is that the passage will add depth and maturity to our faith once the passage is properly understood*. We must be willing to take the passage seriously, invest time and energy into proper study, and set aside any pre–determined assumptions and conclusions.

The second question is this: what do followers of God do with unclear passages? The Westminster Confession provides helpful interpretive direction for us when the passage's meaning is unclear:

> All things in Scripture are not alike plain in themselves nor alike clear unto all … The infallible rule of interpretation of Scripture is the Scripture itself. When there is a question about the true and full sense of any Scripture (which is not manifold, but one), it must be searched and known by other places that speak more clearly.[83]

Stated in more modern terms, when a passage is vague or contains ambiguities that are difficult to explain, the interpreter should seek other passages that are clearer on the topic and let those more explicit passages be the "controlling" passages.

There are passages in Scripture that cannot mean what they plainly say. An example is 1 Corinthians 14:33b–35 (ESV):

> As in all the churches of the saints, the women should keep silent in the churches. For they are not permitted to speak, but should be in submission, as the Law also says. If there is anything they desire to learn, let them ask their husbands at home. For it is shameful for a woman to speak in church.

---

81   Ibid, 17.

82   John H. Walton, *Ancient Near Eastern Thought and the Old Testament: Introducing the Conceptual World of the Hebrew Bible.* 2nd Edition, (Baker Academic, 2018), 47–72.

83   Van Dixhoorn, *Creeds, Confessions, and Catechisms,* 186–187.

This passage is in direct conflict with what Paul wrote earlier in the same letter (1 Corinthians 11:4–5 ESV):

> Every man who prays or prophesies with his head covered dishonours his head, but every wife who prays or prophesies with her head uncovered dishonours her head since it is the same as if her head were shaven.

The issue under discussion right now is not about the head covering or the role of women in the church. The issue is one of a passage that does not mean what it plainly says: in 1 Corinthians 11, Paul assumes women are praying and prophesying in the local assembly of the believers. Nevertheless, in chapter 14, Paul writes that women must remain silent when the believers are assembled. Both cannot be true at the same time. So, the plain reading of one (or both) of these passages cannot mean what the raw syntax says.

Relying on the Westminster Confession again, the confession provides helpful interpretive direction for the interpreter when the passage's meaning is unclear: "All things in Scripture are not alike plain in themselves nor alike clear unto all … The infallible rule of interpretation of Scripture is the Scripture itself. When there is a question about the true and full sense of any Scripture (which is not manifold, but one), it must be searched and known by other places that speak more clearly" (Van Dixhoorn, 2022:186–187).

Furthermore, to the elaboration above stated in more modern terms, when a passage is vague or contains ambiguities that are difficult to explain, the interpreter should seek other passages that are clearer on the topic and let those more explicit passages be the 'controlling' passages. In addition, it may be helpful to appeal to the 'arc' of Scripture as a basis for understanding individual passages. Vanhoozer writes:

> The parts interpret the whole, and the whole interprets the parts because what needs to be known is clearly taught in some places even if not in others."[84]

If no clear passages exist to explain the vague passage, then the interpreter should remember that the clarity of Scripture does not teach that every passage is equally clear, but only that each passage has enough clarity to provide the interpreter with what is necessary for salvation and growth. Unclear passages may need to be viewed with a tentative perspective. I do not believe building prescriptive patterns or practices from vague passages alone without clear teaching from other passages is wise or prudent.

If more clear passages cannot be found, we are advised to do our best, given what is presented in the passage(s). We should learn all that can be learned about the historical

---

84   Kevin J. Vanhoozer. "The Sufficiency of Scripture: A Critical and Constructive Account." *Journal of Psychology & Theology*, 2021. 49(3):222.

and literary context, read comparative studies, exegete the Greek or Hebrew text well, acknowledge the difficulties, resist eisegesis, admit to tentative conclusions, and move on. It is worse to impose onto a passage a meaning that cannot be determined than to admit that one's conclusions are tentative or have limitations that cannot be immediately overcome.

Despite the supernatural events, dissimilar cultures, or the vague, difficult–to–understand passages we find in the Scriptures, followers of Yahweh should not shy away from honest attempts at interpretation while admitting limitations. These problematic passages often provide a greater understanding of the whole context (both natural and supernatural) of humanity's existence on this earth and our faith in God.

THE NECESSITY OF SCRIPTURE

"The necessity of Scripture means that the Bible is necessary for knowing the gospel, for maintaining spiritual life, and for knowing God's will, but is not necessary for knowing that God exists or knowing something about God's character and moral laws."[85] The necessity of Scripture is an expression of God's love for mankind. The necessity for God to express himself through Scripture is due more to God's condescension to mankind's finite condition than to any constraint that was placed on God[86] to communicate to mankind about his persona: "The Creator willingly chose to address human beings, who possessed no power to compel him to communicate with them."[87] Barrick posits the following regarding the necessity of Scripture:[88]

- The image of God in man requires communication between God and man
- Natural revelation's insufficiency to teach the nature of God makes Scripture necessary
- The complexity of divine truth would require a written revelation even if humankind had never sinned
- The fall of man made oral tradition even more difficult because a corrupt humanity is prone to distort what is oral
- Written revelation is how God has chosen to do his work in human lives
- Therefore, a written revelation from God is necessary

Barrick's points are persuasive: God's image within man requires communication between God and man, and the complexity of divine truth would have required a written revelation even if humanity had never sinned. Because of the way God created humanity, a written

---

85 Grudem, *Systematic Theology*, 116.

86 No constraint can be placed on God. He is immutable, impassible, simple, and independent. For further learning in this area, I recommend Herman Bavinck, *The Doctrine of God*. Translated by William Hendriksen. Baker Books, 1979, 145ff.

87 William Barrick. "The Necessity of Scripture." *The Master's Seminary Journal*, 2004, 15(2):151–164.

88 Barrick, *Necessity of Scripture*, 151.

form of communication was eventually necessary if humanity was going to know God and know how to connect with God personally and corporately.

Warfield agrees with Barrick and appeals to the complexity of divine truth as a basis for the necessity of Scripture. Warfield postulates that even after a man is redeemed, man could never "interpret revelational facts correctly and fully. Hence the necessity of Scripture."[89]

Barrick's work quietly counters the enlightenment notion that an independent path to gaining salvific truth about God can be found through reason alone.[90] Romans 1:16–18 (NIV) supports the notion that general characteristics of God can be gleaned through reason and that knowledge is enough to condemn one who does not believe:

> For what can be known about God is plain to them because God has shown it to them. For his invisible attributes, namely, his eternal power and divine nature, have been clearly perceived, ever since the creation of the world, in the things that have been made.

Humanity can learn something about God and God's attributes through reason and observation of nature. Even though a design hypothesis to explain how life and the world came to be may date back centuries,[91] that hypothesis does not negate the need for Scriptures to know God covenantally. The necessity of Scripture asserts that to know *salvific* truth and the will of God, one will need God's special revelation[92] found in God's word. The Scriptures are necessary if followers of Yahweh are to know God covenantally. Romans 10:13–17 (ESV) is more direct on this point:

> [13] For "everyone who calls on the name of the Lord will be saved." [14] How then will they call on him in whom they have not believed? And how are they to believe in him of whom they have never heard? And how are they to hear without someone preaching? [15] And how are they to preach unless they are sent? As it is written, "How beautiful are the feet of those who preach the good news!" [16] But they have not all obeyed the gospel. For Isaiah says, "Lord, who has believed what he has heard from us?" [17] So faith comes from hearing, and hearing through the word of Christ."

89   Benjamin B. Warfield. *The Inspiration and Authority of the Bible.* (Presbyterian and Reformed. 1964), 33.

90   Ada Palmer. "Humanist Lives of Classical Philosophers and the Idea of Renaissance Secularization: Virtue, Rhetoric, and the Orthodox Sources of Unbelief." *Renaissance Quarterly*, 2017, 70(3):935–976.

91   Vargas Sandino, Caccamo, M., Hashim, S., Eng., O. "The Evolution of Intelligent Design: Between Religion and Science." *Revista Científica General José María Córdova*, 2018, 16(22):61–80.

92   *Special revelation is the teaching about God and his works that he has given to us through the prophets and apostles and which is now contained primarily or exclusively in the Bible,* Faithlife, "Special Revelation." In *Logos Bible Study Factbook.* June 8, 2024. https://ref.ly/logos4/Factbook?id=ref%3abk.%25specialRevelation.

God's word is essential to knowing and maintaining a consistent walk with God (Deuteronomy 8:3). His word is essential to preaching and sharing the Christian faith. His word is necessary if we are to find our way to God.

THE SUFFICIENCY OF SCRIPTURE

"The sufficiency of Scriptures means Scripture contains all the words of God he intended his people to have at each stage of redemptive history, and that it now contains everything we need God to tell us for salvation, for trusting him perfectly, and for obeying him perfectly."[93] The Bible is sufficient for its given purposes: it tells humanity all humanity needs to know to be saved and live righteously before God. It does not tell us all we want to know or satisfy all our curiosities.[94]

In areas where the Bible is silent, the Christian is free to make choices as desired, as long as those choices do not violate any command of Scripture. When Christians make choices where the Scriptures are silent or unclear, others in the body should be charitable, not critical, toward those choices. The Evangelical Free Church of America (EFCA) is an example of such charity. In the headline of its' distinctives, the EFCA writes, "In essentials, unity. In non–essentials, charity. In all things, Jesus Christ."[95]

Some will not accept placing doctrines that they consider of primary importance and the principle tests of orthodoxy in the category of charitable tenants when subordinated to the clear commands of Scripture.[96] The sufficiency of Scripture calls for Christians to extend the hand of fellowship to those who may believe differently in areas where the Scriptures are unclear or silent. Such differences may include church membership, political beliefs, the role of women in the church, spiritual warfare, or baptism. Due to differing beliefs, there should be no second–class members inside the body of Christ.

Moreover, the sufficiency of Scripture rules out the need for external revelation supplements to live blamelessly before God.[97] The sufficiency of Scripture gives the follower of God great comfort in knowing that as long as the follower obeys the law of God, that follower is blameless before God:

> Blessed are those whose way in blameless, who walk in the law of the Lord! (Psalm 119:1 ESV)

---

93   Grudem, *Systematic Theology*, 127.

94   Vanhoozer, *Sufficiency of Scripture*, 221.

95   Evangelical Free Church of America. "Disctinctives of the Evangelical Free Church of America," Accessed 06/22/2024. https://www.efca.org/distinctives/

96   Arnold T. Olson. *The Significance of Silence*. (Free Church Press, 1981), v2, 6.

97   Scott R. Swain, *Trinity, Revelation, and Reading: A Theological Introduction to the Bible and Its Interpretation*. (T&T Clark, 2011), 84.

Any other blame or shame that a follower of God experiences when obeying God's law is faux blame or shame.

The sufficiency of Scripture also implies that God has not hidden his will in heaven. His commands are not beyond our reach. Through the Bible, God's word is near and readily accessible:

> "Now what I am commanding you today is not too difficult for you or beyond your reach. It is not up in heaven, so that you have to ask, "Who will ascend into heaven to get it and proclaim it to us so we may obey it?" Nor is it beyond the sea, so that you have to ask, "Who will cross the sea to get it and proclaim it to us so we may obey it?" No, the word is very near you; it is in your mouth and in your heart so you may obey it." (Deuteronomy 30:11–14 NIV).

The sufficiency of Scripture is sometimes confused with Sola Scriptura (Scripture alone), which is one of the three Solas that act as a popular shorthand for some denominations (the other two being Sola Gratia (grace alone) and Sola Fide (faith alone).[98] But these two concepts, while perhaps complementary, are distinct in that Sola Scriptura focuses on authority, whereas the sufficiency of Scripture is more about the breadth of the content itself: what is found in the Bible is sufficient, and the followers of God need no more revelation.

Adding to or subtracting from Scripture to improve Scripture is an implicit admission that one does not believe Scripture to be sufficient. In addition, the sufficiency of Scripture depends on a strong definition of the canon of Scripture, since to add to or subtract from the canon is tantamount to violating the sufficiency of the corpus.[99]

THE INERRANCY OF SCRIPTURE

"The Inerrancy of Scripture means that Scripture in the original manuscripts does not affirm anything contrary to fact."[100] Restated in other terms, the Bible is truthful concerning everything about which the Bible discusses. This principle does not affirm that the Bible is an exhaustive reference work for any topic or domain of study. But when the Bible talks about a topic, what the Bible says about that topic is true.

---

98 Timothy Schmeling, "Sola Scriptura: The solas and Martin Luther." *Logia*. 2018, 27(4):15–22; Scott Manetsch ("Is the Reformation Over? John Calvin, Roman Catholicism, and Contemporary Ecumenical Conversations." *Themelios*. 2011, 36(2):199) adds two more, Solus Christus (Christ alone) and Soli Deo Gloria (glory to God alone).

99 "corpus": *All the writings or works of a particular kind or on a particular subject.* Merriam Webster. *Corpus*. Accessed 6/22/2024. https://www.merriam–webster.com/dictionary/corpus.

100 Grudem, *Systematic Theology*, 90.

In addition, God cannot lie or speak falsely. Therefore, all the words in Scripture are claimed to be wholly accurate and without error in any part because the words of Scripture are God's words. Because there is no higher authority to tether this line of reasoning, God, through the Bible, makes claims about his words, which will require faith to believe. Again, God is his own reference point. The self–referencing claims about the truthfulness of God's words are numerous in the Bible: Numbers 23:19, Psalm 12:6, Psalm 119:89, Proverbs 30:5, 2 Samuel 7:28, Titus 1:2, and Hebrews 6:17–18 (not an exhaustive list).

Importantly, inerrancy is not negated by ordinary speech. A narrator can speak of the sun rising or the rain falling because, from the writer's perspective, this is what happened. Ordinary speech is not to be technically pressed too much. As a present–day illustration, when interpreting law, Justice Scalia wrote that "words are to be understood in their ordinary, everyday meanings—unless the context indicates that they bear a technical sense."[101] In law and theology and interpretation of the Bible, words should be given the meaning they had when written or spoken.

Minor variations in ordinary speech should not be pressed into significant theological meanings. Pedant conclusions are not advocated by inerrancy. To refine this point, the interpreter should remember that excessive concern with minor details used to build significant meaning from a passage is in danger of violating the inerrancy of Scripture rather than being supported by inerrancy.[102]

In addition, we should adopt the principle to favor an interpretation that reveals rather than obfuscates a passage. Based on this principle, an interpretation invalidating other parts of Scripture is to be rejected, not only because of this principle but also because to do so would passively violate the inerrancy of Scripture.

Humans wrote the Bible. However, their writing does not negate inerrancy, even though humans always err at some point. Church history confirms that human interpretation can err while the Bible is inerrant.[103] Conversely, inerrancy does not negate human influence on these Scriptures. If one accepts the inspiration of the Scriptures, one can understand how inerrant writing could be achieved when the writer was operating under the inspiration of God.

---

101   Anthony Scalia and Bryan Garner, *Reading Law: The Interpretation of Legal Texts.* (Thomson/West, 2012), 1172.

102   Grudem, *Systematic Theology*, 90–98.

103   For examples of how human interpretations of Scripture have changed over time, see Kevin Giles. "Post–1970s Evangelical Responses to the Emancipation of Women." *Priscilla Papers* 2006, (20):4, 50 and his discussion of how egalitarian views of women have evolved. Another example is the (right) rejection of racism that was held so prominently by some Christians in America: "The Sbjt Forum: Racism, Scripture, and History." *Southern Baptist Journal of Theology*. 2004, 8:(2):82.

INSPIRATION OF SCRIPTURE

The inspiration of Scripture means "the writings of the Bible are the product of divine power and therefore carry divine authority."[104] Logos defines inspiration as " That extraordinary or supernatural divine influence vouchsafed to those who wrote the Holy Scriptures, rendering their writings infallible."[105] Inspiration is closely linked to authority, but they are disparate ideas.

The influence of God on the writers was such that God became the author of the Scriptures through the human writers. Yet, the writers did not become passive scribes. The writers used their minds and backgrounds while keeping their thought processes and personalities intact:[106]

> The Spirit did not suppress the personality of the human writer, but raised it to a higher level of activity (John 14:26). And because the individuality of the human author was not destroyed, we find in the Bible a wide variety of style and language.[107]

Jesus reference to David in Mark 12:35–36 (NIV) (cf. Matthew 22:43) is an excellent example of the balance between the 'human–ness' of the authors and the divine inspiration from God:

> [35]While Jesus was teaching in the temple courts, he asked, "Why do the teachers of the law say that the Messiah is the son of David? [36] David himself, speaking by the Holy Spirit, declared...

Christ did not deny David's personality in writing inspired words from the Holy Spirit but assumed that both could be present and true when the Scriptures were written. [108]

In addition, inspiration is claimed by the Scriptures for the Scriptures in 2 Timothy 3:16–17 (ESV):

---

104   John F. Walvoord, "Is the Bible the Inspired Word of God?" *Bibliotheca Sacra.* 1959, 116(461):6.

105   Faithlife, "Inspiration." In *Logos Bible Study Factbook.* Accessed June 22, 2024. https://ref.ly/logos4/Factbook?id=ref%3abk.%25inspiration.

106   Jimmy Millikin, "Forming a Doctrine of Scripture." *The Journal of Mid–America Baptist Theological Seminary,* Spring 2014, v1, 69–81.

107   William Hendriksen and Simon J. Kistemaker, *Exposition of the Pastoral Epistles*, New Testament Commentary (Baker Books, 1953–2001), 302.

108   Recall that the Holy Spirit does not speak on his own, The Holy Spirit speaks only what he hears from Christ and God (John 16:12–15).

[16]All Scripture is breathed out by God and profitable for teaching, for reproof, for correction, and for training in righteousness, [17] that the man of God may be complete, equipped for every good work.

Stott says the Greek word "breathed out" means that Scripture was brought into existence by God's breath (literally, the exhaling).[109] Warfield highlights the nuance better: the Scriptures are not a corpus "breathed into by God," presumably while being written. Instead, the corpus is a result of God breathing out, "breathed out by God, "God–breathed," the product of the creative breath of God.[110] Mysteriously, God's life is in the words of Scripture. I cannot explain why this is true. But I accept it by faith.

The mechanics of how inspiration happened is not given to us in the Bible. Sometimes, God spoke directly to a human, as with Moses on Mount Sinai. Other times, Scriptures were written as God worked through the writer. Nevertheless, whatever mode was used, there remains a mystery that includes both a human element and the element of divine infallibility.[111]

In the Old Testament, when a prophet would say, "Thus says the Lord, "the prophet was claiming to be a messenger from God and that the words which followed this phrase were the reliable words of God."[112] This claim would mean God inspired the prophets' words. The apostle Peter made this point clearly (2 Peter 1:19–21 NIV):

[19] We also have the prophetic message as something completely reliable, and you will do well to pay attention to it, as to a light shining in a dark place, until the day dawns and the morning star rises in your hearts. [20]Above all, you must understand that no prophecy of Scripture came about by the prophet's own interpretation of things. [21] For prophecy never had its origin in the human will, but prophets, though human, spoke from God as they were carried along by the Holy Spirit.

"The writer has used a maritime metaphor here indicating that the prophets were carried along by the Holy Spirit as ships were carried along by the wind in their sails."[113] The

---

109   John Stott, *Guard the Gospel the Message of 2 Timothy*, The Bible Speaks Today (InterVarsity Press, 1973), 101.

110   Benjamin B. Warfield, "Inspiration," in *The International Standard Bible Encyclopedia, Revised*, ed. Geoffrey W Bromiley (Eerdmans, 1979–1988), 840.

111   Walvoord, *Is the Bible*, 7.

112   Gruden, *Systematic Theology*, 74.

113   David Strange, *An Exegetical Summary of 2 Peter*, 2nd ed. (SIL International, 2008), 88.

"carried along" language indicates divine inspiration for the prophet's messages that are understandable both to the speaker and hearer.[114]

Hence, the inspiration of Scripture asserts that as God breathed out the words he wanted written, he breathed through writers that he chose, carried them along through the Spirit as they wrote, worked through their intellect and personalities, and produced the most holy book this world has ever seen or will ever see again.

PRESUPPOSITIONS AND GOALS

One's worldview may place a grid over Scripture that proper interpretation of the text will challenge. Being challenged to think and believe differently through more alignment with the Bible is good. Osborne writes:

> We need to bracket our preunderstandings and allow the text to deepen or challenge and even change those already established ideas. As readers, we want to place ourselves in front of the text (and allow it to address us) rather than behind it (and force it to go where we want). The reader's background and ideas are important in the study of biblical truth; however, this must be used to study meaning rather than to create meaning that is not there.[115]

Grudem echoes Osborne when he asserts that studying the bible should result in us knowing "what to believe about each topic."[116] The believing CBO's worldview should not be read eisegetically into the text. Rather, the CBO's worldview is to be changed to align with the meaning of the text that is drawn out exegetically. This book is written by starting with the Bible and engaging proper exegesis. We will apply what the Scriptures say to our decisions and attitudes as CBOs.

I presuppose all people share everyday human experiences with others who lived long ago and in vastly different cultures.[117] Hence, the word of God is not divorced from real life.[118] Nothing can be more "real–life" than for our Savior to share human life by living among us.[119]

---

114 Peter H. Davids. *The Letters of 2 Peter and Jude*. The Pillar New Testament Commentary. (Eerdmans, 2006), 215.

115 Grant R. Osborne, *The Hermeneutical Spiral: A Comprehensive Introduction to Biblical Interpretation*. (Intervarsity, 2006), 29.

116 Grudem, *Systematic Theology*, 21.

117 Klein, *Biblical Interpretation*, 419.

118 Osborne, *Hermeneutical Spiral*, 158.

119 David DeSilva, "Embodying the Word: Social Scientific Interpretation of the New Testament." In *The Face of New Testament Studies*. Ed. Scott McKnight & Grant Osborne. (Baker Books, 2004), 118.

It is important to note that Christ was fully God and fully man. This truth is why followers of Jesus Christ can be confident that Christ himself has experienced their life experiences, and he carries these experiences now as part of his persona. The truth of his full Godhead and full humanity is expressed in Colossians 1:15–20 (ESV):

> He is the image of the invisible God, the firstborn of all creation. For by him all things were created, in heaven and on earth, visible and invisible, whether thrones or dominions or rulers or authorities—all things were created through him and for him. And he is before all things, and in him all things hold together. And he is the head of the body, the church. He is the beginning, the firstborn from the dead, that in everything he might be preeminent. For in him all the fullness of God was pleased to dwell, and through him to reconcile to himself all things, whether on earth or in heaven, making peace by the blood of his cross."

"All the fulness of God" dwells in Christ. "Everything that God is, Jesus is."[120] Jesus is the full embodiment of God's attributes and saving grace[121] which is why God is "able to reconcile to himself all things." When Hebrews 1:3 says that Christ is the "exact representation" of God, that verse says the same thing Paul said in Colossians 1:15–20: Christ embodies the divine essence.[122]

If Christ were not fully human, then there would be, in some sense, a diminishment of Christ's shared experiences with humanity. Hence, even though modern humans share everyday experiences with those who lived long ago, we cannot be certain that Christ had all the experiences of being human unless he was fully human. But since Christ was fully human, those who come to him can have confidence that the events and emotions they experience are shared and understood by the Savior who lived fully as a human.[123]

Hence, taking into account the characteristics of Scripture and the presuppositions of the believer, the complex but achievable goal of our efforts is to "arrive at the meaning of the text that the biblical writers or editors intended their readers to understand"[124] and then living out what is taught in the text.

---

120   Richard R. Melick, *Philippians, Colossians, Philemon*, The New American Commentary (Broadman & Holman, 1991), 224.

121   Max Anders, *Galatians–Colossians*, Holman New Testament Commentary (Broadman & Holman, 1999), 284.

122   David J. MacLeod, "The Finality of Christ: An Exposition of Hebrews 1:1–4." *Bibliotheca Sacra* 2005, 162(646):221.

123   The only human experience Christ did not share was to engage in sin (Joseph G Sahl. "The Impeccability of Jesus Christ." *Bibliotheca Sacra* 1983, 140(557):11–54), though he did experience separation from God near the end of his life while hanging on the cross (Craig Blomberg. *Matthew*. The New American Commentary. (Nashville: Broadman & Holman Publishers, 1992), 419).

124   Klein, *Biblical Interpretation*, 224.

SUMMARY

The Christian business owner should learn that the characteristics of Scripture matter when interpreting Scripture. We also recognize the supernatural aspect of discerning the text's true meaning when the Holy Spirit works within our minds and enables us to believe and obey what we have learned. Finally, a CBO is a student of God's word and knows the Bible better than his profession.

CHAPTER 2

COVENANTS AND BUSINESS OWNERSHIP

While no Biblical center for Christian theology has been proposed that seems to be satisfactory to most Christians (especially academics),[125] God's implementation of his redemptive plan through covenants serves as an excellent starting point for this theology of business ownership.

Covenants serve as a biblical center and prominent theme uniting Scripture.[126] Covenants govern the life of a CBO and create an eternal perspective in which the CBO lives. Covenants inform our stewardship role before God. God's invitation to mankind is extended through those who covenant with God to those who

---

125 Daniel J. Brendsel, "Plots, Themes, and Responsibilities: The Search for a Center of Biblical Theology Reexamined." *Themelios* 35, no. 3 (2010), 411–12. There are a number of propositions for the center of Biblical theology for those interested in this discussion. One example is James Hamilton, *God's Glory in Salvation Through Judgment*, (Crossway, 2010). Another is J. Scott Duvall and J. Daniel Hays, *God' Relationsl Presence: The Cohesive Center of Biblical Theology*, (Baker Academic, 2019.) Consider also T. Johnson Chakkuvarackal, "Towards a Spirit–centered Biblical Theology: The 'From Below' Aspects of the Holy Spirit." *Bangalore Theological Forum*, 2003 Vol35: 1–30. For an older discussion, see Henning Graf Reventlow, *Problems of Biblical Theology in the Twentieth Centure*, trans. John Bowden. (Fortress, 1986), 154–64.

126 Thomas McComiskey, The Covenants of Promise: A Theology of Old Testament Covenants. (Wipf & Stock, 1985), 10.

need God. Covenants are not contracts and the two should not be confused.

In this chapter, I will suggest that the connection between covenants and business ownership is profound. I will demonstrate that one's covenant with God has practical and significant tentacles into a Christian's business ownership role. The organizing principle for the life of a Christian business owner (and for every Christian) is our covenant with God.[127]

GENERALLY SPEAKING, A covenant may be defined as a sacred kinship bond between two voluntary parties, ratified by swearing an oath.[128] One part[129] of a covenant is the promise (if a promissory covenant)[130] or the stipulations (if an obligatory covenant).[131] The promise can be one-sided, in which one party commits to fulfilling his promises to the other party (promissory covenant). Or the promise can be two-sided, in which both parties agree to fulfill their promises to the other (obligatory covenant). The Abrahamic covenant (Genesis 12, 15, 17, 22) is an example of a promissory covenant.[132] The Sinai covenant (Exodus 19.1–31.18) is an example of an obligatory

---

127 For a discussion of the view that covenants are an addendum to God's election in the Old Testament, see Duane Garrett, *The Problem of the Old Testament: Hermeneutical, Schematic & Theological Approaches.* (IVP Academic, 2020), 181ff.

128 Faithlife, "Covenant." In *Logos Bible Study Factbook.* (Faithlife, October 16, 2024.) https://ref.ly/logos4/Factbook?id=ref%3abk.%25covenant.

129 The two parts of a covenant (promise or stipulations and administration) are common to most forms of a covenant in the ANE. Often, the administration of a covenant is broken explicitly into blessings and curses. Various ANE coveant forms were comprised of different essential elements. For example, a Hittite covenant usually had seven parts, whereas the Assyrian covenant had four parts. The other standard elements of covenants may include a prelude, prologue, witnesses, and the oath. For a good discussion about various covenant forms and standard elements, see George R. Law, "The Form of the New Covenant in Matthew." *American Theological Inquiry* 5, no. 2 (2012). For purposes of this book, I am most interested in the promise/stipulations and administrative elements of a covenant.

130 A promissory covenant is generally a unilateral covenant based solely on one party's promise and sealed with that party's oath. The receptor party generally is not required to do anything special to receive the benefits of the promise. For an excellent discussion of God's everlasting promise expressed in the Abrahamic covenant, see Bernhard W. Anderson, *Contours of Old Testament Theology.* (Fortress Press, 2011), 98–99.

131 An obligatory covenant is generally a bilateral covenant based on both party's promises to each other and sealed by an oath from both parties. For a good discussion of promissory and obligatory covenants, see René Lopez, "Israelite Covenants in the Light of Ancient near Eastern Covenants (Part 1 of 2)." *Chafer Theological Seminary Journal Volume 9,* 2003, 92–111.

132 Some will argue that the promises to Abraham in Genesis 12 were not strictly a covenant until they were ratified as a covenant in Genesis 15. See McComiskey, *Covenants of Promise,* 59ff.

or bilateral covenant.[133] Many scholars view the Davidic covenants as promissory[134] (or Grant Covenants).[135] Many also view the book of Deuteronomy as an obligatory or bilateral covenant.[136]

A second part of a covenant is administering how obedience and disobedience are punished or rewarded. Often, curses and blessings were used to administrate obedience and disobedience.[137] Interestingly, Dr. McComiskey finds the new covenant to be administrative only since the promise of the Abrahamic covenant is eternal, and no new promise was given in the New Testament that replaced the promise given to Abraham.[138] I agree with Dr. McComiskey. If one looks closely at the elements of the new covenant,[139] one finds these elements are administrative, not a change or modification of the eternal promise given to Abraham in Genesis 12, 15, and 17.

The forming of the covenants described in the Bible was not unique to Israel. Their use would make sense. If one were going to develop a treaty with God, or if God were going to develop a treaty with His people *at that time*, they would use a common, accepted format so that it would be credible and understood. The notion that the covenant forms were borrowed from other sources does not diminish their validity or effectiveness when used by God.[140] Covenant forms were commonly known and accepted in the ancient Near East.[141] God used the common form of a covenant to make His covenant with His people.

A BRIEF REVIEW OF REDEMPTIVE COVENANTS IN THE BIBLE

God has implemented his redemptive plan through a series of covenants in both testaments. Covenants are vital to understanding the redemptive history of the Bible and a Christian's covenant relationship with God. God's rule is extended through covenants to his people

---

133 McComiskey, *Covenants of Promise*, 63.

134 J. Robert Vannoy. "Samuel, First and Second, Theology Of." In *Evangelical Dictionary of Biblical Theology*, Electronic ed., Baker Reference Library. (Baker Book House, 1996), 703–8.

135 M. Weinfeld, "The Covenant of Grant in the Old Testament and in the Ancient Near East." *Journal of the American Oriental Society*, 1970. 90(2):184–203.

136 Joseph P. Healey, "Faith: Old Testament." In *The Anchor Yale Bible Dictionary*, edited by David Noel Freedman. (Doubleday, 1992), v2, 746.

137 René Lopez, "Israelite Covenants in the Light of Ancient near Eastern Covenants." *Chafer Theological Seminary Journal Volume 10*, 2004, 72–106.

138 I find McComiskey's argument that the new covenant is administrative in nature compelling. To read his thinking, please see McComiskey, *Covenants of Promise*, 153–61.

139 A good outline of these elements can be found in Brian Collins, "The New Covenant." In *Lexham Survey of Theology*, edited by Mark Ward, Jessica Parks, Brannon Ellis, and Todd Hains. (Lexham Press, 2018.)

140 See the *Baker Encyclopedia of the Bible*, on page 617 in the section "The Case for Mosaic Authorship." Walter Elwell, General Editor. Baker Book House (1988).

141 Peter Gentry and Steven Wellum, God's Kingdom through God's Covenants: A Concise Biblical Theology. (Crossway, 2015), 49–50. For a good review of an outline of covenant structures, see G.R. Lanier, "Davidic Covenant" in The Lexham Bible Dictionary. John Barry, Editor. (Lexham Press, 2016.)

and creation.[142] By evaluating the covenants and God's faithfulness to God's followers, one can conclude that one characteristic of God is that he is covenantal in his relationships with humanity.[143]

Covenant of Redemption

The foundational covenant in the Scriptures is the Covenant of Redemption, which is a "…pre–temporal, intra–trinitarian agreement among the Father, Son, and Holy Spirit to plan and execute the redemption of the elect."[144] The members of the Trinity agreed to the Covenant of Redemption before time, often referred to in Scripture as 'God's eternal plan.' Gentry and Wellum openly admit that the Covenant of Redemption has little Scriptural support if the term 'covenant' is defined solely in ANE suzerain[145]–vassal[146] arrangements. However, if 'covenant' is defined more broadly, God's eternal plan becomes a covenant when restated in covenantal terms.[147] Chafer is more direct: "[The Covenant of Redemption] is sustained largely by the fact that it seems both reasonable and inevitable."[148] Berkhof agrees: "Wherever we have the essential elements of a covenant, namely, contracting parties, a promise or promises, and a condition, there we have a covenant."[149]

A more broadly defined covenant is "…a relationship between two parties involving permanent and serious commitments of faithfulness, loyal love, obedience, and trust."[150] When God's eternal plan[151] (Ephesians 1:3–4, 9–10; Galatians 4:4, 1 Peter 1:19–21; Revelation 13:8) is considered within a broader set of covenant definitions, it is not unreasonable to

---

142   Peter Gentry and Steven Wellum, *Kingdom Through Covenant: A Biblical–Theological Understanding of the Covenants.* (Crossway, 2018), 34.

143   David N. Freedman, "Divine Commitment and Human Obligation: The Covenant Theme." *Interpretation*, (1964). 18(4):419–431.

144   John V. Fesko *The Trinity and the Covenant of Redemption.* (Mentor, 2016), 131–32.

145   Merriam–Webster, "Suzerain": *A superior feudal lord to whom fealty is due.* Accessed 02/03/2024. https://www.merriam–webster.com/dictionary/suzerai

146   Merriam–Webster, "Vassal": *A person under the protection of a feudal lord to whom he has vowed homage and fealty; one in a subservient or subordinate position.* Accessed 02/03/2024. https://www.merriam–webster.com/dictionary/vassal.

147   For a more thorough discussion on the Covenant of Redemption, see Wayne Grudem, *Systematic Theology, Second Edition.* (Zondervan Academic, 2020), 650–51; Francis Turretin, *Institutes of Elenctic Theology.* Dennison, J.T. (Ed.) (New Jersey, 1994), 169–84; Fesko, *The Trinity,* 131–32; Gentry, *Kingdom Through Covenant,* 77–79.

148   Lewis S. Chafer, *Systematic Theology.* (Kregel Publications, 1947), v1, 42.

149   Louis Berkhof, *Systematic Theology.* (Eerdmans, 1938), 266.

150   Gentry, *Kingdom Through Covenant,* 165.

151   For a more thorough discussion on God's eternal plan, see Chafer, *Systematic Theology,* v1, 234–236; Norman L. Geisler, *Systematic theology, volume four: church, last things.* (Bethany House Publishers, 2005), 460–465; Archibald A. Hodge, *A commentary on the confession of faith: With questions for theological students and Bible Classes.* (Presbyterian Board of Publication and Sabbath–School Work), 134–40.

conclude that God's eternal plan is a covenant within the Trinity, generally known as the Covenant of Redemption.

Covenant of Works

The Covenant of Works[152] was God's promise to Adam as head and representative of humanity that Adam would live forever if Adam perfectly obeyed God in the garden.[153] This covenant is inferred from Hosea 6:7 (NIV): "As at Adam, they have broken the covenant; they were unfaithful to me there." The Covenant of Works is also inferred from the elements in the creation story in Genesis 2:15–17 (NIV):

> [15] The Lord God took the man and put him in the Garden of Eden to work it and take care of it. [16] And the Lord God commanded the man, "You are free to eat from any tree in the garden; [17] but you must not eat from the tree of the knowledge of good and evil, for when you eat from it you will certainly die."

Berkhof comments:

> In the case under consideration, two parties are named, a condition is laid down, a promise of reward for obedience is clearly implied, and a penalty for transgression is threatened … When entering into covenant relations with men, it is always God who lays down the terms, and they are very gracious terms, so that He has, also from that point of view, a perfect right to expect that man will assent to them. In the case under consideration, God had but to announce the covenant, and the perfect state in which Adam lived was a sufficient guarantee for his acceptance.[154]

Gentry and Wellum[155] agree with Hodge, McComiskey, and Berkhof concerning the Covenant of Works and offer a compelling argument that Genesis 1:26–31, with certain elements in Genesis 2:4–24, constitute God's first covenant with humanity—the Covenant of Works.

---

152   The Covenant of Works is sometimes referred to by other names, such as the covenant of nature, the covenant of life, or the Edenic covenant (Berkhof, *Systematic Theology*, 211).

153   McComiskey, *Covenants of Promise*, 214; Charles Hodge, *Systematic Theology*. (Logos Research Systems, Inc, 1997), v2, 117.

154   Berkhof, *Systematic Theology*, 213.

155   Gentry, *God's Kingdom*, 215–58

Covenant of Grace

The Covenant of Grace was necessary after Adam violated the Covenant of Works. After Adam sinned (Genesis 3:1–13), God implemented his plan from eternity past—the Covenant of Grace—to give sinful people fellowship with him as humanity had through Adam before the fall.[156] The Covenant of Grace starts in Genesis 3:15 and carries through the rest of Scripture to the end of Revelation. The promise of this covenant was "...progressively revealed and fulfilled in history through variously administered covenants with Noah, Abraham, Israel, and David."[157] Even though there exists a plurality of covenants, there is only one overarching Covenant of Grace (that includes the New Covenant), which is why one must "...view the relationships between the covenants in terms of an overall unity and continuity."[158] Figure 2–1 graphically depicts the progression of the foundational covenants in the Bible.

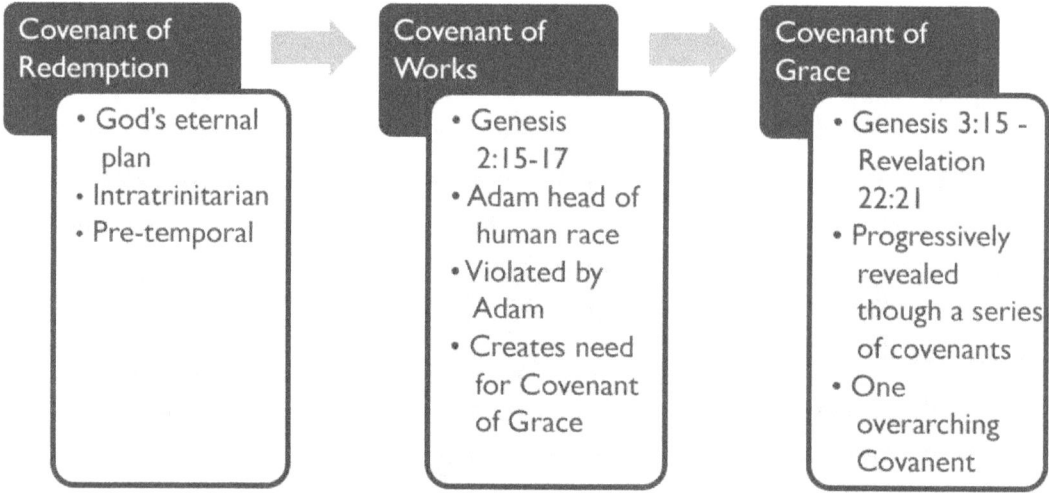

Figure 2–1: Progression of foundational covenants in the Bible

Within the Covenant of Grace are the individual covenants that together form the trajectory of God's saving grace.[159] The individual covenants that constitute the Covenant of Grace are:
- Noahic covenant—Genesis 9:8–17
- Abrahamic covenant—Genesis 12–17

---

156 Wayne Grudem, *Christian Ethics: An Introduction to Moral Reasoning.* (Crossway, 2018), 651.
157 Gentry, *Kingdom Through Covenant*, 84.
158 Gentry, *Kingdom Through Covenant*, 84.
159 Gentry, *Kingdom Through Covenant*, 654.

- Exodus/Sinai covenant—Exodus 19–24[160]
- Mosaic covenant—Deuteronomy 6:4–9[161]
- Davidic covenant—2 Samuel 7:1–29
- New covenant—multiple passages in Isaiah, Jeremiah, Daniel and elsewhere. This covenant culminates in the person of Jesus Christ.

The new covenant is the fulfillment or terminus of the other covenants. Hence, all of these covenants reach their fulfillment in Jesus Christ. Scripture ties kingdom and covenants organically together: through the progression of the covenants, God's saving reign comes to this world in the person of Jesus Christ.

Hence, Christianity is a covenantal religion, and obedience to the Christian faith is covenantal obedience.[162] When Christ calls a person to faith, that individual enters a covenant relationship with God in which there is mutual commitment, love, and faithfulness. Inside this covenant, God graciously gives God's followers a future hope to live in his presence forever. While the beginning of the Covenant of Grace is faith in Christ's work alone, the condition of continuing in that covenant is obedience to God's commands.[163] "A relationship with God entails commands or obligations to be obeyed and fulfilled, but these are always surrounded and supported by the mighty promises of God."[164]

If one's faith in Christ is genuine, it will produce covenantal obedience (James 2:17, 1 John 2:4–6). A Christian business owner stands on the foundations of the Covenants of Redemption, Works, and Grace and works within the practical trajectories of the new covenant to participate in God's eternal plan both for that owner individually, for God's church corporately, and the world globally.

WHY COVENANTS MATTER TO A CHRISTIAN BUSINESS OWNER

Covenants matter to a CBO because, in one way or another, all that a CBO does, thinks, or feels is tethered to his covenant with God, whether inside or outside his business. God's redemptive covenant with us is the core of the theological foundation of business ownership. In addition, covenants provide a basis of business ownership that can be stated as follows:

---

160   Some scholars include all of Exodus 19–40 and continue into Leviticus as the entire Sinai covenant.

161   Some scholars view the entire book of Deuteronomy as a covenant presented in a Suzerain–Vassal Treaty (Gentry, *Kingdom Through Covenant*, 398–99).

162   McComiskey, *Covenants of Promise*, 228.

163   Grudem, *Ethics*, 652.

164   Gentry, *Kingdom Through Covenant*, 269.

Christian business owners live with an eternal perspective derived from the owner's covenant with God and lived out through Biblical stewardship.

EFFECT OF COVENANTS ON BUSINESS OWNERSHIP

At a summary level, the covenant we have with God has several pragmatic effects on what we think, what we value, and how we define our role as business owners:

- Covenants place God at the top of the governance model
- Covenants govern the entire life of the CBO.
- Covenants create an eternal perspective out of which the business owner operates.
- Covenants focus attention on the truly important
- Covenants make it easier to let go of one's business
- Businesses entrusted to Christians are one vector through which God's rule is extended.
- God's offer of salvation to humanity is channeled through those who have covenanted with God
- Covenants create freedom for the business owner.

Governance model

Biblical stewardship is a covenantal stewardship of that which God entrusts to the steward. Because of the CBO's covenant with God, business governance is recast from earthly, legal terms to covenantal terms within the mind of the CBO. Earthly governance structures will indeed remain, but for a CBO, God is the true owner and authority over the CBO's business.

The CBO is not released to disregard earthly laws[165] and regulations,[166] because of the CBOs covenant with God. The CBO maintains compliance[167] to the extent that laws and regulations do not require the CBO to sin. Even though the CBO is the CEO, Founder, or Owner,[168] he is the main servant to God in the business. Figure 2–2 illustrates a conventional wisdom–oriented relationship between business, ownership, and conventional governance. Figure 2–3 extends Figure 2–2 with a covenantal view of governance.

---

165 A law is a statute passed by a legislative process by a duly elected body of representatives.

166 A regulation is a rule promulgated by a governmental authority that operates under the oversight of a duly elected individual or a body of representatives. Rules have the effect of laws, but are not codified in the body of statutes.

167 Compliance is obedience to the laws and regulations adopted by a duly elected legislative body and the governmental agencies that operate under their authority.

168 In many family businesses or those with multiple shareholders, one can be a Christian business owner without having these titles or the authority of a CEO.

Note: Authority increases in Figures 2–2 and 2–3 as one moves from the center to the outside ring.

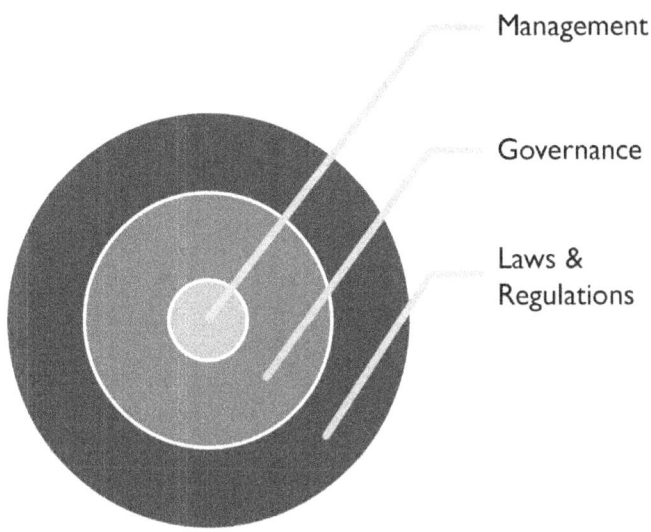

Management

Governance

Laws & Regulations

Figure 2–2: Relationship of business, governance, and the legal system.

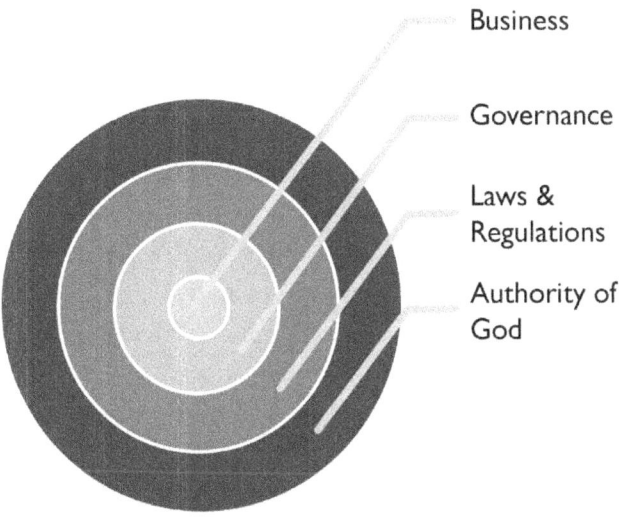

Business

Governance

Laws & Regulations

Authority of God

Figure 2–3: Relationship of business, governance, and authority for a Christian Business Owner.

To the extent that the Scriptures speak to owning and operating a business, the CBO will seek to be obedient first to the commands of Scripture because of the CBOs covenant with God. Thereafter, a CBO will seek to be obedient to the laws and regulations of the State.

It is important to restate that the life purpose of a Christian business owner is about being obedient and faithful to God because of one's covenant with him.

> Note: Perseverance and faithfulness are discussed more fully in Chapter 3, *Stewardship and Entrustments*

Eternal perspective

Because the covenant promises last throughout eternity (Genesis 17:7, 13, 19; 1 Chronicles 16:17; Psalm 105:10), a CBO should align his actions, attitudes, and decisions with his eternal future with Christ. The pragmatic effect of this alignment means that temporal decisions change in quality and intention when choices are evaluated in light of eternity. Things that matter so much to others on earth lose their importance when evaluated through the lens of eternity.

For example, a CBO with an eternal perspective may give away more profits than some would think wise because he is consciously building treasures in heaven. Another example is a CBO who continues to invest in his own development knowing that what he does on this earth is preparation for reigning with Christ in heaven.

Living with eternity in mind means being away of one's mortality. Most of us do not like talking about death or dying. We find it difficult to imagine our existence ending or activities continuing without us.[169] CBOs often kid themselves that they will never leave their business, knowing this is not true, but half believing the lie to comfort and give themselves a sense of relevance as they grow older.

Instead of avoiding the topics of death, a CBO who lives with eternity in mind *looks forward* to passing from this earth into heaven and the presence of God. While none of us look forward to *how* we will die, our covenant with God assures us of a future eternity in God's loving presence. So we can let go of the things of this earth more easily because our covenant gives us the freedom to let go and the security of an assured future.

Focus on the truly important

If you have an assured future with God and understand that his provision for your life is all you need, then winning an earthly contest seems pretty irrelevant. Most professional

---

169 Virginia Morris, *Talking About Death*. (Workman Publishing, 2001), 1–2.

athletes and highly successful business owners enjoy competition. They enjoy being pushed by competition to be better than they are today. They enjoy winning and hate losing.

But in light of eternity, winning and losing do not matter. If you die with $100M or $100, it does not matter. If you build the most successful business in the world, it does not matter. Listen to a portion of Deion Sander's testimony:[170]

> You could sleep in the bed with two and three women and nobody satisfied. You got a hundred suits and can't cover up the pain. You got three, four, five hundred pairs of shoes and you can't take a step in the right direction. You got nine or ten cars in the driveway and you ain't going nowhere. You got a 15,000 square foot house, but you ain't got a home.

Deion Sanders is a modern–day example of the point Christ was making in Matthew 16:24–26 (LEB):

> [24] If anyone wants to come after me, let him deny himself and take up his cross and follow me. [25] For whoever wants to save his life will lose it, but whoever loses his life on account of me will find it. [26] For what will a person be benefited if he gains the whole world but forfeits his life? Or what will a person give in exchange for his life?

In light of eternity, most of what we do and value on this earth pales when interpreted in light of eternity with Christ.

> And the the things of this world will grow strangely dim, in the light of his glory and grace.[171]

I think Helen Lemmel has it just about right.

Let go more easily

Many business owners find it difficult to leave their business after twenty or thirty years because they do not have a future. They have nothing to retire *to*. They have no other purpose in life, so they stick around and work into their eighties or nineties.

---

170   Hey Papi Promotions Network, "Coach Prime 'Deion Sanders' shares his testimony about meeting Jesus!" October 6, 2023. Youtube.com https://youtu.be/MObdBFIRG2U

171   Helen Howarth Lemmel, "Turn Your Eyes Upon Jesus." In *Logos Hymnal Media Resource*. (Lexham Press, 2009.)

However, a CBO who lives with eternity in mind can leave his business because something far greater is in his future. He can view business ownership as a chapter in his life because he has the presence of God on this earth and the assurance of the unfettered presence of God in heaven. What could be better? And if that's not enough, God will give him meaningful work that will be fulfilling and enjoyable—far more fulfilling than the business he owned here on earth.

God's rule is extended

Gentry and Wellum suggest that covenants are the vehicle through which God's rule on earth is established and extended:

> The covenant with Abraham is the basis for all God's dealings with the human race. While the settings and languages differ from the covenants in Genesis 1–3 to the Noahic covenants in Genesis 6–9 and the Abrahamic covenant in Genesis 12–25, the main idea is still that God is establishing his rule in the context of a covenant relationship. Abraham and his descendants will be a light to the nations in this manner.[172]

Because CBOs participate in the covenants between God and his people, CBOs extend God's rule to what the owner owns or rents. The CBO represents God's rule in the marketplace, but it is not extended onto the marketplace. God's rule is not forced on unbelievers in the marketplace; instead, the CBO demonstrates to the marketplace how a Christian behaves, what choices a CBO makes, and lives out what a mature, balanced faith in God looks like. As others are drawn to God, God's rule is extended through others' voluntary acceptance of God's offer of eternal life and forgiveness of sin.

The truth that God extends his rule through covenant is grounded in another truth: man is created in the image of God (Genesis 1:26–28). Bishop notes that

> It is clear that subduing and ruling are one facet of being the image of God, and thus an essential part of what it means to be human. Subduing and ruling the creation, then, are to be done as God's representatives.[173]

Gentry and Wellum nuance this idea of God's rule extending to all people through covenant:

---

172 Gentry, Kingdom through Covenant, 332.

173 Steve Bishop, "Green Theology and Deep Ecology: New Age or New Creation?" *Themelios*, 1991, 16(3):8–14.

The ruling is not the essence of the divine image but rather a result of being made as the divine image … the divine image is correlated with the command to rule as God's viceroy.[174]

When a CBO subdues the earth (Genesis 1:28) by operating a profitable business, that owner works under God's direction to extend God's rule to those parts of the earth the CBO controls. For example, any time a CBO legally owns or rents anything, God's rule is extended to that part of creation for the time the owner legally owns or rents. When an asset or a business is sold, the ownership of those items is transferred to the new owner, but the ownership for the value received from those items is transferred to God via the CBO.

God's offer of salvation

God calls the nations to himself through his people with whom he has covenanted. Calling those who are far from God is an important task for each Christian. Doing so is an act of faithfulness inside our covenant with God. Consider these three passages from Genesis (emphasis added):

> [1] Now the Lord said to Abram, "Go from your country and your kindred and your father's house to the land that I will show you. [2] And I will make of you a great nation, and I will bless you and make your name great, so that you will be a blessing. [3] I will bless those who bless you, and him who dishonors you I will curse, and *in you all the families of the earth shall be blessed.* (Genesis 12:1–3 ESV).

> [17] I will surely bless you, and I will surely multiply your offspring as the stars of heaven and as the sand that is on the seashore. And your offspring shall possess the gate of his enemies, [18] and *in your offspring shall all the nations of the earth be blessed.*" (Genesis 22:17–18 ESV).

> [3] Sojourn in this land, and I will be with you and will bless you, for to you and to your offspring I will give all these lands, and I will establish the oath that I swore to Abraham your father. [4] I will multiply your offspring as the stars of heaven and will give to your offspring all these lands. *And in your offspring all the nations of the earth shall be blessed.* (Genesis 26:3–4 ESV).

---

174   Gentry, Kingdom through Covenant, 223–24.

The context of the covenant community being a blessing to all the nations of the earth is equated with introducing these nations to God and inviting them to live as the covenant community lives: In covenant and communion with God. Gentry and Wellum write:

> The Abrahamic covenant is implemented in the Iron Age, with Israel as Abraham's family, through the Mosaic covenant. Israel—or more particularly, Israel's kind, as the Davidic covenant later makes plain—will be the instrument for renewing the covenant relationship and establishing the instruction and will of Yahweh in the hearts and lives of his people and, through them, in the nations."[175]

As CBOs live and work with others who do not believe in God, we have the opportunity and responsibility to introduce unbelievers to God.

Freedom from performance

Another reflection I will offer is that our covenant with God gives us the safety and security to make mistakes without fearing God's rejection. Covenants are not performance–based relationships, yet paradoxically, covenants give us the freedom to perform better.

Performance–based (transactional) relationships may hinder one's performance because of the insecurities created if one does not perform well enough to meet the standard. The anxieties created in a performance–based relationship can be profound and debilitating. Gregston comments:[176]

> In performance–based relationships, people are valuable because of their actions, accomplishments, and achievements. They are accepted because they meet expectations. Performance–based relationships are conditional and withhold love according to one's performance. These types of relationships hold the bar of expectation too high for most to attain and then maintain. When a [person] fails to meet expectations, they experience an overwhelming sense of disappointment and discouragement, despair, and even despondency."

---

175 Gentry, Kingdom through Covenant, 237.

176 Mark Gregston, "Performance–Based Relationships (Part 1 of 2)." March 8, 2021. Parentingtodaysteens. org. https://parentingtodaysteens.org/articles/devo–10–performance–based–relationships–part–1–of–2/.

While Gregston is writing about teens, his thoughts apply to adults too. Knight echos Gregston in the *Harvard Business Review*:[177]

> When employees lack self–confidence, it can be hard to get them to perform at their best … The challenge is that insecure people are so concerned with how they look and how they are perceived that they either fail to solicit critical feedback or completely ignore it when it's given. And this robs them of the opportunity to improve.

Insecurities are caused by several factors that we carry into the workplace. Most common are the need to be liked, perfectionism, and past failures.[178] Some businesses purposefully prey on employee's insecurities by threatening their job security as a means of motivation.[179] Christian business owners are not immune to the debilitating effects of personal insecurities.[180]

Many Christians carry their insecurities into their covenant with God. They measure 'spiritual growth'[181] through a performance–based filter. (As I will discuss in the next section, *Covenants are not Contracts*; a performance–based Christianity is lethal to fully participating in one's covenant with God.) These individuals are often filled with shame and perfection. CBOs who are insecure often project their performance–based filters onto their employees, compounding the problem for insecure employees.

Christian business owners should manage themselves and their employees through a covenant lens rather than a performance–based model. Metrics matter in business, but relationships matter more. When you are on your deathbed, you likely will not care that production hit its target fifteen years ago, but you will care that you led your production manager to the Lord.

If metrics drive the quality of the relationships, then the owner is acting out of transaction rather than covenant. However, if metrics are enforced while quality relationships

---

177   Rebecca Knight, "How to Manage an Insecure Employee." April 25, 2018, hbr.org. https://hbr.org/2018/04/how–to–manage–an–insecure–employee

178   Melanie Greenberg, "The 3 Most Commo Causes of Insecurity and How to Beat Them." December 6, 2015. Psychologytoday.com. https://www.psychologytoday.com/intl/blog/the–mindful–self–express/201512/the–3–most–common–causes–of–insecurity–and–how–to–beat–them

179   Mindy Shoss, shiyang Su, Ann Schlotzhauer, and Nicole Carusone, "Job Insecurity Harms Both Employees and Employers." September 26, 2022. Hbr.org. https://hbr.org/2022/09/job–insecurity–harms–both–employees–and–employers

180   Cheryl Conner, "Overcoming the Biggest Challenge in Business: Your Own Insecurity." May 10, 2013. Forbes.com. https://www.forbes.com/sites/cherylsnappconner/2013/05/04/overcoming–the–biggest–challenge–in–business–your–own–insecurity/

181   Spiritual growth can generally be thought of as an increase in faith, understanding, holiness, and commitment to God.

are emphasized, the owner can act out of a covenant–flavored relationship while focusing on metrics.

If ones' hiring process is strictly performance–based, which our laws and society encourage, then the employer–employee relationship may become strictly performance–based, stale, and transactional. But to the extent reasonably possible, a CBO, living their lives through the lens of covenant, will focus

- Less on asserting authority and more on building quality relationships
- Less on correction and more on training
- Less on criticism and more on encouragement
- Less on micromanagement and more on delegation and trust

When a CBO is entrusted with a business, the owner has a unique opportunity to build a culture of warmth for employees while remaining tough on process and procedure. *Be tough on process, soft on people.* It is a balance that can and should be pursued to steward well what God has entrusted you.

COVENANTS ARE NOT CONTRACTS

Properly understood, covenants *create* relationships rather than oppression and legalism. The modern reader will likely be far more familiar with the concept of a contract than a covenant. Covenants are not contracts, and the differences between the two are significant. Because covenant theology is so rarely taught in many Christian churches, most Christians view relationships from a transactional perspective rather than through covenant.

Most Christians need to re–program their thinking to think covenentally about their relationship with God instead of transactionally. Table 2–1 compares and contrasts covenants and contracts that clarify and sharpen one's understanding of the biblical idea of a covenant relationship.

Table 2–1: Comparison of Contracts and Covenants[182]

Category	Contract	Covenant
Occasion	Expected benefit: self–interest	Desire for relationship; sacrificial love
Nature	Transactional	Relational

---

182 Adapted from Gentry, *Kingdom through Covenant*, 172–73, and Scott Hahn, "Covenant." In *The Lexham Bible Dictionary.* Barry, J.D. and Beitzel, B.J. (Eds.) (Lexham Press, 2016.)

Category	Contract	Covenant
Basis	Promises exchanged	Sworn by solemn oaths
Focus	Self	Other
Motivation	Profit; self-interest	Self-giving loyalty, sacrificial love
Locus of Control	Externalise duties	Internalise responsibilities
Orientation	Negotiated	Gift
Societal	Emphasize rights	Emphasize responsibilities
Power	Expressed through assertion	Expressed through service
Sacred	Preserving individual rights	Fulfilling responsibilities as an expression of love
Terms	Exchange of property	Exchange of life
Obligation	Performance	Loyalty
Authority	Often asserted	Seldom asserted
Violation	Punishment	Forgiveness
Termination	Temporary	Permanent

Contracts are temporary, while covenant bonds are permanent. Covenants emphasize relational obligations, whereas contracts emphasize rights. Covenant societies emphasize social responsibilities, while contract societies emphasize our private rights.[183] In covenant societies, power is exercised through faithfulness to others. In contract societies, power is exercised by asserting individual rights, sometimes at the expense of another's welfare. In covenant societies, fulfilling responsibilities as an expression of worship to God is sacred. In contract societies, preserving individual rights that limit government power is sacred. Covenants make us "other" focused. Contracts make us "self" focused. Covenants internalize responsibilities. Contracts externalize duties. Covenants are relational. Contracts are transactional. Covenants create safety against lack of performance. Contracts punish lack of performance. Covenants create security that the relationship will last even when difficulties are encountered. Contracts base the security of the relationship on the commitment of both parties to fulfill the terms of their agreement.

183 George E. Mendenhall, *The Tenth Generation: The Origins of the Biblical Tradition.* (Johns Hopkins University Press, 1973), 16–31.

Both covenants and contracts have their place in life. Covenants and contracts are not opposed to each other: each has a positive use in human affairs.[184] Nevertheless, when discussing Biblical covenants and business ownership, one must do so from a framework of covenants, not contracts.

A Transactional View of Marriage: An Example of Covenants vs. Contracts

Sadly, a transactional view of relationships has found its way into the Christian psychological community. Willard Harley, the author of *His Needs Her Needs*, based his marriage counseling practice on the social exchange theory. He makes a compelling argument in his preface for why his methods work. But at the end of the day, his macro argument is that romantic love in a marriage is sustained through thousands of relationship transactions in which the husband meets his wife's needs, and the wife meets her husband's needs:

> If each spouse tried to do whatever it took to make the other happy and avoided doing what made the other unhappy, their feeling of love could be restored. The first couple I counseled with this new approach fell in love again, and their marriage was saved. From that point on, every time I saw a couple, I simply asked them what the other could do that would make them the happiest, and whatever it was, that was their first assignment ... Some surveys have found this book to be the most effective book on marriage ever written. Couples report that by reading this book and following its guidance, their love has been restored and their marriages have been saved. That's because it gets right to the heart of what makes marriages work— the feeling of love and what couples must do to create and sustain that feeling.[185]

I would suggest that marriage is more than transactions focused on meeting the needs of one's spouse. At its core, marriage is a covenant intended to reflect the covenant between the Trinity members. The unity, diversity, and covenant love in the Trinity are to be reflected in the marriage relationship's unity, diversity, and covenant love.

---

184 Hahn, Lexham Bible Dictionary, Covenant.
185 Willard F. Harley, *His Needs Her Needs*. (Revell, 2022), 10.

Yes, meeting the needs of one's spouse is important, but Christians fulfill their marriage responsibilities because of their covenant with each other, whether or not they feel romantic love at any given time and whether or not their spouse is meeting their needs.

By the same token, we should not treat our covenant with God as one comprised of a series of transactions where both sides keep score on how the other is doing.

SUMMARY

One's covenant with God forms the organizing principle to which all of life is tethered. In addition, covenants inform our stewardship role before God and enable us to participate in the great commission (Matthew 28:18–20) by extending an invitation to mankind to covenant with God. Covenants are not contracts, and the two should not be confused.

In the next chapter, I will focus more closely on several aspects of our covenant with God, including God's ownership of all that exists, our relationship with God, and our need to persevere in our allegiance to God faithfully. The next chapter extends the discussions in this chapter in vitally important ways. So, let us turn our attention to stewardship and entrustments.

CHAPTER 3

STEWARDSHIP AND ENTRUSTMENTS

This chapter will outline the inseparable relationship between stewardship and entrustment. Then, I will discuss the five supporting elements of stewardship and entrustment: God's ownership of all, love, presence, perseverance, and faithfulness. The Bible does not explicitly teach that these five elements support stewardship and entrustment, but the connection is so strong logically that it makes sense to conclude as much.

Stewardship is the state of being responsible for someone else's property.[186] Stewardship is about both the material and immaterial. The element of advantaging God's kingdom is at the core of Biblical stewardship, which can be expressed as follows:

Biblical stewards willingly disadvantage themselves to advantage the kingdom of God.

---

186 Faithlife. "Stewardship." In *Logos Bible Study Factbook*. Accessed June 24, 2024. https://ref.ly/logos4/Factbook?id=ref%3abk.%25stewardship.

49

An entrustment is committing something you own to someone else for safekeeping while trusting their fidelity and faithfulness.[187] Stewardship cannot occur without entrustment. Entrustments are given only to stewards. The two are inseparable. There is no stewardship until an owner entrusts material or immaterial elements to a steward. While stewardship can occur within the context of a contract, the spirit of Biblical stewardship is best fulfilled within the context of a Biblical covenant, where perseverance in faithfulness of the steward, not performance, is the definition of success.

Can We Have the Best of Both Worlds?

A strong temptation for CBOs to avoid is the lie that as a CBO, you can have the best of both worlds: you can have all the luxuries and comforts this world offers and all the spiritual blessings that God offers too. The temptation is that you can advantage yourself and God's kingdom at the same time.

Our Christian subculture holds up those who have earned millions in business and have a close walk with God. But too often, those CBOs who do not have both are left to feel inferior or somehow less than those being heralded as the ultimate standard.

I take issue with this line of thinking that we can have the best of both worlds on their earth based on 1 John 2:15–17 (ESV), where he taught us not to believe this lie:

> [15] Do not love the world or the things in the world. If anyone loves the world, the love of the Father is not in him. [16] For all that is in the world—the desires of the flesh and the desires of the eyes and pride of life—is not from the Father but is from the world. [17] And the world is passing away along with its desires, but whoever does the will of God abides forever.

Moreover, Christ reminds us in Luke 12:15 that our life does not consist in the abundance of our possessions. This temptation to "have it

---

187   D.K. McKim, "Entrust." In *The International Standard Bible Encyclopedia, Revised*, edited by Geoffrey W. Bromiley. (Eerdmans, 1979–1988), v2, 107.

all" is overcome through our affections: love God only and leverage the world's system to create wealth for the Kingdom. Disadvantage yourself for the kingdom. Do not love the wealth. Do not desire it. Look at wealth as a tool to accomplish God's purposes and nothing more.

Five elements support Biblical stewardship. These elements include God's ownership of everything, presence, love, perseverance, and faithfulness. Together, these elements create a logical context for stewardship and entrustments.

GOD'S OWNERSHIP OF EVERYTHING

Entrustments cannot occur without ownership. Entrustment in the Scriptures is derived from the truth of God's ownership of everything. The Scriptures clearly articulate God's absolute, undeniable ownership of *everything* on earth. And because he owns everything, he can entrust what he owns to whomever he desires. The Bible attests to God's ownership in multiple passages:

I have no need of a bull from your stall or of goats from your pens, for every animal of the forest is mine, and the cattle on a thousand hills. I know every bird in the mountains, and the insects in the fields are mine. If I were hungry, I would not tell you, for the world is mine, and all that is in it. (Psalm 50:9–12 NIV)

The earth is the Lord's and everything in it, the world, and all who live in it. (Psalm 24:1 NIV)

In anticipation of the coming splendor of the rebuilt temple, God claims in Haggai 2:8 (NIV):

The silver is mine and the gold is mine.

Moreover, according to Old Testament law, land was never sold permanently. Every fifty years, the land reverted to the family who originally owned it. Part of the reason Israelites were not able to sell their land permanently was because God owned it, and as such, this process reminded them that they were foreigners or strangers in the land in which they dwelled:

> The land must not be sold permanently, because the land is mine and you reside in my land as foreigners and strangers. Throughout the land that you hold as a possession, you must provide for the redemption of the land. (Leviticus 25:23–24 NIV)

The Old Testament, which "insists on the difference between possession and ownership," says that "all things are owned by God ... what we possess, we do not own—we merely hold it in trust for God."[188]

In the New Testament, the concept of entrustments is most clearly represented in the parable of the talents in Matthew 25:14–31. In this parable, the Master entrusts his property to his servants. Who owns the property is not in question. The Master is the owner; the servants are not. In entrusting them his property to be managed, he is taking a risk but also showing great trust. Applying this aspect of this parable to Christians, Bruner makes a good observation:

> We are not treated like little children here; we are given large responsibilities and so treated like adults. The grace of the master establishes his servants as mature human beings, called to take initiative and responsibility.[189]

Other Biblical passages illustrate the dynamic of entrustment. For example, the keeper of the prison entrusted everything to Joseph (Genesis 39:22), Pharaoh entrusted everything to Joseph (Genesis 41:41), and Solomon put Jeroboam in charge of the forced labor (1 Kings 11:28). Paul himself said that he had been entrusted with "the glorious gospel" (1 Timothy 1:12). Paul commanded Timothy to "guard the good deposit entrusted to you" (1 Timothy 1:14) and to "entrust these things to faithful men who will be able to teach others also" (2 Timothy 2:2). Interestingly, Jesus did not entrust[190] himself to those who would not believe in him (John 2:24). In addition, Jesus would not entrust that which is holy to those who would defile it. Lack of entrusting is the thrust of not casting what is holy before swine (Matthew 7:6).

---

188 Jonathan Sacks, *The Dignity of Difference: How to Avoid the Clash of Civilizations.* (Continuum, 2002), 114.

189 Fredrick Dale Bruner. *Matthew, Volume 2. The Churchbook.* (Waco, TX: Word Publishing, 1990), 902.

190 In this verse, the word translated *entrust* is ἐπίστευεν from πιστεύω, believe. In a minority of uses, it takes on the flavor of *becoming the recipient of something placed into one's care* (Logos). Examples: Romans 3:2, "the Jews were *entrusted* (ἐπιστεύθησαν)with the oracles of God." 1 Corinthians 9:17, "I am still *entrusted* (πεπίστευμαι) with stewardship." 1 Thessalonians 2:4, "but just as we have been approved by God too be *entrusted* (πιστευθῆναι) with the gospel, so we speak, not to please man, but to please God who tests our hearts." The noun form is πίστις, *faith.*

Entrustment and Ownership within the Trinity

When reading certain passages in the Bible, we find that there is ownership and entrustments within the Trinity. Consider these two sections of Scripture:

> And Jesus came and said to them, "All authority in heaven and on earth has been given to me. Go therefore…" (Matthew 28.18–19 ESV)

and

> I have much more to say to you, more than you can now bear. But when he, the Spirit of truth, comes, he will guide you into all the truth. He will not speak on his own; he will speak only what he hears, and he will tell you what is yet to come. He will glorify me because it is from me that he will receive what he will make known to you. All that belongs to the Father is mine. That is why I said the Spirit will receive from me what he will make known to you. (John 16.12–16 NIV)

In Matthew 28, Christ tells us that all authority in heaven and earth has been given to him. If it was "given," then that authority must have been owned by someone else—God Himself (who else *could* own it?). So, we see God entrusting to Christ "all authority on heaven and earth."

In the John 16 passage, Christ reminds us that everything the Father has is his: "All that belongs to the Father is mine." This is a restatement of Matthew 28. He also teaches us that the Spirit will not speak on his own, he will "only speak what he hears." The Spirit is listening to Christ: "He will receive from me what he will make known to you."

We find that God has entrusted Christ with *authority* and *message*. Christ has entrusted the Holy Spirit with the delivery of messages. When the Spirit speaks, he is not speaking on his own—he only relays what Christ tells him. The message is owned by Christ but relayed to us by the Holy Spirit. Without pressing this too far, there is a sense in which entrustments and stewardship exist within the Trinity.

Each experience we have had is an entrustment from the Lord to be stewarded to further his kingdom. For example, when we comfort another person with the comfort we have received from God and others during suffering we have experienced (2 Corinthians 1:3–4), we are stewarding well an experience entrusted to us to encourage and heal another who is suffering.

In a business context, when we show a new business owner how to build a thirteen-week cash flow forecast so that they can "know their flocks" (Proverbs 27:23) and manage their cash well, we are bringing the wisdom of God into their business and thus furthering the kingdom of God. We are stewarding a simple skill God has entrusted to us and are stewarding that skill well by passing it on to another business owner.

When we pray for one of our employees who does not know God and is going through a difficult time, we engage against the enemy who is trying to destroy them, and thus, we are bringing the authority and power of God into the unseen world around them. We are entrusted with our employees by God and are stewarding his entrustment well by praying for our employees.

That which God makes us aware of, that which He allows us to experience, and the physical things He gives us are all entrustments to be used to further his kingdom through proper stewardship.

Hence, all that we "own" is an entrustment from God. God's entrustments include our business, money, prestige, influence, wealth, power, and authority. All that we have is an entrustment from God.

RELATIONSHIP WITH GOD

Our relationship with God is at the epicenter of our covenant with God. In Chapter 1, *Covenants and Business Ownership,* I looked at covenants from a theological viewpoint and enumerated several practical effects on our role, decisions, and thinking as business owners.

In this section that discusses our relationship with God, I am looking at our covenant with God through interpersonal and emotional lenses. Matthew 25:14–30 is one of the best illustrations of why a robust and positive relationship with God is imperative to healthy Biblical stewardship. I will encourage you to read Matthew 25:14–30 in your Bible before moving forward with my discussion.

In this well-known parable, Jesus describes a master who goes on a long journey and entrusts portions of his property to specific servants. To the first servant, he gives five talents of money, to the second two talents, and another one talent.

The parable describes that the servant who had received five talents put that money to work, gaining five more. Likewise, the one who had been given two talents gained two more. However, given one talent, the third servant dug a hole in the ground to hide his master's money, ensuring that his money would not be lost. He did not create profit on that one talent.

When the master returned from his trip, he wanted to settle accounts with his servants. For the man who had received the five talents and had earned another five, the master commended him for being a good and faithful servant. The same happened to the servant who had been given two talents and had earned two more. For both servants, the master said,

> You have been faithful with a few things; I will put you in charge of many things. Come and share your master's happiness! (Matthew 25:21 NIV)

However, the servant who had received one talent essentially blamed the master for his inability to create another talent of wealth. He said to the master,

> I knew that you are a hard man, harvesting where you have not sown and gathering where you have not scattered seed. So I was afraid and went out and hid your talent in the ground. See, here is what belongs to you. (Matthew 25:24–25 NIV)

The master describes him as a wicked and lazy servant:

> So you knew that I harvest where I had not sown and gather where I have not scattered seed? Well then, you should have put my money on deposit with the bankers, so that when I returned, I would have received it back with interest. (Matthew 25:26–27 NIV)

Ultimately, the servant is described as "worthless" and thrown outside in to the darkness of night.

It appears the relationship of the first two servants with the master was substantively different from that of the third servant. The single variable between the first two servants and the third was their view of the master's person and work. Said a different way, the two commended servants had a good, healthy relationship with the master, and the third did not.

The difference in relationship quality between the two servants and the third necessarily means that the two servants understood the master's heart and intentions. They demonstrated a positive relationship with the master because they understood he was looking for more than an economic return on his investment; he was also looking for a closer relationship with them. That is why their reward was more of his presence and more responsibilities, not more wealth.[191]

---

191   Resist the temptation to eisegetically read into the text a 21st–century assumption that being given more to manage automatically means a higher salary (more wealth) from the master.

The third servant did not understand this dynamic. He had an unhealthy, distant relationship with the master and, as a result, held wrong and harmful views of the master. He did not get close enough to the master or spend enough time with him to understand what was in his master's heart. He did not see the opportunity that was before him. As a result, he was scared because he believed a lie about his master. He did not connect with the master's heart. Terry Austin expounds on this point: [192]

> The difference between the two good stewards and the one worthless steward was their relationship with the master. Everything said about the master implies that he was a generous, trusting man. The word used to describe what he did with his possessions is "entrusted." He handed over all of his possessions to these three men. This appears to be a great act of kindness and an expression of trust. If he did not have confidence in these men, he had other options. We know that he could have put his money in the bank ... The failure of [the worthless steward's] relationship resulted in the failure of his stewardship. He was a worthless steward because he did not have a healthy relationship with the master ... authentic stewardship begins with a proper relationship with the owner.

This passage teaches that a good steward "manages up" by getting to know his master well. *A Christian business owner will take quality time to get to know God and draw close to God's heart.* It is only when the servant has a wrong view of the master that the servant becomes derailed.[193]

LOVE AND PRESENCE

A CBO who stewards well what God has entrusted to him has an abiding love for God that leads to an abiding presence with him (John 15:4–8). I find both love and presence in John 15:5–17, where Christ instructs us to remain in him (5–12) and then immediately follows up with his command that we love one another (13–17).

A CBO who stewards well God's entrustments practices the presence of Jesus and regularly interacts with the Lord throughout the day. Decisions are so varied each day that the CBO understands he must 'check in' with God to know what God would have him do in a particular situation. The more frequently one listens to God, the more love one will

---

192 Terry Austin. *Authentic Stewardship,* (Austin Brothers Publishing, 2010), 111–24.

193 It is possible to have an overly negative or positive view of one's boss, both of which lead to negative results. See Dana Rousmaniere, "What Everyone Should Know About Managing Up." January 23, 2015, hbr.org. https://hbr.org/2015/01/what–everyone–should–know–about–managing–up. See also Caroline Castrillon, "5 Tips to Manage Up at Work." June 28, 2022, Forbes.com. https://www.forbes.com/sites/carolinecastrillon/2020/02/23/5–tips–to–manage–up–at–work/.

develop for the Lord, and the greater one will live in peace and contentment even while life's storms rage on. While at first, this connect does not appear to be obvious, our friend Brother Lawrence found this connection to be true:

> When I prayed during my first years as a monk, I thought mostly about death, judgment, hell, heaven, and my sins. The rest of the day I focused on God's presence even while at work. God was always with me, often as in my heart. The result: my view of God grew far beyond what I could imagine to the point only faith could begin to explain … Since then, I've walked with God simply and in faith. It's a humble path of love. Day after day, I spend my time doing what will please God. When I do this, I hope He'll do what He pleases with me.

One of my life goals is to grow to the point where I can honestly answer my wife's question, "What did you do today?" with this reply: "What God wanted me to do."

Love

Love is a central theme[194] in the Scriptures and Christian theology.[195] Within one's covenant relationship with God, love for God is confirmed through obedience. Such loving obedience is directly discussed by Christ and illustrated in his life via his earthly relationship with God. Even though covenant language is not used in John 5:19–24 (ESV), I find covenant elements of love expressed in a way that we can understand:

> [19] So Jesus said to them, "Truly, truly, I say to you, the Son can do nothing of his own accord, but only what he sees the Father doing. For whatever

---

194   Let us not make the mistake of emphasizing God's love over his other perfections. Emphasizing one perfection over another violates God's simplicity, which means that the "divine Being is uncompounded, incomplex, and indivisible." (Lewis Sperry Chafer. *Systematic Theology*. (Kregel Publications, 1993.), v1, 213). All of God's perfections are equally consistent with each other. Emphasizing one over another creates the notion that God is more one thing and less another, leading to the notion that God is composed of component parts. This is not how God is presented in the Scripture and is not how we should speak of him (Exodus 3:14, John 4:24, Exodus 34:6–7). "All the divine perfections are alike absolute, alike glorious, alike infinite, alike identical with divinity. They are not … to be considered as apart from God, or as properties of the divine subsistence. God's perfections are God himself, and God himself is his perfections." (Thomas Ridgley, *A Body of Divinity*, vol. 1 (New York: Robert Carter & Brothers, 1855), 123.) "God's oneness includes more than his numerical unity. It comprises also his simplicity. This becomes clear when one considers the fact that Scripture in giving us a description of the fulness of God's being uses not only adjectives but also nouns … every attribute is identical with God's being by reason of the fact that every one of his virtues is absolutely perfect." (Herman Bavinck, *The Doctrine of God*. Trans. William Hendriksen. (Baker Books, 1951), 168.

195   Faithlife, "Love." In *Logos Bible Study Factbook*. (Faithlife, October 20, 2024.) https://ref.ly/logos4/Factbook?id=ref%3abk.%25love.

the Father does, that the Son does likewise. [20] For the Father loves the Son and shows him all that he himself is doing. And greater works than these will he show him, so that you may marvel. [21] For as the Father raises the dead and gives them life, so also the Son gives life to whom he will. [22] For the Father judges no one, but has given all judgment to the Son, [23] that all may honor the Son, just as they honor the Father. Whoever does not honor the Son does not honor the Father who sent him. [24] Truly, truly, I say to you, whoever hears my word and believes him who sent me has eternal life. He does not come into judgment, but has passed from death to life.

I want to focus on the "like father, like son" aspect of what Christ models. In Jesus' day, most sons did what their fathers did vocationally. The Jewish culture assumed sons would follow their fathers into the family business or trade.[196] Christ uses this cultural norm to highlight that he only does what he sees God do (5:19b) because he is the Son of God.[197] Christ does what God does (5:20)—like father, like son. God shows Christ all that he is doing because he loves Christ. And Christ does *only* what God does because he loves the Father (John 14:31 ESB): "I do as the Father has commanded me, so that the world may know that I love the Father."

Hence, within the relationship between God and Christ, mutual love is expressed in a perfect father/son relationship. We have God showing his son all that he is doing, and the son delights in the father he loves so much that he does only what he sees his father doing. Both delight in each other's presence as they each receive love from the other. Such delight and love is the model for our covenant relationship with God.

This model is repeated in our relationship with God through Christ. God loves us, and we love God, and part of our entering a covenant relationship with God is that he now calls us "sons of God." (Ephesians 1:5). Repeating the cycle, Christ loves us as God has loved him—perfectly and fully: "As the Father has loved me, so have I loved you." (John 15:9 NIV):

"Thus we move from the intra–Trinitarian love of the Father for the Son, to the Son's love of his people in redemption. Jesus thus becomes the

---

196   D.A. Carson, *The Difficult Doctrine of the Love of God.* (Crossway, 2000), 33.

197   The title "Son of God" as applied to Jesus Christ carries a unique significance beyond its use for angels, kings, or believers in the Old Testament (Douglas J. Moo, "The Christology of the Early Pauline Letters," in *Contours of Christology in the New Testament*, ed. Richard N. Longenecker, McMaster New Testament Studies (Eerdmans Publishing Company, 2005), 187.). While Christians are referred to as "sons of God" by adoption, Christ is described as God's "own Son," suggesting an eternal, unparalleled relationship with God the Father. This title does not literally mean Christ was physically begotten by God, but rather emphasizes His divine nature and virgin birth.

58

mediator of his Father's love. Receiving love, so has he loved. Then he adds, "Now remain in my love. If you obey my commands, you will remain in my love, just as I have obeyed my Father's commands and remain in his love." (John 15:9b–10 NIV)[198]

Hence, our covenant with God is to imitate Christ: we obey Christ as Christ obeyed God. We love[199] Christ (and God) as Christ loved God. We receive God's love as Christ received God's love. We listen to Christ just as Christ listened to God and obeyed him. And we understand that the Holy Spirit is the messenger of Christ to whom we listen as well:

12 "I still have many things to say to you, but you cannot bear them now. 13 When the Spirit of truth comes, he will guide you into all the truth, for he will not speak on his own authority, but whatever he hears he will speak, and he will declare to you the things that are to come. 14 He will glorify me, for he will take what is mine and declare it to you. 15 All that the Father has is mine; therefore I said that he will take what is mine and declare it to you.

In his older years, the apostle John will write the following (1 John 2:3–11 NASB):

[3]By this we know that we have come to know Him, if we keep His commandments. [4]The one who says, "I have come to know Him," and does not keep His commandments, is a liar, and the truth is not in him; [5]but whoever keeps His word, in him the love of God has truly been perfected. By this we know that we are in Him: [6]the one who says he abides in Him ought himself to walk in the same manner as He walked.

In contrast with the gnostics of John's day, who claimed to have special, superior knowledge of God,[200] John confirms we can know God. However, John does not keep love to mere emotion; he connects knowing God with one's moral obedience by imitating Christ's life on this earth. Knowing God is not some "mystic vision or intellectual insight."[201] Instead, knowing God—loving God—must result in moral obedience to him, "for love delights

---

198 Carson, *Difficult Doctrine*, 40.

199 It is important to note that our love for God is meager, finite, fickle, and weak when compared to the fully perfect love that God has for us. Yet God accepts and delights in the love we can express toward him because of his great and perfect love for us.

200 Grant Osborne, Philip W. Comfort, *Cornerstone Biblical Commentary, Vol 13: John and 1, 2, and 3 John*. (Tyndale House Publishers, 2007), 337.

201 Leon L. Morris, "1 John," in *New Bible Commentary: 21st Century Edition*, ed. D. A. Carson et al., 4th ed. (nter–VIarsity Press, 1994), 1401.

to do God's will."[202] Because no one is morally perfect, it cannot be objected that no one knows God, since we all sin.[203] Instead, we should agree with Calvin:

> If any one objects and says, that no one has ever been found who loved God thus perfectly; to this I reply, that it is sufficient, provided every one aspired to this perfection according to the measure of grace given unto him. In the meantime, the definition is, that the perfect love of God is the complete keeping of his law. To make progress in this as in knowledge, is what we ought to do.[204]

I like how Whitacre frames this connection between love and obedience:

> The commands of Jesus are not a set of rules like a traffic code; they are a description of a pattern of life that reflects God's own life transposed into human circumstances. Love for Jesus involves both an attachment to him and a oneness with him and his interests, which naturally leads one to obey him and walk as he walked (1 John 2:6). One obeys what one loves. Indeed, our patterns of obedience reveal what we really love.[205]

D.A. Carson is more succinct: "Mere duty will not generate obedience to Christ; only love for him can do that."[206] While short–term conformity to the commands of God can be achieved through significant human effort, a life patterned after the life of Christ can only come from one who has a real, visceral love for Christ, striving to become mature in deed and love for God—seeking to imitate Christ's likeness—like father, like son. In the long run, CBOs cannot fully obey Christ without true love for him. And without loving obedience, we will not steward well what God has entrusted to us.

The type of love referenced in these verses is expressed in the Greek word ἀγάπη (agapē), which means to have great affection, care for, or loyalty towards another.[207] This love is a self–giving, other–focused love and is the type of love used in the most important command given to us: to love the Lord with all one's heart, soul, and mind. (Matthew 22:37–38). Blomberg describes this love as a

---

202 Morris, *1 John*, 1402.

203 John R. Stott, *The Letters of John: An Introduction and Commentary*. Vol. 19. Tyndale New Testament Commentaries. (InterVarsity Press, 1988), 95.

204 John Calvin and John Owen, *Commentaries on the Catholic Epistles* (Logos Bible Software, 2010), 176.

205 Rodney Whitacre, *John*, 362.

206 Donald A. Carson, *The Gospel According to John*. (Inter–Varsity Press; W.B. Eerdmans, 1991), 505.

207 Faithlife, "Love." In *Logos Bible Study Factbook*. Accessed June 25, 2024. https://ref.ly/logos4/Factbook?id=ref%3abk.%25love.

whole–hearted devotion to God with every aspect of one's being, from whatever angle one chooses to consider it—emotionally, volitionally, or cognitively. This kind of "love" for God will then result in obedience to all he has commanded.[208]

Let us not devolve our love into mere duty. Love is a real emotion we feel toward God. Obedience without love is duty. Love without obedience is a shallow emotion. But when love for God precedes obedience to God's commands, that is evidence of our covenant with God.

There is no substitute or workaround for genuine love for God. You cannot "fake it 'til you make it." There is no "fast track" to loving God. We must spend quality, extended time with God to love him. We will not lay our lives down for God (John 15:13–15), and we cannot live out God's 2nd most important command—to love others as ourselves (Matthew 22:36–40)—without genuine love for him. Loving God is not a task to be completed. It is a comprehensive change in our personas that endures until we die, pervading every aspect of our thoughts, attitudes, and actions.

Presence

Presence is the conduit through which love is passed between God and us. It is difficult to love God if we do not practice the presence of Jesus.[209] Presence can be defined as a state of being or existing in a place.[210] After Adam and Eve sinned, they lost the privilege of God's direct presence (Genesis 3:8ff). In the OT, some of the ways God became present with men were through visions (Genesis 15:1), dreams (Genesis 28:12ff), a burning bush (Exodus 3:2), a pillar of fire or cloud, and the ark of the covenant in the tabernacle.[211]

In the NT, because of the new covenant in which we become sacred space[212] because we each are a sacred temple (1 Corinthians 6:19), God's presence is promised in John 14:23–24 (ESV):

---

208 Craig Blomberg, *Matthew*. (Broadman & Holman Publishers, 1992), 335.

209 There are several books I'll recommend reading for learning about the presence of God. First is Andrew Murray's book, *Daily in His Presence*, (Multnomah, n.d.), second is the time–honored book by Brother Lawrence, *the Practice of the Presence of God* (Public Domain), and third is by A.W. Tozer, *Experiencing the Presence of God: Teachings from the Book of Hebrews*. (Regal, 2010).

210 Faithlife, "Presence." *Logos Bible Study Factbook*. (Faithlife, October 23, 2024.) https://ref.ly/logos4/Factbook?id=ref%3abk.%25presence.

211 E.F. Harrison, "Presence of God." In *The International Standard Bible Encyclopedia, Revised*, edited by Geoffrey W. Bromiley. (Eerdmans, 1979–1988.)

212 To learn more about sacred space in the OT and the new covenant, I recommend listening to Michael Heiser's podcast series on Leviticus. You can learn more at www.nakedbiblepodcast.com.

23 If anyone loves me, he will keep my word, and my Father will love him, and we will come to him and make our home with him. 24 Whoever does not love me does not keep my words. And the word that you hear is not mine but the Father's who sent me.

God making his home with us is as much a statement of presence as anything else. The New Testament writers assume the Spirit lives in us:

[10] But if Christ is in you, although the body is dead because of sin, the Spirit is life because of righteousness. [11] If the Spirit of him who raised Jesus from the dead dwells in you, he who raised Christ Jesus from the dead will also give life to your mortal bodies through his Spirit who dwells in you. (Romans 8:10–11 ESV)

[19] Do you not know that your bodies are temples of the Holy Spirit, who is in you, whom you have received from God? You are not your own. (1 Corinthians 6:19 NIV)

Being *present* with God is a spiritual phenomenon that I do not understand and cannot explain but accept by faith. Loving him and receiving his love includes his presence. Understanding his heart and what he is "all about" requires our steadfast presence with him. We cannot be *present* with God without *loving* him (Matthew 22:37). We can learn a thing or two about abiding in God's presence from Brother Lawrence:

I do know that those who want to know God's full presence need to have their hearts emptied of all worldly stuff. That's because God never shares a heart with anyone or anything. So there's going to be housecleaning if he comes to live in a person's life because He doesn't work to the fullest unless that heart has a "vacancy" sign on its door. I don't know of a better, sweeter life tha an unbroken conversation with God, a life of unlimited free minutes with Him. Only those who are living this kind of life know what I mean. But don't do it just because I'm saying it's sweet. Don't look for the pleasure payoff. It's best to pursue this relationship because we love Him and because it's God's will for us.[213]

---

213 Robert Elmer, *Practicing God's Presence: Brother Lawrence for Today's Reader.* (Navpress, 2005), 45–46.

Personal Testimony of God's Presence

What I write here will resonate more with some readers than others. In a way that is difficult to describe and nearly impossible to quantify or systematize, there are times when I sense God's presence is close and very real when I am

praying. At other times, God's presence seems distant, disconnected, and more of an academic topic than anything else.

I can attest that in those rare moments when I had an unusual sense of God's presence, my love for him grew, my relationship with him was purer, and I understood that the unexplainable could make immense sense in my mind. I can also attest that God's presence cannot be manufactured or produced by some ritual. God is not our cosmic bellhop, waiting at our beckoned call to do as we wish.

I think the overriding characteristic of heaven is God's presence. God's unfettered, direct presence will be the aspect we enjoy more than any material gains. Moreover, I believe that *God's presence answers the most difficult questions we have in life, but the answers are not clarifications or a result of logic. The answers give us a glimpse of God's glory, and the questions diminish in importance.* "And the things of this world will grow strangely dim in the light of his glory and grace."[214]

God's presence is a real source of truth, but it is not a truth that can easily fit into our theological or philosophical structures. In the presence of God, the supernatural will seem natural.[215]

Distraction is lethal to living in God's presence. In personal prayer, distraction—a wandering mind—is often the most challenging hurdle to overcome. While we might be able to focus for hours on details and activities at work, we might also find it difficult to focus on God for

---

214 Helen Lemmel, "Turn Your Eyes Upon Jesus", *The Hymnal for Worship & Celebration*, (Word Music, 1986), 335.

215 R.T. Kendall. *The Sensitivity of the Spirit*. (Charisma House, 2002), 2.

more than a few minutes without our minds wandering off to some other activity, robbing us of intimate time with him or feeling an inner urge to get going on the activities of the day.

Being distracted in prayer is a spiritual battle. The forces who oppose God do not want you or me to connect with him. They want us to focus on anything other than God. They understand that the presence of God can fundamentally transform our minds and spirits and create within us a deep love and commitment for God that cannot be found in other ways. The enemy does not want this, so the battle ensues.

My encouragement to you is this: persevere in prayer. Ask God for focus and concentration. Command the forces opposed to God to be silent. Ask God for unusual sensitivity to his spirit and voice. As you do this more and more, you will find that you can pray for extended periods. You might also find yourself looking forward to your prayer times because you have learned to enjoy the quiet presence of God.

PERSEVERANCE AND FAITHFULNESS

Faithfulness and perseverance are two sides of the same coin. If faithfulness maintains allegiance to duty,[216] then perseverance is faithfulness despite opposition.[217] As I said in the Preface, success is defined in the Bible in terms of faithfulness and perseverance, not financially or through achievements.

Maturity in perseverance is developed through trials and suffering (James 1:1–5, Hebrews 2:9–10). Perseverance is vital for the CBO because a CBO blazing for God *will* experience severe opposition. Such opposition will test the quality of a CBO's faithfulness and perseverance.

Perseverance

Perseverance does not depend on human effort. God works in us to will and work for his good pleasure (Philippians 2:13) and will not allow us to be tempted beyond our strength

---

216 Stuart D. Sacks, "Faithfulness." In *Baker Encyclopedia of the Bible*. (Baker Books, 1988), 1:764–65.

217 Faithlife, "Perseverance." In *Logos Bible Study Factbook*. (Faithlife, October 24, 2024.) https://ref.ly/logos4/Factbook?id=ref%3abk.%25perseverance.

(1 Corinthians 10:13).[218] The power to persevere in our covenantal relationship comes from God. Consider 2 Peter 1:3–8 (NIV):

> His divine power has given us everything we need for a godly life through our knowledge of him who called us by his own glory and goodness. Through these he has given us his very great and precious promises, so that through them you may participate in the divine nature, having escaped the corruption in the world caused by evil desires. For this very reason, make every effort to add to your faith goodness; and to goodness, knowledge; and to knowledge, self–control; and to self–control, perseverance; and to perseverance, godliness; and to godliness, mutual affection; and to mutual affection, love. For if you possess these qualities in increasing measure, they will keep you from being ineffective and unproductive in your knowledge of our Lord Jesus Christ.

God's divine power at work within us gives us all we need for a godly life. Without this power, we cannot live or persevere in our covenant with him. This power is given to us through the indwelling of the Holy Spirit (Ephesians 3:16). It helps us attain all steadfastness and patience (Colossians 1:11). His power will enable us to persevere during significant trials or opposition. We will not be able to persevere as God intends simply through self–reliance. God's power is the *only* way we will be able to persevere.

In the Bible, perseverance is "steadfast, unmovable" (1 Corinthians 15:58). It is something we are called to pursue (1 Timothy 6:11). Perseverance is associated with being patient during afflictions (Revelation 13:10, Romans 5:3–4, 12:12). Trusting in the Lord and perseverance are associated in Psalm 26:1, 57:7, 108:1, and 112:7. Older folks are to be sound in faith, love, and steadfastness (Titus 2:2), which lends credence to the notion that perseverance is learned over time. Those described as "good" soil in Luke 8 will produce a crop a hundred times more than what was sown because they persevered (Luke 8:15).

Perseverance is associated with victory and having authority over the nations (this refers to our participation in the divine council in the new Heaven and the new earth) in Revelation 2:26. Eternal life is promised to those who persevere (Romans 2:7).

In the seven letters to the seven churches in Revelation 2:1–3:22, faithfulness is defined as:
- Love God above all (Revelation 2:4).
- Endure persecution, even to the point of death (Revelation 2:10).

---

218 R.E.O. White, "Perseverance." In *Baker Encyclopedia of the Bible*. (Baker Books, 1988), 2:1647–48.

- Reject idolatry, sexual immorality, and false teaching (Revelation 2:14–16, 2:20–24).
- Identify fully with Christ (Revelation 3:8).
- Being "hot" toward God, as opposed to being "lukewarm" (Revelation 3:15–20).

The rewards for overcoming the temptation to faithlessness are significant. If we overcome, we will be given significant rewards:

- Eat from the tree of life (Revelation 2:7).
- Will not be hurt by the second death (Revelation 2:11).
- Given some hidden manna and a white stone with a new name is known only to us as individuals (Revelation 2:17).
- Authority over the nations and the morning star (Revelation 2:26–27).
- Clothed in white garments and God's promise not to erase our name from the Book of Life. Furthermore, Christ will confess our name before God and his angels[219] (Revelation 3:5).
- The right to sit with Christ on his throne (Revelation 3:21).
- Be granted the right to sit down with God on his throne (3.21).

I will readily grant that some these rewards seem surreal or odd. But in Heaven, they must be important. These rewards are connected to our faithfulness and perseverance in the face of opposition, temptation, and persecution until the end of our lives, when God can say that we have overcome.

Faithfulness

Faithfulness to God always requires submission to God. Hence, faithfulness to God can be produced only by the Spirit of God working in us as we submit to God's commands and leading. Galatians 5:22–24 (NIV) says,

> [22] But the fruit of the Spirit is love, joy, peace, forbearance, kindness, goodness, faithfulness, [23] gentleness and self–control. Against such things, there is no law. [24] Those who belong to Christ Jesus have crucified the flesh with its passions and desires. [25] Since we live by the Spirit, let us keep in step with the Spirit."

---

219 Confessing a name before others is important to God. This reminds me of Matthew 10.32 where Christ said that everyone who "confesses me before men, I will also confess him before my Father who is in heaven" (NASB). See Luke 12.8 as well. It is so important that our salvation is dependent on such confession: "… if you confess with your mouth Jesus as Lord and believe in your heart that God raised him from the dead, you will be saved." Romans 7.16 (NASB).

Faithfulness is the believer's intentionality to keep "in step with the Spirit."[220] To keep in step with the Spirit—to be faithful—is to have congruence between the beliefs and attitudes of the inner man and the outer man.[221] Such congruence is lived out continuously, born in weakness, and demonstrated in dependence on God.[222]

Do not equate faithfulness with perfection. No Christian is perfect, either morally or in his beliefs. While we should strive to grow in our sanctification and holiness, we will never live morally perfect this side of heaven.

The plea of a CBO is for God to transform the owner from the inside out such that there is an increasing congruence between the owner's inner attitudes and beliefs, outer actions and attitudes, and the essence of living in a covenantal relationship with God while on this earth.[223] Such consecration applies to one's role as a business owner as much as any other sphere of life. Our covenant faith in God cannot be compartmentalized or subordinated to a particular role or activity.

Faithfulness to God is not an appendage to our role as business owners.[224] While the world's values will shift and tempt us to drift from our faith, if not deny it, the Scriptures remain constant, and our values do not change. The hope we profess includes our commitment to promises that will be fulfilled in the future,[225] which supports a core tenant of this book: *Christian business owners live with eternity in mind.*

The most miserable people on this earth are those whose behavior violates their inner, deeply held beliefs. I have often observed people who profess one value but act in ways that violate that value. It is the human experience to battle oneself to find congruence between one's values and behaviors. The apostle Paul wrote about this phenomenon in Romans 7:15–8:2, where he openly wrestled with the congruence between his private and public life. The cognitive dissonance, self-doubt, and general anxiety that result from living in ways that violate one's values can be deeply damaging. In one sense, all that faithfulness requires is to live congruently with who one is and what one believes. But this is easier said than done.

---

220 Fredrick F. Bruce, The Epistle to the Galatians: a commentary on the Greek text. (Eerdmans, 1982), 257.

221 Ernest DeWitt Burton., A critical and exegetical commentary on the Epistle to the Galatians. (C. Scribner's Sons, 1920), 322–23.

222 David Bivin, New Light on the Difficult Words of Jesus: Insights from his Jewish Context. (En-Gedi Resource Center, 2007), 138.

223 William Hendriksen, *Exposition of Galatians*. (Baker Books, 1968), 226.

224 Craig S. Keener, *The IVP Bible Background Commentary: New Testament* (InterVarsity Press, 1993), Hebrews 10:23, np.

225 Donald Guthrie, *Hebrews: An Introduction and Commentary*. Tyndale New Testament Commentaries. (InterVarsity Press, 1983), 216–17.

WHEN GOD DISCIPLINES

God's discipline is mentioned over two dozen times in the Bible. The passage that discusses God's discipline most directly and extensively is Hebrews 12:4–11. This section will tie together my discussions of God's love, presence, faithfulness, and perseverance. The Bible teaches that God's discipline produces these characteristics in our personas. Here is the text from the NIV:

> [4] In your struggle against sin, you have not yet resisted to the point of shedding your blood. [5] And have you completely forgotten this word of encouragement that addresses you as a father addresses his son? It says, "My son, do not make light of the Lord's discipline, and do not lose heart when he rebukes you, [6] because the Lord disciplines the one he loves, and he chastens everyone he accepts as his son." [7] Endure hardship as discipline; God is treating you as his children. For what children are not disciplined by their father? [8] If you are not disciplined—and everyone undergoes discipline—then you are not legitimate, not true sons and daughters at all. [9] Moreover, we have all had human fathers who disciplined us and we respected them for it. How much more should we submit to the Father of spirits and live! [10] They disciplined us for a little while as they thought best; but God disciplines us for our good, in order that we may share in his holiness. [11] No discipline seems pleasant at the time, but painful. Later on, however, it produces a harvest of righteousness and peace for those who have been trained by it.

In this passage, the writer of Hebrews[226] asks a rhetorical question, "Have you forgotten?" with an assumed answer: "No, we have not forgotten." This word of encouragement is meant to set the context for the writer's discussion of discipline. Paradoxically, God's discipline should encourage us because his discipline indicates his acceptance of us into his family, preparing us for a greater destiny.[227] God's discipline is confirmation that we are part of his family.

---

226 The author of Hebrews is unknown to us, but expositors have always considered this book significant from the earliest times. See Leon Morris, "Hebrews." In *The Expositor's Bible Commentary: Hebrews through Revelation*, edited by Frank E. Gaebelein, Vol. 12. (Zondervan Publishing House, 1981), 3–7.

227 Craig A. Evans and Craig A. Bubeck, eds. *John's Gospel, Hebrews–Revelation*. First Edition. The Bible Knowledge Background Commentary. (David C Cook, 2005), 248.

Love and Discipline

The writer of Hebrews reminds us that we should not 'make light'[228] or 'lose heart'[229] when God disciplines us.[230] Since we need a role model, we can look to Jesus, who has already walked this path of God's discipline to the extreme point of enduring the cross for us (Hebrews 12:2–3). We are to imitate (John 5:19–24) our Lord's submission to God's discipline, though we can only approximate his example because we have not resisted sin to the point of shedding our blood (vs. 4).[231]

In verses 5–6, the writer quotes Proverbs 3:11–12, which reminds us that God's discipline comes from his deep love for us. Yet, the fact that we are not to grow weary (vs. 5) infers that some discipline lasts longer than one might expect—months or even years. When we endure hardship and trials, one of the ordinary prayers is that God would remove our pain and relieve us of distress. But some lessons take months or years to learn, so God may leave us in a difficult place for long periods. The longer the hardship or trial, the more the writer's command to not become exhausted—to grow weary—applies under the weight of God's discipline.

For lack of a better term, more extended periods of discipline are a type of 'mincing' process where God grinds out of us impurities or wrong beliefs that cannot be removed in other ways. Over time, he matures our faith, and we realize that he is enough to satisfy us. We do not need anything else. God is enough.

Why does God do this? Because of his great and deep love for us (vs. 6). Our trials signify that God deeply loves us.[232] As children of God, we should rejoice in his love expressed for us through discipline. The discipline is temporary, but the spiritual benefits are eternal.[233]

In the book of Revelation, John confirms that God's discipline comes from his deep love for us:

---

228 "Make light:" ὀλιγωρέω, *have little esteem for something* (BDAG), *regard something or someone as of little value* (LN). It occurs once in the NT but roughly 160 times in the Greek classics. "Regard lightly" ESV, NASB; "make light" NIV, LEB; "take the Lord's discipline lightly", CSB.

229 "become weary:" ἐκλύου, from the root λυω, *to loose or untie* (LOGOS). With the preposition ἐκ, *to become weary, give out, to be exhausted in strength* (BDAG). Paul mentions this same idea of not becoming weary in Galatians 6:9, but instead of referencing the Lord's discipline, Paul is referencing good works: *Let us not become weary in doing good* (NIV).

230 "Discipline:" παιδεία, *providing guidance for responsible living* (BDAG), *the imposition of painful consequences or other disadvantages upon someone for their disobedience as part of a process of improving someone's character or actions* (LOGOS). Other uses: Ephesians 6:4, "bring someone up in the *discipline* and instruction of the Lord." 2 Timothy 3:16, "…useful for *training* in righteousness."

231 Grant R. Osborne and George H. Guthrie. *Hebrews: Verse by Verse.* Osborne New Testament Commentaries. (Lexham Press, 2021), 272.

232 Schreiner, *Hebrews*, 383.

233 Osborne, *Hebrews*, 274.

[19] Those whom I love I rebuke and discipline. So be earnest and repent. [20] Here I am! I stand at the door and knock. If anyone hears my voice and opens the door, I will come in and eat with that person, and they with me. (Revelation 3:19–20 NIV)

Confirmation of our Adoption into God's Family

In verses 7–8, the writer returns to the point that God's discipline infers our membership in his family. This truth is stated positively in verse 7 and negatively in verse 8. But the meaning is the same: God disciplines us because we are members of his family.

We are to "endure hardship as discipline (NIV)," meaning we are to endure hardship to the end.[234] In the Scriptures, success for a disciple of Jesus Christ is never defined in monetary terms. Success is always defined in terms of obedience and faithfulness to the end.

In verses 9–10, the writer uses our earthly fathers as an imperfect example of how our heavenly father disciplines us. The writer assumes a healthy father/son relationship here on earth and between ourselves and God. This is the right assumption to make when writing a book like Hebrews. But for those who had abusive, distant, absent, or unloving fathers, the pain of one's past should not be allowed to shroud the main point the writer is making: in a *healthy* father/son relationship, a father will discipline his son to make his son a better person. In our father/son (or father/daughter) relationship with God, he disciplines us so that we can "share in his holiness" (vs. 10). In this context, one can understand Paul's desire to "know Christ" by participating "in his sufferings." Like Paul, we should desire to "gain Christ" and "press on" to "take hold of that for which Christ Jesus took hold of me," including, like Christ, being called "heavenward" to God. (Philippians 3:7–14 NIV).

Those who equate financial prosperity with God's blessings are not likely to find suffering and discipline that leads to sharing "in his holiness" very motivating or enticing. But those with a mature view of God's blessings will know that true satisfaction is found in hungering and thirsting for righteousness (Matthew 5:6), valuing his commands and laws (Psalm 19:10) and our faith in God (1 Peter 1:7) more than earthly wealth. Verse 10 touches on one's affections and allegiances.[235]

Our Response in Delayed Gratification

How we respond to God's discipline makes all the difference to whether or not we draw closer to God. If we respond with repentance and submission to God, he will pour out his

---

234 Schreiner, *Hebrews,* 385.

235 Obsorne equates sharing in God's holiness with 2 Peter 1:4, where we're told that we participate in the divine nature. Osborne, *Hebrews, 277.*

Spirit on us and make his words known to us (Proverbs 1:23). In addition, we will dwell securely and be at ease, living without fearing disaster (Proverbs 1:33).

But if we respond with blame, bitterness, or anger at the unjust and unfair way God is treating us, then we are likely not only to drift farther from God, but also to run into the arms of any belief system that helps us feel better.

The Psalmist reminds us of the good that comes from enduring God's discipline. In Psalms 119:67, 71–72, he wrote:

> ^{67}Before I was afflicted, I went astray, but now I keep your word … ^{71}It is good for me that I was afflicted, that I might learn your statutes. ^{72}The law of your mouth is better to me than thousands of gold and silver pieces. (ESV)

Moreover, in verse 11 (Hebrews 5:11), the writer agrees with the Psalmist when he writes that God's discipline yields "peaceful fruit" and "righteousness" for those who were trained by God's discipline.

All discipline is painful. There is no way to sugar–coat it.[236] I have yet to enjoy the pain of God's trials. But the future "peaceful fruit" of righteousness depends on our faithfulness to endure the hardship and pain of his disciplining hand. To this point, Moses is our example (Hebrews 11:24–27 ESV):

> ^{24} By faith Moses, when he was grown up, refused to be called the son of Pharaoh's daughter, ^{25} choosing rather to be mistreated with the people of God than to enjoy the fleeting pleasures of sin. ^{26} He considered the reproach of Christ greater wealth than the treasures of Egypt, for he was looking to the reward. ^{27} By faith he left Egypt, not being afraid of the anger of the king, *for he endured as seeing him who is invisible.* [emphasis added]

Moses rejected present pleasures and suffered with his people for a future reward.[237] Through his suffering, he was conditioned and shaped by God's discipline. He should inspire us to endure the pain of God's discipline because of the future blessings we will receive in this life and in heaven.

Proverbs 3:11–12

Proverbs 3:11–12 is the Old Testament basis for Hebrews 12:4–11 (ESV). This passage is worth our consideration:

---

236 I like Osborne's transparency on this point. Osborne, *Hebrews*, 277–278.
237 Schreiner, *Hebrews*, 386.

11 My son, do not despise the Lord's discipline or be weary of his reproof,
12 for the Lord reproves him whom he loves, as a father the son in whom
he delights.

The sage uses two words in parallel to refer to God's discipline. The first is the Hebrew word *mûsār* (from *ysr*),[238] translated in the first line of vs. 11 as 'discipline.' In the second line of vs. 11, the writer uses the Hebrew word ykḥ, usually translated as *reproof* (ESV, NASB, LEB) or *rebuke* (NIV). The ideas in both words usually incorporate some aspect of punishment or judgment as a correction to set a person on the right path.

Eliphaz expresses a similar sentiment in Job 5:17–18, but he is more explicit about God being both the discipliner and the healer:

17 "Blessed is the one whom God corrects; so do not despise the discipline of the Almighty. 18 For he wounds, but he also binds up; he injures, but his hands also heal.

The right attitude toward God's discipline is understanding it as an act of love and, thus, not repudiating it. The same God who brings discipline into our lives to keep us from more severe punishments in the future[239] also brings healing and restoration.[240]

The dual role that God fills as both discipliner and healer is expressed in other passages:

See now that I myself am he! There is no god besides me. I put to death and I bring to life, I have wounded and I will heal, and no one can deliver out of my hand. (Deuteronomy 32:39)

Come, let us return to the Lord. He has torn us to pieces but he will heal us; he has injured us but he will bind up our wounds. 2 After two days he will revive us; on the third day he will restore us, that we may live in his presence. 3 Let us acknowledge the Lord; let us press on to acknowledge him. As surely as the sun rises, he will appear; he will come to us like the winter rains, like the spring rains that water the earth. (Hosea 6:1–3)

---

238 "Discipline:" מוּסָר, *training* (HALOT). From יסר, *to instruct, chastise, rebuke* (Logos).

239 Michael V. Fox, *Proverbs 1–9: A New Translation with Introduction and Commentary*. Vol. 18A. Anchor Yale Bible. (Yale University Press, 2008), 152.

240 Duane A. Garrett, *Job*. Edited by David Lamb and Tremper Longman III. Evangelical Exegetical Commentary. (Lexham Academic, 2024), 118.

When God disciplines us, our response of acceptance must include our heartfelt repentance and a recognition that our troubles are divinely sent.[241] He has promised to restore us when we acknowledge our sin and repent.

In addition, God's reproof gives us wisdom (Proverbs 29:15). We are told that the fear of the Lord is the beginning of wisdom, so in some sense, God's reproof builds within us a healthy, mature fear of God. The meaning of Proverbs 29:15 is less about physical life than one's entire life, a life of health that is revived and healed through keeping God's commands.[242] When God disciplines us, his work gives us new life and energy if we respond correctly.

Moreover, Proverbs 15:31 describes God's reproof as "life–giving" (ESV, NIV, NASB, HCB). The Hebrew for "life–giving" comes from a root word with a semantic range that includes *life, nourishment, flourishing, or prosperous*. The pain that God's discipline creates can often mask the life–giving aspect of his discipline. It is usually in retrospect where we see how his discipline is life–giving.

The wisdom literature in the Bible knows that the "righteous do not enjoy uninterrupted blessings."[243] Instead, the righteous understand God's discipline within one's covenant with God wherein God is faithful to us by disciplining us so that we are not left in a state of perpetual, but perhaps unknown, sin (Job 7:17–19, 10:20). In Jewish wisdom literature, discipline was a sign of a father's love for his children[244] and was to be viewed as corrective and educative, not punitive.[245] The writer of Hebrews relies on their cultural view of 'discipline as love' to form the context for his teachings in this passage. Hence, we do not grow weary or make light of God's discipline *because* his discipline is a sign of his love for us (vs. 6).

Within God's discipline, there are always lessons to be learned and blessings to be received. Victory is learning the lessons God has for us and receiving his blessings.[246] By contrast, defeat is growing weary, becoming exhausted, or treating his discipline with contempt and scorn.

An example of the latter is when people interpret God's discipline in moral or justice terms rather than educative and growth terms: "If God truly loved me, he wouldn't allow this (whatever "this" is) to happen," or "If God was a just God, he would not allow this

---

241 Richard D. Patterson and Andrew E. Hill, *Cornerstone Biblical Commentary, Vol 10: Minor Prophets, Hosea–Malachi.* (Tyndale House Publishers, 2008), 39.

242 Mayer, *TDOT,* v4, 334.

243 Allen P. Ross, "Proverbs." In *The Expositor's Bible Commentary: Psalms, Proverbs, Ecclesiastes, Song of Songs,* edited by Frank E. Gaebelein, Vol. 5. (Zondervan Publishing, 1991), 918.

244 Craig S. Keener, *The IVP Bible Background Commentary: New Testament.* Second Edition. (IVP Academic: An Imprint of InterVarsity Press, 2014), np.

245 Thomas R. Schreiner, *Hebrews.* Edited by T. Desmond Alexander, Thomas R. Schreiner, and Andreas J. Köstenberger. Evangelical Biblical Theology Commentary. (Lexham Press, 2021), 383.

246 K. T. Aitken, *Proverbs,* The Daily Study Bible Series (Westminster John Knox Press, 1986), 44.

injustice." Not all suffering should be reduced to a problem with God's justice or his system of morality; some of it must be attributed to his loving discipline.[247]

Trials as Discipline: James 1:2-4

I equate the trials discussed by James with God's discipline. Crises come in all forms, shapes, and sizes. James reminds us to consider all our trials with joy (James 1:2–4 NIV):

> [2] Consider it pure joy, my brothers and sisters, whenever you face trials of many kinds, [3] because you know that the testing of your faith produces perseverance. [4] Let perseverance finish its work so that you may be mature and complete, not lacking anything.

The word for trials in the Greek language means a test or examination given to make one stumble[248] in an attempt to learn the nature or character of the one being tested.[249] These tests are created by God and sent by him into our lives to reveal the dross that exists inside our beings. These tests reveal the thoughts, attitudes, affections, and beliefs that need to be purified through discipline. Once revealed, we can respond by allowing God to clean us out and build us up, or we can become bitter and angry at God and rebuff his attempts to mature us (James 1:5–6). To respond to these examinations with joy is a divine mandate.[250]

We are usually passive at the initiation of these trials.[251] The size and shape of these trials vary from person to person and situation to situation. Some trials are small, others are big. Some are important; some are less important. But each one is sent by God, designed for our growth in godliness.[252]

Sometimes, these trials come into our lives as a crisis that consumes our immediate attention. We often will not see the crisis coming when God uses a crisis to initiate his discipline. The event's significance should drive us to our knees. One request (among others) should be, "Lord, what do you want me to learn from this trial?" A second request is also appropriate, "Lord, please do not release me from this trial until you have accomplished all your purposes in me and I have learned all the lessons you have for me."

---

247 Bruce K. Waltke, *The Book of Proverbs, Chapters 1–15*. The New International Commentary on the Old Testament. (Eerdmans, 2004), 249–250.

248 DBL, #4280.

249 BDAG, 793.

250 Grant R. Osborne, "James." In *Cornerstone Biblical Commentary: James, 1–2 Peter, Jude, Revelation*, edited by Philip W. Comfort. Cornerstone Biblical Commentary. (Tyndale House, 2011), 21.

251 Joseph S. Excell, *The Biblical Illustrator: James*. (Cincinnati; Chicago; Kansas City: Jennings & Graham, n.d.), 5.

252 David Platt, *Exalting Jesus in James*. (Holman Reference, 2014), 7.

Whether your trial is sudden unemployment, a health diagnosis, a spouse asking for a separation or divorce, or something as benign as a car repair bill that you cannot afford, viewing the trial through a spiritual lens where you're open to more of God's discipline is the right approach that will draw you closer and closer to God.

God Restores and Completes: Jeremiah 29:11–14

God's heart and motivations are for our good, not our harm, for our restoration and completeness, not our exile. This thought is expressed in Jeremiah 29:11–14 (NIV):

> [11] For I know the plans I have for you," declares the Lord, "plans to prosper you and not to harm you, plans to give you hope and a future. [12] Then you will call on me and come and pray to me, and I will listen to you. [13] You will seek me and find me when you seek me with all your heart. [14] I will be found by you," declares the Lord, "and will bring you back from captivity. I will gather you from all the nations and places where I have banished you," declares the Lord, "and will bring you back to the place from which I carried you into exile."

Many people read this passage and conclude that God has personalized plans to make them rich based on the word *prosper*. But this conclusion is not warranted.

The word for "prosper" in Hebrew is *šālôm (shalom)*.[253] The LEB and NIV translate this Hebrew word as "prosperity," whereas the ESV, NASB, and CSB translate it as "welfare." The latter is a more comprehensive English term that includes the ideas of restoration and completeness and is the better translation in this context. God plans to restore and complete us, including our finances. But his purpose is to restore us so we seek him with our entire persona. Said differently, we are more able to "seek first the kingdom of God" because he has restored and completed us.

It is proper for us to ask for restoration and completeness, including financial prosperity. But financial prosperity merely frees us up to seek God with our entire being. Since the debtor is a servant to the lender, the financial prosperity we should seek should be financial freedom, which means we are debt–free and can pursue and serve the Lord fully. Once we are no longer under the authority of an earthly lender, we can be entirely under the authority of God. We are not distracted by the demands of a lender or preoccupied with managing our investments. We are free to serve God, depending on him for our daily sustenance. We can be generous, as God directs us to give away our wealth. This is restoration. This is completeness.

---

253 "welfare": עָלוֹם, šālôm; *completeness, intactness* (HALOT), *completeness, soundess, welfare, peace* (BDB), *peace, prosperity, entering into a state of wholeness and unity, a restored relationship* (TWOT).

To strictly read *šālôm* as a financial term in which God promises financial prosperity is a thin interpretation.[254] God's restoration and completeness are also about our affections, beliefs, attitudes, and allegiances. His discipline refines impurities out of our hearts. He disciplines out of us affections for anything that competes with our affection for him. In some senses, this is what he meant in Exodus 20:3, "You shall have no other gods before me." We are told that God's commands are to be desired more than silver or gold (Psalm 19:10), so his discipline, at a minimum, will direct our affections to love his commands more than the temporal things of this earth. Do you love God's commands?

God disciplines us to correct our beliefs so that we believe only the truth and do not hang onto beliefs contrary to Scripture. Restoration and completeness include adjusting our bad attitudes to reflect God's attitudes. His discipline will demand that we give God our complete allegiance ahead of any other allegiances we have on earth, including political affiliations, sports teams, career advancement, etc.

God's plans are more positive and comprehensive toward us than we can believe or comprehend[255] because his purposes are far better than economic luxury. He will make possible what is promised in these verses—to give us a future and hope, to be findable when we seek him with all our hearts, and to restore us from our exiles. He will not abandon us or leave us destitute. He will restore us. It is good and right for us to ask for these things, relying on his promises.

SUMMARY

In this chapter, we have learned about the inseparable relationship between stewardship and entrustment. The five supporting elements of stewardship and entrustments were also discussed. The Bible does not explicitly teach these five elements are supportive to stewardship and entrustment, but the connection is so strong logically that it makes sense to conclude as much.

I suggested that Christian business owners adopt this definition of Biblical Stewardship, that ***Biblical stewards willingly disadvantage themselves to advantage the kingdom of God.*** CBOs willingly give up what God asks of them to advantage his kingdom.

I have spent time discussing God's perfect love for us and how we are to love him in our covenant with him. I have also briefly discussed how God's discipline is an expression of God's love for us. His discipline is intended to mature us and build in us greater perseverance and faithfulness to follow his commands.

---

254 "The Lord sets before the people not merely a future of outward prosperity, but above all a future of internal welfare, without which the former would be altogether inconceivable." (John Peter Lange, Philip Schaff, Carl Wilhelm Eduard Nägelsbach, and Samuel Ralph Asbury. *A Commentary on the Holy Scriptures: Jeremiah*. (Logos Bible Software, 2008), 248.

255 Georg Heinrich August von Ewald. *Commentary on the Prophets of the Old Testament*. Translated by J. Frederick Smith. Vol. 3. (London; Edinburgh: Williams and Norgate, 1878), 239.

In the next chapter, *Contentment and Ambition*, I tackle an entrepreneur's God–given drive to build and succeed. I will examine the motivation for why we do what we do. In addition, I dive into the thorny issue of selfish vs. Godly ambition. There is much to learn, so let's turn the page and keep going.

CHAPTER 4

CONTENTMENT AND AMBITION

In this chapter, I will demonstrate that contentment is a hallmark of a faithful steward before God, and discontent is lethal to Biblical stewardship. Furthermore, I will discuss ambition and conclude that Godly ambition must be grounded in contentment, whereas selfish ambition stands on the foundation of discontent. I will argue that Biblical stewardship cannot be lived out from a spirit of discontent and selfish ambition. Only when a person is led by Godly ambition from a spirit of contentedness will one be able to live out fully one's stewardship role within one's covenant with God.

CONTENTMENT IS BEING satisfied with one's situation.[256] It is wanting what you have rather than what you do not have.[257] Contentment is the opposite of discontentment. It is foundational to Godly ambition, while discontentment leads to complaining and dissatisfaction. Contentment builds one's covenant with God, while discontentment is lethal to one's covenant with God. Figure 4–1 illustrates these opposites and their associated characteristics.

---

256 Faithlife. "Contentment." *Logos Bible Study Factbook*. Accessed July 1, 2024. https://ref.ly/logos4/Factbook?id=ref%3abk.%25contentment.

257 Neil Anderson, *Victory Over the Darkness*. (Bethany House, 2020), 146.

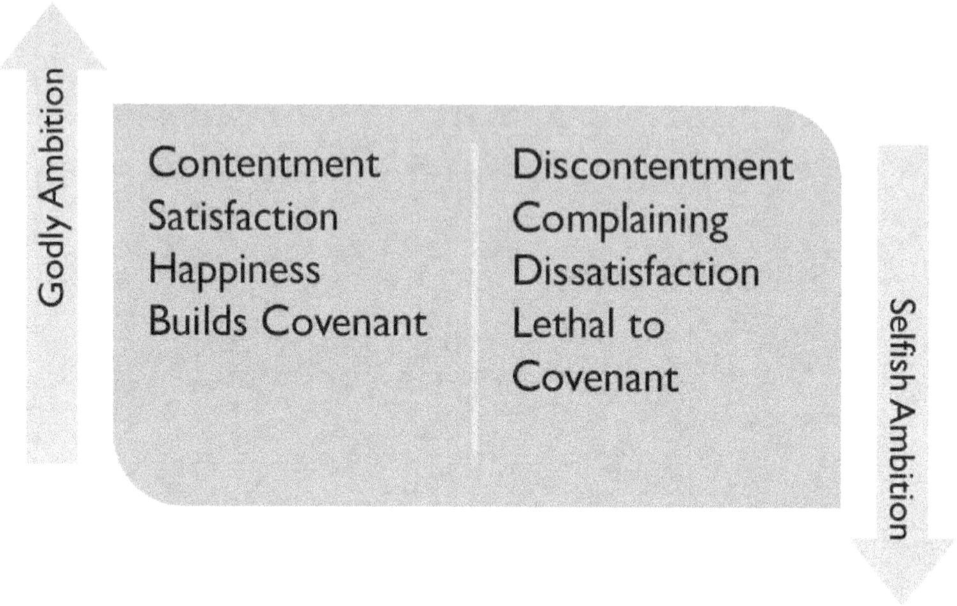

Godly Ambition

Contentment
Satisfaction
Happiness
Builds Covenant

Discontentment
Complaining
Dissatisfaction
Lethal to
Covenant

Selfish Ambition

Figure 4–1: Contentment vs. Discontentment

CONTENTMENT

Contentment is a stewardship choice that affects the quality of our covenant with God. Being content is one hallmark of a faithful Biblical steward. Ecclesiastes 5:10–12, 18–20 (NIV) discusses contentment in the context of work and wealth:

> [10] Whoever loves money never has enough; whoever loves wealth is never satisfied with their income. This too is meaningless. [11] As goods increase, so do those who consume them. And what benefit are they to the owners except to feast their eyes on them? [12] The sleep of a laborer is sweet, whether they eat little or much, but as for the rich, their abundance permits them no sleep ... [18] This is what I have observed to be good: that it is appropriate for a person to eat, to drink and to find satisfaction in their toilsome labor under the sun during the few days of life God has given them—for this is their lot. [19] Moreover, when God gives someone wealth and possessions, and the ability to enjoy them, to accept their lot and be happy in their toil—this is a gift of God. [20] They seldom reflect on the days of their life, because God keeps them occupied with gladness of heart.

Notice that a faithful follower of God is content with the amount and quality of the wealth God has entrusted him. He enjoys his labor and its' fruit by being content with what he has.

In this passage, we learn also that loving money is the path to a life of discontentment. If you love money, you will never be satisfied. No matter how much you have, you will always want more. "Life is wasted when it is spent in a quest for more money."[258]

An increase in wealth only brings an increase in anxiety for the covetous person[259] and leaves an emptiness that cannot be filled apart from God.[260] A particular advantage to being poor is that one can sleep better—something the rich man's wealth cannot purchase.[261]

The other side of discontentment is contentment, which will allow you to find enjoyment in your work. When you enjoy your work, you can enjoy your wealth and be content with it. Enjoying one's work and being content with one's wealth is a gift from God accepted in grateful appreciation.[262] You enjoy the small things in the present and leave the anxieties of the future to God.[263] You are so happy with what you have that you forget you are growing old. Instead of living out your days in anger and bitterness with physical problems, you are content and enjoy your work and the wealth God has given you. Your work and wealth are enough. The ideal for a Christ follower is that one does not regret the past or worry about the future but enjoys God's provision in the present because God fills his heart with joy.[264]

Living a life of contentment is a choice. Contentment is a choice to accept God's presence as enough for a happy and fulfilled life. Contentment is a choice not to compare one's station in life with another. Contentment is a choice to reject the world's belief that you can and should have all that the world offers if you are going to find happiness and fulfillment. In short, a content steward has rejected the world's definition of success. And as mentioned earlier, a disciple of Jesus Christ who is truly content also finds that God is enough in every situation. When one's legitimate needs are not immediately satiated (Exodus 15:23 – 17:7), one will still find that God's presence and holiness are enough for the moment and into the future.

---

258 Duane A. Garrett, *Proverbs, Ecclesiastes, Song of Songs*, vol. 14, The New American Commentary (Nashville: Broadman & Holman Publishers, 1993), 314.

259 Donald R. Glenn. "Ecclesiastes." In *The Bible Knowledge Commentary: An Exposition of the Scriptures*, edited by J. F. Walvoord and R. B. Zuck. (Wheaton, IL: Victor Books, 1985), 989.

260 Derek Kidner. *The Message of Ecclesiastes: A Time to Mourn, and a Time to Dance*. Edited by J. Alec Motyer and Derek Tidball. (The Bible Speaks Today. England: Inter–Varsity Press, 1984), 56.

261 Thomas Krüger. *Qoheleth: A Commentary*. Edited by Klaus Baltzer. Translated by O. C. Dean Jr. Hermeneia—a Critical and Historical Commentary on the Bible. (Minneapolis, MN: Fortress Press, 2004), 121.

262 Adrian Rogers, "A Perspective on Life." In *Adrian Rogers Sermon Archive*. (Rogers Family Trust, 2017).

263 Dennis Kinslaw, "The Book of Ecclesiastes." In *Job–Song of Solomon*, Vol. 2. The Wesleyan Bible Commentary. (Eerdmans, 1968), 620.

264 J. Stafford Wright. "Ecclesiastes." In *The Expositor's Bible Commentary: Psalms, Proverbs, Ecclesiastes, Song of Songs*, edited by Frank E. Gaebelein, Vol. 5. (Grand Rapids, MI: Zondervan Publishing House, 1991), 1170.

AMBITION

So, what about ambition? Can a person be content with what God has given him yet still be ambitious? Is not discontentedness a necessary element of ambition?

Ambition is generally considered a personal drive towards achieving goals important to an individual.[265] Ambition can be negative, such as pursuing goals that are selfish or evil, or positive, such as pursuing goals that will build up the church or further God's kingdom.

Can we be content business owners while also being ambitious to grow our businesses and create more wealth? I believe the answer is "yes." The Bible discusses selfish and godly ambition. Let us discuss both, starting with the negative side of ambition—selfish ambition.

Selfish Ambition

Selfish ambition[266] is the pursuit of a personal agenda that satisfies selfish desires.[267] Selfish ambition is associated with "empty conceit"[268] and "looking out for your own interests." in Philippians 2:3–4. Selfish ambition comes in many forms and has many innocent faces. I ran across this quote while researching for this section. Neill outlines selfish ambition better than I ever could. While he is writing to young ministers, CBOs can easily downstep his warnings into our role as business owners. The desire to be on top, to be noticed, to gain a large social media following, to craft our reputation, to do more so one can be more—these desires cut across all vocations, times, ethnicities, and demographics. While this quote is a bit long, it is worth your attention. I encourage you not to skip reading this quote:

> To enter into the ministry is an exceedingly dangerous thing to do. All Christians are exposed to temptation, but the minister is exposed to many temptations from which other Christians are free … You will be exposed to many temptations and to many sins. There is one sin, however, that can totally destroy your *usefulness as a* minister: ambition … The temptation is to start to look around and to find a slightly bigger and better church. The temptation is to speak in assemblies of ministers, to make yourself remarked, to have people saying about you, "Ah yes, he is a promising

---

265 Faithlife, "Ambition." In *Logos Bible Study Factbook*. (Faithlife, July 3, 2024.) https://ref.ly/logos4/Factbook?id=ref%3abk.%25ambition.

266 "selfish ambition": ἐριθεία. In extra–Biblical literature, *a self–seeking pursuit of political office by unfair means.* BDAG comments: "its meaning in our literature is a matter of conjecture," but finds that *selfish ambition, disputes* or *outbreaks of selfishness* is the most probable sense. *Selfish ambition,* implying *rivalry,* coupled with *hostility,* results in *a feeling of strife for another* (DBL).

267 Steve Deneff, More than Forgiveness: A Contemporary Call to Holiness Based on the Life of Jesus Christ. (Wesleyan Publishing House, 2002), 120.

268 "empty conceit": κενοδοξία. A hapax legomena meaning a vain or exaggerated self–evaluation (BDAG). A state of pride without basis or justification (LN) or pride without proper basis (DBL).

young man." President of a Baptist convention, that sounds pretty good to an Episcopalian. Perhaps it may be the loving wife who says to you, "Darling, your gifts are not really being used here. Can't we look around for something a little better?" Unless your eyes are sharp, you may not see the serpent standing behind Eve with her plausible appeal and expectation. Dear brethren, unless you can be happy preaching the simplest gospel to the simplest people for 50 years in the mountains of Tennessee or the Ozarks, if there really is such a place, you had better not go into the ministry. Ambition, to do well, to be thought well of, to make yourself known, to get on in the church, to build yourself a great tower—that is to build a leaning tower of Pisa which in the end will collapse and be destroyed. You may build up for yourself a treasure of what you think is gold but on the day of judgment it will be revealed as dross. You may clothe yourself in the noble vestments of reputation and approval but on the day of testing these will be shown as filthy rags. Ambition tells you how to get to the top. *Room At the Top,* that is the title of a famous novel by John Braine. But I can assure you that there isn't room at the top. If you get there you will find a gang of prima donnas, each more eager than the rest to push the others down. I only know one place where there is plenty of room. That is at the foot of the cross. There is plenty of room there.[269]

Neill is describing selfish ambition, though he uses only the word "ambition." Pride can be so ambient, so subtle, so disarming. But it is pride, nevertheless. Selfish ambition—thinking of yourself more highly than you should, keeping your own interests first—is the stuff that renders our faithfulness to God impotent.

We find selfish ambition illustrated in the story of James and John in Mark 10:36–40 (ESV):

And James and John, the sons of Zebedee, came up to him and said to him, "Teacher, we want you to do for us whatever we ask of you." And he said to them, "What do you want me to do for you?" And they said to him, "Grant us to sit, one at your right hand and one at your left, in your glory." Jesus said to them, "You do not know what you are asking. Are you able to drink the cup that I drink, or to be baptized with the baptism with which I am baptized?" And they said to him, "We are able." And Jesus said to them, "The cup that I drink you will drink, and with the baptism with which I am baptized, you will be baptized, but to sit

---

269 Stephen Neill, "To Think the Way God Thinks: Philippians 2:1–18," *Faith and Mission* 1, no. 1 (1983): 73–74.

at my right hand or at my left is not mine to grant, but it is for those for whom it has been prepared."

James and John wanted status, so they asked for it. Their ambition was to gain political power, riding the coattails of Jesus.[270] To do this, they needed to reign with Christ and to be at his side when He ascended the political ladder. They wanted privilege and prestige.[271] Their requests show how much they lacked comprehension of Jesus' teaching.[272]

More examples of selfish ambition include the story of Absalom trying to gain control of the throne (2 Samuel 15:1–6) and Adonijah putting himself forward as king (1 Kings 1:5–8). We also have the King of Babylon (Isaiah 14:13–14), the ruler of Tyre (Ezekiel 28:1–2), and an unnamed king (Daniel 11:36) who exalt themselves above God. Of course, in the New Testament, we have the Antichrist, who will "exalt himself over everything that is called God" (2 Thessalonians 2:4).

Selfish ambition comes from pride, which is seen throughout the Bible as the root of selfishness and rebellion. There are obvious parallels between John's broad categorizations of sin (lust of the flesh, lust of the eyes, and the pride of life) and Paul's description of those who preach Christ out of *selfish ambition*.

Selfish ambition can be seen in a heart that "devises wicked schemes" and "feet that are quick to rush into evil" (Proverbs 6.17 NIV). Those of us who have been regenerated by the Holy Spirit and brought into the kingdom of God by accepting Christ through faith (Ephesians 4.6) were once living out a heart of selfish ambition:

> All of us also lived among them at one time, gratifying the cravings of our flesh and following its desires and thoughts. (Ephesians 2:3 ESV)

In Jeremiah 45:5, we are told by God not to seek "great things for yourself" because, if we do, God will need to take time to humble us (Matthew 23:12), and we will render ourselves unproductive in God's kingdom:

> Still others, like seed sown among thorns, hear the word; but the worries of this life, the deceitfulness of wealth and the desires for other things come in and choke the word, making it unfruitful. (Mark 4:18–19 NIV)

The results of selfish ambition are given to us in James 3:13–16 (NIV):

---

270 David E. Garland, *Mark*. The NIV Application Commentary. (Zondervan, 1996), 410–11.
271 Ronald J. Kernaghan, *Mark*. The IVP New Testament Commentary Series. (InterVarsity, 2007), 203.
272 Morna D. Hooker, *The Gospel according to Saint Mark*. Black's New Testament Commentary. (Continuum, 1991), 246.

Who is wise and understanding among you? Let them show it by their good life, by deeds done in the humility that comes from wisdom. But if you harbor bitter envy and selfish ambition in your hearts, do not boast about it or deny the truth. Such "wisdom" does not come down from heaven but is earthly, unspiritual, demonic. For where you have envy and selfish ambition, there you find disorder and every evil practice.

To summarize, selfish ambition focuses on yourself—what you want to achieve. You can be focused on power, wealth, financial security, or even building a strong business or a large church. Selfish ambition seeks great things for itself. Selfish ambition is the cause of wicked schemes and is grown in the soil of pride. Selfish ambition can even use religion to promote itself above God. It seeks position and status. God's response is to humble us, and until we allow him to do this, we will be unproductive for the kingdom, because "God opposes the proud but gives grace to the humble" (James 4:6 ESV). Figure 4–2 illustrates the elements of selfish ambition.

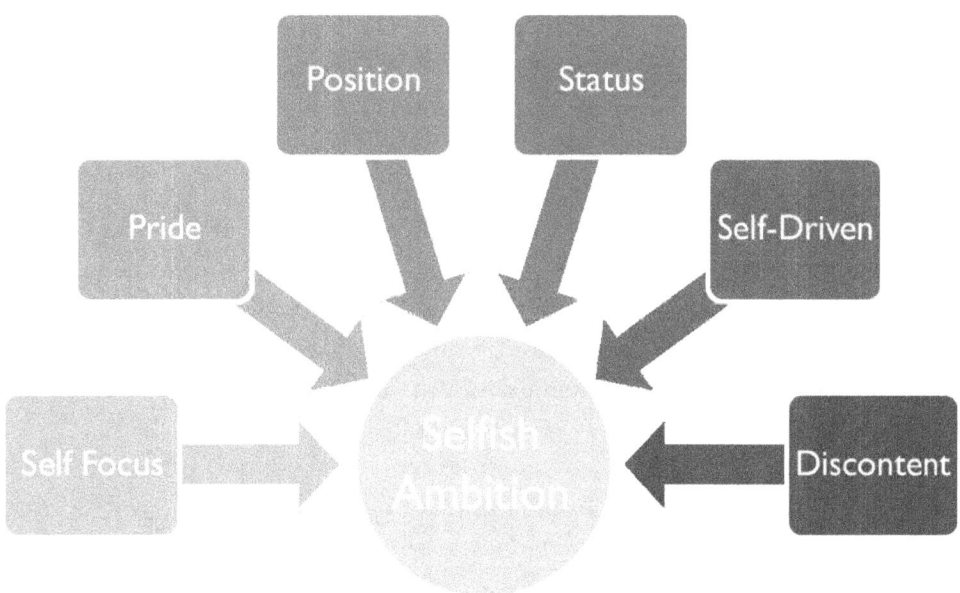

Figure 4–2: Elements of Selfish Ambition

To give up selfish ambition means to give up your dreams of wealth, achievement, prestige, status, and the pride of those achievements. Selfish ambition is nearly impossible to give up unless it is replaced by Godly ambition under the transforming power of the Holy

Spirit. Apart from God's work in one's life, selfish ambition will remain rooted and strong, predictably producing negative results.

Godly Ambition

Instead of being driven by selfish ambition and our agenda, we need to be led by the Spirit of God and focused on God's agenda. This principle is clearly taught in Matthew 6:25-34 (ESV). Christ is teaching us about worry and placing our trust in God, but in the midst of his teaching, he laser-focuses us on seeking God and his kingdom:

> [25] "Therefore I tell you, do not be anxious about your life, what you will eat or what you will drink, nor about your body, what you will put on. Is not life more than food, and the body more than clothing? [26] Look at the birds of the air: they neither sow nor reap nor gather into barns, and yet your heavenly Father feeds them. Are you not of more value than they? [27] And which of you by being anxious can add a single hour to his span of life? [28] And why are you anxious about clothing? Consider the lilies of the field, how they grow: they neither toil nor spin, [29] yet I tell you, even Solomon in all his glory was not arrayed like one of these. [30] But if God so clothes the grass of the field, which today is alive and tomorrow is thrown into the oven, will he not much more clothe you, O you of little faith? [31] Therefore do not be anxious, saying, 'What shall we eat?' or 'What shall we drink?' or 'What shall we wear?' [32] For the Gentiles seek after all these things, and your heavenly Father knows that you need them all. [33] But seek first the kingdom of God and his righteousness, and all these things will be added to you. [34] "Therefore do not be anxious about tomorrow, for tomorrow will be anxious for itself. Sufficient for the day is its own trouble.

Godly ambition always focuses on God's kingdom and righteousness first.

Every time.

In the midst of our busy lives where we worry about so many "cares of this world," that "choke the word of God," (Matthew 13:22), rendering us "ineffective and unproductive" (2 Peter 1:8), Christ tells us to "seek first" God's kingdom and his righteousness, understanding that all these "other things" will be given to us at the right time.

Pragamtically, a CBO filters *every* decision through these two questions:

- Is it best for the kingdom?
- Is it best for righteousness?

Godly ambition means that we want what God wants. We find joy and contentment in letting the Spirit *lead* us into offering new products and services. Just because we can see into the future and envision what *could be* does not mean God calls us to make that envisioned future a reality. Until we sense God is leading us into a new business, product or service line, or some other endeavor, we are content to remain "as is."

Godly ambition means we will learn to be at rest when the Spirit *does not* lead us into a new product or service line. Godly ambition means we walk away from significant revenue-generating opportunities if those opportunities are not best for God's kingdom or his righteousness. Hence, we learn to trust God fully and that when he directs restraint—even amid overwhelming data that says "move forward"—it is best for us personally and our business to stand down. *Like those in full–time vocational ministry who must learn that the need is not the call, Christian business owners must learn that the opportunity is not the call.*

Selfish ambition has difficulty saying "no" to most new shiny objects. Spirit-led business owners see the same opportunities but first ask the Lord if they should pursue the new opportunity. They trust God's direction and find *equal contentment* in a "no" or a "yes" from God.

It is not that spirit–led business owners lack ambition to grow financially. Instead, their ambition is re-oriented to glorify God. They find *more* joy in seeing God glorified than they do in creating a new revenue-generating engine.

They understand that the business and opportunities God entrusts to them *are enough*. Their first ambition is to advantage God's kingdom and his agenda. For the spirit–led Christian business owner, there are no "missed opportunities." They have missed nothing if they are not led to pursue a new opportunity. Christian business owners have learned that just because they *can* does not mean they *should*. Godly ambition is fully compatible with disadvantaging oneself for God's glory.

From a business owner's perspective, ask yourself *why* you got into starting and running a business. For many owners, there was a confluence of knowing their industry, having unique skills or ideas, wanting to make a difference, a drive for independence, and earning enough money to cover their living expenses. In addition, many were simply in the right place at the right time. Some would call this luck—I would call it an entrustment from God.[273]

However, understanding why you got into business ownership is important to assessing your ambition. Those with godly ambition will seek to humble themselves before God and be content with the business God entrusts to them. They will be content with the amount of wealth entrusted to them. And their ambition will be to honor and glorify Christ in their lives and the marketplace. Figure 4–3 summarizes the elements of Godly ambition.

---

273 Christian business owners do not have a concept of "luck" because of God's sovereignty. The Lord decides the outcome of every roll of the dice (Proverbs 16:33).

Figure 4–3: Elements of Godly Ambition

Being content—wanting what you already have—is a choice and a gift from God. Disadvantaging yourself to advantage God's kingdom is also a choice that CBOs make many times over. American culture leads us toward discontent and selfish ambition. We are repeatedly told to follow our hearts,[274] dreams,[275] and believe in ourselves.[276] However, experience indicates that following these three pieces of advice leads to discontent, discord, and selfishness.

For the Christian business owner, we live counter–cultural lives (1 John 5:3–4) because of our covenant with God. We follow the heart of God because we know our hearts are deceitful and wicked (Jeremiah 17:9). We follow the commands of God instead of our dreams because that is where we find true happiness, joy, contentment, and the blessings of God (Psalm 1:1, 94:12ff, Jeremiah 17:7–8).[277] We believe in God, trusting in him for

274 Andrew Matthews, Follow Your Heart: Finding Purpose in Your Life and Work. (Price Stern Sloan, 1997.)

275 Franklin University, "Follow Your Dreams & Aspirations, Not Someone Else's." Accessed 11/01/2024, franklin.edu. https://www.franklin.edu/blog/follow–your–dreams–aspirations–not–someone–elses

276 Tchiki Davis, "How to Believe in Yourself." December 12, 2023, psychologytoday.com https://www.psychologytoday.com/us/blog/click–here–for–happiness/202201/how–to–believe–in–yourself

277 David Platt, Matt Mason, and Jim Shaddix. *Exalting Jesus in Psalms 51–100*. (Holman Reference, 2020), 394.

our sustenance and the security of our future because he is the only one who is trustworthy (Psalm 111:7, 119:138, 40:4, 19:7). In addition, we know that trusting in ourselves places us under a curse from God and indicates that our hearts are no longer aligned with him (Jeremiah 17:5).

From one Christian business owner to another, I urge you to choose contentment and Godly ambition. Not only will you experience the benefit of a happier life, you will enjoy the presence of God more fully.

SUMMARY

Contentment is wanting what you already have. Godly ambition is being led into a new direction where as selfish ambition is being led by your unholy desires. While both types of ambition can look similar on the outside, God looks at our hearts and ambitions. *Why* we do what we do is of paramount importance.

Our real life starts when we die on this earth. In the next chapter, I will look at drawing close to the heart of God and learning to live in his presence daily. Living with his presence in mind helps us prepare for living with God in eternity. Understanding how our work as Christian business owners prepares us for an eternity with God is the subject of my next chapter, so let's turn our attention to Chapter 4, *Preparation for Eternity*.

CHAPTER 5

PREPARATION FOR ETERNITY

Recall from Chapter 2, *Covenants and Business Ownership*, that Christian business owners live their lives with eternity in mind. Living with an eternal perspective includes connecting what we do on this earth to what we will do in eternity. In this chapter, I will argue for one point: what we do on this earth is preparatory for what we will be doing in heaven and our role of reigning with Christ.

IN THE FIELD of hermeneutics, which is the study of how we interpret the Bible,[278] there is a principle to which I ascribe: emphasize what the Scriptures emphasize and de-emphasize what is de-emphasized. I do not wish to imply an over-emphasis on this truth of reigning with Christ in eternity by dedicating an entire chapter to it when it is seldom mentioned in the Scriptures. However, because this truth is rarely taught in our churches or seminaries, I believe it is worth a short chapter to underscore my claim that what we do on this earth is preparatory for our work with Christ in eternity.

In Revelation 5:10, we are told we will reign on earth; in Revelation 22:5, we are told that we will reign forever and ever in the new heaven and earth.

---

278 Faithlife, "Hermeneutics." In *Logos Bible Study Factbook*. (Faithlife, LLC, November 13, 2024.) https://ref.ly/logos4/Factbook?id=ref%3abk.%25hermeneutics.

Turning our focus to the seven letters to the seven churches in Revelation 2:1–3:22, I recognize that each letter addresses a particular situation in a specific church.[279] However, these letters are also relevant to the universal church.[280] Taken from the letter to Thyatyra (Revelation 2:18–29), we learn that if we are faithful to God for the balance of our lives, we will reign with him in eternity. We will reign, "but only because Christ reigns and He is pleased to share his dignity" with us.[281] A steadfast faithfulness to God proves authentic trust in Christ. Here is the text:

> Hold fast what you have until I come. The one who conquers and who keeps my works until the end, to him I will give authority over the nations, and he will rule them with a rod of iron, as when earthen pots are broken in pieces even as I myself have received authority from my Father. And I will give him the morning star. (Revelation 2:25–28 ESV)

When we live a life of faithfulness to Christ—described as "those who overcome" (Revelation 2:26)—we are promised a function of reigning with God in eternity. In the last letter to the church of Laodicea, Revelation 3:20–21 (ESV), John records the words of Christ:

> Behold, I stand at the door and knock. If anyone hears my voice and opens the door, I will come in to him and eat with him, and he with me. The one who conquers, I will grant him to sit with me on my throne, as I also conquered and sat down with my Father on his throne.

The believer's destiny is not only a place in God's home (John 14:1–3) but dominion with Jesus in the new heaven and earth. Dominion with Christ depends on the believer overcoming pressures to accommodate idolatry and taking a low profile in their witness,[282] i.e., unfaithfulness to God.

---

279   Some scholars believe these seven churches were existing churches when John wrote Revelation. However, these scholars believe these seven churches also represent seven different types of churches that have existed throughout the present dispensation, seven types of individuals commonly found in contemporary churches, and seven periods of church history. See M.J. Brunk, "The Seven Churches of Revelation Two and Three," *Bibliotheca Sacra*, 1969. 126(503):240–46. It is also interesting to note that in Revelation, there are seven spirits, angels, churches, seals, trumpets, bowls, beatitudes, and doxologies. (Brendon R. Witte, "Seven Churches." In *The Lexham Bible Dictionary*, edited by John D. Barry, Et Al., (Lexham Press, 2016.)) Because the number seven is a sign of perfection, the seven letters could represent Jesus' perfect revelation to His people (Richard Bauckham, *The Theology of the Book of Revelation*. (Cambridge University Press, 1993), 26–27).

280   Gregory K. Beale, *The Book of Revelation: A Commentary on the Greek Text*. New International Greek Testament Commentary. (Eerdmans; Paternoster Press, 1999), 226.

281   Richard Chenevix Trench, *Commentary on the Epistles to the Seven Churches in Asia*, Fourth Edition, Revised (London: Kegan Paul, Trench, & Co., 1886), 156.

282   Beale, *Revelation*, 309.

Faithfulness is the key. It appeals to our egos to think we will reign with Christ in eternity, but realizing that right requires that we are "all in" while on this earth and that we stay "all in" until the day we die. Our preparation for an eternal reign with Christ depends not on *what* we do but on *our faithfulness to God* in whatever we do, including business ownership. Stated another way, business ownership, *per se*, is not the preparation. Being faithful to God in our role as business owners is what is in view here.

Our reign with Christ will fulfill his original purpose: to have us steward and cultivate the earth, enjoy our work, and enjoy his presence. He will create a new heaven and earth (Revelation 21:1, 2 Peter 3:13, Isaiah 65:17, 66:22) since the earth and heaven we know today will "pass away." We will work with God to subdue the earth and steward that which he will entrust us. Heiser is worth quoting at this point:

> We can see that the tasks of humanity, taken in tandem with the earlier observations that require Eden and Earth to be distinct, distinguish Eden and the earth. It makes no sense to subdue the garden of God. It's already what God wants it to be. There's no place on Earth like it. If it needed subjugation, that would imply imperfection. That's something that cannot be said about Eden, but it's true of the rest of the world. For sure God was happy with the whole creation. He pronounced it "very good" (Gen 1.31). But "very good" is not perfect.[283] Lastly, Eden and Earth must be distinct since, after the fall, Adam and Eve are expelled from it and have to live elsewhere. Unless you believe that they were sent into outer space, you must acknowledge Eden and Earth as distinct... The distinction helps us see that the original task of humanity was to make the entire Earth like Eden. Adam and Eve lived in the garden. They cared for it. But the rest of the earth needed subduing. It wasn't awful—in fact, Genesis 1 tells us that it was habitable. But it wasn't quite what Eden was. The whole world needs to be like God's home. He could do the job himself, but he chose to create human imagers to do it for him. He issued the decree; they were supposed to make it happen. They were to do that by multiplying and following God's direction. Eden is where the idea of the kingdom of God begins. And it's no coincidence that the Bible ends with the vision of a new Edenic Earth (Rev 21–22).[284] [emphasis added]

---

283 I do think the author, as much as I respect him, is splitting hairs here. I take "good" to mean that it was "perfect" in the sense that it was exactly what God wanted it to be at the time He created it.

284 Michael Heiser, The Unseen Realm: Recovering the Supernatural Worldview of the Bible (Lexham Press. Kindle Edition, 2015), 50–51.

It is important to understand that starting, growing, and building a business is part of "subduing the earth" (Genesis 2:18). Through business, we take raw materials and create useful things that better our lives. Innovation and creativity are often expressed within the context of business. As a Christian business owner, when you run your business well, you fulfill God's command to "be fruitful" and "subdue" the earth.

But it is equally important to understand that owning a business is preparatory for what we will be doing in heaven. Taking seriously our stewardship responsibilities is part of the preparatory work to reigning with him. Holding fast to our covenant with him is also part of that preparation work. *We do not primarily prepare ourselves to have a fulfilling career. We prepare to enjoy his presence, learn to be faithful to him, and reign with him in eternity.*

SUMMARY

In this chapter, I have claimed that our work here on earth is preparatory for our work in heaven and our reign with Christ. I have asserted that our destiny is not only a place in God's home (John 14:1–3) but dominion with Jesus in the new heaven and earth. But this dominion depends on us overcoming pressures to accommodate idolatry and become unfaithful to God.

In the next chapter, we'll focus on our identity in Christ, a vitally important topic as we steward a business God has entrusted to us. So, let's turn the page and keep going.

CHAPTER 6

OUR IDENTITY IN CHRIST

Changing our self-image by accepting the truth of our identity in Christ is necessary to live out all that our covenantal relationship with God calls us to. In this chapter, I will suggest that understanding our identity in Christ is necessary to steward what God has entrusted us with. I will outline what is true about each of us who have entered God's covenant. Part of the transformation of our minds and hearts includes a transformation of our identity.

CONVENTIONAL WISDOM

Conventional wisdom[285] has much to say about one's identity—what it is, how to form it, and how to sustain it. Theories about identity abound in the current literature. Examples can be found in philosophy,[286] sociology,[287] and other disciplines, like psychology. The conventional wisdom on identity formation is overwhelmingly noisy. Conventional wisdom starts with the individual and places the individual at the decision-making center of defining who the person is.

---

285 Please refer back to the Preface to recall how this phrase, "conventional wisdom" is being used in this book.

286 Richard Gaskin, "The Identity Theory of Truth." *The Stanford Encyclopedia of Philosophy*. Edward N. Zalta (Ed.). Winter, 2021. https://plato.stanford.edu/entries/truth-identity/.

287 Peter Burke and Jan Stets, *Identity Theory*. (Oxford: Oxford University Press, 2009).

Conventional wisdom's methods of defining identity usually connect one's identity to something unique or inherent in one's physical appearance or ethnic heritage.[288] *Psychology Today* suggests that identity is found in discovering and developing one's potential, choosing a life purpose, and applying one's potential to one's life purpose.[289] Furthermore, identity is also thought to be formed as one sums up one's memories, experiences, relationships, and values.[290]

Developing an identity attempts to merge the parts of our personas into a coherent whole. Vignoles argues that identity is personal and social: identity involves one's relationship with society and oneself.[291] In other words, identity can be ascribed (what society says about us) or achieved (what we do and say about ourselves), but it is likely less ascribed in our culture today than in decades past.[292] Identity is developed over time as one balances sameness and changes subjectively and objectively.[293] Identity considers how one is different from others,[294] what beliefs and values we hold, and even the brands we use.[295]

Conventional wisdom's view of identity formation is not wrong. Who hasn't had the experience of achieving a goal and then incorporated that achievement into how they thought about themselves? Who hasn't had their national heritage shape their identity—even a little—as they grew into adulthood? The factors of identity formation that conventional wisdom discusses are helpful and assist us in developing a mature view of ourselves. But, as we will see throughout this book, conventional wisdom is incomplete. It is a godless wisdom. Our personas are an insufficient reference point for developing a fully coherent identity. We need God to inform us about our true identities as disciples of Jesus Christ.[296]

---

288 Here is an example: Nadine Batchelor–Hunt, "I'm Jewish and black – where do I fit in?" bbc.com. December 26, 2021. https://www.bbc.com/news/uk–59748260.

289 Psychology Today Staff, "Identity." Accessed 07/14/2024, psychologytoday.com. https://www.psychologytoday.com/us/basics/identity.

290 Psychology Today Staff, "Identity." Accessed 11/26/2024, psychologytoday.com. https://www.psychologytoday.com/us/basics/identity#theories–of–identity

291 Vivian Vignoles, "Identity: Personal AND Social." In: *Oxford handbook of Personality and Social Psychology*. 2nd Edition. (Oxford: Oxford University Press, 2017), 1.

292 Gerald Adams, "Personal Identity Formation: A Synthesis of Cognitive and Ego Psychology." *Adolescence*. 2000. 12(46):151.

293 Päivi Fadjukoff, "Identity Formation in Adulthood." *Jyväskylä studies in education, psychology and social research*. Dissertation thesis, University of Jyväskylä, November, 2007.

294 Suzanne Degges–White, "Personal and Social Identity: Who you are Through Other's Eyes." October 15, 2021. psychologytoday.com. https://www.psychologytoday.com/us/blog/lifetime–connections/202110/personal–and–social–identity–who–are–you–through–others–eyes.

295 Skye Jethani, *The Divine Commodity: Discovering a Faith Beyond Consumer Christianity*. (Zondervan, 2009), 52.

296 For the millions who have not entered into a covenant with God, the section in this chapter about who we are in Christ will not apply to them because they are not in Christ.

BUSINESS OWNERSHIP AS IDENTITY

Business ownership breeds its unique kind of identity. Most owners' identities are tightly intertwined with their business and their role as business owners.[297] I have met several highly wealthy men and women nearing the end of their lives who started with nothing and are now worth well over $50M—a few over $200M. I observe that for many (not all of them), their identity is so completely tied to their public persona as a founder or owner of a successful business that they struggle to imagine having any other primary identity, such as a grandfather or grandmother.

However, one thing is clear: they do not identify themselves first or primarily as followers of Yahweh. Of those whom I have met, to a person, their relationship with God was more of an intellectual belief coupled with socially acceptable nods to religion without being too consumed by it. These owners who identify first as business owners and second as Christians sound good, look good, live morally, and are often fun people with whom to spend time. They are intelligent and talented. They are good people to be with. But their hearts are far from God, and their identity is wrapped up in their business.

A Christian's identity is primarily connected to what God says is true about us, how he has gifted us, and who he is transforming us to be. We define ourselves in contrast to who God is, which is both humbling and enlightening. *Faithful CBOs first identify as disciples of Jesus Christ. Business ownership is a distant second.*

DANIEL IS OUR EXAMPLE

In this story, Daniel, Hannaniah, Mishael, and Azariah faced an identity challenge that most of us have never confronted. After being taken captive and exiled to Babylon, their names were changed to reflect the nature of foreign gods.[298] Yet, their core identity as followers of Yahweh never wavered. How did they do this? The answer to that question illustrates what we are discussing in this chapter. Here is the relevant text from Daniel 1:5b–7 (NIV):

297　Robin Waite, "Defining Yourself as a Business Owner: Tips From a Mentor." September 19, 2023, robinwaite.com. https://www.robinwaite.com/blog/defining–yourself–as–a–business–owner–tips–from–a–mentor.

298　I am borrowing this section from my book *Working for a Difficult Boss*. (Bible and Business, 2023).

They were to be educated[299] for three years, and at the end of that time they were to stand before the King. [6] Among these were Daniel, Hananiah, Mishael, and Azariah of the tribe of Judah. [7] And the chief of the eunuchs gave them names: Daniel he called Belteshazzar, Hananiah he called Shadrach, Mishael he called Meshach, and Azariah he called Abednego.

Names in Hebrew and Chaldean Cultures

Having one's name changed as an adult could significantly alter one's identity in Hebrew and Chaldean cultures. The Hebrew names for Daniel, Hananiah, Mishael, and Azariah were changed to Chaldean names by the chief of the eunuchs (vs. 7). In those cultures, names usually "conveyed some impression as to the intrinsic character of the one who bore the name."[300] Changing their names was part of the assimilation program into the Babylonian culture and Nebuchadnezzar's court. It was a way for the Chaldeans to say, "What we say about you is more important than anything else."

It was common for Assyrian, Babylonian, and Egyptian kings to take new names on special occasions or give new names to their royal family members.[301] For example, in Genesis 41:45, Pharoah gave Joseph the name Zaphenath–Paneah.[302] In 2 Kings 23:34, Pharoah Neco changed Eliakim's name to Jehoiakim. And in 2 Kings 24:17, Mattaniah's name was changed to Zedekiah.

Name changes were common in the Hebrew culture, too. For example, Abram's name was changed to Abraham, Jacob to Israel, Hadassah to Esther (Esther 2:7), and Solomon to Jedidiah. In our culture today, we do not change our names when something significant occurs. We change titles but not names.

299 "educated": לדג, *to make great, to cause to be of major significance or importance* (Logos); *to grow up, become great* (BDB); *be exalted, i.e., be in a state of honor, glory and so have high status* (DBL). The word is used to indicate a state of physically growing larger (Genesis 21:8, Isaiah 44:14, Jonah 4:10) but is more often used in conjunction with growing in status (Genesis 12:2, 2 Samuel 7:22). If one understands this word as primarily referring to physical growth, then the concept of nourishment makes sense. But if one understands that in the Chaldean mind, these unsophisticated foreigners were going to be made "great" in status, then the concept of training would make more sense. What jumps off the page at me is the Chaldean's hubris in believing they could program a person into "greatness." This is directly the opposite of how we become "great" in the kingdom of God. We become "great" by becoming the least, becoming last, humbling ourselves before God. We do not become "great" by completing a three–year training program—a temptation to which many Christian seminary students have fallen prey.

300 Lewis Sperry Chafer, *Systematic Theology*. (Grand Rapids, MI: Kregel Publications, 1993), v1, 261.

301 Camden M. Cobern, *Ezekiel and Daniel*. Edited by D. D. Whedon. Vol. VIII. Commentary on the Old Testament. (The Methodist Book Concern, 1901), 330.

302 Scholar's dispute what this name means (K.A. Mathews. *Genesis 11:27–50:26. The New American Commentary*. (Broadman & Holman Publishers, 2005), v1B, 764, but all agree that his name was Egyptian in character (James K. Hoffmeier, *Israel in Egypt: The Evidence for the Authenticity of the Exodus Tradition*. (Oxford University Press, 1997), 87.

All four young men bore names that honored Yahweh, the God of Israel.[303] Their new Chaldean names were probably assigned arbitrarily,[304] though some think their names were chosen deliberately to mock Yahweh.[305] For sure, their new names were intended to separate them from their national and Jewish identity.[306] Table 6–1 presents the essence of these changes:

Table 6–1: Change of Names and Meaning[307]

Hebrew Name	Meaning	Chaldean Name	Meaning
Daniel	"My judge is God."	Belteshazzar	"Bel, protect his life" or "Lady, protect the King."
Hananiah	"Yahweh has shown grace," or "The Lord is gracious."	Shadrach	"The command of Aku" 308 or "I am fearful of a god." 309
Mishael	"Who is what God is?" or "Who is like God?"	Meshach	"Who is what Aku is?"
Azariah	"Yahweh has helped"	Abednego	"Servant of Nebo"

303 Dwight J. Pentecost, "Daniel." In *The Bible Knowledge Commentary: An Exposition of the Scriptures*, edited by J. F. Walvoord and R. B. Zuck. (Victor Books, 1985), 1330.

304 Later on in this study, we'll look at the story that focuses on Daniel's three friends being thrown in the fire as a punishment for not bowing down to an idol. The story is usually told to our children using their Chaldean names. It seems to me that we ought to use their Hebrew names since these are their real, original names.

305 LaGrone, Jessica. *The Rewritten Life Leader Guide: When God Changes Your Story.* (Abingdon Press, 2017), n.p.

306 Matthew Bryce Ervin and Joel Richardson, *The Divine Messenger: Appearances of the Son of God in the Old Testament* (Eugene, Oregon: Wipf and Stock, 2023). n.p.

307 This table is compiled from several sources: Gleason L. Archer, "Daniel." In *The Expositor's Bible Commentary: Daniel and the Minor Prophets*, edited by Frank E. Gaebelein, Vol. 7. (Zondervan Publishing, 1986), 34; Camden M. Cobern, *Ezekiel and Daniel*. Edited by D. D. Whedon. Vol. VIII. Commentary on the Old Testament. (The Methodist Book Concern, 1901), 330; Pentecost, *Bible Knowledge Commentary*, 1330; Stephen R. Miller. *Daniel*. Vol. 18. The *New American Commentary*. (Broadman & Holman, 1994), 65; Eugene Carpenter, "Daniel." In *Cornerstone Biblical Commentary: Ezekiel & Daniel*, edited by Philip W. Comfort, Vol. 9. (Tyndale House, 2010), 318.

308 "Aku": A Sumerian or Elamite moon–god, Archer, *Expositor's Bible Commentary*, 34.

309 Pentecost, Bible Knowledge Commentary, 1330.

Whenever they heard their Chaldean names, they were reminded of their slavery and that they were cut off from their people and homeland.[310] For example, when Daniel heard his name, Belteshazzar, he heard, "Bel protects his life." *Bel* is Marduk, a prominent Babylonian god.[311] So, instead of having an identity where Yahweh is my judge, and I am accountable to him, Daniel now has to hear that some false god nicknamed Bel will protect his life. After hearing this a few thousand times, one might be tempted to believe it.

The comparisons are just as striking for Hananiah, Mishael, and Azariah. Instead of hearing that Yahweh has been gracious to him, Hananiah now hears that another Babylonian god, Aku, has command over him. For Mishael, instead of hearing "Who is like God?" where the assumed answer is "none but Yahweh himself" (Yahweh is the incomparable God—Exodus 15:11, Deuteronomy 3:24, 1 Kings 8:23, Psalm 97:9), he now hears the same question about Aku, presumably with a similar assumed answer.

For Azariah, instead of hearing that Yahweh is his helper, he hears he is the servant of Nebo, another Babylonian god.

Yet, despite their name changes, they never forgot who they were or where they came from. They never internalized their Babylonian identities. They rejected what others said about them in favor of what they knew to be true as followers of Yahweh. How were they able to do this? By firmly grounding their identity in their relationship with God.

Daniel Identified with God

We are given clues inside this book of Daniel that show he firmly grounded his identity in Yahweh. First, in Daniel 2:23 (ESV), he refers to God as the "God of my fathers":

> To you, O God of my fathers, I give thanks and praise, for you have given
> me wisdom and might, and have now made known to me what we asked
> of you, for you have made known to us the King's matter.

Notice that Daniel connects his pedigree with the God of his ancestors. This phrase emphasizes a personal and generational relationship with God, as seen in the story of Jacob, who referred to "the God of your father, God of Abraham, God of Isaac, and God of Jacob" (Exodus 3:6) and underscores God's commitment to individuals and families across generations, serving as a protector and provider.[312] By using this phrase, he says (in essence), "God was with my fathers—He disclosed himself to them. He rescued them from bondage. They trusted and walked with him. They devoted themselves to him. He has

---

310 John Calvin and Thomas Myers. *Commentary on the Book of the Prophet Daniel.* (Logos Bible Software, 2010), 95.

311 Carpenter, Cornerstone Biblical Commentary, 318.

312 John Goldingay, *Old Testament Theology: Israel's Gospel* (IVP Academic, 2003), 244.

done the same with me. This is my ethnic and familial heritage. This is also my spiritual heritage. I am one of them. I am a follower of Yahweh."

Second, in Daniel 6:22 (ESV), Daniel says:

> My God sent his angel and shut the lions' mouths, and they have not harmed me, because I was found blameless before him.

In this story, after King Darius learns Daniel is alive after spending the night with hungry lions, Daniel refers to God as "my God." God was not just *a* god. He was "*my* God."[313] By comparison, after Daniel interprets Nebuchadnezzar's dream in the second chapter, we learn that Daniel's interpretation impressed Nebuchadnezzar. Still, Nebuchadnezzar had not yet submitted himself to Yahweh because he used the phrase "your God":

> The King answered and said to Daniel, "Truly, your God is God of gods and Lord of kings, and a revealer of mysteries, for you have been able to reveal this mystery. (Daniel 2:47 ESV)

Yet after his sanity was restored, Nebuchadnezzar lost the phrase "your God" and instead exalted God directly himself:

> But at the end of those days, I, Nebuchadnezzar, looked up to heaven, and my sanity returned to me. Then I praised the Most High and honored and glorified Him who lives forever: For His dominion is an everlasting dominion, and His kingdom is from generation to generation. [35] All the inhabitants of the earth are counted as nothing, and He does what He wants with the army of heaven and the inhabitants of the earth. There is no one who can hold back His hand or say to Him, "What have You done?" [36] At that time my sanity returned to me, and my majesty and splendor returned to me for the glory of my kingdom. My advisers and my nobles sought me out, I was reestablished over my kingdom, and even more greatness came to me. [37] Now I, Nebuchadnezzar, praise, exalt, and glorify the King of heaven, because all His works are true and His ways are just. He is able to humble those who walk in pride. (Daniel 4:34–37 HCSB)

---

313 Such personalization of Yahweh in a monotheistic system is counter–cultural to Babylon's polytheistic culture. For their entire time in Babylon, Daniel and his friends would have been immersed in polytheism. Yet Daniel and his friends remained monotheistic and faithful to Yahweh, which is an example we all should emulate.

While it is not recorded that Nebuchadnezzar used the phrase "my God," the strength of his exultations shows he had identified himself with Yahweh in more than an intellectual sense: he had given his heart and allegiance to God. He identified himself as a follower of Yahweh.

Daniel's example shows that we can choose to base our identity on our relationship with God and not accept the world's assessment of our person and work. If we are successful (by the world's definition of "success"), we may hear the world's accolades and applause. Such noise can intoxicate our pride and pull us away from God. Let us be sure to focus on the approval of God as we build our identity in contrast to who God is, what he says about us, and what he has done in our lives.

WE ARE NEW CREATIONS

What God says is true about us can and should form the core of our identities. Let us start by considering the reality that we are a new creation. The foundation for any Christian's new identity is the truth that God has transformed each of us into a new creation (2 Corinthians 5:16–17 ESV):

> [16] From now on, therefore, we regard no one according to the flesh. Even though we once regarded Christ according to the flesh, we regard him thus no longer. [17] Therefore, if anyone is in Christ, he is a new creation. The old has passed away; behold, the new has come.

The term "new creation" …

> … is often thought of in exclusively personal terms…It is taken to refer to a person's conversion to Christ when the old life is exchanged for a new relationship to the Lord. This is undoubtedly part of Paul's meaning, but there is more. Recent scholars see here a cosmic setting; hence "new creation," recalling the old created world marred by human sin. In Christ a new order of existence is called into being, and believers enter by faith into that new world with a fresh orientation and outlook on life with the promise of resurrection to God's final world. This is called an eschatological hope and entails the dawn of a new age, promised by God in the OT prophetic hope.[314]

When people come to Christ, they should see themselves differently *because they are a new person—a new creation* with a *new future grounded in their relationship with Christ*. This

---

314   William Baker, Ralph P. Martin, and Carl N. Toney, *Cornerstone Biblical Commentary: 1 Corinthians, 2 Corinthians*. (Tyndale House, 2009), 384.

realization is not a wishing–something–into–existence; it is simply acknowledging the truth. We view ourselves as a new creation with a new future *because that is who we are.* We base our identity on the truth that we are a "new creation" and have exchanged our old lives for a new relationship with Christ.

Without this truth transforming our identity, God's call and gifting in our lives will be random and optional. But if we learn that our gifting and calling are grounded in being a new creation, they take on a new meaning and imperative as we live for God and express our love for him through obedience.

In addition, as a new creation, we no longer look at others as we did before ("according to the flesh"). Instead, we now see others

> according to their standing with Christ…When we see that we are all sinners dead in our sins and needing reconciliation from God, and when we accept Christ's shameful death on the cross as our death, then all previous canons we used to appraise others must be scrapped.[315]

We consider others through God's eyes. We look at ourselves as new creations. We are fundamentally different than we were before. Nothing can change that truth. Yet there is more, much more.

MORE TRUTH OF WHO WE ARE IN CHRIST

I will suggest that our identity formation in Christ must include these truths:[316]
- John 1:12: I am God's child
- John 15:15: I am Christ's friend
- Romans 5:1: I have been justified
- 1 Corinthians 6:17: I am united with the Lord, and I am one spirit with Him
- 1 Corinthians 6:20: I have been bought with a price. I belong to God
- 1 Corinthians 12:27: I am a member of Christ's body
- Ephesians 1:1: I am a saint
- Ephesians 1:5: I have been adopted as God's child
- Ephesians 2:18: I have direct access to God through the Holy Spirit
- Colossians 1:14: I have been redeemed and forgiven of all my sins
- Colossians 2:10: I am complete in Christ. I Am Secure
- Romans 8:1–2: I am free from condemnation

---

315 David E. Garland, *2 Corinthians*, The New American Commentary. (Broadman & Holman, 1999), 284.

316 This list is taken directly from Neil T. Anderson. *Victory Over the Darkness: Realize the Power of Your Identity in Christ.* Revised and Updated. (Bethany Publishing, 2020), 36–37, Kindle Edition.

- Romans 8:28: I am assured all things work together for good
- Romans 8:31–34: I am free from any condemning charges against me
- Romans 8:35–39: I cannot be separated from the love of God
- 2 Corinthians 1:21–22: I have been established, anointed, and sealed by God
- Philippians 1:6: I am confident that the good work God has begun in me will be perfected
- Philippians 3:20: I am a citizen of heaven
- Colossians 3:3: I am hidden with Christ in God
- 2 Timothy 1:7: I have not been given a spirit of fear but of power, love, and discipline
- Hebrews 4:16: I can find grace and mercy in time of need
- 1 John 5:18: I am born of God, and the evil one cannot touch me
- Matthew 5:13–14: I am the salt and light of the earth
- John 15:1, 5: I am a branch of the true vine, a channel of his life
- John 15:16: I have been chosen and appointed to bear fruit
- Acts 1:8: I am a personal witness of Christ
- 1 Corinthians 3:16: I am God's temple
- 2 Corinthians 5:17–21: I am a minister of reconciliation for God
- 2 Corinthians 6:1: I am God's co–worker (see 1 Corinthians 3:9
- Ephesians 2:6: I am seated with Christ in the heavenly realm
- Ephesians 2:10: I am God's workmanship
- Ephesians 3:12: I may approach God with freedom and confidence
- Philippians 4:13: I can do all things through Christ who strengthens me

I'd like you to go back and read that list again.

Then read it every day for 60 days.

If you take the time to bake into your identity what is true about you, you will be changed forever for the better.

Let God shape the core of your identity by accepting what is true about you since you have entered into a covenant with God. And let these truths infuse your gifting and God's call on your life.

In the same way, when we enter the workplace, we should not forget who we are in Christ. We should remember that we are a new creation. We should never forget that we have been rescued from Satan's kingdom and brought into the kingdom of God (Colossians 1:13).

We should view ourselves first as new creations grounded in our identity in Christ, then second as business owners. If you get these two identity elements out of order, you will have difficulty stewarding what God has entrusted you well, and you will likely drift very far from God.

God wants to raise a new generation of Christian business owners who build their identities on their covenant relationship with Christ before identifying as business owners.

Viewing ourselves first as followers of God and stewards of his entrustments to us is the basis for learning to think theologically before we think professionally and learning to disadvantage ourselves to advantage the kingdom of God. What I am suggesting we embrace as CBOs is an entire mind-shift that is part of a larger, more pervasive revival as we seek to draw closer to God.

SUMMARY

Christian business owners ground their identity in their covenant relationship with God. We identify as a new creation in Christ. We accept all that God says in true about us.

Business ownership is an entrusted role to us. Business ownership is not our identity. Others may see us primarily through our role as business owners, but we see ourselves first and primarily as God sees us: a person who has been redeemed, transformed, justified, sanctified, and set apart to God for fellowship with him and to do what God's calls us to do to further his kingdom on this earth.

In the next chapter, we'll learn how God communicates with us. Learning about those communication channels will teach us how to listen to him.

CHAPTER 7

LISTENING TO GOD

Listening to God's communications is visceral to walking closely with him and making wise decisions as Christian business owners. I argued earlier in Chapter 3, *Stewardship and Entrustments*, that God's presence is the conduit through which love is passed between us. Moreover, I have suggested that it is difficult to love God if we do not practice the presence of Jesus. In this chapter, I will assume that God's presence includes his communications with us, both through and outside of Scripture. I will indicate that the Scriptures teach that God is communicating with us continually in ways consistent with Scripture. I will further claim that God expects us to listen to his communications.

CONVENTIONAL WISDOM ON HEARING GOD'S VOICE

Some have studied people who hear God's voice. Their research concluded that a person's ability to hear God's voice might indicate a spiritual experience, but psychologists find this unlikely. Instead, these voices should be explained through the model of mental illness or a variety of other scientific models.[317] One study suggested that porosity[318] and absorption[319] blur the boundaries between inner sensory events and the outer world. In effect, people who think they hear the voice of God are predisposed to outside influences on their minds (porosity) and are less discriminating about the source of what they experience (absorption). What they attribute to God are nothing more than experiences they created in their minds.[320] Research further observes that the power of culture and individual differences may result in vivid sensory experiences interpreted as evidence of gods and spirits rather than mental processes wrongly interpreted.[321]

As one reviews the psychological literature on hearing God's voice, one is reminded of just how much resistance there is in the psychological community to finding any validity in spiritual beliefs. The modern practice of psychology in America is genuinely godless. As a Minnesota licensed psychologist (MA, LP),[322] I have long observed the arrogance and anti–religious attitudes of prominent psychological associations and their members.[323] Remember, spiritual things are foolish to those who do not know God (1 Corinthians 2:14), so explaining or defending one's listening to God's communications to those who do not know the Lord likely will be fruitless.

BIBLICAL WISDOM ON GOD'S COMMUNICATION WITH US

For the balance of this chapter, I will propose a balanced and Biblically–based view of God's communication activities with us.

---

317 Christopher C.H. Coo, "Chapter 7 Hearing the voice of God" In *Hearing Voices, Demonic and Divine: Scientific and Theological Perspectives.* (Routledge, 2019.)

318 "porosity" from "porous:" *permeable to outside influences.* Accessed 07/24/2024. Merriam–webster. com. https://www.merriam–webster.com/dictionary/porous

319 "absorption:" *the process of absorbing something or of being absorbed.* Accessed 07/27/2024. Merriam–webster.com. https://www.merriam–webster.com/dictionary/absorption

320 Tanya Marie Luhrmann, Kara Weismana, Felicity Aulinoa, Joshua D. Brahinskya, John C. Dulina, Vivian A. Dzokoto, Cristine H. Legare, Michael Lifshitz, Emily Ng, Nicole Ross–Zehnder, and Rachel E. Smith, "Sensing the presence of gods and spirits across cultures and faiths." *Proceedings of the National Academy of Sciences.* 2021. 188(5):7.

321 Luhrmann, *Sensing*, 7–8.

322 LP–5769. I am licensed at the time of this writing.

323 An interesting side note is that all of the personality theories I know of assume an evolutionistic foundation to the development of their theory. I don't know of anyone who has developed a theory of personality that is based on the Biblical truth that we are each created in God's image and that those who have entered a covenant with God somehow participate in the divine nature (2 Peter 1:4). God would need to raise up a person or persons to do this work, which can easily consume a lifetime of effort and toil, but it would be interesting to see how a theory of personality that incorporates the truth of sin, image of God, and so forth would differ from the theories offered today.

Does God Communicate with Us?

The short answer is yes.

Now for the longer answer.

God communicates with us in at least four ways. The first way that God talks to us is through general revelation (Psalm 19:1–4, Romans 1:18–20). The second way is through Jesus Christ (Matthew 5:17; Luke 24:27; Hebrews 1:1–2). Third, God speaks to us through the Holy Spirit (John 16:12–15). Finally, God speaks to us through the Bible (John 1:14, 5:39; 1 Timothy 3:16). God is not limited to these four methods, but these are the four most often used methods by God.[324] All four of these methods of communication *require more effort and intentionality on our part to listen and understand.* Figure 7–1 illustrates these four methods.

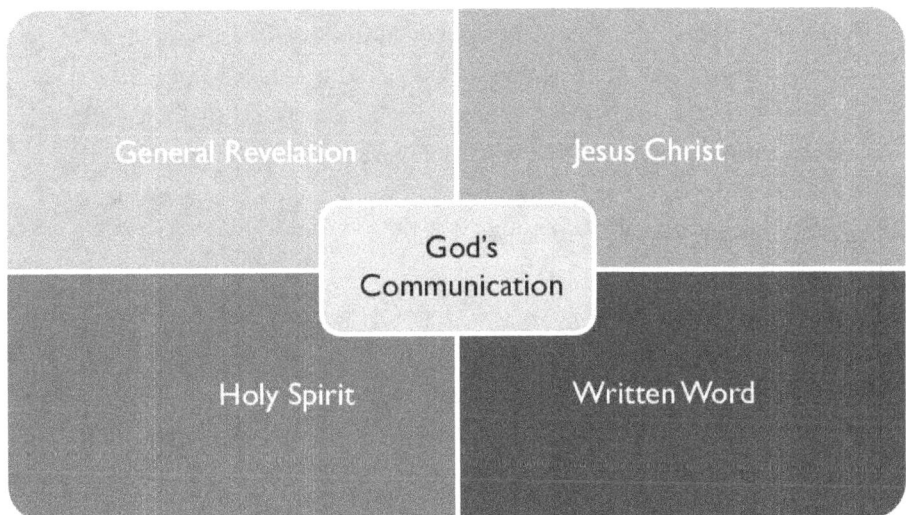

Figure 7–1: Four Ways God Communicates with Us

---

324 Dreams and visions are two other ways outlined in Scripture that God can speak to us, but those are used less often in my limited experience. What I will reject is that God communicates with us in myriad or unlimited ways. I had a friend once tell me that she felt a special message from God after an eagle landed in a tree by her dock on the lake at her cabin. She took that eagle's presence as God talking with her and she was sure she heard the message correctly. Squire Rushnell has made popular the notion of *godwinks,* and his book discussed the power of coincidence to guide one's life (*When God Winks,* Howard Books, 2001.). "It might be said, in fact, that Godwinks are the best way for God to make Himself known in your life and to provide encouragement." (*When God Winks,* p. 4). This is a lie. God does not communicate through coincidences, though the Spirit can give us discernment in how to respond to them. Coincidences are not given to us as a communication path in Scripture and should not be regarded as a method of how God communicates us. Coincidences differ from "open" or "closed" opportunities (sometimes called "doors", such as "open doors" or "closed doors.") A closed door can never tell you what you ought to do, but it sure can tell you what you can and cannot do. The same applies to open doors: they can never tell you what you ought to do, but they are possibilities that should be prayed over as we seek God's direction.

General Revelation

General revelation is truth about God which he gives to all mankind.[325] Two passages immediately come to mind: Psalm 19:1–4 (CSB) and Romans 1:18–19 (CSB).

> [1] The heavens declare the glory of God, and the sky proclaims the work of His hands. [2] Day after day they pour out speech; night after night they communicate knowledge. [3] There is no speech; there are no words; their voice is not heard. [4] Their message has gone out to all the earth, and their words to the ends of the world.

> [18] For God's wrath is revealed from heaven against all godlessness and unrighteousness of people who by their unrighteousness suppress the truth, [19] since what can be known about God is evident among them, because God has shown it to them. [20] For His invisible attributes, that is, His eternal power and divine nature, have been clearly seen since the creation of the world, being understood through what He has made. As a result, people are without excuse.

The Psalm 19 passage teaches that we can discern the glory of God by looking at the stars—the heavens—which are the "work of his hands." Though their voice is inaudible, their speech reaches all nations, "poured forth" every night, and their message is equally intelligible to all.[326] Psalm 19 is quoted in Romans 10:18 and is thought to be the basis of Paul's argument in Romans 1:18–20 that God's eternal power and deity are clearly perceived by that which is made.[327]

Creation itself testifies to God's power and divine nature. Implied in Romans 1:19–20 is the notion that a person with no extraordinary capacities can discern there is a God, that this God is eternal, that he has a divine nature, and that he is not silent.[328] This incomprehensible God is knowable,[329] but we must *actively listen* because every day, God

---

325   Faithlife, "General Revelation." In *Logos Bible Study Factbook*. (Faithlife, October 7, 2024.) https://ref.ly/logos4/Factbook?id=ref%3abk.%25GeneralRevelation.

326   Allen P. Ross, "Psalms." In *The Bible Knowledge Commentary: An Exposition of the Scriptures*, edited by J. F. Walvoord and R. B. Zuck. (Victor Books, 1985), 807.

327   Derek Kidner, *Psalms 1–72: An Introduction and Commentary*. Tyndale Old Testament Commentaries. (InterVarsity Press, 1973), 115.

328   Francis A. Schaeffer, *The Complete Works of Francis A. Schaeffer: A Christian Worldview*. (Crossway Books, 1982) v1, 326.

329   Herman Bavinck, *The Doctrine of God*. Translated by William Hendriksen. (Baker, 1977), 13.

communicates to mankind through his creation about who he is. "No day passes in which God does not show some signal evidence of his power."[330]

Yet we should not assume that man, in his fallen state with a corrupt mind, can correctly interpret what God is communicating through nature.[331] For example, just by looking at the stars, God's eternality, power, and divine existence can be demonstrated (Romans 1:20).[332] God's eternal power and divine nature are "clearly seen" because God took the initiative to "show" his attributes to us through his creation.[333] "People cannot miss God's revelation of himself, because he is actively making his revelation 'fully known, evident, and clear.'"[334]

Yet, many continue to posit the notion that a God, as described in the Bible, does not exist.[335] Their minds are so blinded by the enemy that they cannot discern obvious truth (2 Corinthians 4:4). When they look at the stars, they do not find a God who is consistent, eternal, powerful, and reliable.[336] Instead, they look at the stars and see everything else except the message God is communicating.[337]

Special revelation

Special revelation is the teaching about God and the works he has given us through the prophets and apostles, which is now contained primarily or exclusively in the Bible.[338] For many, part of God's special revelation is learning to listen to God's voice.

God's audible voice is illustrated in the Bible, especially in the OT. For example, God called to Moses from the burning bush (Exodus 3:4), from a cloud (Exodus 24:16), and a voice from between the cherubim (Numbers 7:89). In Psalm 68:33, God speaks with a mighty voice; the voice of the Lord sounded like many waters (Ezekiel 43:2, Revelation

---

330 John Calvin and James Anderson, *Commentary on the Book of Psalms*, (Logos Bible Software, 2010), v1, 310.

331 Wayne Grudem, *Systematic Theology: An Introduction to Biblical Doctrine.* 2nd Edition. (Zondervan Academic, 2020), 144.

332 Francis Turretin, *Institutes of Elenctic Theology.* Translated by George Musgrave Giger, Edited by James T. Dennison. (P&R Publishing, 1992), v1, 169.

333 Richard Alan Young, "The Knowledge of God in Romans 1:18–23: Exegetical and Theological Reflections." *Journal of the Evangelical Theological Society* 43, no. 4 (2000): 695–707.

334 Bruce A. Baker, "Romans 1:18–21 and Presuppositional Apologetics," *Bibliotheca Sacra* 155 (1998): 287.

335 Ravi Zacharias, *The Real Face of Atheism.* (Baker Books, 2004), 19–34.

336 Tremper Longman, III, ed., *Psalms Thru Song of Songs.* Vol. 5. Layman's Bible Commentary. (Barbour Publishing, 2010), 20.

337 Major Gherman Titov, a Soviet Astronaut, reportedly claimed that God did not exist since he saw "no God or angels" during his seventeen orbits of the earth. *The New York Times.* May 7, 1962. https://www.nytimes.com/1962/05/07/archives/titov–denying–god–puts–his–faith–in–the–people.html#

338 Gerald Bray, "Special Revelation," in *Lexham Survey of Theology*, ed. Mark Ward et al. (Lexham Press, 2018).

111

1:15) and God's voice came from Heaven (Daniel 4:31; Matthew 3:17; Mark 1:11; Luke 3:22; John 12:28–30).[339]

However, the Bible does not always describe God's voice as audible. Instead, the Bible teaches that there is an inaudible voice that we can "hear." This voice is God's authentic voice. Christ–followers can listen to his soundless voice because his spirit talks to us through our spirit. Consider Isaiah 30:19–21 (NIV):

> People of Zion, who live in Jerusalem, you will weep no more. How gracious he will be when you cry for help! As soon as he hears, he will answer you. Although the Lord gives you the bread of adversity and the water of affliction, your teachers will be hidden no more; with your own eyes you will see them. Whether you turn to the right or to the left, your ears will hear a voice behind you, saying, 'This is the way; walk in it.'

Here, we learn that the teachers we can see and hear will instruct us on which decisions to make, which path to walk, and which course of action to follow. Faithful teachers will instruct us on the right path to follow, which is one choice in front of us. We must choose to obey and follow God's voice.[340]

Moreover, the writer of Hebrews says:

> So, as the Holy Spirit says. 'Today, if you hear his voice, do not harden your hearts as you did in the rebellion, during the time of testing in the wilderness. (Hebrews 3:7–8 NIV).

This quotation from Psalm 95:7–11 is instructive since the classic failure of Israel at Kadesh Barnea led to their 40–year wandering in the wilderness. Had Israel obeyed God's voice instead of hardening their hearts, they would not have perished under his punishment.[341] Notice the conditional clause "if"—"*if* you hear his voice." This conditional clause implies our ability to hear, which could be negated by our unwillingness to listen. However, disciples of Christ do not ignore the voice of God. Disciples of Christ hear God's voice through the Spirit and immediately obey.

In addition to God's voice is his word, written for us and contained in the Bible's 66 books and letters. God's word is authoritative, clear, necessary for salvation, sufficient, inspired, and inerrant. While general revelation informs us that a God presides over all, special revelation is required to come to a place of entering a covenant with him.

---

339 A.C Day, *Collins Thesaurus of the Bible*. (Logos Bible Software, 2009). np.

340 Edward Young, *The Book of Isaiah, Chapters 19–39*. Vol. 2. (Eerdmans Publishing Co., 1969), 357–58.

341 Zane Hodges, "Hebrews." In *The Bible Knowledge Commentary: An Exposition of the Scriptures*, edited by J. F. Walvoord and R. B. Zuck. (Wheaton, IL: Victor Books, 1985), 786–87.

More Info: To learn more about the Bible and its characteristics, please see Chapter 1, *The Six Characteristics of Scripture*. Chapter 1 should be considered a backdrop of this discussion on special revelation.

Person of Christ

The writer of Hebrews tells us that God has "spoken to us by his son" and that Christ is the *exact* representation of God's being (Hebrews 1:1–4) The perfections of God he has chosen to reveal to us become visible in Christ.[342] The same God who spoke through the prophets in times past has spoken to us through his son, Jesus Christ. Hence, if you want to know what God is like—how he thinks, feels, and what he values—look at the person of Jesus Christ in the gospels. Look at the evidence for Christ's claims. Look at what Christ did and what he said. In the gospels, you will find meekness and majesty, manhood and deity, a God who kneels in humility to wash our feet, and learns obedience even to the point of death on a cross.[343] My friend, this is your God—and he communicates every moment of every day through the written accounts of Jesus Christ in the Bible.

Through the Holy Spirit

I suspect this is the most controversial method, at least at first blush. Here is the text that is the focus of this section, John 16:12–14 (CSB):

> [12] "I still have many things to tell you, but you cannot bear them now. [13] When the Spirit of truth comes, He will guide you into all the truth. For He will not speak on His own, but He will speak whatever He hears. He will also declare to you what is to come. [14] He will glorify Me because He will take from what is Mine and declare[344] it to you. (John 16:12–14 (CSB))

Scholars are all over the map on what "all truth" means. For example, Ryrie concludes that the Spirit's "all truth" teaching means "Christian doctrine including prophecy" and applies this generally to all Christians.[345] Grudem limits the Spirit's breadth of activity to

---

342 Raymond Brown, *The Message of Hebrews: Christ above All*. The Bible Speaks Today. (InterVarsity Press, 1988), 31.

343 Graham Kendrick, "Meekness and Majesty." Accesed 10/08/2024. Grahamkendrick.co.uk. https://grahamkendrick.co.uk/meekness–and–majesty–this–is–your–god/

344 "declare": from ἀναγγέλλω, *to carry back information, to report, disclose, proclaim, teach* (BDAG), *inform, tell, announce* (DBL), *to provide information with possible focus upon the source of the information* (LN).

345 Charles Caldwell Ryrie, *Basic Theology: A Popular Systematic Guide to Understanding Biblical Truth* (Moody Press, 1999), 132.

the disciples, who are given "amazing gifts to enable them to write Scripture."[346] Whitacre limits "all truth" to "all the truth in Jesus,"[347] whereas Hendriksen and Kistemaker have a more expanded definition of "all truth" that includes all Christian doctrine: "The Holy Spirit never rides a hobby. He never stresses *one* point of doctrine at the expense of all the others. He leads into *all* the truth."[348] Whitacre, Henriksen, and Kistemaker apply this passage to all Christians. Wiersbe combines John 16:13 with John 14:26 to form a trilogy that Wiersbe believes applies generally to all Christians:

> The Spirit would remind them of what Jesus had taught them; this gives us the four Gospels. The Spirit would also "guide" them into all truth; and this would result in the epistles. "He will show you things to come" refers to the prophetic Scriptures, especially the Book of Revelation.[349]

Plummer believes John 16:13 implies that "all Christians are assured of the supernatural presence of the Holy Spirit, who will teach them and protect them from all error." Arp finds this passage is a "situation promise" that applies only to the disciples.[350] At the other end of the spectrum, we have William Barclay who takes "all truth" at face value: "God's revelation to men and women is a revelation of *all* truth. It is quite wrong to think of it as confined to what we might call theological truth."[351]

I find myself more on the end of the spectrum with Barclay, where "all truth" means "all truth." Let's take the phrase at face value. I do not limit "all truth" to only theological truth. From where I sit, "all truth" includes the spirit enlightening us about the truth of our present–day situation, giving us wisdom when we ask for it (James 1:1–5), and guiding us to apply all of Scripture to our situation.

The Holy Spirit guides us to make the decisions and have the attitudes that mimic Christ. He only speaks what he hears—he never speaks on his own. He hears from Christ, who has been given all authority in heaven and earth (Matthew 28:18–20). His guidance is internal in our minds, and our spirit is giving us confirmation that his leadership is authentic. Satan will try to mimic the Holy Spirit and deceive us into a destructive path. Through our spirits, the Holy Spirit will guide us into the right path—the truthful path—but we must pay attention and be willing to follow his guidance.

---

346 Wayne A. Grudem, *Systematic Theology: An Introduction to Biblical Doctrine.* (InterVarsity Press; Zondervan, 2004), 59.

347 Rodney A. Whitacre, *John.* Vol. 4. The IVP New Testament Commentary Series. (IVP Academic, 1999), 391.

348 William Hendriksen and Simon J. Kistemaker, *Exposition of the Gospel According to John*, vol. 2, New Testament Commentary (Baker Books, 1953–2001), 328.

349 Warren W. Wiersbe, *The Bible Exposition Commentary*, vol. 1 (Victor Books, 1996), 362.

350 William Arp, "Illumination: What Is the Role of the Holy Spirit in Interpretation?" *Journal of Ministry and Theology* 16, no. 1 (2012).

351 William Barclay, *The Gospel of John*, vol. 2, The New Daily Study Bible (Edinburgh, 2001), 228.

I believe the Spirit takes the truth of Christ's persona and the Scripture and applies them to many decisions, beliefs, attitudes, and actions in our lives. If the Spirit does not apply truth and its implications to the many areas of our lives and communicate the thoughts of Christ to us, then we are left to live righteously strictly based on our human abilities to apply Scripture to our unique situations without any guidance. Such a non–Spirit–led proposition is unacceptable.

Listening to God for a Christian Business Owner

This chapter is not intended to solve all the theological issues about how one listens to God. I have friends everywhere along the spectrum of how they believe the Holy Spirit communicates with us. One friend is a "Bible–only" friend who does not believe the Spirit talks directly to us. Another friend routinely hears God's voice in decision–making and tends not to move forward without clear "direction" from God. Regardless of where you land on that continuum, there is common ground to be found in the teachings of Scripture.

So, in the balance of this chapter, I will be transparent and tell you where I am on this topic. I trust my discussion will be helpful to you. I land in a somewhat ambiguous place when listening to God's communications. What I believe today, as I write this, will likely change as I grow older and closer to God. Only in the last few years have I come to appreciate the supernaturalness of listening to God's communications. But listening requires much humility, calmness, devotion to quality time with God, and a predisposition to obey when God directs. God doesn't speak when he knows we're going to disobey. Here are my thoughts about listening to God's communications with us—in no particular order.

The Scriptures are the final authority for life

I find no difference between God's authority and the Scripture's authority. Hence, any communication from God will align and not contradict any teaching in the Bible. This is non–negotiable.

Personal experience should never be taught as prescriptive for all Christians

Only the Scriptures are inspired and inerrant (also discussed in Chapter 1, *The Six Characteristics of Scripture*), meaning my experiences are not inerrant or inspired. While I can learn from my experiences as part of my journey to growing closer to God, I should never make my experiences prescriptive for other Christians. Experience is what it is, but it is not a source of truth for the church.

In addition, *how* God communicated with Biblical characters is *descriptive* of what occurred, but is not *prescriptive* for us today. For example, the fact that God placed a bright light on Saul and spoke to him audibly as he was traveling to Damascus does not mean that God will shine a bright light on you or me and then talk to us audibly. There is no Biblical passage that indicates the Damascus road encounter or Peter's vision of what was considered clean and unclean is *prescriptive* for how we live with God today. If they were prescriptive, the Scriptures would have made that clear. God doesn't hide his commands from us (refer back to the *Clarity of Scripture* in Chapter 1). If there is a command to follow, God has made that clear to us.

The Holy Spirit does live inside me

The life–giving presence of the Spirit is a reality for every Christian. Remarkably, the Holy Spirit lives *inside* us, not only *with* us (1 Corinthians 6:19).[352] The Spirit's indwelling presence in the believer is one of the hallmarks of the New Covenant. In the Old Testament, God was *with* his people by dwelling *among* them, which still had a sanctifying effect on them.[353] But after the resurrection of Christ and the advent of the Holy Spirit in Acts 2, the Spirit indwelled the believer physically.[354] It seems strange to me that the Spirit would reside in me and yet not communicate with me.

Guidance requires communication

It is best to believe the spirit guides us in many decisions not directly discussed in the Bible. His guidance is based on the truth of who Christ is, the truth presented in God's word, and what he hears from Christ in real time. All guidance requires communication. The Spirit cannot guide without also communicating with us.

Development of the canon required hearing from the Holy Spirit apart from the Scriptures

Bible–only proponents of God's communications are going to have a problem here. Because God did not give us an explicit list of writings to be regarded as canonical, various councils and individuals engaged in thoughtful processes, debates, discussions, prayer, and so forth to develop the writings we consider sacred today.

---

352 Frederick Dale Bruner, *The Letter to the Romans: A Short Commentary*. (Eerdmans, 2021), 110.

353 James Hamilton, *God's Indwelling Presence: The Holy Spirit in the Old & New Testaments*. NAC Studies in Bible and Theology. Series Editor: E. Ray Clendenen. (B&H Academic, 2006), 51.

354 James Leo Garrett, Jr., *Systematic Theology: Biblical, Historical, and Evangelical*. Fourth Edition. Vol. 1. (Wipf & Stock, 2014), 231.

Different segments of Christianity consider different books or letters written by the ancients as authoritative for faith and practice today. For example, Catholic, Coptic, and Eastern Orthodox churches consider the Old Testament Apocrypha—a collection of writings included in older versions of the Old Testament that were not included in the Masoretic Text of the Hebrew Bible[355]—part of the current Old Testament. However, Protestant Christians do not consider the Apocrypha part of the canon.[356]

Klein, Blomberg, and Hubbard do a good job of laying out how we got our canon of 66 books today.[357] But what cannot be denied is that over several hundred years, consensus was achieved through much discussion, study, debate, and *listening to the Holy Spirit*. The source of truth upon which we rely so much was developed through methods denied today by Bible–only proponents. This fact should not go unnoticed.

PUTTING IT TOGETHER

Listening to God's communications will be experienced differently by different Christians. At the core of this discussion about listening to God's communications is that God constantly communicates with us. But what is not explicitly taught or commanded in Scripture is how we receive those communications or that we *must* receive his communications in one way or another.

Hence, based on experience plus the four ways God communicates with us, I will suggest that some will hear better through studying the Bible while others will hear better through being in nature or observing it. Others will "hear" an inaudible voice in their minds or spirits, while others will draw closer to God through the stories of Christ in the gospels. I am comfortable acknowledging that some "hear" using one method better than others. For me, I sometimes hear in my mind and my spirit. But I also hear through the intentional study of God's written word. Being in nature does little for me.[358] We should have theological freedom in this area to allow Christians to express their God–given ways of connecting with him.

---

355 Douglas Estes, "Apocrypha, Old Testament," *The Lexham Bible Dictionary*. Barry, J.D., et al. (Eds.) (Lexham Press, 2016.)

356 David deSilva, "Apocrypha and Pseudepigrapha." In *Dictionary of New Testament Background: a Compendium of Contemporary Biblical Scholarship. 2000*. Porter, S. and Evans, C. (Eds.) (Intervarsity Press, 2000.)

357 William Klein, Criag Blomberg, and Robert Hubbard, *Introduction to Biblical Interpretation*. Third Edition. (Zondervan Academic, 2017), 165–180.

358 Here is a quick story: I have friends who hunt deer and talk about becoming part of nature when sitting in a deer stand. They love the peaceful quiet of the wood. That was not my experience. I have only hunted deer twice. The last time, not only did I not see any deer, I did not see any *animals*, and that led me to conclude that I should not be in a deer stand ever again!

SUMMARY

In this chapter, I have suggested that the Scriptures tell us that God communicates in four primary ways, though he is not limited to those ways. I have also indicated that different Christians "hear" (predominantly) in one or more of these ways. How one Christian "hears" from God should not become prescriptive for how another Christian receives God's communications.

In the next section of this book, we will dive into a series of discussions about decisions that CBOs face and what the Bible says about those decisions. Let's move forward and learn what God has for each of us.

PART II

BIBLICAL THEOLOGY APPLIED TO EVERY–DAY DECISIONS THAT A CHRISTIAN BUSINESS OWNER FACES

IN THE SECOND part of this book, I focus on practical matters that every business owner faces. The theology we have been learning will now form the context for our topical discussions. Christian theology will be ambient to these discussions. The Scriptures are relevant to every area of business. In this section—which will comprise the balance of this book—I will illustrate that the commands and theologies found in the Bible have numerous connections to the role of a business owner and the decisions an owner makes. I will look at the following areas:

- Money and wealth
- Leadership
- Core Ideology
- Receiving advice
- Planning
- Governance, Risk, and Compliance
- Ethics and legal considerations
- Supply chain and vendor management

- Marketing
- Human resources
- Finishing well

In these discussions, conventional wisdom will be filtered through Biblical wisdom to understand what God intends a Christian business owner to think, do, and believe. The filtering process will also indicate which parts of conventional wisdom are acceptable in Biblical wisdom's view and which parts should be rejected.

In the *BetterMan* series, we are taught that one of the four elements of Biblical manhood is to "courageously follow God's word."[359] CBOs—both men and women—should understand that following God's word is not for the faint of heart. Courage will be required. Some of what we learn will be easy to implement, but other commands will require a gut-check decision: either you will obey God or you will not. As we work our way through this section, I pray that God will draw your heart to himself and that you will be transformed by his word and the Holy Spirit's work in your heart, mind, and soul.

There is much to learn, so I will start by looking at what the Bible says about money and wealth.

359 BetterMan, *A Real Man Courageously Follows God's Word*, Session 7, BetterMan Core. https://betterman.com/betterman-defined.

CHAPTER 8

MONEY AND WEALTH

The purpose of this chapter is to demonstrate several claims. First, conventional wisdom on money, wealth, and investing is sound generally and, for the most part, should be heeded by a Christian business owner. Second, because the temptations to love money and wealth are so subtle, it is best not to pursue wealth accumulation. Third, the prosperity gospel is antithetical to Biblical Christianity and should be avoided. Fourth, assuming debt is not sinful but should be avoided if possible. Fifth, saving too much for the future is hoarding, so philanthropy or God-led reinvestment should be employed to prevent hoarding by those whom God entrusts with much wealth. Last, you cannot have the best of God and the best of this world. If you try to pursue both, eventually, you will be forced to choose where your affections and allegiances lie.

This chapter will be divided into four sections: A) Wealth and Prosperity, B) Debt, C) Saving, and D) Greed.

IN ALL FOUR ensuing conversations about money and wealth, let's not lose sight of the notion that we are to seek first God's kingdom and his righteousness (Matthew 6:33) and that our true satisfaction is found in living righteousness (Matthew 5:6).

In addition, as stewards of God's entrustments, we voluntarily disadvantage ourselves, if necessary, to advantage God's kingdom.

WEALTH AND PROSPERITY

Wealth is an abundance of goods or money.[360] Many fathers of our faith were wealthy. Some examples are Abraham, Joseph, Job, David, and Solomon. But being rich did not ensure they were strong with God. Many other fathers of our faith were not known to be rich, such as Isaiah, Jeremiah, Ezekiel, most of the minor prophets, the disciples, and Jesus Christ.

Conventional Wisdom

Thousands of books and millions of words have been written about wealth and money from an American viewpoint. Here is a brief overview of conventional wisdom regarding happiness, investing, and Americans' views of the wealthy.

Money and happiness

Conventional wisdom is conflicted on whether or not wealth brings happiness and satisfaction. One study suggests that an increase in wealth does bring an increase in happiness.[361] Yet, Senik found that if an individual becomes wealthy, that individual will be happy, fulfilled, and satisfied.[362] But is the accumulation of wealth all it's purported to be? Perhaps not.

Other research has shown that a preoccupation with accumulating wealth leads to compromised psychological and relational health.[363] One study suggested valuing money over other things likely hampers happiness and well–being.[364] In addition, materialistic individuals may become trapped by their adaptation levels relative to wealth, fulfillment, and satisfaction. They will likely demand increasing levels of stimulation merely to maintain old levels of pleasure. For example, if USD 5,000 made an individual happy yesterday, perhaps USD 5,200 will be needed today to experience the same level of happiness. With a

---

360 Benjamin I. Simpson, "Wealth," in *The Lexham Bible Dictionary*, ed. John D. Barry et al. (Lexham Press, 2016).

361 Matthew A. Killingsworth, "Money and Happiness: Extended Evidence Against Satiation." July 17, 2024. *Happiness Science*. https://happiness–science.org/money–happiness–satiation/#results.

362 Claudia Senik, "Wealth and Happiness." *Oxford Review of Economic Policy*. 2014. 30(1):92.

363 Brian J. Sherman, "The Poverty of Affluence: Addition to Wealth and its Effects on Well–Being." *Graduate Student Journal of Psychology*. 2006. 8:30–32.

364 Lora Park, Deborah Ward, and Kristin Naragon–Gainey, "It's All About the Money (For Some): Consequences of Financially Contingent Self–Worth." *Personality and Social Psycholgy Bulletin*. 2017, 43(5):601–622. See also M.J. Monnot, "Marginal Utility and Economic Development: Intrinsic Versus Extrinsic Aspirations and Subjective Well–Being Among Chinese Employees." *Social Indicators Research*. 2017, 132(1):155–185.

continual need for more materialistic stimulation to maintain previous levels of satisfaction, an individual can become stuck on the 'hedonic treadmill,' demanding more and more from life to be as happy and satisfied as before.[365]

Saving and investing

The conventional wisdom on how to build wealth is more consistent. Conventional wisdom teaches that building wealth takes time, effort, and discipline.[366] Conventional wisdom recognizes that wealth can be lost in the market. However, it assumes that understanding how to invest wisely through a diversified portfolio is the best way to protect oneself from board market downturns that lead to financial loss.[367] Conventional wisdom believes one can secure one's financial future through consistent saving and intelligent investing.[368]

Conventional wisdom recognizes financial risks exist when investing. As the amount of money one holds increases, the amount of injury represented by these risks increases too.[369] Still, conventional wisdom believes these risks can be controlled to minimize damage to one's investment portfolio during market downturns. There is much good to learn from conventional wisdom when building and managing wealth.

American's Views of the Wealthy

American society's view of wealth is somewhat schizophrenic. Our version of capitalism provides opportunities for upward economic mobility that rewards individual effort and skill with new wealth.[370] Yet, the system providing these opportunities creates wealth inequalities that our society increasingly finds repugnant.[371] Americans generally admire those who are rich yet report that others admire the rich "too much." Many believe that hard work, ambition, and family connections drive opportunities to create new wealth,

---

365 P. Brickman and D.T. Campbell, "Hedonic relativism and planning the good society." In: *Adaptation Level Theory: A Symposium.* Appley, M.H. (Ed.) (Academic Press, 1971), 287–302.

366 Adam Hayes, "Principles of Building Wealth." March 25, 2024, Investopedia.com, https://www.investopedia.com/managing–wealth/simple–steps–building–wealth/

367 Ibid.

368 The Federal Reserve Bank of Dallas, "Building Wealth: A Beginner'sGuide to Securing Your Financial Future." Accessed 06/29/2024. https://www.dallasfed.org/-/media/microsites/cd/wealth/index.html

369 Adam Hayes. "Understanding Financial Risk Plus Tools to Control It." June 15, 2024. Investopedia. com. https://www.investopedia.com/terms/f/financialrisk.asp

370 Isabel Sawhill and John Morton, "Economic Mobility: Is the American Dream Alive and Well?" May 1, 2007, The Brookings Institute. https://www.brookings.edu/articles/economic–mobility–is–the–american–dream–alive–and–well/

371 Ana Hernández Kent and Lowell R. Ricketts, "U.S. Wealth Inequality: Gaps Remain Despite Widespread Wealth Gains." February 7, 2024, The Federal Reserve Bank of St. Louis. https://www.stlouisfed.org/open–vault/2024/feb/us–wealth–inequality–widespread–gains–gaps–remain

while poor life choices, drugs, family breakdown, and lack of a hard work ethic drive poverty. [372] We respect and admire individual billionaires but rage against the "top 1%".[373] A general summation of the literature is that we all want to be rich, but we sometimes harbor negative feelings toward others who are rich.

Conventional wisdom views wealth mainly through political and social class lenses. It rarely incorporates a transcendent God who has given commands for mankind to follow. Conventional wisdom views the wealthy as having philanthropic, societal obligations.[374] A Christian view will mostly supplant societal obligations with Biblical stewardship to use wealth as God directs, which usually includes giving to one's community and to God's kingdom.

Biblical Wisdom

Some of what conventional wisdom suggests aligns with Biblical teaching regarding saving and investing. For example, the concept of saving regularly in small amounts to build wealth over time is advocated by both conventional wisdom[375] and Proverbs 13:11 (NIV): "Dishonest money dwindles away, but whoever gathers money little by little makes it grow."

Yet, some of conventional wisdom is built on assumptions that contradict Scripture. For example, the belief that one can create financial security is a ruse from a Biblical viewpoint. There is no such thing as economic security, though some who claim to follow Christ espouse it and work hard to achieve it.[376] Proverbs 23:4–5 (NIV) reminds us that wealth can dissolve swiftly, without warning, and we can do nothing about it. So do not tire yourself to obtain something so fleeting in nature and duration:

> Do not wear yourself out to get rich; do not trust your own cleverness.
> Cast but a glance at riches, and they are gone, for they will surely sprout
> wings and fly off to the sky like an eagle.

372 Emily Ekins. "What Americans Think About Poverty, Wealth, and Work." September 24, 2019, Cato institute. https://www.cato.org/publications/survey–reports/what–americans–think–about–poverty–wealth–work

373 Jesse Walker, Stephanie Tepper and Thomas Gilovich, "People are more tolerant of inequality when it is expressed in terms of individuals rather than groups at the top." October 18, 2021. *Proceedings of the National Academy of Sciences*. 118(43):np.

374 Columbia University Libraries, "Philanthropy of Andrew Carnegie." Accessed 08/24/2024, Library. columbia.edu. https://library.columbia.edu/libraries/rbml/units/carnegie/andrew.html

375 Alex Gailey, "Over half of Americans are struggling to save. These 8 charts show how small savings can add up to big money." January 29, 2024, Bankrate.com. https://www.bankrate.com/banking/see–how–to–save–money–through–small–savings–over–time/

376 Jonathan Baer. "The Soil of the Prosperity Gospel." *9Marks Journal*, 2014. v1:22–25.

In the ancient world, the figure of a bird flying off symbolized fleeting wealth.[377] I have lost wealth quickly, and many who read this book have experienced something similar. Placing one's trust and confidence in fleeting wealth seems to be unwise.

The Bible views wealth less in political or social terms and more in moral or spiritual terms. Wealth is often seen as a blessing from God, frequently linked to God's covenant with Abraham (Genesis 12:1–3, 15:1–7). Moses stipulates that wealth will come to Israel if they carefully obey God's commands (Deuteronomy 28:1–14).[378]

But wealth is also seen as a temptation to drift from God and become filled with pride. Jesus warns that it is impossible to love God and love wealth (Matthew 6:24). Hoarding wealth is evidence of diminished devotion toward God and a lack of faith in his provision.[379]

Hence, much conventional wisdom about building wealth can be adopted by a Christian without accepting the premise that one can become financially secure. In addition, I bristle at the phrase "financial independence" because I do not believe that either you or I should be independent from God.[380] But if, by "financial independence," one means to be debt–free, then I heartily endorse pursuing that goal.

One of the more misused concepts in the Bible is that of prosperity. So, at this point, it is a good use of time and page space to learn what prosperity is, how a Christian should view it, and why the prosperity gospel (as it is commonly termed) is heretical and damaging to Biblical Christianity.

Prosperity

Prosperity is a state of abundance and economic growth.[381] Prosperity is God's generosity in response to our covenantal obedience to him.[382] Consider these passages that connect covenantal obedience to God and material prosperity:

---

377 Allen P. Ross. "Proverbs." In *The Expositor's Bible Commentary: Psalms, Proverbs, Ecclesiastes, Song of Songs*, edited by Frank E. Gaebelein, Vol. 5. (Zondervan Publishing House, 1991), 1068.

378 Benjamin I. Simpson. "Wealth." In *The Lexham Bible Dictionary*, edited by John D. Barry, David Bomar, Derek R. Brown, Rachel Klippenstein, Douglas Mangum, Carrie Sinclair Wolcott, Lazarus Wentz, Elliot Ritzema, and Wendy Widder. (Lexham Press, 2016.)

379 Ibid.

380 If a Christian is given so much wealth by God that this individual could live comfortably without ever needing to depend on God again, I believe it is an act of discipleship to give enough wealth away that dependence on God is re-created.

381 Faithlife, "Prosper." In *Logos Bible Study Factbook*. July 16, 2024. https://ref.ly/logos4/Factbook?id=ref%3abk.%25prosper.

382 Andrew E. Hill, "Prosper; Prosperous." In *The International Standard Bible Encyclopedia, Revised*, edited by Geoffrey W. Bromiley. (Eerdmans, 1979–1988), v3, 1012.

Therefore keep the words of this covenant and do them, that you may prosper[383] in all that you do. (Deuteronomy 29:9 ESV)

And keep the charge of the Lord your God, walking in his ways and keeping his statutes, his commandments, his rules, and his testimonies, as it is written in the Law of Moses, that you may prosper in all that you do and wherever you turn. (1 Kings 2:3 ESV)

[1] Blessed is the one who does not walk in step with the wicked or stand in the way that sinners take or sit in the company of mockers, [2] but whose delight is in the law of the Lord, and who meditates on his law day and night. [3] That person is like a tree planted by streams of water, which yields its fruit in season and whose leaf does not wither— whatever they do prospers. (Psalm 1:1–3 ESV)

[10] All the ways of the Lord are loving and faithful toward those who keep the demands of his covenant. [11] For the sake of your name, Lord, forgive my iniquity, though it is great. [12] Who, then, are those who fear the Lord? He will instruct them in the ways they should choose. [13] They will spend their days in prosperity, and their descendants will inherit the land. (Psalm 25:10–13 NIV)

These four passages illustrate the association between obedience to God's commands and prosperity. Other passages make this association too, including Deuteronomy 5:33, 2 Chronicles 24:20, and Joshua 1:8.

Visceral to the Hebrew concept of prosperity were the spiritual and ethical dimensions of obedience to God before there is an experience of God's blessings. True prosperity was linked to the blessings of covenantal obedience before God. In other words, God bestows prosperity on those who keep and do his commands. More generally, prosperity in the OT connotes the accomplishment of goals, success in labor, living in peace and safety, enjoying family, and acquiring material goods.[384]

When God blesses us with material wealth, we are commanded to enjoy those blessings and be content with them:

---

383 "prosper": from the root שׂכל, *to instruct, teach, give insight, be smart.* (HAOLT). All but two occurrences of this word in the OT are in the Hif'il, hence, *to underand, prosper* (TWOT), *be prudent* (BDB), *to have a capacity for understanding as a result of proper teaching* that can lead to *accomplishing an activity thoroughly and with success, to succeed or prosper* (DBL).

384 A. E. Hill, "Prosper; Prosperous." V3, 1011.

126

[19] This indeed is a gift of God: everyone to whom God gives wealth and possessions, he also empowers him [to enjoy them], to accept his lot, and to rejoice in *the fruit of* his toil. [20] For he does not remember the *brief* days of his life, for God keeps his heart preoccupied with enjoyment *of life.* (Ecclesiastes 5:19–20 LEB)

God gives both wealth and the power to enjoy that wealth. Our world assumes these two elements invariably go together, but experience would indicate otherwise. The man without God may be rich and yet live a life of pain and emptiness. But the man of God will be happy and content with the wealth God has entrusted to him because he is happy with God first.[385] Two quotes will help bring clarity to this discussion. "No amount of prosperity can make up for a life without joy,"[386] and "It is no part of biblical faith to espouse a view of life which bans enjoyment and pleasure. It is, indeed, a misunderstanding of the facts of the case that those who live according to God's laws are unhappy people."[387] When God gives you prosperity, take time to enjoy it!

But as you're enjoying your prosperity, pay attention to avoiding two common temptations that prosperity brings. The first is to refuse to acknowledge God as the source of one's prosperity. When we think we created our wealth (Deuteronomy 8:10–18), we are likely to lack generosity toward the poor, ignoring that God has been generous to us. As a result, we will not continue to enjoy God's generosity:

[49] Now this was the sin of your sister Sodom: She and her daughters were arrogant, overfed, and unconcerned; they did not help the poor and needy. [50] They were haughty and did detestable things before me. Therefore I did away with them as you have seen. (Ezekiel 16:49–50 ESV)

If we do not connect our prosperity to God's active blessing and generosity with our responsibility to be generous toward others, then our prosperity may foster an attitude of self–sufficiency, which is antithetical to covenantal obedience (Revelation 3:17; Luke 12:13–21) and we will incur God's discipline.

We should learn to be content with the amount and nature of wealth God entrusts to us. We should learn to be content with the size of the business God gives us. And we should never conclude that those with larger, more profitable companies are somehow better than us or favored more by God. Recall the parable of the talents (Matthew 25:14–31).

---

385 Michael A. Eaton, *Ecclesiastes: An Introduction and Commentary.* Tyndale Old Testament Commentaries. (InterVarsity Press, 1983), 119.

386 Duane A. Garrett, *Proverbs, Ecclesiastes, Song of Songs*, The New American Commentary (Broadman & Holman, 1993), 315.

387 J. A. Thompson, *Deuteronomy: An Introduction and Commentary*, Tyndale Old Testament Commentaries (InterVarsity Press, 1974), 153.

The servant given two talents and created two more through economic activity received the same reward as the one given five talents. In God's economy, the size of business and wealth pale compared to one's faithfulness to God.

This is such an important point that the definition of success used in this book bears worth repeating here:

Success is defined as faithfulness to God and perseverance in obedience because that is how success is defined in the Bible.

When we love money, all kinds of evils will be present in our lives, not the least of which is apostasy as we give up our faith in favor of our wealth (1 Timothy 6:9–10 ESV):

> But those who desire to be rich fall into temptation, into a snare, into many senseless and harmful desires that plunge people into ruin and destruction. 10 For the love of money is a root of all kinds of evils. It is through this craving that some have wandered away from the faith and pierced themselves with many pangs.

Honestly, *having a strong desire to create significant wealth and yet walk closely with God is a very difficult balance to achieve.* Doing both is not out of the question, but in my experience, relatively few can wholly love God and yet create significant wealth through their business. To walk closely with God, one must give up earthly desires, including the perks that come with wealth. It's very easy to love those perks and drift from God.

The Prosperity Gospel

The second temptation to sin is to believe that the Bible teaches that God baked into the universe laws and principles that, if learned and applied, will lead to us living without physical ailments in the lap of luxury.[388] The *prosperity gospel* (PG) (also known as the word–faith movement) teaches that "God wants all Christians to be both healthy and wealthy and that there are certain 'laws of prosperity' that, when applied correctly, inevitably produce these results."[389]

One of the laws often discussed within the PG movement is that faith is released through the spoken word. As words of faith are spoken, we can obtain anything we want: health, wealth, success, and more.[390] The PG asserts God wishes everyone to be healthy and

---

388 Walter C. Kaiser, "The Old Testament Promise of Material Blessings and the Contemporary Believer." *Trinity Journal*, 1988, 9(2): 151–169.

389 Robert A. Sirico, "The Entrepreneurial Vocation," *Journal of Markets & Morality (Spring and Fall)*, 2000, 3(1 & 2):11.

390 Gary Gilley, "The New Look of the Prosperity Gospel: Joel Osteen Offers You Your Best Life Now." Edited by Kurt Goedelman. *The Journal of Modern Ministry*, 2010. 7(2): 93–109.

wealthy.[391] These two quotes from Kenneth Copeland—one of the most prominent preachers of this heresy—illustrate well the thinking of those in the prosperity gospel movement:

> Abraham, Moses, David, and Solomon … why did God bless these men? Why have so few men found the blessings of God in finance? … In the book of Deuteronomy, we see the predominant rule to remember in living a prosperous life: "And though say in thine heart, My power and the might of mine hand hath gotten me this wealth. But thou shalt remember the Lord they God: for it is he that giveth thee the power to get wealth that he may establish his covenant which he swore unto they fathers, as it is this day." (Deuteronomy 8:17–18). The predominant rule: God gives the power to get wealth. Why? To establish his covenant … Since God's covenant has been established and prosperity is a provision of this covenant, you need to realize that prosperity belongs to you now![392]

Economic hardship is thought to be a result of sin because God does not want his people to be economically poor. If financial prosperity is not present in the lives of professing Christians, it is assumed that God's blessing is not upon them, and they are not spiritually successful.[393] Sarles writes:

> Advocates of the prosperity gospel claim that it is God's will for every believer to be prosperous. The implication is that a sick or poor believer is outside God's will for his life. Not only is the nature of God's will for believers on earth refashioned, but also an enormous load of guilt falls on followers of the movement who are terminally ill or financially handicapped … the prosperity gospel claims that both physical healing and financial property have been provided for in the Atonement.[394]

The notion that God establishes his covenant by gifting wealth is entirely false. The purpose of the covenant was to give mankind a way to commune with God after Adam and Eve sinned. The purpose was not to provide us with wealth on this earth. God's covenant is established because he wants to be with those who believe in him. Our salvation is the reason for God's covenant with us, not our comfort or personal balance sheet.

---

391 David W. Jones, "The Bankruptcy of the Prosperity Gospel: An Exercise in Biblical and Theological Ethics." *Faith and Mission*, 1998. 16(1):79–84.

392 Kenneth Copeland, *The Laws of Prosperity*. (Kenneth Copeland Publications, 1974), 38–39, 51.

393 Russell S. Woodbridge, "The Bankruptcy of Prosperity Theology: An Unprofitable Gospel." *Theology for Ministry*, 2008. 3(1):5–26.

394 Ken L. Sarles. "A Theological Evaluation of the Prosperity Gospel." *Bibliotheca Sacra*, 1986, 143(4):329.

The prosperity gospel contains grains of Biblical truth, but these truths are significantly distorted. Russell Woodbridge and David Jones have outlined[395] how the prosperity gospel twists Biblical theology:[396]

- Our covenant with God is a means to material entitlement
- Jesus atonement extends to the "sin" of material poverty
- Christians give to gain material goods from God
- Faith is a self–generated force that leads to prosperity
- Prayer is a tool to force God to grant prosperity

Moreover, the Lausanne Theology Working Group has published a paper contrasting how the prosperity gospel twists good theology into heresy.[397] Table 8–1 outlines the thrust of the group's work.

Table 8–1: Contrasts between Biblical Theology and the Prosperity Gospel

Affirm	Reject
Miraculous grace and power of God; the power of the Holy Spirit	God's miraculous power can be treated as automatic or be beckoned by human techniques
There is a Biblical vision of human prospering; God's blessings include material goods.	Spiritual warfare can be measured in material terms, or wealth is always a sign of God's blessings.
The importance of hard work and the positive use of the resources God gives us	That success in life is entirely due to our striving, wrestling, or cleverness; that self–help techniques can achieve wealth; that the PG is wholly focused on individual wealth without needing community accountability.
Political and social systems exist that oppress millions into terrible poverty, robbing people of the hope of a better future.	Any Biblical teaching that A) enriches those who preach the PG while leaving the masses no better off than before, B) does not address the injustices and exploitations that exist, C) further victimizes the poor by making them feel that their poverty is their fault due to lack of faith, D) fails to provide a sustainable answer to the real causes of poverty.

395   David W. Jones and Russell S. Woodbridge. Health, Wealth, and Happiness: How the Prosperity Gospel Overshadows the Gospel of Christ. (Kregel Publications, 2017).

396   David W. Jones. "Errors of the Prosperity Gospel." *9Marks Journal*, 2014. v1:34–38.

397   Chris Wright, Kwabena Asamoah–Gyadu and the Theology Working Group, "Statement on the Prosperity Gospel." Ed. John Azumah. January 16, 2010, Lausanne.org. https://lausanne.org/content/a–statement–on–the–prosperity–gospel

Affirm	Reject
The entire counsel of God must be considered when developing a theology of prosperity.	A method of Biblical interpretation that is distorted, selected, and manipulative of Biblical passages
Centrality of the Cross of Christ	The centrality of individual wealth
Humble, quiet, holy life lived by leaders in positions of public fame	Flamboyant and extravagant lifestyles
Call to repentance and faith in Christ	Call to give more money to the leader
Warnings in Scripture about the dangers of wealth and the idolatrous sin of greed	Ignoring or contradicting the Biblical teachings on the dangers of wealth and the idolatrous sin of greed
Preach the whole gospel message of sin, repentance, faith, and eternal hope.	Failure to preach the whole gospel message of sin, repentance, faith, and eternal hope.
Spending quality time on evangelism	Replacing time for evangelism with fundraising and appeals

Eisegetically infusing a meaning into Biblical texts from the personal experience of an affluent religious leader who is living in the most affluent generation of the most affluent nation this world has ever seen is the height of cruelty against those oppressed into poverty. In addition, according to the standards of the Bible, much of what the PG preachers teach has the marks of false prophets.[398]

The prosperity gospel cannot be lived out in all parts of the world in all periods. True biblical theology can be obeyed and lived out, however difficult, in all seasons and times across all peoples and languages. Those in abject poverty could never live a life of luxury due to the economic and political systems in which they find themselves. Even if we account for wealth being relative to one's culture, the prosperity gospel cannot be lived out in all parts of the world in all periods.

Furthermore, the notion that God would have us all be financially successful is contradictory to Hebrews 11, in which our forefathers are reported to have been tortured, mocked, scourged, imprisoned, sawn in two, put to death, destitute, afflicted, ill-treated, wandered in deserts, or lived in holes in the ground. They are remembered for their faithfulness to God. I doubt they would have been called out in Scripture as heroes and examples had they lived outside God's will and blessing. But they certainly lived without material wealth.

---

398 Lausanne, Statement on the Prosperity Gospel, Online.

Christ himself grew up in an impoverished family. Later, He would say he had nowhere to lay his head (Matthew 8:20). When he died, his only earthly possession was the clothing he was wearing, which was divided by lots among the Roman soldiers while he was hanging on a cross, suffocating to death. The example of his life is incompatible with the prosperity gospel.

Finally, a prosperity gospel robs us of a healthy theology of suffering—a theology that is already lost in most Evangelical churches in America today.

Wealth and Temptations to Sin

With wealth comes temptations to sin, usually in the form of drifting from God and becoming arrogant. The temptation of drifting and pride is addressed in Deuteronomy 8:10–20. In this passage, Moses reminds the Israelites that there is a significant temptation when one becomes wealthy: to drift from God and grow arrogant, thinking that we are the source of our wealth (please read Deuteronomy 8:10–20 in your Bible before reading further in this chapter and leave your Bible open for this discussion).

The temptation to forget God is grounded in pride and arrogance. Put bluntly, rich people tend to forget how hard it is to be poor or be under the oppression of debt. They forget the hard life from whence they came. A past reality is rarely experienced as strongly as a present reality. They may minimize God's role in finding freedom from their bondage and forget that it was God who brought them out of their misery. They may forget that it was God who gave them their wealth. Instead, they may recall all the long days of hard work, the risks they took to succeed, or the sheer persistence they displayed to achieve and conclude, 'I did this myself.'[399]

The descriptions of Israel's state (11–16), as predicted by Moses, could easily apply to America and other affluent countries in the 21st century. Consider:

- "Eat and are satisfied": Most Americans have plenty of food, as evidenced by the obesity rate in the United States, which is at an all-time high.[400]
- "Build fine houses": America has the largest house sizes in the world,[401] especially compared to European homes.[402]

399 John A. Thompson, *Deuteronomy: An Introduction and Commentary.* Tyndale Old Testament Commentaries. (InterVarsity Press, 1974), 153.

400 Niall McCarthy, "U.S. Obesity Rates Have Hit an All-Time High." October 16, 2017. Forbes.com. https://www.forbes.com/sites/niallmccarthy/2017/10/16/u–s–obesity–rates–have–hit–an–all–time–high–infographic/.

401 Joe Pinsker, "Why Are American Homes So Big?" September 12, 2019. The Atlantic. https://www.theatlantic.com/family/archive/2019/09/american–houses–big/597811/

402 Alan Wood, "Which Region Dominates? 74 Essential Comparisons of American and European Homes." May 11, 2023. Global Watchdog, https://gwmac.com/74–essential–comparisons–american–and–european–homes/

- "Herds and flocks grow large": in today's vernacular, "Your business is growing and becoming more profitable."
- "Silver and gold increase": in today's vernacular, we would say, "Your investment portfolio is doing well."
- "All you have is multiplied": in today's vernacular, we would say, "That overall, I am living my best life."

When we can
- eat when and what we want
- in homes that are comfortable and large
- with a growing business that is producing more profits
- and an investment portfolio is consistently growing
- living a life of comfort and convenience,

perhaps it is easy to see how we could forget God and attribute our financial success to our own efforts.

The real challenge of affluence is not hoarding vs. philanthropy, not slavery vs. freedom, it is remaining dependent on God vs. forgetting him.[403] The real test of the quality of your faith in God comes when you, the business owner, become affluent and you have wealth like you have never had before. If you remember that it is God "who gives you the ability to produce wealth" and stay humble (vs. 18), then you will confirm that your covenant with God is real and authentic (vs 19).

God does not promise us wealth but may bless us with wealth because of his generosity. Wealth and prosperity can never be regarded as a natural right. They are a gift from God.[404] Merrill writes:

> The connection between covenant and blessing is clearly affirmed in v. 18, where Moses commanded his hearers to remember the Lord inasmuch as the success they enjoyed was confirmation of his covenant favor and the covenant relationship was the source of their blessing. In other words, there is a reciprocal dynamic in which covenant produces blessing and blessing proves the reality of covenant ... Material (or any other kind of) success is a concomitant of covenant fellowship. It provides evidence that the covenant relationship exists, but it is by no means its prerequisite.[405]

---

403 Jonathan Sacks, Covenant and Conversation: Deuteronomy: Renewal of the Sinai Covenant. (Maggid Books, 2019), 77.

404 Thompson, *Deuteronomy*, 154.

405 Eugene H. Merrill, *Deuteronomy*, The New American Commentary (Broadman & Holman Publishers, 1994), 187–188.

Remembering God is the opposite of forgetting (disregarding) God. The Hebrew word for 'remembering' means more than merely recalling a fact, as if one is playing a board game or regurgitating a historical fact. The use of this word in the Old Testament more often focuses on actions, not mental activity. For example, "to remember" may mean that a "person did a favor for someone, helped them, or was faithful to a promise."[406] *Remembering God means that we recall what God has done for us, keeping in mind that he is rescuing us from the power of sin to give us freedom in the power of his Spirit. We interpret our reality through the lens of covenant and God's generosity toward us.*

Moreover, despite our efforts, risk-taking, or persistence, we should recall that if we are talented, it is because the Lord created us that way. If we are persistent, it is because God gave us that trait. If we can tolerate more risk than others, it is because God has designed us this way. If we are smart, it is because God gave us our intelligence. If we are creative—that's from God, too. If we have significant opportunities to create wealth, it is because the Lord has positioned and gifted us to do so. If we have been given considerable wealth through inheritance, it is because the Lord has been generous to us. If we have a new product idea, it is because the Lord gave us that idea. *There isn't anything that you or I can point to in business or life and say, "I did that on my own." All of life starts with God, comes from God, and ends with God.*

Some business owners who read this book will have tens of millions in disposable cash. Other business owners who read this book cannot rub two nickles together. Regardless of how much or little wealth you have, remembering God is a choice we make, and that choice reflects whether or not we are living in a covenant with God. Remembering God reveals where our allegiances and affections lie. If we think we created our wealth, then we are living in pride, in opposition to our covenant with God. But if we attribute our wealth to God's generosity, despite our efforts and risk–taking, then we live in humility in alignment with our covenant with God.

Moving on, assuming debt is part of being a business owner. Few business owners reading this book have not personally guaranteed a line of credit or some other debt instrument. The Bible has important things to say about debt, so let's focus on learning about a Biblical view of debt.

DEBT AND LENDING

Debt is the ability to consume today and what you will produce tomorrow. Debt is an obligation to pay in the future for a benefit gained in the present.[407] Debt cannot exist

---

406   Lois Tverberg. Listening to the Language of the Bible: Hearing It Through Jesus' Ears. (En–Gedi Resource Center, 2006), 15–16.

407   Faithlife, "Debt." In *Logos Bible Study Factbook*. (Faithlife, October 30, 2024.) https://ref.ly/logos4/Factbook?id=ref%3abk.%25debt.

without another party acting as the lender. Lending is taking our current resources and entrusting them to another, assuming *his* future wealth will be able to pay us back.[408] I will first discuss conventional and Biblical wisdom regarding debt, then turn our attention to lending.

Conventional Wisdom

Conventional wisdom separates 'good debt' from 'bad debt.' Good debt is debt that one assumes will help achieve meaningful growth in one's life. Examples of good debt are student loans, loans to start a business, and mortgages.[409] Credit card debt and high–interest loans are usually considered bad debt.[410] Too much good debt can become bad debt, so it is advisable not to assume debt unless absolutely necessary.[411]

American culture encourages debt as a means to happiness and fulfillment. For example, our consumer culture often encourages Americans to spend beyond their means to achieve the American dream,[412] even though it is increasingly difficult for many Americans to achieve.[413] Saltzman believes debt is the cultural issue of our time—a time in which we value our credit scores more than our quality of life.[414] If one looks carefully at the idealized versions of others' lives presented on social media, one will find that those lives cannot be economically sustained without either significant debt or income that is well beyond their station in life.

Americans often ignore the connection between debt and financial freedom. While the short–term benefits of taking on debt give us a product or service we think we need, debt's long–term injury is realized too late. Small amounts of debt might be helpful to achieve specific goals. However, long–term, persistent pain will ensue if we accumulate too much debt.

408 Faithlife, "Lending." In *Logos Bible Study Factbook.* (Faithlife, October 30, 2024.) https://ref.ly/logos4/Factbook?id=ref%3abk.%25lending.

409 Louis DeNicola, "Good Debt vs. Bad Debt: What's the Difference?" September 13, 2024, Experian.com. https://www.experian.com/blogs/ask–experian/good–debt–vs–bad–debt–whats–the–difference/

410 Fidelity Smart Money, "Good vs. Bad Debt: How to Tell the Difference." October 8, 2024, fidelity.com. https://www.fidelity.com/learning–center/smart–money/good–debt–vs–bad–debt

411 Schwab Moneywise, "Good Debt vs. Bad Debt." Accessed 11/02/2024, schwabmoneywise.com. https://www.schwabmoneywise.com/essentials/good–debt–vs–bad–debt

412 The American dream is the association of upward mobility with enough economic success to lead a comfortable life. See Sarah Churchwell, "A Brief History of the American Dream." *The Catalyst, A Journal of Ideas from the Bush Institute.* Winter, 2021: Online. Bushcenter.org. https://www.bushcenter.org/catalyst/state–of–the–american–dream/churchwell–history–of–the–american–dream

413 Tchiki Davis, "4 Ways American Culture is Influencing Happiness." May 17, 2018. Psychologytoday.com. https://www.psychologytoday.com/intl/blog/click–here–happiness/201805/4–ways–american–culture–is–influencing–happiness

414 Jason Saltzman, "Why I Believe Debt is an Issue of our Culture." September 28, 2022. Rollingstone.com. https://www.rollingstone.com/culture–council/articles/why–i–believe–debt–is–issue–of–our–culture-1234599835/

For example, if we have too much debt, our ability to borrow can be negatively affected.[415] In addition, if we have high–interest debt, the interest can accumulate to the point where one's debt is unmanageable.[416] Too much debt will make it much harder to save for the future, build an emergency fund, or take a vacation.[417]

Debt providers, such as banks and credit card companies—who do not care about your financial freedom despite what they claim in their marketing[418]—make it easy to go into debt. Banks and other debt providers make money by putting or keeping you in debt. They depend on the psychological and persistent connections between using a credit card and one's willingness to spend.[419] They understand that using credit cards activates reward centers in our brains[420] and creates perks that the card user can earn that accelerate our use of the cards, a phenomenon called "chasing credit card rewards." Such chasing is common. Research shows that two–thirds of Americans in debt try to maximize their credit card rewards, even though they cannot pay off their credit card each month.[421]

Moreover, the Net Cost of Credit (NCC)—the total cost of credit after accounting for the value of earned rewards—continues to be negative for most debt holders, meaning that the benefits of reward programs fail to exceed the costs of credit.[422] In addition, it is not uncommon for credit card companies to promise upfront benefits only to bury complex, vague terms in the fine print and change the value of the rewards after people sign up to

---

415 Michael Reynolds, "How Debt Can Sabotage Your Financial Future: Understandin the Negative Effects of Debt." May 6, 2024, elevationfinancial.com. https://www.elevationfinancial.com/how–debt–can–sabotage–your–financial–future–understanding–the–negative–effects–of–debt

416 U.S. Bank Wealth Management, "Financial Leverage: What is Good Debt vs. Bad Debt?" Accessed 11/01/2024, Usbank.com/wealth–management. https://www.usbank.com/wealth–management/financial–perspectives/financial–planning/financial–leverage–what–is–good–debt–vs–bad–debt.html

417 Reynolds, How Debt Can Sabotage.

418 Ryley Amond, "Why You Want to be a Credit Card Deadbeat." November 2, 2024, cnbc.com https://www.cnbc.com/select/credit–card–deadbeat/

419 Joe Boden, Erik Maier, and Robert Wilken, "The Effect of Credit Card vs. Mobile Payment on Convenience and Consumers' Willingness to Pay." *Journal of Retailing and Consumer Services*. Volume 52, January, 2020. See also Drazen Prelec and Duncan Simester, "Always Leave Home Without It: A Further Investigation of the Credit–Card Effect on Willingness to Pay." *Marketing Letters*. 2001, 12:5–12. https://doi.org/10.1023/A:1008196717017

420 Drazen Prelec and Sachin Banker, "How Credit Cards Activate the Reward Center of our Brains and Drive Spending." June 9, 2021, mitsloan.mit.edu. https://mitsloan.mit.edu/experts/how–credit–cards–activate–reward–center–our–brains–and–drive–spending. See also Sachin Banker, Derek Dunfield, Alex Huang, and Drazen Prelec, "Neural Mechanisms of Credit Card Spending." *Scientific Reports*. February 18, 2021. 11:4070. https://doi.org/10.1038/s41598–021–83488–3.

421 Katie Kelson, "2 in 3 Americans with Debt are Chasing Credit Card Rewards." March 11, 2024, bankrate.com. https://www.bankrate.com/credit–cards/news/chasing–rewards–in–debt/

422 Consumer Financial Protection Bureau, "Credit Card Rewards." May, 2024, consumerfinance.gov. https://files.consumerfinance.gov/f/documents/cfpb_credit–card–rewards_issue–spotlight_2024–05.pdf, See also Consumer Financial Protection Bureau, "The Consumer Credit Card Market." October, 2023, consumerfinance.gov, https://files.consumerfinance.gov/f/documents/cfpb_consumer–credit–card–market–report_2023.pdf

earn them.[423] Since many Americans define themselves by the material things they own, combined with the easy availability of expensive credit dressed in the glitter of rewards, it is no wonder that nearly half of all Americans carry credit card debt to achieve what they feel they deserve.[424]

But consumer debt is not our greatest worry. At every level, America is awash in debt, and no one seems to have an answer. So, the mountain of debt continues to enlarge. At the time of writing this content (September, 2024), the following debt amounts in America are true:

- Federal debt, including debt held by the public and intragovernmental holdings, is in excess of $36 trillion.[425]
- Combined state and local government debt is estimated to be $3.3 trillion.[426]
- Over the next 75 years, we have an estimated $73 trillion of unfunded obligations to ourselves through Medicare and Social Security.[427]
- Home mortgage debt is $12.52 trillion.[428]
- Commerical mortgage debt stands at 4.7 trillion.[429]
- States have unfunded pension debts roughly totaling $1 trillion.[430]
- Nonfinancial corporate debt in Q2 of 2024 was $13.9 trillion.[431]
- Americans owe $1.6 trillion in auto loan debt.[432]

---

423 Consumer Financial Protection Bureau, "CFPB Report Highlights Consumer Frustrations with Credit Card Rewards Programs." May 9, 2024, consumerfinance.gov. https://www.consumerfinance.gov/about–us/newsroom/cfpb–report–highlights–consumer–frustrations–with–credit–card–rewards–programs/

424 46% of households in America held debt on credit cards in 2022. See Yu–Ting Chiang and Mick Dueholm, "Which U.S. Households Have Credit Card Debt?" May 20,2024, stlouisfed.org. https://www.stlouisfed.org/on–the–economy/2024/may/which–us–households–have–credit–card–debt

425 U.S. Department of Treasury, "Debt to the Penny." Accessed 11/01/2024. Fiscaldata.treasury.gov. https://fiscaldata.treasury.gov/datasets/debt–to–the–penny/debt–to–the–penny

426 Russell Pustejovsky and Jeffrey Little, "Annual State and Local Government Finances Summary: 2021." August, 2023, census.gov. https://www2.census.gov/programs–surveys/gov–finances/tables/2021/2021al-finsummarybrief.pdf

427 Romina Boccia, "Medicare and Social Security are Responsible for 100 Percent of US Unfunded Obligations." March 20, 2024, cato.org. https://www.cato.org/blog/medicare–social–security–are–responsible–100–percent–us–unfunded–obligations

428 Federal Reserve Bank of New York, "Household Debt and Credit Report." Q2, 2024. Newyorkfed.org. https://www.newyorkfed.org/microeconomics/hhdc

429 Jamie Woodwell, "Commercial and Multifamily Mortgage Debt Outstanding Increased in Q1 2024." July 29, 2024, multihousingnews.com. https://www.multihousingnews.com/commercial–and–multifamily–mortgage–debt–outstanding–increased–in–first–quarter–2024/

430 Joanna Biernacka–Lievestro and Joe Fleming, "States' Unfunded Pension Liabilities Persist as Major Long–Term Challenge." July 7, 2022, pewtrusts.org. https://www.pewtrusts.org/en/research–and–analysis/articles/2022/07/07/states–unfunded–pension–liabilities–persist–as–major–long–term–challenge

431 Federal Reserve, "Financial Accounts in the United States – Z.1" Q2, 2024, federalreserve.gov. See the section titled "U.S. Nonfinancial Debt." https://www.federalreserve.gov/releases/z1/20240912/html/recent_developments.htm

432 Maggie Davis, "Average Car Payment and Auto Loan Statistics: 2024." September 20, 2024, lendingtree.com. https://www.lendingtree.com/auto/debt–statistics/

- Americans owe $1.1 trillion in credit card debt.[433]
- Americans owe $1.7 trillion in student loan debt.[434]

Asserting that America's balance sheet has more than enough assets to cover the debt is a problematic counter argument. The average net worth of an American is just over $1M,[435] yet 10.4% (~13 million) households have a negative net worth.[436] Overall, the picture is a bit brighter. The Fed estimates our household and non-profit net worth is $170 trillion for Q3, 2024.[437] Rising equity values and home equity account for much of our asset values.[438]

So, what happens when the government can no longer fund its activities through borrowing? Few contemplate this scenario, but those who do paint an unhappy picture. The most difficult scenario is that the Federal government defaults on its obligations, leading to severe distrust and loss of confidence. Specifically, treasury securities would lose value or become unacceptable as collateral, disrupting short-term funding markets. The FDIC's (Federal Deposit Insurance Corporation) deposit insurance funds are invested in treasury securities. Suppose banks were to become stressed at a sufficient number, which is not an unlikely scenario. In that case, the agency may be unable to obtain enough funds from the Department of the Treasury to protect bank customers, unless the Treasury via the Fed created hundreds of billions of dollars electronically, which would likely raise the inflation rate. Moreover, a government default could trigger financial market distress, causing financial institutions to preserve their cash, raise lending rates, and cut back on new loans. The cutbacks would trigger a slowdown in the auto, housing, and business finance markets, causing companies to cut back operations, slow down or eliminate hiring, and perhaps lay off thousands to preserve cash. A recession or depression could ensure that the world would gradually shift away from the US Dollar being the world's reserve currency. At

---

433 Matt Schulz, "2024 Credit Card Debt Statistics." November 1, 2024. Lendingtree.com. https://www.lendingtree.com/credit-cards/study/credit-card-debt-statistics/

434 Matt Schulz, "Student Loan Debt Statistics." August 16, 2024, lendingtree.com. https://www.lendingtree.com/student/student-loan-debt-statistics/

435 Emily Sherman and Jessica Walrack, "What is the Average American Net Worth by Age?" March 28, 2024, usnews.com. https://money.usnews.com/money/personal-finance/articles/what-is-the-average-american-net-worth-by-age

436 Shehryar Nabi, "Thirteen million US households have negative net worth. Will they ever move from debt to wealth?" May 25, 2022, aspeninstitute.org. https://www.aspeninstitute.org/blog-posts/thirteen-million-us-households-have-negative-net-worth-will-they-ever-move-from-debt-to-wealth/

437 Federal Reserve, "Balance Sheet of Households and Nonprofit Organizations, 1952-2024." September 30, 2024, federalreserve.gov. https://www.federalreserve.gov/releases/z1/dataviz/z1/balance_sheet/chart/

438 Tuan Nguyen, "American household net worth sets record, bringing debt-to-asset ratio to a 50-year low." December 13, 2024, realeconomy.rsmus.com. https://realeconomy.rsmus.com/american-household-net-worth-sets-record-outpacing-debt/. The macro picture is meaningless if you are one of those 13 million families with a negative networth.

that point, we lose our super-power status and may need to obligate ourselves to another country to pay our debts.[439]

Leaving out the unfunded obligations to ourselves through Medicare and Social Security, Americans owe nearly $76 trillion dollars. Our annual GDP[440] (Gross Domestic Product), which is a comprehensive measure of all U.S. economic activity for each year, stands at 29.35 trillion. To pay off all of our debt (including interest) would consume the entire output of our economy for nearly three years. If one included the unfunded Medicare and Social Security Obligations and paid forward the mandates in present value terms, America would need to consume at least five years of our total GDP to pay off our debt. And that just gets us to break-even.

Why do these numbers matter? When a country accumulates too much debt—as America has—it can experience significant economic problems, including slower economic growth, reduced government ability to provide essential services, increased borrowing costs, decreased investor confidence, and potentially a sovereign debt crisis if the government becomes unable to repay its debts, potentially leading to currency devaluation and financial instability.[441]

Given America's debt picture, when our children produce wealth tomorrow, they will receive little for the fruit of their labor because *we have already consumed their wealth*. Rather than leaving our children with an inheritance that will help them thrive, we are leaving them a debt so large that they will struggle to survive, let alone improve their economic well–being.

Neither political party in America is seriously discussing our unsustainable fiscal position. So, we continue to incur more debt not only because of the dollar's privileged status as the world's reserve currency,[442] but also because there is no constitutional governor on spending. Western democracies redistribute so much wealth through the use of debt that

---

439 Government Accounting Office, "Debt Limit: Statutory Changes Could Avert the Risk of a Government Default and Its Potentially Severe Consequences." December 11, 2024, gao.gov. https://www.gao.gov/products/gao-25-107089.

440 Bureau of Economic Analysis, Gross Domestic Product. https://www.bea.gov/data/gdp/gross–domestic–product

441 Tobias Adrian, Vitor Gaspar, Pierre–Olivier Gourinchas, "The Fiscal and Financial Risks of a High–Deebt, Slow–Growth World." March 28, 2024, imf.org. https://www.imf.org/en/Blogs/Articles/2024/03/28/the–fiscal–and–financial–risks–of–a–high–debt–slow–growth–world

442 The dollar became the world's reserve currency in 1944 at the conclusion of World War II. Under this system, the dollar was supposed to have been tied to the gold, but President Nixon took us off the gold standard in 1971, leaving the entire world operating our currencies based mainly on trust in the fiscal stability of the United States. See Federal Reserve History, "Creation of the Bretton Woods System." July 1944, federalreservehistory.org. https://www.federalreservehistory.org/essays/bretton–woods–created. See also *Money for Nothing: Inside the Federal Reserve,* Directed and written by Jim Bruce, featuring Live Schreiber, Paul Volcker, Janet Yellen and others. Amazon Prime Video. The Bretton Woods agreement that created the dollar as the world's reserve currency is discussed starting at 17:54 (of 1:25:48) in the documentary. https://www.imdb.com/title/tt2752724/

139

"politicians who argue for cutting expenditures nearly always run into the well–organized opposition of one or both of two groups: recipients of public sector pay and recipients of government benefits."[443]

Conventional wisdom has no solution to the debt problem. Resolving the debt problem would mean having the older generations admit they have treated the younger generations very poorly.[444] Acknowledging the inter–generational inequities would ignite such unrest that it is better to live the charade that we are passing to the next generation a financially stable country when, in reality, we are passing a country closer to bankruptcy than ever before.[445]

Obviously, spending needs to be reduced, and revenue needs to be increased to the point where no more debt is being created. That is the first step. But there is virtually no political will to do either, so we kick the can down the road, increasing the likelihood of a complete financial collapse coupled with significant inter–generational conflict and social unrest. What we are doing to the younger generations is immoral and cannot be justified by any measure.

By way of planning, Christians should try to become as debt–free as possible. During the coming financial crisis,[446] the number of sick and homeless will be in the millions. The opportunity for Christians to show the love of Christ to a lost world in crisis will never be more ripe. Millions could come to know Christ through the coming financial crisis. While I do not want the crisis to occur, I want people to come to Christ even more. So my willingness—the church's willingness—to reach out to the lost while we are suffering greatly needs to be a decision we have already made.

Biblical Wisdom

I'll present the Biblical wisdom about debt in propositional statements. The first is this: debt enslaves the borrower to the lender. This Biblical wisdom is found in Proverbs 22:7 (CSB): "The rich rule over the poor, and the borrower is a slave to the lender." To the extent a person is in debt, that person has forfeited a measure of freedom and self–determination to the lender. While it is not wrong to borrow money, it is best to be

---

443 Niall Ferguson, *The Great Degeneration: How Institutions Decay and Economies Die.* (Penguin Publishing Group. Kindle Edition), 44.

444 Ferguson, Great Degeneration, 45.

445 The government's own balance sheet for 2023 showed total assets at $5.4 trillion dollars, but total liabilities at $42.898 trillion. Any business in America that had six dollars of liabilities for every dollar of asset would be considered bankrupt. See the Bureau of the Fiscal Service, "Financial Report of the United States Government." Accessed 11/02/2024, fiscal.treasury.gov. https://fiscal.treasury.gov/reports–statements/financial–report/balance–sheets.html

446 Yes, this is an assumption. Am I too pessimistic? Perhaps. I'll plead guilty. But most signs point in this direction. I think it is difficult to conclude otherwise.

debt–free. To the extent that we borrow money, we become a slave to that lender until the debt is paid fully.

Debt limits one's availability to God's call to full–time ministry. Understand that the more debt you have, the less money and work cycles you have available for the Lord's work.[447]

Avoid borrowing unless necessary. What constitutes "necessary" is anyone's opinion, but this principle does ask us to evaluate the difference between a 'need' and a 'want.' By focusing on genuine needs rather than wants, Christians can potentially avoid financial stress and mismanagement of their finances.[448]

Avoid signing surety for a loan. The Scriptures speak to signing for another's debt in Provbers 6:1–5 (CSB) and 22:26–27 (NIV):

> My son, if you have put up security for your neighbor or entered into an agreement with a stranger, ² you have been trapped by the words of your lips — ensnared by the words of your mouth. ³ Do this, then, my son, and free yourself, for you have put yourself in your neighbor's power: Go, humble yourself, and plead with your neighbor. ⁴ Don't give sleep to your eyes or slumber to your eyelids. ⁵ Escape like a gazelle from a hunter, like a bird from a fowler's trap.

> Do not be one who shakes hands in pledge or puts up security for debts; if you lack the means to pay, your very bed will be snatched from under you.

This prohibition also appears in Proverbs 11:15; 17:18; and 20:16. It is foolish to cosign for another's debts and become entangled in their financial problems.[449] The reasoning behind this prohibition is clear: If your assets cannot satisfy the obligations, the creditors will take even the most intimate of your assets, as indicated by the phrase "your very bed will be snatched from under you."[450]

---

447 I understand that all work is worship and that there is no divide between secular and sacred. Yet, this point remains because God cannot call some to full–time vocational ministry because of their debt. Debt can be a constraint on God's call on one's life.

448 Zoltán Szallós–Farkas, "Ethical Challenges in Marriage: Chronic Illnesses and Finances," in *Family: With Contemporary Issues on Marriage and Parenting*, ed. Elias Brasil de Souza and Ekkehardt Mueller, vol. 3 of *Biblical Research Institute Studies in Biblical Ethics* (Review and Herald Publishing Association; Biblical Research Institute, 2023), 250.

449 Sid S. Buzzell, "Proverbs." In *The Bible Knowledge Commentary: An Exposition of the Scriptures*, edited by J. F. Walvoord and R. B. Zuck. (Victor Books, 1985), 955.

450 Bill English, Biblical Wisdom for Business Leaders: Thirty Sayings from Proverbs. (Bible and Business, 2022), 40–43.

Taking on the responsibility to pay another's debt if they default is associated with being foolish,[451] arrogant,[452] and impulsive.[453] When you sign for another's debt, you get all the liability and none of the power. Pledging another's debts is a foolish decision, and the sage placed this passage in conjunction with other representations of what foolishness looks like.[454]

The sins of greed and lying can turn good debt into bad debt by harming the lender/borrower relationship.[455] The lending/borrowing relationship is a resource–sharing, cooperative relationship. The temptation to overestimate our ability to repay or to lie to the other party is always present. The temptation to borrow for a want instead of a need is also always present. These two sins of pride and lying contradict the covenant characteristics of love and faithfulness.

Matthew 5:25–26 (NIV) instructs us on how to manage a lender/borrower relationship that has been harmed. The instruction assumes we are the borrower, and the onus is placed on us to settle matters quickly:

> [25] "Settle matters quickly with your adversary who is taking you to court. Do it while you are still together on the way, or your adversary may hand you over to the judge, and the judge may hand you over to the officer, and you may be thrown into prison. [26] Truly I tell you, you will not get out until you have paid the last penny.

The emphasis on immediate action when someone has a grievance against us is present in this passage. When we are conscious of a broken relationship, we must take the initiative to mend it. This instruction is difficult but important to follow if we are to represent Christ well in this world.[456]

Grace and forgiveness are necessary for lending to work in a sinful world.[457] This point is directed toward lenders in Matthew 18:21–35 (please read this parable in your Bible). The parable's end is that we should forgive others for their offenses against us because of

---

451   Allen P. Ross, "Proverbs." In *The Expositor's Bible Commentary: Psalms, Proverbs, Ecclesiastes, Song of Songs*, edited by Frank E. Gaebelein, Vol. 5. (Zondervan Publishing, 1991), 931.

452   H.A. Ironside, *Notes on the Book of Proverbs*. (Loizeaux Bros, 1908), 62.

453   Bruce Waltke, *The Book of Proverbs, Chapters 1–15*. The New International Commentary on the Old Testament. (Eerdmans Publishing, 2004), 331.

454   Lindsay Wilson, *Proverbs: An Introduction and Commentary*. Edited by David G. Firth. Vol. 17. Tyndale Old Testament Commentaries. (Inter–Varsity Press, 2017), 105–106.

455   Leonard D. Van Drunen, "Debt, Risk, and Grace." *Journal of Markets & Morality (Spring and Fall 2015)* 18, no. 1 (2015): 61–76.

456   John R. W. Stott. The Message of the Sermon on the Mount (Matthew 5–7): Christian Counter–Culture. The Bible Speaks Today. (InterVarsity Press, 1985), 86.

457   Van Drunen, Debt, Risk, and Grace, 61–76.

how much more Christ has forgiven us. Christ uses the comparison of money and sin to illustrate this point.

If a borrower does not repay us, must we forgive? Yes. Whether the borrower is a brother or not, we must forgive.[458] If we become the unforgiving servant (18:23–34), we become subject to God's wrath (vs. 35) because we have been forgiven far more (our sin) than we can ever forgive in someone else (a broken promise to repay a debt).[459] Implied is the notion that if we don't forgive others when their sin harms us, we treat God's forgiveness of our sin with contempt.

I find grace is expressed in Matthew 5:42 (NIV): "Give to the one who asks you, and do not turn away from the one who wants to borrow from you." When someone is distressed—even if their own foolish decisions cause their distress—we do not turn a deaf ear to their plight. An attitude that "they get what they have coming" is antithetical to Christian forgiveness.[460] Instead, we give generously, not grudgingly; lend liberally, not selfishly; and show loving-kindness to those who have harmed us.[461] Joseph is an excellent example of being generous in forgiveness: he was generous and forgiving of his brothers (Genesis 50:19–21), who had not treated him very kindly (37:18–28) and were in desperate need of economic, culinary, and material assistance.

Furthermore, I find grace in Psalm 112:5 (ESV), "It is well with the man who deals generously and lends; who conducts his affairs with justice." Lending can be predatory or generous. The implied comparison in this verse is that an evil lender can plunder the poor through usury while keeping up the pretense of assisting the distressed, thus being unjust to those he enslaves in debt. But the Christian who lends does so generously, out of compassion for their situation, and can conduct his affairs with justice.[462]

Never lend more than you are willing to lose. This principle is more Bill than the Bible. It is just common sense. Whether through a formal loan instrument or extending credit to customers, never lend more than you are willing to lose.

Get to know the personal situations of those who owe you money (Matthew 12:7). When you loan someone money, you are loaning God's resources to that person. A faithful steward will not loan money in haste despite his generous lending. God will hold *you* responsible for

---

458 Dan Doriani, "Forgiveness: Jesus' Plan For Healing And Reconciliation In The Church (Matthew 18:15–35)." *Southern Baptist Journal of Theology*. 2009, 13(3):22–33.

459 Donald A. Carson, "Matthew." In *The Expositor's Bible Commentary: Matthew, Mark, Luke*, edited by Frank E. Gaebelein, Vol. 8. (Zondervan Publishing, 1984), 406.

460 Can we sue a Christian brother who has defaulted on his debt payments to us? I do not think so. But I'll defer this conversation to Chapter 14, *Ethics and Legal Considerations*. At this point, I will say that If you think there is a reasonable chance that you will not be repaid, then offer to do some or all of the work *pro bono* or give your products away because generosity is more valued in Scripture than lending.

461 William Hendriksen and Simon J. Kistemaker, *Exposition of the Gospel According to Matthew*. Vol. 9. New Testament Commentary. (Baker Books, 1953–2001), 311.

462 John Calvin and James Anderson. *Commentary on the Book of Psalms*. (Logos Bible Software, 2010), 325–26.

lending money unwisely or hastily. The best practice is to know the personal and business situations of those who will owe you money before you lend them money.

SAVING

Conventional Wisdom

Conventional wisdom on saving money is outlined in these ten pithy sayings, which comprise good advice for anyone to follow:[463]

- Never spend money before you have it
- Spending is quick; earning is slow
- A fool and his money are soon parted
- Creditors have better memories than debtors
- Rather go to be supperless than rise in debt
- If you buy what you don't need, you steal from yourself
- Save for a rainy day
- A penny saved is a penny earned
- Interest on debts grows without rain
- Lend your money and lose your friend

Conventional wisdom is remarkably optimistic about saving money consistently, little by little, over time, and using compound interest to continue building one's investments. (compound interest is the principle of earning interest on interest.)[464] When combined with dollar–cost averaging, which is the practice of investing a consistent dollar amount in the same investment instrument(s) at regular intervals,[465] the results of these combined efforts are consistent returns, mitigation of the highs and lows of market fluctuations, and over time, earning more on savings than what you earn in your job.

Often, conventional wisdom focuses savings on meeting one's financial goals, which generally include living off the interest of one's investments during one's retirement years

---

463 Jesse Campbell, 10 Financial Proverbs that are Still True Today." September 14, 2024. Moneymanagement. org. https://www.moneymanagement.org/blog/financial–proverbs–that–are–still–true–today

464 U.S. Bank Wealth Management, "Why Compound Annual Growth Matters." May 10, 2024. Usbank.com. https://www.usbank.com/financialiq/invest–your–money/investment–strategies/why–compounding–matters.html

465 Poonkulali Thangavelu, "Dollar–Cost Averaging: Pros and Cons." October 31, 2023, Investopedia. com. https://www.investopedia.com/articles/forex/052815/pros–cons–dollar–cost–averaging.asp

and creating a life of economic freedom. Minimizing stress in one's later years is a byproduct of regular saving over time, plus having your own safety net for unexpected emergencies.[466]

Conventional wisdom defines hoarding as a mental health condition that causes one to accumulate too much stuff.[467] However, hoarding, as a mental health issue, is generally not connected to excessive savings. There is the recognition that people can save too much money out of fear of never having enough to meet their needs. Conventional wisdom does find that a person can have too much money. The pathology lies in the fear of never having enough, even though one may have millions in the bank. The disconnect between feelings and reality is thought to be the main problem for over–savers. In addition, *over–savers* tend to have poor investment performance due to overly active trading coupled with purchasing too much insurance. Because of their fears, these people often have difficulty spending money on the most basic necessities.[468]

Biblical Wisdom

While Christian stewardship is much more than good money management, it does include managing our wealth well. Saving can be viewed as a core strategy of financial planning that anticipates economic adversity and the opportunity to give above and beyond normal giving levels. Wise investing is part of saving for the future.[469] When it comes to saving for the future, I believe the Scriptures teach the following:

- We save in the present to pay for future expenses
- We save in the present to give more in the future
- We balance spending and saving

Save to pay for future expenses

I'll start this section by noting that generosity and saving for future expenses are not at odds with each other. It is good stewardship to set aside wealth generated today so that you can bear a known expense in the future. As an example of saving for the future, let us start with Joseph in Genesis 41:46–49 (ESV):

---

466 Rene Bennett, "7 Top Reasons to Save Your Money." November 6, 2024, bankrate.com. https://www.bankrate.com/banking/savings/top–reasons–to–save–money/

467 American Psychiatric Association, "What is Hoarding Disorder?" Accessed 11/13/2024, psychiatry.org. https://www.psychiatry.org/patients–families/hoarding–disorder/what–is–hoarding–disorder

468 Kelly Long. "Yes, There is Such a Thing as Saving too Much." Accessed 11/14/2024, financialblisscoach.com. https://www.financialblisscoach.com/post/there–s–such–a–thing–as–saving–too–much

469 Paul H. Wright. "Financial Planning." In *Holman Illustrated Bible Dictionary*, edited by Chad Brand, Charles Draper, Archie England, Steve Bond, E. Ray Clendenen, and Trent C. Butler. (Holman Bible Publishers, 2003), 574–575.

[46] Joseph was thirty years old when he entered the service of Pharaoh king of Egypt. And Joseph went out from the presence of Pharaoh and went through all the land of Egypt. [47] During the seven plentiful years the earth produced abundantly, [48] and he gathered up all the food of these seven years, which occurred in the land of Egypt, and put the food in the cities. He put in every city the food from the fields around it. [49] And Joseph stored up grain in great abundance, like the sand of the sea, until he ceased to measure it, for it could not be measured.

Joseph's preparation for famine in Egypt is a prime example of seeing one's need for money and resources and saving for the future out of one's abundance in the present. Based on the king's dream, Joseph *knew* the lack of grain in the future would be severe, so the king allowed Joseph to save up grain out of the seven–year abundance. The principle to learn here is that *proper saving attempts to match future needs out of present abundance.*

Save to give more in the future

A Christian who saves more than needed to avoid being generous is committing the sin of hoarding. There is a balance that needs to be struck between saving for future expenses and being generous in the present. Ultimately, only God knows our hearts. Yet it is a balance that needs to be struck.

The Corinthian believers who laid aside money to help the poor in Jerusalem is in focus here. Consider 1 Corinthians 16:1–3 (ESV):

[1]Now concerning the collection for the saints: as I directed the churches of Galatia, so you also are to do. 2 On the first day of every week, each of you is to put something aside and store it up, as he may prosper, so that there will be no collecting when I come. 3 And when I arrive, I will send those whom you accredit by letter to carry your gift to Jerusalem.

Clearly, Paul is instructing the Corinthian believers to set aside a small amount of money each week so that they can give generously to the poverty–oppressed Christians in Jerusalem when he comes. The principle to learn is that *proper saving attempts to build a fund that can be given toward needs in the body of Christ.*

It is honorable to God to set aside a portion of your wealth with the express intention of giving it away. While I can't point to chapter and verse, it seems that the thrust of what pleases God is for us to structure our lives so that after reasonably saving for the future, we give the balance of our wealth away. This is one of many ways to disadvantage ourselves to advantage the Kingdom of God.

Spending too much vs. saving too much

The Bible presents those who spend too much as fools and encourages those who save to do so using the best of their resources:

> The wise store up choice food[470] and olive oil, but fools gulp theirs down. (Proverbs 21:20 NIV)

This verse contrasts a wise person's continual saving that results in long–term abundance and the fool's instant gratification.[471] Restraint characterizes the wise, allowing them to accumulate wealth naturally.[472] Fools care only for the present and give little thought to the future. As Christians, CBOs should balance spending with saving, which will require us to sometimes make tradeoff decisions in favor of the expenditure and other times in favor of saving. Proverbs 21:20 applies to both personal and business activities. CBOs show restraint and balance in personal and business spending and saving activities.

In contrast to conventional wisdom, where hoarding is viewed as a mental health issue and refers only to the accumulation of material things, saving too much is called hoarding in the Bible. James addresses this topic in his open letter to the Jewish community (James 5:1–5 NIV):

> Now listen, you rich people, weep and wail because of the misery that is coming on you. ² Your wealth has rotted, and moths have eaten your clothes. ³ Your gold and silver are corroded.[473] Their corrosion will testify against you and eat your flesh like fire. You have hoarded wealth in the last days. ⁴ Look! The wages you failed to pay the workers who mowed your fields are crying out against you. The cries of the harvesters have reached the ears of the Lord Almighty. ⁵ You have lived on earth in luxury and self–indulgence. You have fattened yourselves in the day of slaughter.

James presents the wealth of the rich as rotted and their clothing as decaying. The wealth itself was decaying because it was hoarded due to the sin of oppression in which the rich were engaging. They trusted their wealth to save them ("You have hoarded wealth in the last day"). "Trusting in wealth because it supposedly "retains its value"

---

470   "Choice food" is translated as "precious treasure" in the ESV.

471   "It is tempting to think of the fool as one large digestive tract." (Bruce K. Waltke, *The Book of Proverbs, Chapters 15–31*. The New International Commentary on the Old Testament. (Eerdmans, 2005), 183.)

472   Duane A. Garrett, *Proverbs, Ecclesiastes, Song of Songs*. The New American Commentary. (Broadman & Holman Publishers, 1993), 182–183.

473   "corroded": κατιόω, become rusty, tarnished, corroded (BDAG).

is trusting in a charade. The rituals of amassing wealth and curating precious objects are a dance of death."[474] Landfills are full of material things that once were new but now are decaying.

The decay concept introduced by James is interesting since gold and silver do not decompose in the sense that they rot or wither away. While they are susceptible to oxidation and can corrode and tarnish, they are immune to decay.[475] "The tarnish indicated how long the hoarded wealth had lain idle.[476] The wealth that could have been used to help others and further God's kingdom sat idle and unproductive due to the selfishness of its owner. I connect the hoarded wealth in James 5 with the one talent the wicked servant hid in the ground in Matthew 25. In both instances, wealth was not put to use for the Kingdom. At a minimum, idle wealth is an indication of poor stewardship.

Wealth is a renewable resource, but the owner sins when the owner acts like life is a zero–sum game and hoards wealth instead of using it to benefit others (either through investment or philanthropy). CBOs cannot be faithful stewards of God's entrustments to them and yet hoard wealth. The two are mutually exclusive.

Investing in something that naturally decays over time is foolish. Hence, build wealth for yourself in heaven, where "neither moth nor rust destroys and where thieves do not break in and steal." (Matthew 6:20 ESV). The wise CBO connects generosity toward God with building wealth in heaven. Under the direction of the Holy Spirit, the wise CBO gives sufficient velocity to wealth that could be excessively saved by passing it on to those who need it, thus fulfilling God's purposes for business and furthering God's kingdom on earth.

Check yourself. Do you love your earthly wealth? Would you feel intense sadness or insecurity if you lost your wealth? Would you be embarrassed to downgrade your standard of living? Would you sell everything you had and give it to the poor to follow Christ? Are you hoarding wealth?

After you have saved enough for future expenses, give your money away as God directs. Build treasures for yourself in heaven. Just because we *can* save more than we need does not mean we *should* do this. From where I sit, *there is something healthy about giving away enough wealth to create an evergreen dependence on God for our future needs.*

---

474 Kurt A. Richardson, *James*, vol. 36, The New American Commentary (Broadman & Holman Publishers, 1997), 206.

475 Ampex Knowledge Center, "Do Silver and Gold Decay?" May 24, 2022. Ampex.com. https://learn.apmex.com/learning–guide/science/do–silver–and–gold–decay/.

476 Donald W. Burdick, "James," in *The Expositor's Bible Commentary: Hebrews through Revelation*, ed. Frank E. Gaebelein, vol. 12 (Zondervan Publishing, 1981), 199.

One College President "Gets it"

Recently, I had coffee with the President of a Christian College in the upper Midwest. We were discussing endowments and their role in funding the operations of his college. We compared the endowment sizes of some Ivy League schools with those of Christian colleges.

He told me that while he is trying to grow the college's endowment, he does not want it to grow past a certain size because he does not want his college to lose dependence on God to supply their daily provisions.

This President "gets it." This President understands the balance between appropriate saving and maintaining dependence on God.

What if you cannot save?

Saving for the future assumes you have some disposable income to set aside in a savings account. Some do not enjoy this luxury. I would guess that most people worldwide cannot save for the future. They barely have enough to live on in the present moment. So what I offer in this section is more 'Bill than Bible', but I offer it with a clear mind from the Spirit.

Payoff your bad debt. If you have bad debt, your savings plan is to pay off your bad debt. View these payments as a forced savings plan because you will be required to make regular payments on your bad debt.

Do not take on more debt. Avoid all debt as much as possible. I understand that sometimes debt is hoisted on us—medical bills, car repair bills, etc.—but do not take on more debt unless absolutely necessary.

Do not stop being generous toward God. If your heart is right with God, you naturally will want to be generous toward him. Do not accept the lie that you do not have enough money to tithe or to be generous. The parable of the widow's mite (Mark 12:41–44) is sufficient to disabuse us of this lie.

Be content with what God has given you. Contentment will lead you away from temptations to overspend and take on more debt.

Do not feel inferior to your friends who may be more wealthy than you. This is a tough one. Your friends may take vacations to exotic places, drive the latest cars, or enjoy season tickets to sporting events—luxuries you ma desire but cannot afford. Do not measure your worth or success by comparing yourself to them. Remember our definition of success, which was offered in the preface: success is defined *as faithfulness to God and perseverance in obedience.* Success is never defined in monetary terms. Live for an audience of one – God himself.

Ask God to prosper you. While I detest the prosperity gospel and regard it as heresy (see the section *The Prosperity Gospel* earlier in this chapter), there are reasons from the Bible to ask God to prosper us. In brief, there are three points to note:

- We are commanded to ask for good gifts, so we should ask
- We ask because we know that God's heart is to give good gifts
- We ask for moderation, not extravagance

Let's elaborate on these three points. First, we are *commanded* to ask, seek, and knock. Here is Matthew 7:7–12 (CSB):

> [7] "Keep asking, and it will be given to you. Keep searching, and you will find. Keep knocking, and the door will be opened to you. [8] For everyone who asks receives, and the one who searches finds, and to the one who knocks, the door will be opened. [9] What man among you, if his son asks him for bread, will give him a stone? [10] Or if he asks for a fish, will give him a snake? [11] If you then, who are evil, know how to give good gifts to your children, how much more will your Father in heaven give good things to those who ask Him! [12] Therefore, whatever you want others to do for you, do also the same for them—this is the Law and the Prophets.

Notice that God's motivation is to give us good things if we ask! What we ask for must have righteous motives (James 4:2–3),[477] and it must be in line with seeking the kingdom of God and his righteousness first.[478] The two questions I use to evaluate my motives are this: "Is this best for the Kingdom of God?" and "Is this best for righteousness?" Other questions include, "Does this disadvantage God's kingdom?" or "Does it advantage me

---

477   In this context, righteous motives would be the opposite of asking wrongly, "to spend it on your passions." The idea is gratifying one's selfish desires instead of spending our wealth to further God's kingdom. (Donald W. Burdick, "James." In *The Expositor's Bible Commentary: Hebrews through Revelation*, edited by Frank E. Gaebelein, Vol. 12. (Zondervan Publishing, 1981), 193.) Again, the sin is advantaging ourselves instead of advantaging God's kingdom.

478   Charles L. Quarles, *Matthew.* Edited by T. Desmond Alexander, Thomas R. Schreiner, and Andreas J. Köstenberger. Evangelical Biblical Theology Commentary. (Lexham Academic, 2022), 203.

while disadvantaging God's kingdom?" Also, "Is it best?", "Does it bind?" and "Does it build?"[479] Before you ask, filter your request(s) through these questions.

Jesus assures us he can and will provide the means for the impossible.[480] *A Godly request will often ask for more than we can imagine (Ephesians 3:20) and will create further dependence on him, not independence from him.*

Secondly, it is good and right to ask for moderation, not extravagance—which is how I define *balanced prosperity*. We should ask for enough prosperity to live at the average of the community in which God has placed us. I derive this principle from Proverbs 30:7–9 (NIV):

> [7] "Two things I ask of you, Lord; do not refuse me before I die: [8] Keep falsehood and lies far from me; give me neither poverty nor riches, but give me only my daily bread. [9] Otherwise, I may have too much and disown you and say, 'Who is the Lord?' Or I may become poor and steal, and so dishonor the name of my God.

There are temptations with both extreme poverty and wealth that can be avoided by living a middle–class life.[481] Agur recognizes these temptations, so he asks for an economic station that keeps him from becoming deceitful (vs. 8a) and self–sufficient (vss. 8b–9). A life of balanced material blessings—balanced prosperity—is what is requested from God.[482] Let us use Agur's example of the level of prosperity to ask of God.

This last point limits the previous point. We can be fully restored and completed without financial extravagance. In fact, I would argue that extravagance may work against full restoration and completeness because of the inherent temptations of having much wealth.

Trust God to supply your needs. Repeatedly, God has provided for Mrs. English and me in miraculous ways. God is generous toward us and supplies the needs of those who follow him (Philippians 4:10–19, Psalm 23:1). Trust in the character of God, who never denies himself by not being faithful to his promises toward us.

---

479   G. Campbell Morgan, "The Limitations of Liberty – 1 Corinthians 6:12 and 10:23." Accessed 11/16/24, biblenotes.online. https://biblenotes.online/resources/sermonscampbellmorgan/docs/wp01–01.docx

480   D.A. Carson, "Matthew." In *The Expositor's Bible Commentary: Matthew, Mark, Luke*, edited by Frank E. Gaebelein, Vol. 8. (Zondervan Publishing, 1984), 186.

481   George M. Schwab, "The Book of Proverbs." In Cornerstone Biblical Commentary, Vol 7: The Book of Psalms, The Book of Proverbs. (Tyndale House, 2009), 645.

482   Allen P. Ross, "Proverbs." In *The Expositor's Bible Commentary: Psalms, Proverbs, Ecclesiastes, Song of Songs*, edited by Frank E. Gaebelein, Vol. 5. (Zondervan Publishing, 1991), 1120.

GREED

Conventional Wisdom

"The point is, ladies and gentlemen, that greed—for lack of a better word—is good." This is a famous quote from the 1987 movie *Wall Street*.[483] Conventional wisdom is a bit divided on greed.

Generally, most Americans view greed as morally wrong. Greed is often associated with selfishness, exploitation, and unethical behavior, as well as materialism, envy, and self–interest.[484] Most people do not want to be called 'greedy' because of its negative connotations.[485]

Defining what greed is can be a bit complex. In the business literature, the words *excessive* or *insatiable* are often associated with the concept of greed. In addition, some literature discusses whether greed can exist beyond material goods (can one be greedy for sex?) and if harm to others must be involved for greed to be present.[486]

While fewer voices find greed to be good, they are no less important. For many, greed is considered normal, even if it is morally wrong.[487] Greed is associated with superior economic outcomes, and many believe that without greed, our country would decline in to poverty and anarchy.[488] The summation is that most recognize that greed exists; some think it is healthy or has good outcomes, but most don't want to be known as greedy. How many Americans view greed as a moral issue is difficult to discern.

Biblical Wisdom

Greed is an "excessive desire to acquire or possess more wealth than one needs or deserves."[489] In Psalm 10:2–3, the arrogant, wicked man "boasts of the cravings of his heart" while blessing the greedy and reviling the Lord. In Romans 1:29, those who have been given over

---

483 The movie "Wall Street." Quote from the character Gorden Gekko. Accessed 11/13/2024, 1987, imdb.com. https://www.imdb.com/title/tt0094291/.

484 Ronald E. Riggio, "Is Greed Good or Bad?" March 1, 2024, psychologytoday.com. https://www.psychologytoday.com/us/blog/cutting–edge–leadership/202403/is–greed–good–or–bad

485 S.W. Gilliland and J.S. Anderson, "Perceptions of greed: A distributive injustice model." In *Emerging Perspectives on Organizational Justice and Ethics*. (Information Age Publishing, 2011), 137–166.

486 K. Hoyer, M. Zeelenberg, & S.M. Breugelmans, (2024). "Greed: What Is It Good for?" *Personality and Social Psychology Bulletin*, 50(4), 597–612. https://doi.org/10.1177/01461672221140355

487 Bruce Levine, "Greed and Hustle Have Become Virtues." January 16, 2014, nytimes.com. https://www.nytimes.com/roomfordebate/2014/01/16/why–we–like–to–watch–rich–people/greed–and–hustle–have–become–virtues

488 Neel Burton, "Is Greed Good? The Psychology and Philosophy of Greed." June 23, 2024, psychologytoday.com. https://www.psychologytoday.com/us/blog/hide–and–seek/201410/is–greed–good

489 Faithlife, "Greed." In *Logos Bible Study Factbook*. (Faithlife, November 13, 2024.) https://ref.ly/logos4/Factbook?id=ref%3abk.%25greed.

to their sinful lusts by the Lord are filled with "every kind of wickedness," including greed (see also 1 Corinthians 5:10). Greed is associated with being eager for money and wandering from the faith (1 Timothy 6:1–10). In Mark 7:21–22 (see also Matthew 15:19–20), greed is listed as one element that makes a man "unclean."

Greed is not requisite to creating wealth. When two parties freely agree to an economic transaction beneficial to both, this is not greed but self-preservation. If greed were at the root of all financial transactions in a free market, then we could not fulfill our duties (as illustrated in Luke 19 or Matthew 25 in the parables of the talents) to return a profit to the Lord without sinning. A business can be incubated, grown, and sustained without greed.

God condemns greed in the Scriptures because it contradicts Biblical stewardship and God's generosity toward us. Greed is the antithesis of disadvantaging oneself to advantage God.

Christian leaders are not to be greedy. Lack of greed is a requirement for those desiring to be elders in the church. 1 Timothy 3:2–3 states that Christian leaders should not be "lovers of money." You can find similar commands in Titus 1:7 and 1 Peter 5:2.

Greed should be considered normal for those whom the Holy Spirit has not regenerated. Without the transforming power of the Holy Spirit in one's heart, money and wealth often occupy the throne of one's life. Hence, greed is sometimes considered a "respectable" sin by those who do not know the Lord. For them, any ethical conundrum associated with greed is usually related to a pragmatic exercise of capitalism.[490]

Greed cannot thrive within one's covenantal relationship with God. Greed is entirely self-focused and is the antithesis of faithfulness to God. Greed is faithfulness to oneself. There is no room for greed in the life of a Christian business owner who is serious about living faithfully for God within the owner's covenantal relationship.

The Scriptures contain several examples of greed. One example is in Joshua 7, where Achan wrongfully took some of the sacred things from the plunder in Israel's victory over Jericho. Achan's greed was costly: Achan and his family were put to death as a result of his sin. Greed cannot coexist within a covenant with God. Greed is entirely self-focused and is the antithesis of faithfulness to another. There is no room for greed in the life of a CBO who is serious about living faithfully for God.

Judas Iscariot's greed was mentioned in passing in John 12:1–6 (NIV):

> Six days before the Passover, Jesus came to Bethany, where Lazarus lived, whom Jesus had raised from the dead. [2] Here a dinner was given in Jesus' honor. Martha served, while Lazarus was among those reclining at the table with him. [3] Then Mary took about a pint of pure nard, an expensive perfume; she poured it on Jesus' feet and wiped his feet with her hair. And

---

490 John Paul Rollert, "The Moral Ambivalence of Gordon Gekko". *Chicago Booth Review*. August 18, 2017. https://www.chicagobooth.edu/review/moral–ambivalence–gordon–gekko.

the house was filled with the fragrance of the perfume. [4] But one of his disciples, Judas Iscariot, who was later to betray him, objected, [5] "Why wasn't this perfume sold and the money given to the poor? It was worth a year's wages." [6] He did not say this because he cared about the poor but because he was a thief; as keeper of the money bag, he used to help himself to what was put into it.

Greed that masquerades as altruism is still greed. And like Judas Iscariot, greed will foster in the persona of a CBO a selfish view of an opportunity cost that is appropriate in God's kingdom.[491] Other passages related to greed that we should read and follow include Exodus 20:17, Deuteronomy 5:12, Ezekiel 18:8–17, and Romans 13:9.

A good parable that teaches against greed is in Luke 12:16–21 (NIV):

And he told them this parable. "The ground of a certain rich man yielded an abundant harvest. He thought to himself, 'What shall I do? I have no place to store my crops.' "Then he said, 'This is what I'll do. I will tear down my barns and build bigger ones, and there I will store my surplus grain. And I'll say to myself, "You have plenty of grain laid up for many years. Take life easy; eat, drink and be merry." ' "But God said to him, 'You fool! This very night your life will be demanded from you. Then who will get what you have prepared for yourself?' "This is how it will be with whoever stores up things for themselves but is not rich toward God.

This story is the parable of the rich man who was successful in business and decided to build bigger barns to hold more grain (wealth). The rich man was so successful that there was not enough room for all the harvested grain. So, the rich man built larger barns to hold the additional grain. Nothing in this story suggests the rich man acquired wealth unethically or illegally.

The man's words revealed the man's heart (Luke 6:44–45): "I'll say to myself, 'You have plenty of good things laid up for many years. Take life easy; eat, drink, and be merry." To the man's way of thinking, this new wealth was all about his comfort, security, and pleasures. Yet, he is described by God as a "fool" because his supreme investments in life were in temporal things that could be taken in an instant.

His actions alone would have revealed what was in his heart. But his words confirmed it: "I will say to myself, 'You have plenty of good things laid up for many years. Take life easy; eat, drink, and be merry." Life was all about his money, wealth, comfort, security, and enjoyment. But little did he know that he could die and not take one thing with him into

---

491 Colin G. Kruse, *John: An Introduction and Commentary*. Vol. 4. Tyndale New Testament Commentaries. (InterVarsity Press, 2003), 259.

eternity. He is described by God as a "fool" because his supreme investments in life were in temporal things that could be taken from him in an instant. He did not even consider creating treasures in Heaven.

This man believes he has achieved financial security. He has managed his business well and has generated significant wealth because of his management skills. Moreover, he believes that his wealth will take care of him for the balance of his life. But, wealth has one major weakness: it has no purchasing power after death.[492] His greed to retain all his wealth works against him by ensuring, through death, that someone else will get all that he has, and they will have not worked for one cent of it.

To apply the parable of the rich man to us Christian business owners, I would be remiss if I did not ask the obvious question: when we make more and more money, do we move to more expensive neighborhoods and build bigger homes? When we generate more profit, do we hoard our wealth in asset purchases such as a second home, expensive sports cars, or certain investment instruments? Do we disadvantage God's kingdom by spending our wealth on unnecessary memberships or expensive season tickets? Do we miss the opportunity to build treasures in heaven by being generous toward God? If our business has a blowout year in terms of profits, do we go on a blowout shopping spree? Check yourself. Do you act more like the rich man than you do like the college President? Are you focused more on the temporal or the eternal?

In my observation, significant financial success is difficult to handle in a godly way. Financial success will reveal what is in a person's heart much faster than financial failure. I believe God gives wealth to relatively few people with developed hearts who can handle such success. God knows that much wealth would ruin most of his followers, so he protects us by not giving much wealth to us.

Let us see our role as Christian business owners to generate wealth that is used to further God's kingdom. Let us disadvantage ourselves to advantage God's work on this earth. Let us understand that it is better to create treasures in heaven than on this earth. And let us hold our wealth with an open hand before God, without greed.

SUMMARY

The purpose of this chapter was to demonstrate several conclusions. First, conventional wisdom on money, wealth, and investing is sound generally and, for the most part, should be heeded by a Christian business owner. Second, because the temptations to love money and wealth are so subtle, it is best not to pursue wealth accumulation beyond becoming debt–free and saving for future expenses. Third, the prosperity gospel is antithetical to Biblical Christianity and should be avoided. Fourth, assuming debt is not sinful but should

---

492 Trent C. Butler. *Luke*. Vol. 3. Holman New Testament Commentary. (Broadman & Holman Publishers, 2000), 204.

be avoided if possible. Fifth, saving too much for the future is hoarding, so philanthropy should be employed to prevent hoarding by those whom God entrusts with much wealth. It is best to give enough away to create purposefully dependence on God for the future. Last, you cannot have the best of God and the best of this world. If you try to pursue both, eventually, you will be forced to choose where your affections and allegiances lie.

In the next chapter, I dive into the subject of leadership. Like it or not, if you're a CBO, you're a leader. I will propose that we lead the way Christ leads us. So, let's turn to Chapter 9, *Leadership*, and see what God has in store for us.

CHAPTER 9

LEADERSHIP

Christian business owners lead their businesses as Christ leads his church. To lead otherwise invites potentially unethical or immoral ways of leading those God has entrusted us. Before those whom we lead, all that is in our hearts is laid bare for them to see.

In this chapter, I will propose a simple leadership model for Christian business owners based solely on how Christ led when he was on this earth and how he leads his church today. I will argue that much of the leadership in the Christian church is based on an unhealthy preoccupation with authority rather than a healthy reflection of how Christ leads the church. I will also offer you a way to develop your leadership philosophy. I will briefly discuss the sensual temptations that can significantly harm your role as a leader in business and the church. Finally, I will advise you on handling yourself when your employees do not follow you.

MANY CHRISTIAN BUSINESS owners do not see themselves as leaders. Yet they swiftly learn that ownership is leadership when they hire their first employee or contractor.

CONVENTIONAL WISDOM

Leadership is a noisy, crowded space in the current literature. It is impossible to overview the current literature on business leadership briefly. But I will cover a few high points.

Thousands of studies have been conducted on leader behavior, focused on determining which behaviors are effective and ineffective.[493] Winston and Patterson reviewed 160 articles and books on leadership to categorize all the distinct leadership dimensions available in the literature. They eventually categorized 91 different dimensions (whew!).[494] There are dozens of leadership styles offered in the current literature.[495] In addition, how leaders are developed continues to be a topic of conversation and research.[496] Most leaders have a default style of leading,[497] and they need to develop certain personal qualities to be effective leaders.[498] The qualities that various sources find significant seem to blur together into a master list that no mere mortal could ever comprehend or attain.

But if there are problems with the sheer number of qualities a good leader should have, there is also real danger in reducing the qualities needed to basic characteristics like competence or likability. Research shows that hiring authorities for leadership positions and many others often confuse confidence and likeability with competence and real leadership skills. For example, traits like self-absorption and overconfidence should be red flags, not indicators of leadership potential. Overconfident people are often abrasive toward others while staying "very much in awe of themselves." Overvaluing their talents and contributions, after a few achievements, their confidence can morph into narcissism. They will often over-rely on themselves and diminish the significance of other's contributions.[499] They live out, in spades, common phrases such as "believe in yourself," "don't worry about what

---

493 Gary Yukl, "Effective Leadership Behavior: What We Know and What Questions Need More Attention." *Academy of Management Perspectives.* 26(4):66.

494 Bruce E. Winston and Kathleen Patterson, "An Integrative Definition of Leadership." *International Journal of Leadership Studies.* 2(1):online. Accessed 07/17/2024. https://www.regent.edu/journal/international–journalof–leadership–studies/an–integrative–leadership–definition/

495 One example of dozens of articles is this: Rebecca Knight, "6 Common Leadership Styles—and How to Decide Which to Use When." April 9, 2024. *Harvard Business Review.* https://hbr.org/2024/04/6–common–leadership–styles–and–how–to–decide–which–to–use–when. Another example is this: Letsroam.com, sa, "12 Effective Leadership Styles for Your Team's Success." Accessed 07/08/2024. Letsroam.com. https://www.letsroam.com/team–building/resources/leadership–styles/

496 Kavitha Sethuraman and Jayshree Suresh, "Effective Leadership Styles." *International Business Research.* 7(2014):165.

497 Minute Tools Content Team, "Leadership Styles." Minute Tools, Feb, 2017. https://expertprogrammanagement.com/2017/02/leadership–styles/

498 Micela Leis and Stephanie Wormington, "12 Essential Qualities of Effective Leadership." July 3, 2024. The Center for Creating Leadership. https://www.ccl.org/articles/leading–effectively–articles/characteristics–good–leader/. See also Erin Wike. "20 Leadership Qualities that Make a Great Leader (With Tips)." April 30, 2023. Indeed.com. https://www.indeed.com/career–advice/career–development/leadership–qualities–that–make–a–great–leader.

499 Theodore Millon, *Disorders of Personality.* 3rd Edition. (John Wiley & Sons, 2011), 375.

others think of you," "follow your heart," and the all-encompassing phrase that gives jerks all the permission they need to be jerks, "just be yourself."[500] Mental health issues[501] and personality disorders[502] are a real problem in the business owner community, and Christian business owners are no exception.

In such a diverse and over-studied space, I think it is wise to turn to the Scriptures and see what we can learn about leadership. We have examples in the Bible of those born with leadership attributes but who still needed to be developed. For example, David was a natural leader. But David also needed to learn how to lead. Some estimate that at least 20 years passed between the time David was anointed king over Israel by Samuel and before the Northern tribes accepted him as king.[503] During these years, David needed to learn valuable leadership lessons to make him the king he became.[504]

Moses is another example. Moses was raised in Pharaoh's house and was educated in all the wisdom (polytheism) of the Egyptians. He was powerful in speech and action (Acts 7:22), yet he needed to spend 40 years in the desert as a shepherd before he was ready to be Israel's leader and rescuer.

Conventional wisdom has much to offer when it comes to learning about leadership. Much of what conventional wisdom offers should be adopted by Christian business owners. However, most conventional wisdom on leadership is godless because it does not account for a transcendent God who can transform the heart and mind of a leader to be more like Christ and, thus, a more effective leader.

Our world today has a false assumption that leadership is mostly about enjoying power and subduing people. Those with selfish ambitions like the idea of power and control, which often leads to conflicts, insecurities, and leadership voids among those who are led.[505] Jesus never overpowers his followers. He never "lords" anything over us. He never "makes a final decision," expecting everyone to "fall in line." Instead, Christ serves, but he serves with authority. Let us focus on learning how Christ leads and apply what we learn to our roles as business owners.

---

500 Tomas Chamorro-Premuzic, *Why Do So Many Incompetent Men Become Leaders? (and how to fix it)*. (Harvard Business Review Press, 2019), 3-4.

501 M.A. Freeman, P.J. Staudenmaier, M.R. Zisser, *et al.* "The prevalence and co-occurrence of psychiatric conditions among entrepreneurs and their families." *Small Business Economics,* 2019, 53:323–342. https://doi.org/10.1007/s11187-018-0059-8

502 Tomas Chamorro-Premuzic, "1 in 5 business leaders may have psychopathic tendencies—here's why, according to a psychology professor." April 8, 2019, cnbc.com. https://www.cnbc.com/2019/04/08/the-science-behind-why-so-many-successful-millionaires-are-psychopaths-and-why-it-doesnt-have-to-be-a-bad-thing.html

503 Henry D. M. Spence–Jones, *2 Samuel*. The Pulpit Commentary. (Funk & Wagnalls Company, 1909), 127.

504 If you want to learn more about the leadership lessons David needed to learn before he was anointed king, I recommend R.T. Kendall, *A Man After God's Own Heart: God's Relationship with David and with You*. (Christian Focus Publications, 2002.)

505 Jey J. Kanagaraj, "Johannine Jesus: The Supreme Example of Leadership: An Inquiry into John 13:1–20." *Themelios,* 2004. 29(3):16.

HOW DOES JESUS LEAD?

One could be forgiven if one equates servant leadership with how Christ leads his church. At first blush, they probably seem similar. Robert Greenleaf developed the servant–leadership model in the 1970s and suggested that authentic, ethical leaders are servants first.[506] Greenleaf's model has evolved into a multi-dimensional leadership theory that builds on a desire to serve coupled with an intent to lead and develop others to achieve a higher purpose objective.[507]

However, some do not believe the servant leadership model fits well with Christ's example of leadership. Babyak suggests that an analysis of how Jesus led does not fit into the construct of a servant leader.[508] Niewold concluded that even a Christianized form of servant leadership results in a distorted Christology.[509] Whether or not Christ's leadership fits with a modern–day leadership philosophy is a discussion that appeals mainly to academics who study such things. In the real world, what matters is faithfulness to God and modeling Christ as much as possible in our day–to–day interactions. The labels we use are less important.

Hence, I suggest we start with the Scriptures rather than conventional wisdom and learn a few lessons from Jesus that we can emulate as Christian business owners.[510] I suggest that when it comes to leadership, CBOs should emulate Christ in the following ways:

- Value each person equally
- Lead out of mission and purpose
- Serve those you lead
- Be oriented toward the truth
- Be Spirit–led

Value each person equally

Leadership becomes oppression if you do not value and respect those whom you lead. Oppressors demean and disrespect, but leaders value and respect those they lead.

When Christ washed the feet of his disciples, he modeled a powerful example of a leader who valued equally each of his followers (John 13:1–5 ESV):

---

506 Don M. Frick, *Robert K. Greenleaf: a Life of Servant Leadership*. (San Francisco: Berrett–Koehler, 2004), 5.

507 Michael F. Coetzer, Mark Bussin, and Madelyn Geldenhuys, "The Functions of a Servant Leader" *Administrative Sciences*. 2017. 7(1):5.

508 Andrew T. Babyak, "Toward a Theory of Biblical Leadership." *Journal of Biblical Integration in Business*. 2018. 12(1):55–66.

509 Jack Niewold, "Beyond Servant Leadership." *Journal of Biblical Perspective*. 2007. 2(1):118–134.

510 What I propose here is far from exhaustive and may disappoint many who live in the leadership vertical.

[1]Now before the Feast of the Passover, when Jesus knew that his hour had come to depart out of this world to the Father, having loved his own who were in the world, he loved them to the end. 2 During supper, when the devil had already put it into the heart of Judas Iscariot, Simon's son, to betray him, 3 Jesus, knowing that the Father had given all things into his hands, and that he had come from God and was going back to God, 4 rose from supper. He laid aside his outer garments, and taking a towel, tied it around his waist. 5 Then he poured water into a basin and began to wash the disciples' feet and to wipe them with the towel that was wrapped around him.

We are told that the devil had already prompted Judas Iscariot to betray him. Yet, Jesus washed his betrayer's feet, too. Jesus treated the one who would betray him equally with those who would eventually give their lives for him.[511] CBOs value every employee, vendor, partner, and stakeholder equally. Each person is to be valued because God's image is in each person.

Lead out of mission and purpose

Everything Jesus did was connected to his mission and purpose. Christ led with a vision of what things would look like when he completed his mission.[512] Recall that we live with an eternal perspective derived from our covenant with God. Similarly, Christ led knowing what was to come and aligned his decisions with what was coming in the future.

Thus, it is good to ask, "Why did Jesus leave heaven and come to the earth?" His decisions aligned with why he was sent to this earth:[513]
- Preach (Mark 1:38, Luke 4:43)[514]
- Put God before family (Matthew 10:34–36)

---

511   Colin G. Kruse, *John: An Introduction and Commentary*. Vol. 4. Tyndale New Testament Commentaries. (Downers Grove, IL: InterVarsity Press, 2003), 275.

512   Gene Wilkes, *Jesus on Leadership: Timeless Wisdom on Servant Leadership*. (Carol Stream, IL: Tyndale House, 1998), 9–11.

513   Benjamin B. Warfield, "Jesus' Mission, according to His Own Testimony (Synoptics)." *The Princeton Theological Review* 1915. 13(4):513–586. See also J. Dean Cameron. *Sermon Outlines for Special Occasions*, Dollar Sermon Library Series (Grand Rapids, MI: Baker Book House, 1976), 43.

514   Jesus came to preach, but the miracles Christ performed when he preached confirmed his message. (William Hendriksen and Simon J. Kistemaker. *Exposition of the Gospel According to Mark*. Vol. 10. New Testament Commentary. (Grand Rapids: Baker Book House, 1953–2001), 73.) Christ didn't come to be a miracle–worker, he came to be our savior. (Alan R. Cole. "Mark." In *New Bible Commentary: 21st Century Edition*, edited by D. A. Carson, R. T. France, J. A. Motyer, and G. J. Wenham, 4th ed., (Inter–Varsity Press, 1994), 957.)

- True peace through division (Luke 12:49–53)[515]
- Fulfill the law (Matthew 5:17–18)[516]
- Call sinners to righteousness (Mark 2:17, Matthew 9:12–13, Luke 5:31, 19:10). Note that saving some from their sins involves condemning others who do not believe (John 9:39).[517]
- Receive God's full wrath and punishment for sin as mankind's substitute (Matthew 1:21, 20:28, Mark 10:45)[518]
- Give abundant life (John 10:10)
- To bear witness to the truth (John 18:37)
- To do God's will (John 6:38)

Jesus was fully aware of his divine origin and destiny (Isaiah 61:1–3, Luke 4:18–19).[519] Jesus knew why he was on earth and what he needed to do to accomplish God's will. When he led his disciples, he led out of his vision and purpose. Christian business owners should lead others out of their purpose and calling. And your mission and purpose should never be derived from selfish ambition.

Serve those you lead

In Luke's gospel, Christ uses the disciples' arguments about who was the greatest to clarify his role with them—as one who serves (Luke 22:24–27 ESV):

> [24] A dispute also arose among them, as to which of them was to be regarded as the greatest. [25] And he said to them, "The kings of the Gentiles exercise lordship over them, and those in authority over them are called benefactors. [26] But not so with you. Rather, let the greatest among you become as the youngest, and the leader as one who serves. [27] For who is the greater, one who reclines at table or one who serves? Is it not the one who reclines at table? But I am among you as the one who serves.

515   The coming of God's kingdom necessarily divides people into two camps: one camp follows God, the other camp opposes him. Robert H. Stein, *Luke*. Vol. 24. The New American Commentary. (Broadman & Holman Publishers, 1992), 364.

516   Christ "will bring the law to its intended goal." Craig Blomberg, *Matthew*. Vol. 22. The New American Commentary. (Broadman & Holman Publishers, 1992), 103.

517   Carson, *John*, 377.

518   See Grudem's excellent summary of Christ's atonement in Wayne Grudem. *Systematic Theology: An Introduction to Biblical Theology*. (Inter–Varsity Press; Zondervan Publishing, 2004), 570–77.

519   Merrill C. Tenney, "John." In *The Expositor's Bible Commentary: John and Acts*, edited by Frank E. Gaebelein, Vol. 9. (Zondervan Publishing, 1981), 136.

Greatness in the world's eyes involves being served by others.[520] But greatness in the kingdom of God comes through serving (i.e., being the youngest) instead of being served. Coupled with the foot–washing story we just read about in John 13:12–17, we learn that even though one may be entitled to a position by virtue of age or another characteristic, such position does not constitute greatness. Instead, "faithful service in a lowly place is itself true greatness."[521] Dr. Osborne's words are instructive: "None of us dare allow ourselves to feel self–important. Every achievement is actually a gift from God for the sake of the church and for his glory."[522]

Christ's call to lead through service is one of the most difficult aspects of stewardship.[523] His call demands a deep, personal humility counter-cultural to the selfish, cost-benefit, what–is–legal leadership philosophy where the leader protects his status and compensation above the needs of his company and employees. Christian business owners must avoid the intoxication of self–importance or taking the best while leaving employees with less. Hence, we serve our employees, for example, by letting them go through the buffet line first, letting them have better offices, or helping them sweep the factory floors. We serve. We do not exercise an authoritarian style of lordship over them.[524]

Be oriented toward the truth

Just because we focus on serving our employees does not mean we lack authority. Because of our role as business owners, every time we speak, we're exercising authority. Because of our position, we can implement change when needed.

Our inherent authority is one reason we must be oriented toward the truth. If we're dealing in fantasy instead of the truth (there is no middle ground), we'll drive our business into bankruptcy and hurt countless employees, partners, and vendors. In other words, if we make decisions based on what we hope will be in the future or how we wish it were in the present, we'll make wrong decisions. We must lean into reality and how things are and

---

520   Robert H. Stein, *Luke*. Vol. 24. The New American Commentary. (Broadman & Holman Publishers, 1992), 549.

521   Leon Morris, *Luke: An Introduction and Commentary*, Tyndale New Testament Commentaries (InterVarsity Press, 1988), 326.

522   Grant R. Osborne, *Luke: Verse by Verse*, ed. Jeffrey Reimer, Elliot Ritzema, and Danielle Thevenaz, Awa Sarah, Osborne New Testament Commentaries (Bellingham, WA: Lexham Press, 2018), 507.

523   John C. Hutchison, "Servanthood: Jesus' Countercultural Call to Christian Leaders." *Bibliotheca Sacra,* 166 (2009).

524   The idea here is one of ruthless authority exercised as self–centered leadership. William Hendriksen and Simon J. Kistemaker, *Exposition of the Gospel According to Luke*. Vol. 11. New Testament Commentary. (Baker Books, 1953–2001), 971.

base our decisions on the unvarnished truth of the present. To do otherwise will damage us worse than had we faced reality head-on.[525]

In my experience of running businesses, I have learned that *the truth is never the problem*.[526] Instead, the truth will bring freedom to your situation (John 8:36), no matter how difficult the truth might be. As one friend said to me, some babies *are* ugly. The truth is never the problem.

Be Spirit-led

All four gospels make it clear that Jesus' ministry did not begin until after his baptism at the Jordan River with his cousin, John, and the descent of the Holy Spirit on him.[527] Immediately after his baptism, the Spirit led Christ into the wilderness to be tempted by the devil (Matthew 4:1, Mark 1:12, Luke 4:1). After being tempted and yet not sinning, Christ returned to Galilee in the power of the Spirit (Luke 4:14). Christ knew the Holy Spirit was on him (Luke 4:18) and was able to act with authority against evil spirits who were oppressing people (Luke 4:33, Matthew 8:16, Mark 1:26–27).

The same spirit that was on Christ has been sent to us (John 14:26, 15:26, 16:13) and lives in us (John 14:17, 1 Corinthians 6:19). It is recorded that Peter was filled with the Holy Spirit (Acts 4:8), that unnamed men working in the early church were filled with the Spirit (Acts 6:3) and Saul was filled with the Spirit when Ananias laid hands on him to receive Christ. The Holy Spirit (Acts 9:31) encouraged the early church, and Jewish believers were stunned that the Holy Spirit had been given to Gentile believers (Acts 10:45, 15:8).

It is the Spirit who sets us free from sin and death (Romans 8:2) and thus, we set our minds on the things of the Spirit instead of the flesh (Romans 8:5). The Holy Spirit helps us pray and intercedes for us (Romans 8:26–27). The Spirit assigns our gifts that build and edify the church (1 Corinthians 12:11) and we are to eagerly desire the Spirit's gifts (1 Corinthians 14:1).

The Holy Spirit living in us is a "deposit," guaranteeing our future in heaven (2 Corinthians 5:5). The Spirit has discernable "fruit" in our lives (Galatians 5:22) and the Spirit's desires are in direct opposition to the desires of the flesh (Galatians 5:17). We are commanded to be filled with the Spirit (Ephesians 5:18), to pray in the Spirit on all occasions with all kinds of prayers and requests (Ephesians 6:18) and sing in the Spirit with songs the Spirit gives us (Colossians 3:16).

---

525 Henry Cloud, Integrity: The Courage to Meet the Demands of Reality. (Harper Collins, 2000), 100–05.

526 Jeff VanVonderen, Tired of Trying to Measure Up: Getting Free from the Demands, Expectations, and Intimidation of Well-Meaning People. (Bethany House Publishers, 1980), 27.

527 Hwa Yung. *Leadership or Servanthood? Walking in the Steps of Jesus.* (Cumbria, UK: Langham Publishing, 2021), np.

The Spirit can be quenched (1 Thessalonians 5:19) and some will abandon the Christian faith to follow deceiving spirits and things taught by demons (1 Timothy 4:1). It is the Holy Spirit's presence that makes a woman beautiful (1 Peter 3:4). The work of the Holy Spirit ensured that the prophetic word was preached with power (2 Peter 1:21). To this end, as the Spirit fills us, we find the Spirit gives us power, love, and self–discipline (2 Timothy 1:7). Finally, it is the Spirit who invites us to God, to have our thirst quenched and to take hold of the free gift of the water of life (Revelation 22:17).

The Spirit of God humbles Christian business owners. The Spirit teaches us what to think and the attitudes to hold. Christian business owners understand that differences in gifting come from the Spirit, so CBOs respect and encourage differences in employees and others.

We lead through the Spirit because we are (or should be) filled with the Spirit. When we lead in the Spirit, we lead with love, joy, peace, patience, kindness, goodness, faithfulness, gentleness, and self–control (Galatians 5:22). It is difficult to imagine that one can be authoritarian, angry, controlling, condescending, disrespectful—essentially a horse's petute—and exhibit the characteristics of the Spirit.

PROPER USE OF AUTHORITY

The Christian church today in America is in a similar boat as we were coming out of the safe and conventional 1950s and moving into the turbulent 1960s and 1970s.

The 60s and 70s were a time of rapid and disorienting cultural change for most Christians. All many could think to do was to play the separation card and to set up as many boundaries as possible against a culture they were convinced was going to hell in a handbasket and posing a considerable threat to the wellbeing and faith of Christian young people. Separation was the prophylactic against the godless sex, drugs, and rock and roll of that era.

Of course, Christians discovered that you cannot escape from culture entirely. When you try to separate from mainstream culture, you inevitably set up a parallel culture with its own ambiguities and problems.

One of the older generations' failings was an unhealthy preoccupation with authority, most notably represented in the Bill Gothard movement and teachings.[528] In those homes and churches that followed Gothard, we established authorities that were not to be questioned and were always to be obeyed. This unhealthy exercise of authority was a response to the blatant rebellion against the establishment and the church during that time. Even if the authority was failing or wrong, if that authority was on "our side," they were given

---

528 https://billgothard.com/. Many were injured emotionally and spiritually by his teachings. See "Shiny, Happy People." Accessed 11/20/2024. Imdb.com https://www.imdb.com/title/tt27715627/

a pass. Such authorities were given license to be harsh, shaming, and sometimes abusive, even inside the church.

This type of authority has survived in some Christian circles even to this day. Over the last 10–15 years, we have been witnessing what happens when these unhealthy and sinful authorities rule homes, churches, and even entire denominations. Tens of thousands of Christians have been harmed by one or more authorities that were allowed to operate without culpability.[529] Christ speaks against such authoritarianism in Luke 22:25–26 (NIV):

> [25] Jesus said to them, "The kings of the Gentiles lord it over them; and those who exercise authority over them call themselves Benefactors. [26] But you are not to be like that. Instead, the greatest among you should be like the youngest, and the one who rules like the one who serves.

The Greek word for the phrase "lord it over" means to exercise rule and control,[530] but improperly, by being ruthless[531] and tyrannical.[532] 1 Peter 5:3 warns elders against this type of authority. Here, Christ tells us that the values of authoritarianism so prevalent in the pagans should not characterize Christians. We rule through service. We rule through devolution.

A proper use of authority operates within the notion that all authority on earth is delegated by God (Romans 13:1–2). No authority exists in any absolute sense other than God's authority. Those who manage through ungodly methods forget that their authority is an entrustment and should be used to build up others while accomplishing the mission and vision of the organization.

---

529 Two examples come to mind. First is Mark Driscoll, pastor of Mars Hill, who fell to the perils of power, conflict and Christian celebrity. Not only was his ministry shipwrecked, his personal life was injured a thousands were left disillusioned by his actions. See *The Rise and Fall of Mars Hill*, Christianity Today, https://www.christianitytoday.com/podcasts/the-rise-and-fall-of-mars-hill/. Also consider how the leaders of the Southern Baptist Convention protected hundreds of pastors who were sexually abusing children. Terry Gross, "How the Southern Baptist Convention Covered up its Widespread Sexual Abuse Scandal." June 2, 2022, National Public Radio. https://www.npr.org/2022/06/02/1102621352/how-the-southern-baptis t-convention-covered-up-its-widespread-sexual-abuse-scand. For more stories like these, see julieroys.com, ministrywatch.com and thechristianpost.com.

530 BDAG, 576.

531 William Hendriksen and Simon J. Kistemaker, *Exposition of the Gospel According to Luke*. Vol. 11. New Testament Commentary. (Baker Books, 1953–2001), 971 and Craig Keener, *The IVP Bible Background Commentary: New Testament*. Second Edition. (IVP Academic: An Imprint of InterVarsity Press, 2014), 237.

532 For the parallel use of this phrase in 1 Peter 5:3, see E.H. Plumptre, *The General Epistles of St Peter and St Jude, with Notes and Introduction*. The Cambridge Bible for Schools and Colleges. (Cambridge: Cambridge University Press, 1890), 154 and Greg W Forbes, *1 Peter*. Edited by Andreas J. Köstenberger and Robert W. Yarbrough. Exegetical Guide to the Greek New Testament. (B&H Academic; WORDsearch, 2016), 168–69.

A proper use of authority operates within the notion that being vested with authority does not mean being vested with superiority. Having authority is a role, not a right. Oppressive behavior toward those who lack authority is clearly sin (Proverbs 22:22–23).

A proper use of authority operates within a system of accountability. Luke 12:42–48 indicates that even if an earthy authority has no earthly accountability, there is an accountability to God that will occur someday.

A proper use of authority operates out of one's character much more than one's position. As a leader, who you are is much more important than your position as a business owner. Asserting authority because of one's position usually means the battle for trust and character has been lost.

DEVELOPING YOUR LEADERSHIP PHILOSOPHY

While the discussion in this section might seem like an academic exercise, if you take it seriously and communicate the results to your employees, you will find your leadership taking a significant step forward. Here is what I suggest you do.

First, take some time off from work, between one and two days. Then, work through this section, element by element and reflectively build your personal leadership philosophy. After creating your leadership philosophy, share it with your spouse and close friends. Ask for their feedback and refine it. At all times, submit your philosophy to the Lord and ask him what he wants to say to you about your leadership philosophy.

Second, live by your philosophy without fail or excuse.

Third, communicate your philosophy to your staff and let them hold you accountable for living it out every day.

Elements of a leadership philosophy

Writing your leadership philosophy will force you to consider what you believe about leadership and what you believe to be true about yourself.[533] A leadership philosophy includes:
- Summary leadership statement that is personalized to yourself
- Your definition of leadership
- Outline your leadership values and operating principles
- Articulation of what you will expect from yourself and others
- Transparent admittance of your personal idiosyncracies
- Let's discuss each section individually.

---

533   If you need help with the tasks in this section, contact Bill English through bibleandbusiness.com or onpathcoaching.com.

Summary leadership statement

Write your leadership philosophy in one statement. It needs to be succinct and to the point. For example, my summary statement about leadership is this:

Know yourself. Know your people. Know your stuff.

My leadership summary statement combines self–awareness, connecting with others, and competence in my leadership role. This statement is the last element to write and should not be attempted until the other tasks below are completed.

Your definition of leadership

In this section, you will write a broader definition of leadership that can be the basis for your leadership summary statement. If you are unsure what to write here, look at incorporating a variety of ideas and then pair them down into a more verbose definition of leadership. When I went through this exercise, this is where I landed:

Leadership is influencing people by providing purpose, direction, and motivation while operating to accomplish the organization's goals in ways that improve the organization.

You may lead because of God's call on your life to ownership. You may find inspiration in God's purposes for business (see Chapter 10, *Core Ideology,* and the section titled *Biblical View on the Purpose of Business*) as you write your definition. Consult some books and resources. Think through how Christ leads us today and what a proper use of authority looks like. Do not rush this process. It is important that what you produce is both quality and reflective of who you are.

Values and Operating Principles

Take time to write out your leadership values. You will fail from time to time at living them out, but you will not be sorry that you have these and that you asked your staff to hold you accountable to them. When I went through this exercise, Table 9–1 was where I landed.

Table 9–1: Values and Operating Principles

Values	Operating Principles
Connect authentically with each person on staff	Assume trust that flows both ways
Be oriented toward the truth	See things the way they are, not the way I wish they were.
Work hard to finish jobs/projects and get results	Do what I say, when I say I will do it or communicate early when problems or timelines adjust the timing and/or quality of results
Embrace, engage, and deal with the negative	Work to end, resolve or transform problems
Grow personally and professionally	Coach others to grow personally and professionally
Have fun	Have fun
Work for a transcendent purpose	Fulfilling transcendent purpose is more important than profits or industry recognition – what is your transcendent purpose?

What I Expect From Myself and Others

Next, write out what you expect from your employees and what they can expect from you. Doing this latter part will help your employees hold you accountable. Table 9–2 is where I landed when I did this exercise.

Table 9–2: What I Expect from Myself and Others

What I expect	What I will Ask
Honesty: Speak the truth with love and respect	Please do not minimize or exaggerate Please do not gossip Please express disagreements – with respect & care Communicate 100%
Maturity: Own your words and actions	"Own" your words and actions first
Unifier: Contribute to unity of staff and purpose	Please do not be an agent of discord or dissension Please participate in company fun activities when you can do so

What I expect	What I will Ask
Growth: Own your professional growth	Please pursue education, resources, authority, and direction to grow in your leadership and skills
Respect and Trust: Assume the best in others	Seek first to understand the other person Assume good intentions in the other person Be careful to protect the reputation of others
Competence: Follow through and get the job done right and on time.	I'll ask that you always ask questions of me if my tasks or assignments are unclear I'll ask that you let me know early if you need additional time to complete a project or get results from a goal that I have set I'll ask that you do this with your manager too
Innovation: creative leadership	Look for creative ways to solve problems Realize that our industry is constantly changing – decisions often change as new information or opportunities arise

Personal Idiosyncrasies

Finally, as odd as it might sound, this part asks you to be honest with yourself. Writing this section without unvarnished feedback from people who know you best is also difficult. A good way to find out your idiosyncrasies is to ask this question: "What is it like to be on the other end of <enter your name here>? Often, our idiosyncrasies are blind spots, so some of their feedback may hurt. Be sure to have close friends who will support you and allow you to process what you're learning about yourself.

When I did this exercise, I landed with these idiosyncrasies:
- My moods go up and down.
- I tend to "feel" (sometimes profoundly) the ebb and flow of the organization
- External processor – I think out loud
- If I "suggest" something, that means "do it."
- I am an intermittent perfectionist.
- I am transparent, sometimes too transparent.
- I think (ruminate?) about conversations and decisions and may later change my mind based on those conversations.
- I have learned to trust my instincts, meaning I will think I am right even without clear evidence to support my position.
- I am not good at holding others accountable for day–to–day task completion. I think people should finish their stuff on time and with excellence.

- Pacing & Decision–Making—my pacing varies depending on what I'm hearing or not hearing from the Lord

SUMMARY

Christian business owners lead their businesses as Christ leads his church. To lead otherwise invites potentially unethical or immoral ways of leading those God has entrusted us. Before those whom we lead, all that is in our hearts is laid bare for them to see.

In this chapter, I proposed a simple leadership model for Christian business owners based solely on how Christ led when he was on this earth and how he leads his church today:

- We value each person equally
- Lead out of mission and purpose
- Serve those we lead
- Oriented toward the truth
- Led by the Spirit as we lead others

I also suggest that a proper use of authority recalls:

- Our authority is delegated to us by God, hence it is an entrustment
- We are not superior to others
- We lead within a system of accountability
- We lead out of character more than position

Christian leadership looks and feels differently than worldly leadership. While there is much we can learn from conventional wisdom, there is more to learn from Christ's leadership in the Gospels.

I have also suggested that you take a few days away from the office and develop your personal leadership philosophy. Take the time to write it out and ask for feedback from your closest friends and family. While doing this may hurt at times, you will emerge on the other side as a much better owner because you're a better leader.

How you lead will continually reinforce or detract from what you value. Your core values and God's purposes for business should inform all of your decisions as a leader. In the next chapter, we will examine your business's core ideology. There is much to learn, so let us keep going.

CHAPTER 10

CORE IDEOLOGY

The core ideology of a business "consists of two distinct parts: core values, a system of guiding principles and tenants; and core purpose, the organization's most fundamental reason for existence.[534] A core ideology is the glue that keeps a company on track as it grows and changes.

CORE VALUES

Core values are widely discussed and accepted in the conventional wisdom literature. Much of what is written is helpful and should be considered by the Christian business owner.

Conventional Wisdom

Core values are an organization's essential tenets—the values it would hold even if they became a competitive disadvantage. Core values express an organization's beliefs about life and business. Core values are one of the most fundamental components of an organization's

---

534 Jim Collins & Jerry Porras, "Building Your Company's Vision." 1996. Accessed 10/20/2023. https://hbr.org/1996/09/building–your–companys–vision.

culture.[535] The most successful companies pursue their core values as much as they pursue anything else, such as product innovation, customer retention, or profits.[536]

Core values are non-negotiable, even under significant duress. Sticking with one's values will create risk and pain at some point, both for the organization and the business owner. Core values are a rallying point and a positive constraint on the organization's decisions and plans.[537]

In a privately held business, the owner's values will become the company's core values, even when the owner articulates one set of values but lives out a different set day–to–day. It does not matter what values are plastered on the wall in printed form. The values that the owner lives out become the organization's core values and can have a strong, positive or negative impact on the culture and direction of the organization.[538]

In privately held companies, the owner's values are often vaguely articulated, seldom published, and ambiguously communicated. The result is that value gaps are created, and employees are left to intuit the values of the owner and the organization. The owner must fill these gaps by articulating his core values and consistently living them out. Doing so will benefit him in crisis management, strategic change, key decisions, and growth management.[539]

Values and purpose differ in that purpose states the "why" of the business.[540] In contrast, values focus on the ethical and moral principles that guide how those working in the business will behave.[541] Given this basic difference between values and purpose, the reader should not expect the core values of a business to be like God's purposes for business, which are discussed later in this chapter.

Conventional wisdom will often gravitate toward common core values such as (not an exhaustive list) honesty, integrity, teamwork, accountability, loyalty, compassion, kindness, curiosity, or humility. Conventional wisdom views core values pragmatically and egocentrically. On the pragmatic front, one researcher suggests that "core values define the overarching concepts that summarise the identity of the corporate brand and as guiding

---

535 Jerzy Smolicz, "Core values and cultural identity." *Ethnic and Racial Studies*. 1981. 4(1): 75–90.

536 Jim Collins & Jerry Porras, *Built to Last: Successful Habits of Visionary Companies*. (HarperCollins, 2004), 8.

537 Patrick M. Lencioni, "Make Your Values Mean Something." *Harvard Business Review*. July, 2002:5–9.

538 Katherine Dean, "Values–Based Leadership: How Our Personal Values Impact the Workplace." *The Journal of Values–Based Leadership*. 2008. 1(1):1–7.

539 Richard L. Osborne, "Core Value Statements: The Corporate Compass." *Business Horizons*. 1991. 34(5):28–34.

540 Jen Croneberger, *Vision, Mission and Purpose: The Difference*. Forbes.com, 2020. Accessed 08/19/2023. https://www.forbes.com/sites/forbescoachescouncil/2020/03/04/vision–mission–and–purpose–the–difference.

541 Daniela Kirova, *What is the Difference Between Values, Purpose, Mission and Vision?* Startwithvalues.com, 2023. Accessed 08/19/2023. https://values.institute/what–is–the–difference–between–values–purpose–mission–and–vision.

lights for the brand building process.[542] Hence, core values are viewed as a building block to attaining a brand from which the market will purchase goods or services.

Biblical View of Core Values

For a CBO, the question is not which values the owner should select from a list generated through conventional wisdom. The question is more focused: "What should the CBO value more than anything else in business?" Asked differently, does the Bible give us a set of values that the CBO should follow?

The Bible directs the attention of the CBO to place an incomparably greater value on one's faith in Christ over any other aspect of a business. The comparison the Bible uses is between one's faith in God and the possession of wealth. Paul makes the comparison in a passing comment in 1 Peter 1:7 (ESV):

> So that the tested genuineness of your faith—more precious than gold that perishes though it is tested by fire—may be found to result in praise, glory, and honor at the revelation of Jesus Christ.

A Christian's faith—which cannot perish or fade away and is guarded by God's power—is far more valuable than gold, even gold refined by fire.

> For all its value, the natural world will cease. Faith (as the genuine, proven character of the person) is of incredibly greater value because it is imperishable and will go into eternity.[543]

This comparison between faith and wealth is also mentioned in Psalm 119:72 (LEB):

> The law of your mouth *is* better to me than thousands of gold and silver *coins*.

Both 1 Peter 1:7 and Psalm 119:72 are comparisons. We're taught to value faith and God's commands over what the world says is most valuable – gold. These comparisons are more common in the Bible that what we might initially think. It is incumbent on a CBO to follow the Bible's instructions on what to value when inculcating core values into his business. Table 10–1 surfaces Scripture passages that prescribe a CBO to value one thing over another.

---

542 Mats Urde, "Core value–based corporate brand building." *European Journal of Marketing* 2001. 37(7):1017–1040.

543 Grant R. Osborne, "1 Peter," in *Cornerstone Biblical Commentary: James, 1–2 Peter, Jude, Revelation*, ed. Philip W. Comfort, Cornerstone Biblical Commentary (Tyndale House Publishers, 2011), 155.

Table 10–1: Scripture Passages that Teach a Business Owner What to Value Most

Value	Biblical Citation	Potential Core Value Names	Opposite Core Value Names
Faith more than money	1 Peter 1:6–7	Faith in God	Faithlessness Disloyalty
God's commands more than money	Psalm 119:72; Proverbs 3:14, 8:10	Trust in God	Doubt Distrust
God's wisdom more than money	Proverbs 16:16, James 1:5–8; Ecclesiastes 4:13	Wisdom	Ignorance Thoughtlessness
God's kingdom more than wealth	Matthew 13:44–45	Eternal Perspective	Transient Temporary
Hard work over empty boasting	Proverbs 12:29;	Diligence	Sloth Laziness
Relationship with God over earthly relationships	Matthew 10:37	Stewardship	Carelessness Negligence
God's praise over man's praise	John 12:43	Humility	Pride Arrogance
Knowing Christ over achievement.	Philippians 3:4–20	Stewardship	Carelessness Negligence
Wisdom above all other desires	Proverbs 8:11	Wisdom	Ignorance Thoughtlessness
Obedience to God more than religious traditions	1 Samuel 15:22	Holiness	Wickedness
Being with God more than doing anything else	Psalm 84:10	Intimacy with God	Enmity
Fear the Lord over great wealth	Proverbs 15:16	Fear of the Lord	Pride Arrogance
Poor with loving relationships than to be rich with much hatred and strife	Proverbs 15:17	Honesty Integrity Authenticity	Lying Corruption Inauthentic Hypocritical

Value	Biblical Citation	Potential Core Value Names	Opposite Core Value Names
Poor with peace and quiet over wealth with strife	Proverbs 17:1; Ecclesiastes 4:6	Honest Peace	Strife Discord
Good name/good reputation more than wealth	Proverbs 22:1	Reputation	Ill Repute
Walk blamelessly and yet be poor than to be wealthy with perverse ways	Proverbs 28:6	Holiness	Wickedness
Contentment with what one has more than discontentment with what one does not have	Ecclesiastes 6:9	Contentment	Discontentment
Being killed than causing a follower of God to sin	Luke 17:2	Holiness Purity	Wickedness Impurity
Trust in God rather than trusting in man	Psalm 118:8–9	Trust in God	Trust in Man Trust in Self
Patience over a display of strength; self–control over domineering others	Proverbs 16:32; Ecclesiastes 9:16–18	Patience Self–Control	Impatient Impulsive
Diminishing oneself in the presence of the powerful than lifting up oneself in the presence of the powerful	Proverbs 25:6–7	Humility Respect	Pride Arrogance Disrespect
To not vow than to vow and not fulfil one's vow	Ecclesiastes 5:4–5	Reliable Prudent	Unreliable Imprudent
Listen to the rebuke of a friend more than the praise of those who do not know you.	Ecclesiastes 7:5	Teachable Coachable	Stubborn
Show proper respect rather than extravagant revelry.	Ecclesiastes 7:2	Respect Decorum	Disrespect Rudeness Impropriety

CBOs should ensure that at least some of these values given in the Bible are represented in the core values of the owner's business. At a minimum, opposite values should never be embraced. Moreover, a prudent CBO will use these values as a guide to interview potential candidates. Value-based interviewing aims to weed out candidates who look good and may be highly talented but will not support the organization's core values.[544]

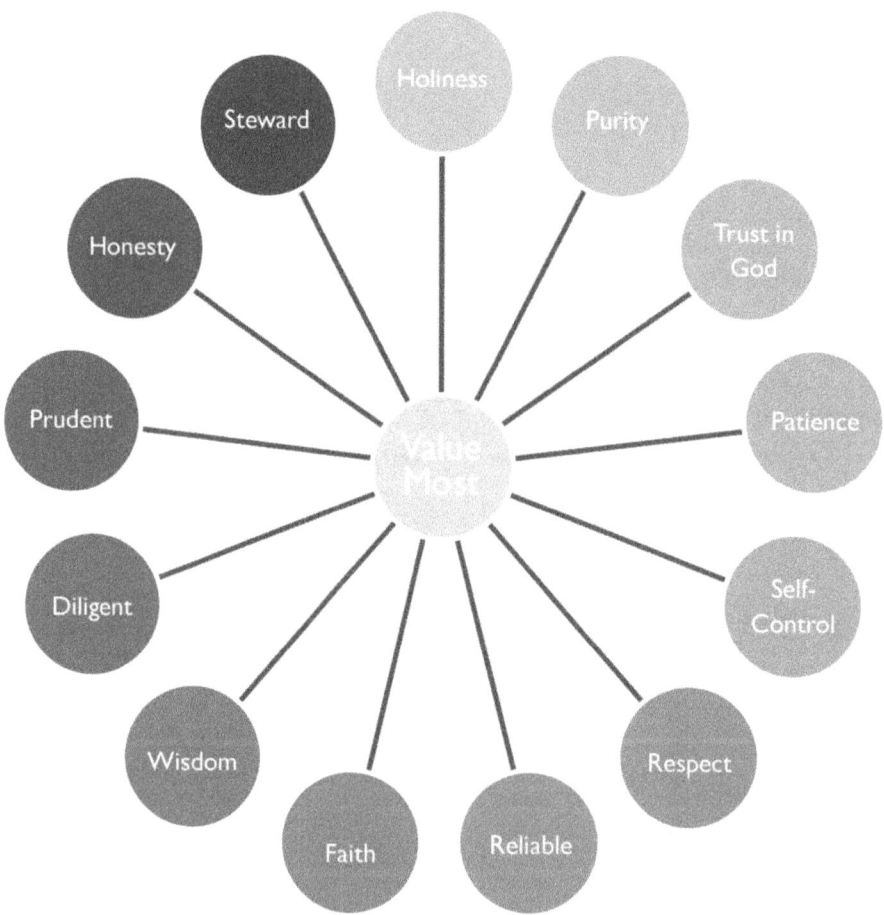

Figure 10–1 visually depicts what Christian business owners should value most.

A temptation to sin occurs when a CBO chooses core values to appease employees, stakeholders, market onlookers, or conventional wisdom. Selecting core values simply because the core value is the value *Du jour* makes a mockery of the values God has given to the CBO in the Scriptures. The values selected should be deeply nested in the owner's persona

---

544 Sam Miller, "Values–based recruitment in health care." *Nursing Standard.* 2015. 29(21):37–41.

and walk with God. Figure 10-1 visually depicts Table 10-1's essence by showing what the Scriptures say CBOs (and all Christians) should value most.

PURPOSE

This section is the second part of the larger discussion about a company's core ideology. We will discuss God's purposes for business, adopting a biblical worldview rather than accepting the conventional wisdom of American business thought leaders.

Conventional Wisdom

Milton Friedman is often credited (or blamed) for launching the shareholder–focused management orientation in corporate America.[545] Although others have argued that this hyper–focus on shareholders had more to do with an unprecedented wave of hostile takeovers and was sustained by a dramatic shift toward incentive–laden executive pay,[546] most have felt that Friedman's approach to the purpose of business was too profit and shareholder–focused.

There is a general lack of agreement among business academics and thought leaders on the macro purpose of business. General themes can be identified across authors. For example, Naert believes the purpose of business is to create "both economic and societal value."[547] Parikh believes the purpose of business is to further the welfare of others, use resources judiciously, and innovate to meet economic and social expectations.[548] For Zakaullah, preserving religion, life, reason, descendants, and property is the purpose of business.[549] Moll, interviewing Van Duzer, noted that the purpose of business is twofold: to provide goods and services and to provide meaningful and creative jobs.[550] In addition, Van Duzer wrote,

545 Milton Friedman, "The Social Responsibility of Business is to Increase Its Profits." *The New York Times Magazine*, September 13, 1970. https://www.nytimes.com/1970/09/13/
archives/a–friedman–doctrine–the–social–responsibility–of–business–is–to.html

546 Brian R. Cheffins, "Stop Blaming Milton Friedman!" *Washington University Law Review*. 2021. 98(6):1607–1644.

547 Philippe Naert, Dean Panel Response, "What is the Purpose of Business?" In: *The Purpose of Business: Contemporary Perspectives from Different Walks of Life*. Erisman, A. and Gautschi, D. (Eds.) (Palgrave MacMillan, 2015), 35.

548 Indira J. Parikh, ibid., 48.

549 Muhammad Zakaullah, "Business and Religion: Religious Perspectives on Business from Buddhism, Christianity, Judaism, and Islam." In: *The Purpose of Business: Contemporary Perspectives from Different Walks of Life*. Erisman, A. and Gautschi, D. (Eds.) (Palgrave MacMillan, 2015), 168–69.

550 Rob Moll and Jeff Van Duzer. "The Meaning of Business: Christians in the Marketplace, Says Jeff Van Duzer, Are Not Second–Class Citizens of the Kingdom." *Christianity Today*, 2011. 55(1):24–26.

The purpose of business is still to serve. It is to serve the community by providing goods and services that will enable the community to flourish. And it is to serve its employees by providing them with opportunities to express at least a portion of their God–given identity through meaningful and creative work.[551]

Fassin believes business is about money, power, achievement, and success.[552] Usually, some combination of profits and being good to others blend to form the conventional wisdom on the purpose of business.

Biblical View on the Purpose of Business

Van Duzer, due to his working within a Christian framework, goes further than others and ties his twin purposes for business to God's redemptive plan:

> Business must concern itself with redemptive as well as creative work … Those goods and services that enable a community to flourish will now often take on a redemptive quality. Rather than simply adding to a community's stockpile of available goods, Christians in business will need to look for opportunities where the service or product they provide may be used to heal or restore.[553]

Others who have considered God's purposes for business align with VanDuzer. For example, Vu asks,

> Is there a creational, redemptive view of business? … How about if we make the purpose of business to make communities flourish and to create opportunities for people to express their God–given capacities in meaningful ways?[554]

In addition, Grudem notes that no economic activity is presented in the Scriptures from an exclusively "earthly" perspective. Business, like every other human activity, has a spiritual aspect that needs our attention. Grudem notes:

---

551 Jeff Van Duzer, Why Business Matters to God: (and what still needs to be fixed). (InterVarsity Press, 2015), 97.

552 Yves Fassin, "The Reasons Behind Non–Ethical Behaviour in Business and Entrepreneurship." *Journal of Business Ethics*, 2005. 60(3):265–279.

553 Van Duzer, Why Business Matters, 113.

554 Andy Crouch, "Here's to the Misfits: How Silicon Valley Entrepreneurs Are Taking a Leap of Faith to Create Technology that Makes You More Human." *Christianity Today*, 2013. 57(1–10):44–49.

All economic activities—working, saving, spending, giving—are to be done while mindful of God and conscious of "spiritual" or "heavenly" rewards and punishments to be received sometimes in this life and sometimes in the life to come.[555]

Moreover, "people should produce goods and services for the benefit and enjoyment of mankind."[556] Claar and Klay support this dual foci on products and people by writing:

Because God continuously sustains and unfolds new potential in creation, the gift of human creativity is essential for society to thrive, especially in continuous change. In their exercise of stewardship, human beings are called to develop resources and apply their talents.[557]

In these various discussions on the purpose of business, one can discern themes of creativity, serving one's fellow man, and generally improving the lives of those in one's community. Surprisingly, no author that this researcher read connected the purpose of business to proper stewardship of that which God has entrusted to his stewards.

Perhaps this lack of connection between stewardship and the purpose of business is because of our self-imposed constructs of stewardship as an individual pursuit and business (generally speaking) as a corporate pursuit. Only when a business is viewed as a tool through which a Christian steward lives out the steward's role and responsibilities does the connection between the individual pursuit of stewardship and the corporate aspects of a business come into a connected focus. Hence, I suggest that God's purposes for business must be connected to the owner's stewardship role. God's purposes for business must emanate from his entrustment of economic activity to his stewards.

> Note: In this discussion, I will focus on business as an institution, not the purpose of any individual company. Individual purposes are usually expressed through mission or vision statements that define their purpose.

The order in which these five purposes are presented is arbitrary. No one purpose is more or less important than the other four. Figure 10–2 visually illustrates these five purposes.

---

555 Wayne Grudem, "Can an Economic System be Compatible with Scripture?" In: *Biblical Principles & Economics: The Foundations Volume 2*. Chewning, R. C. (Ed.) (NavPress. 1989), 29.

556 Grudem, *Economic System*, 31.

557 Victor Claar and Robin Klay, Economics in Christian Perspective: Theory, Policy and Life Choices. (InterVarsity Press. 2007), 27.

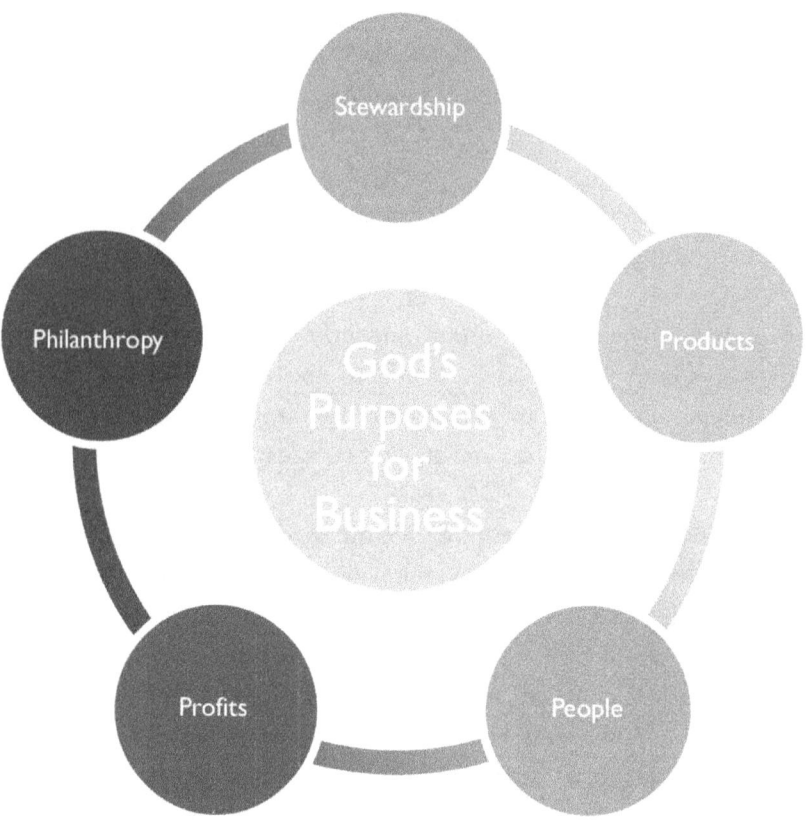

Figure 10–2: God's five purposes for business

Purpose #1: Stewardship

Business exists to provide the owner with an outlet to fulfill God's call on the owner's life to steward a company to the glory of God.

Every Christian is called to steward that which God entrusts to him. When God entrusts a business to an individual, that individual becomes a business owner and can pursue stewardship in a way consistent with God's call on the owner's life.

It seems odd to assert that God has a distinct call and purpose for a business owner yet does not have a purpose for the business which God has entrusted to the steward. One purpose of business is to provide a way to live out God's call to stewardship.

Purpose #2: Products

Business exists to provide a means to produce products and services that enable the community to flourish.[558]

"Flourish" combines the concepts of increase, health, and success. CBOs focus on producing products that contribute to the flourishing of their community. As stated more robustly, CBOs produce products and services that help the community increase and grow in health and wellness and contribute to the overall success of the owner's community. CBOs do not work toward the owner's success without helping others succeed.

Biblical Passages on Products

The Bible is not silent on the creation of products. While I could not find direct biblical instruction about this purpose, the Bible indirectly discusses this principle through narrative and stories. Upon reflection, a Bible student can conclude that in the Scriptures, talent put in the service of ungodly ends is condemned, and talent used to glorify God is commended.

For example, even though the artistry may be of high quality, when talent is used to service ungodly goals, that talent is condemned by God:

> [8] They are both stupid and foolish, instructed by worthless idols made of wood! [9] Beaten silver is brought from Tarshish, and gold from Uphaz from the hands of a goldsmith, the work of a craftsman. Their clothing is blue and purple,[559] all the work of skilled artisans. [10] But Yahweh is the true God; He is the living God and eternal King. The earth quakes at His wrath, and the nations cannot endure His rage. [11] You are to say this to them, "The gods that did not make the heavens and the earth will perish from the earth and from under these heavens." (Jeremiah 10:8–22 CSB).

The skills and abilities of the craftsmen who created these idols were positively evaluated as quality work: "all made by skilled workers." Yet, no amount of high–quality work could change the truth that these idols were impotent, worthless, empty, and vain, especially when

---

558 Van Duzer, *Business Matters*, 39.

559 Colors of royalty and divinity. Cf. Victor Matthews, Mark W. Chavalas, and John H. Walton, *The IVP Bible Background Commentary: Old Testament*. Electronic ed. (InterVarsity Press, 2000), np.

they were compared to God's majesty.[560] "Jehovah is the one only living and true God, and to set up any other in competition with Him is the greatest affront."[561] No amount of human effort can change this truth.

Just because the work output of a skilled worker is high quality does not mean it is valuable in the eyes of God. If the output leads people away from God, if the work product is not in alignment with God's character and moral will, if the work product displays a disdain for God, then no matter the quality or the skill that was used to create the product, it is a "worthless wooden idol." Habakkuk asks this insightful question (Habakkuk 2:18 NIV):

> Of what value is an idol carved by a craftsman? Or an image that teaches lies? For the one who makes it trusts in his own creation; he makes idols that cannot speak.[562]

The implied answer is negative. The Hebrew construction stresses the idols' lack of value in whatever way they were made.[563]

Because God gives people the talents and ability to create products, those whose work product is intended for an evil purpose bring God's condemnation to themselves. The product's intended use is in view here, not the quality of the craftsmanship.

Conversely, the Bible discusses high–quality products being used to glorify God. For example, real skill was needed to help rebuild the walls of Jerusalem:

> Then Moses said to the Israelites, "See, the Lord has chosen Bezalel son of Uri, the son of Hur, of the tribe of Judah, and he has filled him with the Spirit of God, with wisdom, with understanding, with knowledge and with all kinds of skills— to make artistic designs for work in gold, silver and bronze, to cut and set stones, to work in wood and to engage in all kinds of artistic crafts. And he has given both him and Oholiab, son of Ahisamak and of the tribe of Dan, the ability to teach others. He has filled them with the skill to do all kinds of work as engravers, designers, embroiderers in blue, purple, scarlet yarn, fine linen, and weavers—all of them skilled workers and designers. So Bezalel, Oholiab and every skilled person to whom the Lord has given skill and ability to carry out all the

---

560 Tremper Longman, III, *Isaiah Thru Ezekiel*. Vol. 6. Layman's Bible Commentary. (Barbour Publishing, 2013), 83.

561 Keith Brooks, Summarized Bible: Complete Summary of the Old Testament (Logos Bible Software, 2009), 169.

562 "cannot speak:" "literally, *dumb nothings*." Frederick Carl Eiselen, *The Minor Prophets*. Vol. IX. Commentary on the Old Testament. (Jennings & Graham; Eaton & Mains, 1907), 493.

563 Richard D. Patterson and Andrew E. Hill, *Cornerstone Biblical Commentary, Vol 10: Minor Prophets, Hosea–Malachi*. (Tyndale House, 2008), 424.

work of constructing the sanctuary are to do the work just as the Lord has commanded. (Exodus 35:30–36:1 NIV)

There are three themes running through this passage. First, this was the Lord's work and no one else's. This work was being accomplished through the skills he had given (35:31–35; 36:1–2). Secondly, the work was done by many different people who had been specifically chosen and gifted by the Lord, who in turn were able to empower other people as well. And thirdly, everyone had something to contribute, if not to the project, then certainly to the Lord.[564]

Driver reminds us that "in the OT, [the Holy Spirit was regarded] as the source of any *exceptional* power or activity of man, as well as of supernatural spiritual gifts.[565] The workers were given wisdom, knowledge, and understanding about their skills and the materials with which they were working. The Spirit of God was "on" the workers, working through their skills to release unusual creativity and excellence in a work product that glorified God.

This story teaches that *any* work (that is not sin) can be performed under the anointing of God (1 Corinthians 10:13). The dichotomy created between clergy and laity over the last two thousand years must be diffused in favor of concluding that all work is ministry for the Christian.[566] The Bible does not differentiate between some works that are holy and others that are secular. All work can be either—it depends on the individual performing the work, the intended use of the work product, and the individual's relationship with God.

Work products can be restorative in nature or destructive in nature. The Bible commends work products that restore people to a right relationship with each other and with God. Any business owner's work can be restorative and draw people to God.

Considerations on Producing Products

How should a CBO apply what has been presented? What follows here are several practical applications.

When producing a product, keep the customer's best interests in mind. Two passages will highlight this principle. The first is James 4.17 (CSB), which says, "It is a sin for the person who knows to do what is good and doesn't do it." Consider also Philippians 2:4 (CSB): "Everyone should look out not only for his own interests, but also for the interests of others."

---

564 Allen Ross and John N. Oswalt, *Cornerstone Biblical Commentary: Genesis, Exodus*, vol. 1 (Tyndale House, 2008), 545.

565 S. R. Driver, *The Book of Exodus in the Revised Version with Introduction and Notes*, The Cambridge Bible for Schools and Colleges (Cambridge University Press, 1911), 342.

566 Charles H. Spurgeon, "Sympathy and Song." In *The Metropolitan Tabernacle Pulpit Sermons*. (Passmore & Alabaster, 1916), 62:289–300.

Understanding your customers' needs and the needs of those who live or work with them is a hallmark of a CBO who is interested in being good to others. Understanding how all the moving parts affect each other and having the emotional intelligence to put oneself in the other's shoes to experience (to some degree) what they experience provides a vital context for looking out for other's interests.

In addition, products should bring healing or restoration to broken situations when possible. This consideration goes to the concept of health. Van Duzer writes:

> Rather than simply adding to a community's stockpile of available goods, Christians in business will need to look for opportunities where the service or product they provide may be used to heal or restore. In other words, a business should seek to serve its community by providing not only additive products but also products that reach back and help to redeem broken situations. For example, a business could provide services to help clean up polluted waterways and toxic dumps. It could provide aesthetically pleasing designs for urban renewal projects. It could produce vaccines for diseases that are decimating communities, make available Internet access to economically oppressed communities or publish books that will increase understanding between tween communities torn apart by racial hatred, and so on.[567]

So, we do not shy away from creating restorative products. Restorative products and services always have the other's best interests in mind.

A product whose use injures or destroys relationships does not enable the community to flourish. For example, offering a service that encourages financial infidelity, such as gambling or get–rich–quick schemes, is an example of a product that destroys relationships. Another example is lawyers who encourage lawsuits to earn an income. Businesses that encourage marital infidelity fall into this consideration, too.

A product sold without sharing needed information enables one party to win at the expense of another does not enable the community to flourish. Healthy economic transactions are fully voluntary and meet the needs and interests of both parties. This consideration means the seller discloses enough information to make the transaction voluntary. In addition, we do not use deception in our negotiations. Voluntary transactions must have a proper disclosure of truthful information flowing both ways.

A product with addictive qualities such that your customers become dependent and keep purchasing your product is not a product that will allow the community to flourish. Products with an addictive quality enslave your customers into an unhealthy,

---

567 Van Duzer, *Business Matters*, 114.

involuntary relationship with your company. This consideration can be applied to a wide range of products, such as gambling or prescription drugs. However, this consideration can also be applied to food additives, alcohol, and other products that (essentially) cause a person to want that product repeatedly, to their detriment. CBOs pay attention to their products' effects and understand how customers use those products and they take action when needed.

Purpose #3: People

Business enables individuals to develop and express their God-given creativities and passions.

Every business needs people to perform all sorts of tasks. So, investing in employees is essential to building the business and making it profitable. Treating people well brings Christ to the marketplace. Helping one's employees be the best they can be will demonstrate God's heart.

Biblical Passages on Being an Employer

The Scriptures have much to say to employers. This section will outline what the Bible says about being an employer. Employers have significant obligations to employees. When owners fulfill their obligations to employees, God is glorified, and the owner is fulfilling his stewardship role to the Lord.

Be fair to one's employees. Job 31:13–15 (LEB) defended himself by saying:

> [13] "If I have rejected my male or female slave's case when their complaint *was* against me, [14] then what shall I do when God rises up? And when he enquires, how shall I answer him? [15] Did not he *who* made me in the womb make them? And did not one fashion us in the womb?

Also, consider how Job defended himself in 31:38–40 (LEB):

> [38] If my land has cried out against me, and its furrows have wept together, [39] if I have eaten its yield without payment, or I have caused *the* breath of its owners to die, [40] let thorns grow in place of wheat and noxious weeds in place of barley."

Job knows he can sin by A) denying justice to his employees, B) demoralizing his employees, or C) not paying them their full wages on time. These three temptations are called out by Job as sin. He knows God will ask him about this, so he discerns a connection between his actions as an employer and God watching his behavior. This passage applies to business owners today. God is watching each owner's behavior. We should consider the day when God calls us each to account for our stewardship of his business.

In addition, Job states a theological truth: the employer and employee are equally valuable to God because both are made in God's image (Ephesians 6:9). Gender, race, or economic status—none of these demographics creates inequality before God. Biblical Christians do not divide over that which is sacred: gender, ethnicity, economic entrustments, or individual talents. Instead, CBOs find the hand of God in the other's persona and celebrate God's goodness to them.

Fairness before God between employer and employer is mentioned in the New Testament:

> Masters, grant your slaves justice and fairness, knowing that you also have
> a master in heaven. (Colossians 4:1 LEB).

Our master in heaven (God) has been more than fair with us. So, in our stewardship role, we should reflect God's fairness by being fair to our employees. Fairness is difficult to define and is clearly a flexible concept. Cultural values, in part, will determine what is fair. But in the long run, it is "Christ who is the ultimate arbitrator of whether some action is just and fair,"[568] and the Lord is unconditionally righteous and fair.[569]

Part of treating an employee fairly is to avoid threats directed toward employees:

> And masters, treat your slaves the same way, without threatening them,
> because you know that both their Master and yours is in heaven, and
> there is no favoritism with Him. (Ephesians 6:9 CSB)

Christian owners refrain from threatening employees because they recognize that both the owner and the employee are equal before God. Business owners should not misuse their authority by issuing punishment threats. Threats are a weapon that the powerful wield over the powerless. A relationship based on threats is not a Christian relationship at all.[570] So,

---

568 Harold W. Hoehner, Philip W. Comfort, and Peter H. Davids, *Cornerstone Biblical Commentary: Ephesians, Philippians, Colossians, 1&2 Thessalonians, Philemon.*, vol. 16 (Tyndale House, 2008), 293.

569 Gustav Stählin. "Ἴσος, Ἰσότης, Ἰσότιμος." In *Theological Dictionary of the New Testament*, edited by Gerhard Kittel, Geoffrey W. Bromiley, and Gerhard Friedrich. (Eerdmans, 1964), 3:343–55

570 John R. W. Stott, *God's New Society: The Message of Ephesians*, The Bible Speaks Today (InterVarsity Press, 1979), 254.

Christian business owners avoid using threats. Besides, employees who are believers have a real defender who will protect them should we, the owners, get out of line.[571]

To summarise, fairness means:

- Paying full compensation on time
- Ensuring justice is enforced for your employees
- Accepting and dealing fairly with employee grievances against you, the owner
- Make sure that you do not demoralize your employees

Never Defraud Your Employees. This consideration is similar to the previous consideration of being fair to one's employees, but it has a more narrow focus on the fraudulent activity of wrongly withholding compensation due to one's employees.

> Do not defraud or rob your neighbor. Do not hold back the wages of a hired worker overnight. You shall not oppress your neighbor or rob him. The wages of a hired servant shall not remain with you all night until the morning" (Leviticus 19:13 NIV).

> Now to the one who works, his wages are not counted as a gift but as his due" (Romans 4:4 NIV).

It is good that we accrue unpaid wage liabilities on the balance sheet. Such accrual reflects God's heart. Wages are not charity but a liability for the employer (Deuteronomy 24:14, Proverbs 11:16). Because a business owner cannot have a payroll liability to the owner's self, business owners pay themselves last, not first. The owner has no moral obligation to pay herself. And while an argument from silence, I find it interesting that the Bible never portrays masters as getting paid before their workers.

Do Not Exploit Your Employees. Exploitation occurs when employers use their power to extract more value from their workers than is given in compensation, creating a situation in which the workers are unfairly paid and oppressed. There is also the element of a power imbalance. The employees accept less than fair compensation because they have little choice in agreeing to the terms of employment. The Bible compares employers who oppress employees by not paying wages that are due to those who have sexual affairs, engage in sorcery, are mean to the powerless, and do not fear God:

> Then I will draw near to you for judgment. I will be a swift witness against the sorcerers, against the adulterers, against those who swear falsely,

---

571 William Hendriksen and Simon J. Kistemaker, *Exposition of Ephesians*. Vol. 7. New Testament Commentary. (Baker Books, 1953–2001), 265.

against those who oppress the hired worker in his wages, the widow and the fatherless, against those who thrust aside the sojourner, and do not fear me, says the Lord of hosts" (Malachi 3:5 ESV).

These groups are not good company to keep. Christian business owners should be aware of the severity of not being fair with employee wages.

Considerations on Employment and Wages

There are several principles to consider regarding not exploiting one's employees. First, there exists a market rate for competent work. Christians who employ others should strive to pay market rates, even if the power imbalance with an employee might allow you, the owner, to negotiate the employee's labor at a less–than–market rate. A Christian business owner's standard is not how cheaply the rate is at which the owner can hire good talent. Instead, the standard is how best we can use our inherent power as an employer to be fair with each employee's compensation.

Many employers—even Christian employers—view compensation through a legal lens. However, CBOs should be far more concerned about what God thinks than what a judge might think. Regardless of the legal options available to the owner, the owner should first be concerned with obeying God by not exploiting employees.

Secondly, the Scriptures do not differentiate between for–profit and nonprofit entities. There is no concept of a corporation in the Bible and no concept of a non–profit entity. So, the for–profit/non–profit nuance is irrelevant regarding compensation. Fairness in compensation applies to ministry work, too. Church boards are put on notice. Scripture does not justify paying pastors less simply because they are in full–time vocational ministry. *When church members enrich themselves by not giving their whole tithe and then ask their pastors to work for less compensation than they, themselves, would accept for employment, this is hypocrisy and a form of oppression, exploitation, and stealing* (1 Timothy 5.17).

Third, the Scriptures do not differentiate race, gender, or pedigree. It is a sin to pay different wages to different people for the same work output and quality simply because they have a different skin tone, different X/Y chromosomes, or come from a lower or higher class in society. CBOs do not do this.

Purpose #4: Profits

Businesses exist to create profits.

Profits provide sustainability and allow the owner to fulfill the other four business purposes. A variation of profits can be a good indicator of excesses in the other four purposes. Profits will suffer if one of the other purposes gets out of balance. When profits suffer, the owner should see if another purpose is being over– or under–emphasized.

Profits in the Parable of Five Talents in Matthew 25:14–30

The Scriptures have much to say about economic profits. God expects a financial return on his economic–based entrustments to us. The parable of the five talents from Matthew 25:14–30 is helpful to us for understanding how God views profits. I rely on this parable because it is difficult to properly exegete the text and yet allegorize the profits mainly to spiritual gifts. I believe a more plain reading makes more sense and creates fewer questions.[572]

The master gives his servants real money. The faithful servants used that money to create more financial wealth. The newly created wealth was given back to the master. The master rewarded his faithful servants with more of his presence and management responsibilities (this latter point is emphasized more in Luke's account of this parable (Luke 19:11–26)).

The overall focus of the parable is faithfulness.[573] The amount of wealth both faithful servants created was less important than their faithfulness to generate wealth with what the master had given them. For a business owner entrusted with the ability to create wealth, not making a profit is an abdication of that owner's stewardship responsibility, while creating profit is living out God's entrustment to the owner.

While an argument from silence, this parable illustrates that profits are a renewable resource. The master assumed the servants could create more profit and trusted the servants to do this. Any argument about economics that assumes a fixed pie—a zero-sum game—is inconsistent with Scripture. Profits have always been renewable, given suitable political and economic systems.

It is biblical to hold to the notion that profits are good when earned legally and ethically. Profits are a social, economic, and spiritual good. CBOs should not be ashamed to run profitable businesses. Without the wealth–creating engine of business, nonprofit entities would not exist. All non–profit organizations are supported, ultimately, by profitable companies. Non–profit corporations are not strengthened when for–profit businesses are injured.

More Biblical Teaching on Profits

Several familiar stories in the Bible could not have occurred without the presence of profit. For example, the story of the good Samaritan (Luke 10:30–37) could not have happened

---

572 Donald A. Carson, "Matthew." In: *The Expositor's Bible Commentary: Matthew, Mark, Luke.* F. E. Gaebelein (Ed.) (Zondervan Publishing, 1984), 516.

573 Michael Green, *The Message of Matthew: The Kingdom of Heaven.* (InterVarsity Press, 2001), 261.

without the Samaritan's financial ability to pay for the wounded man's care. At some point in Samaritan's life, a profitable business existed.

Recall Boaz in the book of Ruth. Boaz was a man of means, employing servants and owning fields from which his servants harvested. Boaz purchased from Naomi all the property of Elimelek, Kilion, and Mahlon, and in the transaction, acquired Run, Mahlon's widow (Ruth 4:1–12). Boaz had the financial ability to make these purchases. Boaz had margin. Having profit and savings enabled Boaz to fulfill his duties.

Another example is Joanna and Susanna in Luke 8:1–3. Joanna and Susanna financially supported the ministry of Christ. These funds may have come from savings. These women may have scaled back personal spending to give more to Christ's ministry, but either way, Joanna and Susanna had access to funds, and at least a portion of those funds were used to support Christ's ministry. Those funds, at some point, must have come from a profitable business, though, with Joanna's husband being the household manager for Herod, some of the funds may have come from a large salary earned by Chuza.

Profits are a result of hard work. The first two stewards in the parable of the five talents (Appendix G) worked effectively to create profit. But they are not alone. The connection between work and profit is taught in at least two passages: Proverbs 14:23 (ESV) and 21:5 (NIV):

> In all toil there is profit, but mere talk tends only to poverty. (14:23)

> The plans of the diligent lead to profit as surely as haste leads to poverty. (21:5)

These two verses in Proverbs teach that diligent work is needed to achieve economic profit. Creating profits will require hard work. And the hard work will need to be committed over a sustained period. Profits come to those who persist in hard work.

Get–rich–quick (GRQ) opportunities are not in view here. The whole idea of a GRQ is that one can become rich without working hard. GRQ's are a lazy man's way to wealth. The Scriptures never condone GRQ schemes and they condemn laziness.

Hard work and laziness are inimical to each other. Laziness produces salt without savor (Matthew 5:13) and makes it hard to find salvation (Matthew 7:14).[574] Laziness is associated with wickedness engaged by an unprofitable servant. Genius has been conquered by this sin and laziness only produces mediocrity. The life of Christ is a non–verbal rebuke of laziness, given how hard he worked for three years to bring good

---

574   W. B. Frankland, "Indolence." In *A Dictionary of Christ and the Gospels: Aaron–Zion*, edited by James Hastings. (T&T Clark; Charles Scribner's Sons, 1906.), 822.

news to the masses and train his disciples to get them ready to establish the church.[575] Laziness—a staple of an American view of retirement—should never be characteristic of a Christian business owner.

Profits are sometimes withheld as a result of sin. This principle is best illustrated in Haggai 1:1–10 (NIV):

> In the second year of King Darius, on the first day of the sixth month, the word of the Lord came through the prophet Haggai to Zerubbabel son of Shealtiel, governor of Judah, and to Joshua son of Jozadak, the high priest. This is what the Lord Almighty says. "These people say, 'The time has not yet come to rebuild the Lord's house.' Then the word of the Lord came through the prophet Haggai. "Is it a time for you yourselves to be living in your panelled houses, while this house remains a ruin?" Now this is what the Lord Almighty says. "Give careful thought to your ways. You have planted much but harvested little. You eat, but never have enough. You drink, but never have your fill. You put on clothes but are not warm. You earn wages, only to put them in a purse with holes in it." This is what the Lord Almighty says. "Give careful thought to your ways. Go up into the mountains and bring down timber and build my house, so that I may take pleasure in it and be honoured," says the Lord. "You expected much, but see, it turned out to be little. What you brought home, I blew away. Why?" declares the Lord Almighty. "Because of my house, which remains a ruin, while each of you is busy with your own house. Therefore, because of you the heavens have withheld their dew and the earth its crops. I called for a drought on the fields and the mountains, on the grain, the new wine, the olive oil and everything else the ground produces, on people and livestock, and on all the labor of your hands."

Human flourishing generally occurs when we honor God and follow His commands. Their obvious lack of flourishing was a result of their disobedience.[576] They have planted, but not harvested. They have eaten, but were not satisfied. They have drunk liquids, but are still thirsty. They have clothes, but are not warm. They have produced wealth, but have no money to show for their efforts. "All these figures speak of the hardship that befalls

---

575 John Legge, "Slothfulness." In *A Dictionary of Christ and the Gospels: Aaron–Zion*, edited by James Hastings. (T&T Clark; Charles Scribner's Sons, 1906), 642–43.

576 Micah Fries, Stephen Rummage, and Robby Gallaty, *Exalting Jesus in Zephaniah, Haggai, Zechariah, and Malachi*, ed. David Platt, Daniel L. Akin, and Tony Merida, Christ–Centered Exposition Commentary (Holman Reference, 2015), 51.

people who have not included the Lord in their plans and who are preoccupied with their own interests."[577]

This Haggai passage illustrates the Biblical principle that God may withhold wealth when sin is present in the believer's life. When CBOs put God's agenda, wants, and desires behind their own, they may see themselves generate much profit only to find they do not have enough money to meet their expenses.

Profits created through wickedness and oppression do not last. Consider Job 20.12–23 (ESV),

> [12] Though evil is sweet in his mouth, though he hides it under his tongue, [13] though he is loath to let it go and holds it in his mouth, [14] yet his food is turned in his stomach; it is the venom of cobras within him. [15] He swallows down riches and vomits them up again; God casts them out of his belly. [16] He will suck the poison of cobras; the tongue of a viper will kill him. [17] He will not look upon the rivers, the streams flowing with honey and curds. [18] He will give back the fruit of his toil and will not swallow it down; from the profit of his trading he will get no enjoyment. [19] For he has crushed and abandoned the poor; he has seized a house that he did not build. [20] "Because he knew no contentment in his belly, he will not let anything in which he delights escape him. [21] There was nothing left after he had eaten; therefore his prosperity will not endure. [22] In the fullness of his sufficiency he will be in distress; the hand of everyone in misery will come against him. [23] To fill his belly to the full, God will send his burning anger against him and rain it upon him into his body."

The wicked man enjoys sin for as long as possible, "getting out of it everything he can."[578] But once wickedness is fully accounted for in an individual's life ("yet his food is turned in his stomach"), that initial sweetness becomes bitter and perhaps even poisonous.

For CBOs, such wickedness will cause the owner to give back what the owner has attained. Why? Because the owner has oppressed the poor ("he has crushed and abandoned the poor"). The owner has left the poor destitute and wrongfully taken the homes of the poor. Because the owner's greed knew no rest, the owner would not retain or save anything he desired ("vomits them up again"). The owner will continually be discontented, empty, and full of cravings that can never be satisfied. Reyburn writes:

---

577   Robert L. Alden, "Haggai," in *The Expositor's Bible Commentary: Daniel and the Minor Prophets*, ed. Frank E. Gaebelein, vol. 7 (Zondervan Publishing House, 1986), 581.

578   William David Reyburn, *A Handbook on the Book of Job*. (United Bible Societies, 1992), 375.

This line is idiomatic; "to know no quietness in the belly" is the equivalent of saying "his insides are never at ease," that is, "he is always gluttonous, greedy, piggish." This line may be rendered, for example, "his appetite is never satisfied," "He can never get enough," or "He always wants more than he gets."[579]

When Christians avoid profits that were attained through oppressive ends, Christians prosper. Proverbs 28:16 (ESV) says:

A ruler who lacks understanding is a cruel oppressor, but he who hates unjust gain will prolong his days.

Isaiah 33:15–16 (ESV) says:

He who walks righteously and speaks uprightly, who despises the gain of oppressions, who shakes his hands, lest they hold a bribe, who stops his ears from hearing of bloodshed and shuts his eyes from looking on evil, he will dwell on the heights; his place of defense will be the fortresses of rocks; his bread will be given him; his water will be sure.

Those with a visceral disdain for profits gained unjustly and who keep from doing so will endure, be secure, and be resourced well by God.

Using religion to create personal wealth is an abomination in the sight of God. The commercialization of Christianity can be quite profitable. Christian businesses in media, trinkets, and swag (sometimes called "Jesus Junk"[580]), music, cards, and books can be highly profitable.[581] Those who use godliness as a means to financial gain are false teachers and should be called out as such (Philippians 1:12–18).[582]

---

579   Reyburn, *Handbook,* 380.

580   Jason Janz, "Jesus Junk." August 24, 2006. Sharperiron.org. https://sharperiron.org/article/jesus–junk.

581   Tim Stafford, Surprised by Jesus: His Agenda for Changing Everything in A.D. 30 and Today. (IVP Books, 2006), 160.

582   Robert Black and Ronald McClung, *1 & 2 Timothy, Titus, Philemon: A Commentary for Bible Students.* (Wesleyan Publishing House, 2004), 115–16.

An example of using faith to create business profit and how abhorrent it is to God for us to conduct business (and predatory business no less) in his sacred space[583] is found in John 2:12–16 (LEB):[584]

> [12] After this he went down to Capernaum, and his mother and brothers and his disciples, and they stayed there a few days. [13] And the Passover of the Jews was near, and Jesus went up to Jerusalem. [14] And he found in the temple *courts* those who were selling oxen and sheep and doves, and the money changers seated. [15] And he made a whip of cords *and* drove *them* all out of the temple *courts*, both the sheep and the oxen, and he poured out the coins of the money changers and overturned their tables. [16] And to the ones selling the doves he said, "Take these *things* away from here! Do not make my Father's house a marketplace!

Remember that Israel was still under the Old Testament sacrificial system when Christ walked on this earth. However, the system has become dependent on commercial business to make it easier for the laity to bring an appropriate sacrifice at the temple.

This story occurs during Passover, so the crowds were inflated much like those at a state fair or a sporting event. Many had come from long distances and needed to purchase their animal(s) to participate in the rituals so common to their faith. Because there was no common currency, money changers—similar to what we find in ports of entry and exit—were exchanging foreign currencies into the local currency (Tyrian silver) acceptable to the Jewish leadership to pay the temple tax.[585]

The outer court—the court of the Gentiles—had been turned into what must have resembled a stockyard,[586] though there were stalls and small buildings outside

---

583 For the most part, the concept of sacred space is foreign to present day Christians, but it was well known to 1st century Jews. Sacred space is where God dwells, so if you're a 1st century Jew, you understand that you do not casually enter God's space. You must be accepted by God and enter with a seriousness and awe befitting entrance into God's space. You must be both ritually and morally pure to enter his space. "The Jerusalem temple was the locus of God's special presence among his people. It was a symbol of God's choice of the Jewish people as his own, and its priests were the official representatives mediating God's presence to the people." (Tim Wardle, "Place: Holy (Earliest Written Evidence)." In *The Eerdmans Encyclopedia of Early Christian Art and Archaeology*, edited by Paul Corby Finney, (Eerdmans Publishing, 2017), 2:340–41. To learn more about sacred spaces, listen to Michael Heiser's podcast, "Introducing Leviticus." August 21, 2015, nakedbiblepodcast.com. https://nakedbiblepodcast.com/podcast/naked–bible–63–introducing–leviticus/.

584 A temple cleansing occurs a second time in Matthew 21:12 (also recorded in Mark 11:17).

585 Grant R. Osborne, *John: Verse by Verse.* Edited by Jeffrey Reimer, Elliot Ritzema, Danielle Thevenaz, and Rebecca Brant. Osborne New Testament Commentaries. (Lexham Press, 2018), 67.

586 William Hendriksen and Simon J. Kistemaker, *Exposition of the Gospel According to John.* Vol. 1–2. New Testament Commentary. (Baker Books, 1953–2001), 122.

the temple that were typically used to buy and sell animals.[587] Because of the outsized demand for animals, the stalls and tables had spilled into the Court of the Gentiles—a sacred space.

In this story, John presents the main problem of conducting business in the temple's sacred space.[588] In the second occurrence,[589] Christ calls out the predatory motivations of the vendors ("cave of robbers" (Matthew 21:13 LEB)). Not only were predatory prices charged for animals to those who have traveled long distances, but the money changers were charging predatory service fees to exchange foreign currencies for the local currency acceptable to the Jewish leadership.

Across both stories, we learn that God is offended by business being conducted in sacred space (his space) and is doubly offended by price gouging and selfishness of the vendors that prey on the vulnerable. The temple had been defiled,[590] and Jesus drove them out of the temple not only because of their unethical and sinful practices but also because of their defiling presence.[591]

I cannot find any place in the Scriptures where those who make a profit from the beliefs and symbols of Christianity sin. But as in all aspects of business, when their greed exceeds their pursuit of God's kingdom (Matthew 6:33), their love for God (Deuteronomy 6:4–6), and their faithfulness to God through stewardship, then they sin. Our worship of God must be pure and undefiled by greed and hypocrisy. I think Stafford sums this up well:

> I do not mean to suggest that people do wrong to make a profit. Even if people grow rich practicing ministry, I am not sure they sin. They do wrong when greed rises above the righteousness of the kingdom of God. Some of them publish books or develop seminars that pander to the Christian market. They know what people want to hear, and they provide it. Some are frankly cynical about the calculations of what will sell. Woe to them! Woe to publishers who are most concerned to catch a publishing trend. Woe to writers whose sales figures are their greatest source of delight. Woe to speakers who command such high fees that they never experience the grit of ordinary church life. Woe to Christian businesses that measure success by the bottom line. Nothing does more damage to God's kingdom in America than this commercialism. Can anyone imagine Jesus living

---

587 Urban C. von Wahlde, *The Gospel and Letters of John: Commentary on the Gospel of John*. Vol. 2. The Eerdmans Critical Commentary. (Eerdmans Publishing, 2010), 99.

588 Wahlde, *John*, 100.

589 Osborne, *John*, 68.

590 Osborne, *John*, 68.

591 Leon Morris, *The Gospel according to John*. The New International Commentary on the New Testament. (Eerdmans Publishing, 1995), 172.

this way? Greedy religion does not walk in Jesus' steps, and it undercuts those believers who seek to do so.[592]

Moving on, there are other examples of greed and hypocrisy revealed as people try to use religion to turn a profit. For instance, in Numbers 22:16–17, Balaam is allowed to get rich by placing a curse on Balak's enemies. This phenomenon is equivalent to using a religious position to create profit. The same temptation to get rich was offered to Peter and John in Acts 8:18–24 when Simon sees the positive effects in others who have received the Holy Spirit and thinks he can buy that ability to give the Holy Spirit to others.

In 1 Samuel 2:12–17, Eli's sons (considered the heirs apparent of Eli's priesthood) extorted money from the offerings people brought to the temple. The result was death in the 1 Samuel and the Acts 8 story. Eli's sons did not repent in 1 Samuel, and God put them to death in battle (1 Samuel 4:11). Ironically, Eli also died the same day—God put an end to Eli's dynasty because of the sin of Eli's sons.

God detests the use of religion for personal gain when that gain is grounded in greed and hypocrisy. It is an abomination to him. When religious leaders personally profit from the money entrusted to their ministry, these leaders are sinning and, frankly, should not be in ministry.

However a business owner does not sin by engaging in profitable business when the products or services are the beliefs or symbols of Christianity. However, the owner must know how close to the line the owner lives. The owner should be constantly aware of how quickly and subtly greed and hypocrisy can enter his heart. Owners who traffic at the intersection of profits and religion should err on either holding down profits through lower pricing or being more philanthropic than usual. If a business turns out to be highly profitable, purposeful self–denial is a good response.

I cannot point to chapter and verse, but my sense from the Spirit, as I write this, is that greed to make a profit when trafficking in the beliefs and symbols of Christianity is more abhorrent to God than plain old greed for wealth and money. God's purposes for business do not change when applied to a business that profits from religion, but I think a stricter judgment awaits that owner in the afterlife.

It is not a sin to be wealthy. Many forefathers of the Christian faith were wealthy, and one will search the Scriptures in vain to find a condemnation for their wealth. For example, Job, considered one of the most wealthy then, followed God closely. He is never condemned for being rich. The mere possession of wealth is never condemned in the Bible. While this is an argument from silence, it remains a strong argument.

Profits never last. Earlier, I noted that profits are a result of hard work. Over the years, I have witnessed significant profits melt away because the owner became incrementally

---

592 Stafford, *Surprised by Jesus*, 160.

more and more lazy or entrusted the business to a person who could not continue to create more profits. Just because a company has been profitable for years does not mean it will be profitable automatically moving forward.

Wealth created from profits is never to be trusted for one's security. A CBO's financial security is always grounded in the CBO's covenant relationship with God. One's security is based on God's promises to provide for the needs of God's followers.

Purpose #5: Philanthropy

A business's purpose is to give business owners unique opportunities to be financially generous toward God.[593]

The conventional wisdom on why people are generous focuses on the more psychologically mature element of compassion,[594] where the giver has the capacity and desire to walk in another's shoes and give because the donor understands the connections between all the moving parts. In addition, the giver has grown in maturity to the point of giving out of her beliefs and conclusions about life.[595] Other motivations toward generosity include tax breaks, sheer altruism, and what economists call "image motivation"—giving makes the donor look good to those whose opinions they care about.[596]

For the Biblical steward, philanthropy is engaged because God has been generous with us (John 3:16). In turn, we are generous to those in need. Christ reminds us of this truth in Matthew 5:42, where we are instructed to give to the one who asks for something from us.

CBOs view philanthropy through a covenant worldview rather than a tax–treatment strategy coupled with social benefits. Recall that covenants are inherently life–giving and relationship–forming. When CBOs are generous by giving to those in need, they mirror, in a small way, the generosity of God toward themselves.

If every regular attender and member of Christian churches would *tithe*, then not only would every congregation be free of financial worries, but their salt and light (Matthew

---

593 I preached a four–part sermon series on generosity at my local church. Those sermons are now published in a short book, *The Transformative Power of Generosity Toward God.* (Bible and Business, 2023.) https://www.bibleandbusiness.com.

594 Lake Institute on Faith and Giving, *The Generosity Equation: Donors, Faith & Avenues to Giving.* Lake Institute on Faith and Giving Lecture Series. June 19, 2019. https://lakeinstitute.org/resource–library/why–the–generations–approach–generosity–differently/

595 Jennifer Jones, "Beyond Generosity: The Action Logics in Philanthropy." (PhD Diss., University of San Diego, 2015), 313–19.

596 The Economist, "Looking good by doing good: Why are people so generous." The Economist, 2009. 390:76.

5.13) influence would be much greater in this lost and broken world. They could feed and house the poor. They could walk with those who lost their jobs. They could be more effective at building ministries that are sorely needed. Pastors could be paid at an average of what their elder boards earn, and we would have less pastoral attrition due to financial stress.

However, in most churches, most attendees never give one penny to support their church ministries.[597] If every Christian tithed 10 percent of their income, faith–based organizations would have an extra $139 *billion* each year.[598] Divide that by roughly 400,000 churches in America, and this would mean an average of $347,500 of additional funds per church per year to support and extend their ministries. Our influence would broaden, and those who oppose us would need to stand back and admit that we are living out our faith.

But we do not give. We spend our money elsewhere, demonstrating that we love worldly things more than God (Matthew 6:19–21). So the world around us shrugs their shoulders and moves on. Nothing to see here. I believe R.T. Kendall is correct when he writes:

> The world is unimpressed with the church because the church has not commanded the world's attention and respect … Why should they, when we don't respect God – or his ways? We show how much we care by how much we give. If [our faith] has not touched our checkbooks, then Voltaire got it right when he said: "When it is a question of money, everybody is of the same religion." [599]

Jesus said:

> Whoever can be trusted with very little can also be trusted with much, and whoever is dishonest with very little will also be dishonest with much. So if you have not been trustworthy in handling worldly wealth, who will trust you with true riches? And if you have not been trustworthy with someone else's property, who will give you property of your own? No one can serve two masters. Either you will hate the one and love the other, or you will be devoted to the one and despise the other. You cannot serve both God and money. (Luke 16:10–13 NIV)

It is sheer folly to attempt to draw closer to God if you bypass "the least" of giving and generosity. This phenomenon is why teaching the unambiguous biblical principles of stewardship

---

597 Churchtrac, "The State of Church Giving: Trends and Statistics (2024)." Accessed 08/28/2024, churchtrac.com https://www.churchtrac.com/articles/the–state–of–church–giving.

598 Vanco, "51 Church Giving and Growth Statistics." In: *The Definitive Guide to Churchgoer Giving: Key Trends in Online Giving, Attendance, and Engagement.* eBook accessed 08/28/2024. https://www.vanco-payments.com/egiving/asset–church–giving–statistics–tithing

599 R.T. Kendall, Tithing: Discover the Freedom of Biblical Giving. (Zondervan, 1982), 13–14.

and generosity is so important. We confront the sin of robbing God (Malachi 3:14) and ask our laity to choose: are you going to love God or love the things of this world, because you cannot do both (1 John 2:15). *The reason some Christians rarely witness, pray, read their Bibles, individually worship and praise God, or give generously to God is because their affections are divided between trying to love God and the things of this world. They believe their best life is found in having all of God and all of the world. This duality results in a lukewarm person whom God will reject if this person does not repent and fully turn to God* (Revelation 3:14–22).

Christ said show me where your money is, and I'll show you what you love (Matthew 6:19–24). If you do not give to God once you have learned about the importance of generosity, then you must not love him (1 John 2:15). Dr. Kendall correctly observes:

> To put it another way: who among us at one time or another has not sought to use one form of obedience to offset a deficiency in another area? "I don't tithe, but I go to church!" or "I don't tithe, but I bring people to church." Does it work? No, it does not. We who do "more" when we are aware of some form of disobedience in our Christian lives are not talking to God but to ourselves. We really project upon what we hope He is thinking. It is nothing but playing games with God – and ourselves…How we respond to the light that God throws on our paths when it comes may well determine whether or not we are given more light in which to walk. For if we do not walk in the light that God kindly sheds on our paths and our minds and in our hearts, it is not likely we will get further light for other matters.[600]

Believing one can compensate for disobedience through a notable number of righteous acts requires an impressive level of distorted thinking. The lie one accepts is that sin and righteousness can be summed through some spiritual calculator, which will show God that, on balance, we are not *that* bad. Once this calculation process is accepted, we give ourselves the freedom to believe the lie that God is making the same calculation. We hope God will overlook our disobedience in generosity as a tradeoff for the other good things we are doing. In other words, we think God will put up with a "small" sin in one area because He is pleased with how well we are doing in so many other areas. And besides, it is not that big of a deal, right? As Dr. Kendall wrote, we're just playing games. God doesn't make such tradeoff decisions.

Christian business owners who love God do not just tithe—they are *generous*. Of all the demographics in our churches, *we* have the most wealth to give. Our generosity could enable our churches to fund their ministries and do much good in our communities.

---

600 Kendall, *Tithing.* 15–16

But more importantly, becoming generous would *unleash* our walk with God. We would become free from the sin of hoarding. It would emancipate us to live on fire for Christ. We would learn contentment (1 Timothy 6:1–10) and the joy of giving. We would mature in our covenant relationship with God: "Tithing is so essential to your development as a Christian that nothing will be its adequate substitute."[601]

Now, to be sure, there have been and are high-profile Christian business owners who have had positive influence and demonstrated generosity, such as Dave Thomas, who founded Wendy's; Truitt Cathy, who founded Chick-fil-A, James Cash Penny, who was a partner in the founding of the Golden Rule Store, which was later renamed JC Penny's in 1914, and Sam Walton, the founder of Walmart. (an interesting trivia is that Sam Walton started in business by working as a clerk at JC Penny[602].) Forever 21 prints John 3:16 at the bottom of its bags. Tyson Foods employs more than one thousand chaplains to provide pastoral care to its employees. Alaska Air, Interstate Batteries, and others have distinct Christian roots because of their founders.[603]

But as influential as these and others like them have been, we need more than a couple dozen large companies owned by Christians to achieve the revival I hope God grants for this nation. We need a sea change in those smaller businesses owned by Christians with fewer than one hundred employees. The change needed is for Christian business owners to understand, accept, and live out their stewardship roles and responsibilities before the Lord and become generous toward him. Without stewardship, contentment, covenant, and generosity, I find it difficult to see how God will entrust to us the "true riches" of his presence and winning others to him.

Biblical Passages on Philanthropy

Philanthropy is discussed often in the Bible. Financial giving and generosity are constant themes in the Old and New Testaments. Some passages discuss or illustrate being generous; other passages teach generosity directly. I will discuss the lessons CBOs should learn from the Scriptures regarding financial giving and generosity.

Voluntarily meeting the needs of the poor is visceral to Biblical philanthropy and Christian stewardship. CBOs accept the God-given responsibility to meet the poor's needs under the Holy Spirit's direction. Rabbi Sacks says it well:

> A world where the few prosper and many starve offends our deepest sense of fairness and human solidarity. You do not have to be a convinced egalitarian

---

601 Kendall, *Tithing,* 18.

602 Tim Parker. "High Profile Christian Business Leaders." May 28, 2024. investopedia.com. https://www.investopedia.com/financial-edge/0912/high-profile-christian-business-leaders.aspx.

603 Drake Baer. "18 Extremely Religious Big American Companies." December 11, 2014. Businessinsider.com. https://www.businessinsider.com/companies-that-are-extremely-religious-2014-12

to know that disparities of vast, concentrated wealth alongside widespread suffering is intolerable. The real problem is one of responsibility. No one planned this outcome. It happened as a result of billions of transactions, investments and purchasing decisions."[604]

Sacks notes that "no one" planned this outcome. No one is responsible. He is correct. However, we business owners can help solve this problem through intelligent philanthropy. CBOs accept that philanthropy, as directed by God, is a core purpose of God's call on the CBO's life and business. Sacks bases his call to philanthropy on the dual concepts of justice and charity. He asserts that one cannot exercise the whole meaning of justice (not mere legal justice) without compassion and charity. For Sacks, justice is tempered by compassion, for one does not do only what the law requires but what is morally right.[605] One goes beyond the mere call of duty to answer the call of flourishing. One does not just tithe; one is generous. One example illustrates the combination of justice and compassion for our fellow man, Deuteronomy 24:10–13 (CSB):

[10] "When you make a loan of any kind to your neighbor, do not enter his house to collect what he offers as security. [11] You must stand outside while the man you are making the loan to brings the security out to you. [12] If he is a poor man, you must not sleep in the garment he has given as security. [13] Be sure to return it to him at sunset. Then he will sleep in it and bless you, and this will be counted as righteousness to you before the Lord your God.

Respect for the poor man is given in two ways. First, the rich do not invade the poor man's home to grab what is legally theirs—collateral for the loan. Instead, they stand outside, waiting patiently and respectfully while the poor man brings out the garment to give to the lender. Secondly, the lender returns the garment at night so that the poor man does not shiver in his sleep due to the cold temperatures.

It is fair to obtain collateral for a loan. However, compassion shows respect and ensures that the poor man's welfare is elevated above the lender's need for collateral. CBOs love first and enforce the regulations of the law second. We value the person more than the rule.[606]

---

604 Jonathan Sacks, The Dignity of Difference: How to Avoid the Clash of Civilizations. (Continuum, 2002), 111.

605 Jonathan Sacks, *Covenant and Conversation: A Weekly Reading of the Jewish Bible. Deuteronomy, Renewal of the Sinai Covenant.* (Maggid Books, 2019), 40.

606 Eugene Merrill, *Deuteronomy.* Vol. 4. The New American Commentary. (Broadman & Holman, 1994), 321–22.

Generosity eliminates social and economic distinctions. Some rely on passages like Acts 4:32–37 (LEB) to suggest that Christianity is best lived out in a socialistic economic system:

> ^{32} Now the group of those who believed were one heart and soul, and no one said anything of what belonged to him was his own, but all *things* were theirs in common. ^{33} And with great power the apostles were giving testimony *to* the resurrection of the Lord Jesus, and great grace was on them all. ^{34} For there was not even anyone needy among them, because all those who were owners of plots of land or houses were selling *them* *and* bringing the proceeds of the things that were sold ^{35} and placing *them* at the feet of the apostles. And it was being distributed to each as anyone had need. ^{36} So Joseph, who was called Barnabas by the apostles (which is translated "son of encouragement"), a Levite of Cyprus by nationality, ^{37} sold a field that belonged to him *and* brought the money and placed *it* at the feet of the apostles.

This passage (and Acts 2) can not be used to justify political systems like socialism or communism, where private ownership is effectively outlawed.[607] Instead, Luke used these events to teach that in the body of Christ, economic and social distinctions should be minimized, if not erased, through Christian friendship built on our common bond in Christ. The rich initiated the elimination of these distinctions, who would give the poor some of the benefits they took for granted.[608] Even today, it is a gift of God to a body of believers when they enjoy a Spirit–filled unity as described in Acts 4.[609]

So, while this passage is descriptive of what the early church did and is not necessarily prescriptive for how CBOs should behave today, I believe that God is pleased when business owners mirror the heart attitude of the generosity of Barnabas in this story. CBOs do what is reasonably possible to meet the needs of the poor.

CBOs are generous with another who has become poor through unforeseen events. Leviticus 25:35–38 (CSB) speaks to this situation:

> ^{35} "If your brother becomes destitute and cannot sustain himself among you, you are to support him as a foreigner or temporary resident, so that he can continue to live among you. ^{36} Do not profit or take interest from him, but fear your God and let your brother live among you. ^{37} You are

607   Michael Heiser, "Acts 4 and 5." Nakedbiblepodcast.com. May 27, 2015. https://nakedbiblepodcast.com/wp–content/uploads/2015/04/Transcript–42–Acts–4–5.pdf.

608   Alan C. Mitchell, "The Social Function of Friendship in Acts 2:44–47 and 4:32–37." *Journal of Biblical Literature*. 1992. 111(2):258.

609   Allison Trites and William J. Larkin, *Cornerstone Biblical Commentary, Vol 12: The Gospel of Luke and Acts*. (Tyndale House, 2006), 414.

> not to lend him your silver with interest or sell him your food for profit.
> [38] I am Yahweh your God, who brought you out of the land of Egypt to give you the land of Canaan and to be your God.

The Leviticus passage commands those wealthy to sustain their brother when "his hand gives way," i.e., becomes destitute. Do not let him fall even further, so it will be even more difficult for him to get back up.[610] Instead, come alongside him and support him by giving him aid and not charging any interest when money is lent to him. Do not take any profit or cause him to enter into more and more debt that he may not be able to pay.[611]

Sometimes, people become poor without behavior that can be faulted. Becoming poor can happen through sudden unemployment, medical bills, a house fire, an automobile accident, or another calamity. Moses commanded the Israelites to be generous toward others who became poor and could not self–support. CBOs should be generous toward their brother, who has become poor.

The amounts given are less important than the attitude of the giver. Consider Mark 12:41–44 (ESV) and the story of the widow who gave two mites:

> And he sat down opposite the treasury and watched the people putting money into the offering box. Many rich people put in large sums. [42] And a poor widow came and put in two small copper coins, which make a penny. [43] And he called his disciples to him and said to them, "Truly, I say to you, this poor widow has put in more than all those who are contributing to the offering box. [44] For they all contributed out of their abundance, but she out of her poverty has put in everything she had, all she had to live on.

When Christ said that the widow who gave two small copper coins gave more than the others, he was not referring to the amount given but to her heart of generosity. Because of her great sacrifice, her contribution demonstrated a heart saturated in love for God and trust in his provisions.[612] Christ "does not look at the size of the gift but at the dimensions of the sacrifice behind it."[613]

Others, Christ noted, gave out of an abundance of wealth. One wonders if the wealthy even "felt" their gifts in a sacrificial sense. The widow gave all that she owned. A rare attitude of

---

610 Michael Carasik, *Leviticus: Introduction and Commentary*. Translated by Michael Carasik. First edition. The Commentators' Bible. (The Jewish Publication Society, 2009), 212–13.

611 Mark Rooker, *Leviticus*. Vol. 3A. The New American Commentary. (Broadman & Holman, 2000), 308.

612 William Hendriksen and Simon J. Kistemaker. *Exposition of the Gospel According to Mark*. Vol. 10. New Testament Commentary. (Baker Book House, 1953–2001), 507–508.

613 David Turner and Darrell L. Bock, *Cornerstone Biblical Commentary, Vol 11: Matthew and Mark* (Tyndale House, 2005), 515.

generosity and trust can be discerned in the widow's giving. CBOs should have a "widow's heart" of love for God and trust him. We should be willing to sacrifice greatly if God calls us to do so.

God gives more to those who are generous toward God so the generous disciples can be blessed by giving even more. This is the thrust of what Paul meant when he wrote:

> [6] Remember this: The person who sows sparingly will also reap sparingly, and the person who sows generously will also reap generously. [7] Each person should do as he has decided in his heart—not reluctantly or out of necessity, for God loves a cheerful giver. [8] And God is able to make every grace overflow to you, so that in every way, always having everything you need, you may excel in every good work. [9] As it is written: 'He scattered; He gave to the poor; His righteousness endures forever.' [10] Now the One who provides seed for the sower and bread for food will provide and multiply your seed and increase the harvest of your righteousness. [11] You will be enriched in every way for all generosity, which produces thanksgiving to God through us. (2 Corinthians 9:6–11 CSB).

God's generosity toward us is unlimited and not measured out. Hence, our response is to show abundant generosity to others and be ready to give, not hold to a mindset of reluctance.[614] As a business owner is faithful in a few things (supplies seed to the sower), God gives the owner more material resources (will supply and multiply your seed for sowing) so the owner can understand God's heart more and is more transformed by learning more about God (you will be enriched in every way), which results in greater generosity (to be generous in every way). CBOs do not give to get more money; CBOs give financially to get more of Christ (harvest of your righteousness).

When the recipient can work, God's call to be generous does not replace the recipient's work. This is why a CBO carefully considers the persona and situation of the recipient. Giving is a holy act of stewardship and should not be undertaken from immature motivations like tax breaks or an improved image. Matthew 7:6 (ESV) says,

> Do not give dogs what is holy, and do not throw your pearls before pigs, lest they trample them underfoot and turn to attack you.

In this verse, Jesus checks the disciple's zeal to help others unbridled. This command counsels disciples not to be stupid.[615]

---

614 Paul Barnett, *The Message of 2 Corinthians: Power in Weakness.* The Bible Speaks Today. (InterVarsity Press, 1988), 152.

615 Frederick Dale Bruner, *Matthew, Volume 1 The Christbook Matthew 1–12.* (Word Publishing, 1987), 275.

There is a form of generosity that urges giving at every opportunity. Biblical stewardship bears in mind the eternal effects of "insensitive giving." When philanthropy accomplishes for others what they could achieve on their own, that charity is harming, not helping them:

> While poor people mention having a lack of material things, they tend to describe their condition in far more psychological and social terms than our North American audiences. Poor people typically talk in terms of shame, inferiority, powerlessness, humiliation, fear, hopelessness, depression, social isolation, and voicelessness. North American audiences tend to emphasize a lack of material things such as food, money, clean water, medicine, housing … This mismatch between many outsiders' perceptions of poverty and the perceptions of poor people themselves can have devastating consequences for poverty–alleviation efforts.[616]

When philanthropy is viewed solely in financial terms, donors and recipients create a poverty of spiritual intimacy with God in which materialism takes center stage instead of developing a relationship with God. When recipients do not work (when they can do so) and yet receive financial help, they lose the dignity that comes with honest work. Insensitive giving encourages the sin of laziness. Recipients can become self–centered and demand that others give to them out of a sense of entitlement. Biblical philanthropy must take a multi–faceted view of giving within a larger context of connecting the recipients to God (alleviating spiritual poverty), to work (alleviating stewardship poverty), and to the community (alleviating community poverty by becoming a productive member of society).[617]

Connecting work to philanthropy is supported in Scripture. Consider Leviticus 19:9–10 (ESV):

> [9] When you reap the harvest of your land, you shall not reap your field right up to its edge, neither shall you gather the gleanings after your harvest. [10] And you shall not strip your vineyard bare, neither shall you gather the fallen grapes of your vineyard. You shall leave them for the poor and for the sojourner: I am the Lord your God.

CBOs do not take the (holy) wealth God has entrusted to them and give it away simply because of a need. *The need is not the call.* Even though a need may be directly in front of the owner, and the owner can meet that need, the owner must also assess A) if the recipient is going to use the gift as intended and B) if giving the gift harms the recipient. What I

---

616   Steve Corbett & Brian Fikkert, *When Helping Hurts.* (Moody, 2012), 50.
617   Corbett, *Helping Hurts,* 57.

am teaching here is completely in line with James 4:17. If our giving harms the recipient, we are not doing good.

Disciples are entrusted with being both generous and smart. Do not give that which is holy to those who will misuse the gift. Jesus counsel "do not judge" (Matthew 7:1) does not mean "do not think."[618]

SUMMARY

In this chapter, I have discussed the values that a Christian business owner should adopt. Those values should inform the owner's selection of core values for his business. I have also reviewed God's five purposes for business and gave ample Biblical evidence for each of these purposes.

In the next chapter, we'll shift our focus to that of receiving advice as an owner. To whom should the owner turn when he needs advice? What kind of advice should he accept? These and other questions will be answered in the next chapter, so let's keep going.

---

618 Bruner, *Matthew*, 275.

CHAPTER 11

RECEIVING ADVICE

Who your advisors are is of paramount importance to the decisions that you make. Understanding what the Bible says about giving and receiving advice is equally important. Your trusted advisors should understand Christian stewardship and God's purposes for business. Otherwise, their advice will lead you down paths of planning that will not support your stewardship role before God.

ADVICE IS A recommendation on a decision or course of action.[619] Counsel is essential for gaining wisdom and obtaining guidance before making important decisions. Advice is something all of us need from time to time.

Our ability to succeed in life depends on the quality of the relationships that we build throughout our lives. Both personal and professional relationships *matter*. Most books on success will focus on *your* skills, *your* brains, and *your* efforts. But our performance and success in business and life are either improved or diminished by the people with whom we associate, extending to the advice we receive and accept.[620]

---

619 Merriam–Webster, "Advice." Accessed 08/30/2024. https://www.merriam–webster.com/dictionary/advice

620 Henry Cloud, *The Power of the Other: The Startling Effect Other People Have on Your, From the Boardroom to the Bedroom and Beyond—and What to do About it.* (Harper Business: 2016), 8–10.

CONVENTIONAL WISDOM ON TRUSTED ADVISORS

Not all business relationships are created equal. When it comes to receiving advice, some business relationships will be vendor–only relationships that hold little power over us. However, some vendor or professional relationships will mature through a process where the other person is rightly termed a *trusted advisor*. That process is graphically depicted in Figure 11–1. [621]

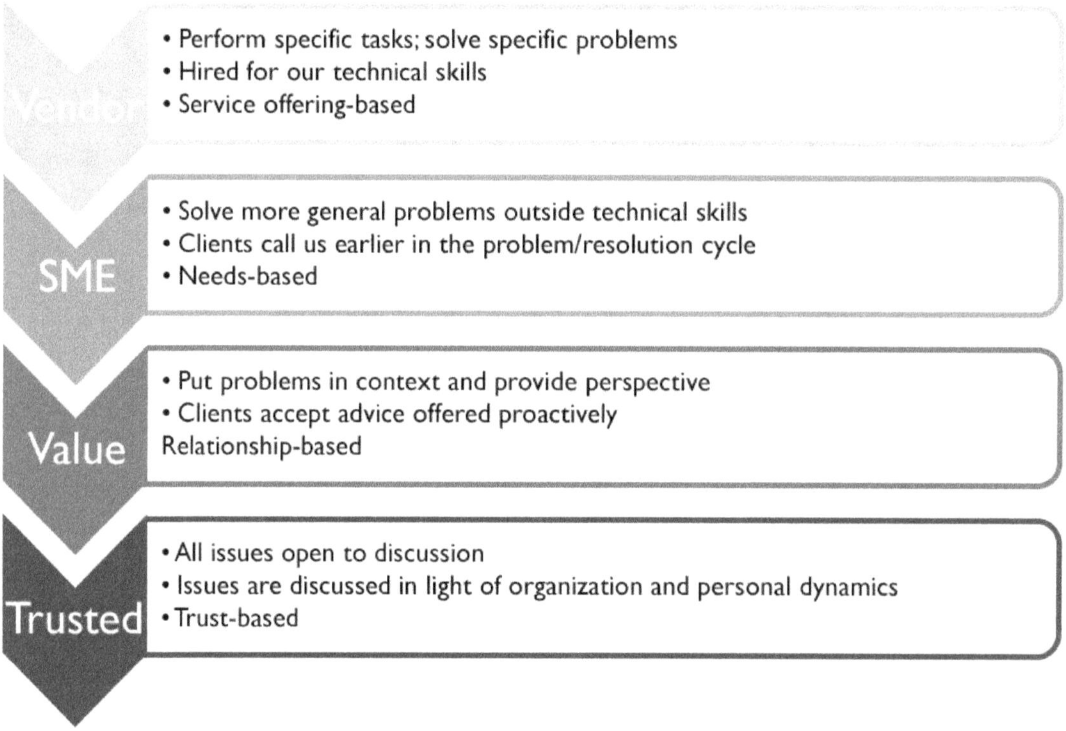

Vendor
- Perform specific tasks; solve specific problems
- Hired for our technical skills
- Service offering-based

SME
- Solve more general problems outside technical skills
- Clients call us earlier in the problem/resolution cycle
- Needs-based

Value
- Put problems in context and provide perspective
- Clients accept advice offered proactively
- Relationship-based

Trusted
- All issues open to discussion
- Issues are discussed in light of organization and personal dynamics
- Trust-based

Figure 11–1: From Vendor to Trusted Advisor

A trusted advisor is a person whom you listen to when an issue first arises, often in times of great urgency. The issues discussed with a trusted advisor usually involve organizational and personal dimensions. You have learned over time that this person is competent in his or her field, understands you and your situation, has the emotional intelligence to be calm when you are not, and can keep secrets and confidences.

---

621   David H. Maister, Charles H. Green, and Robert M. Galford, *The Trusted Advisor*. (Free Press, 2000), 7–10.

Trusted advisors have certain characteristics CBOs should look for as they build their panel of trusted advisors. These characteristics are unsurprising but essential to the advisor-advisee relationship. Figure 11–2 illustrates the core characteristics of a trusted advisor. [622]

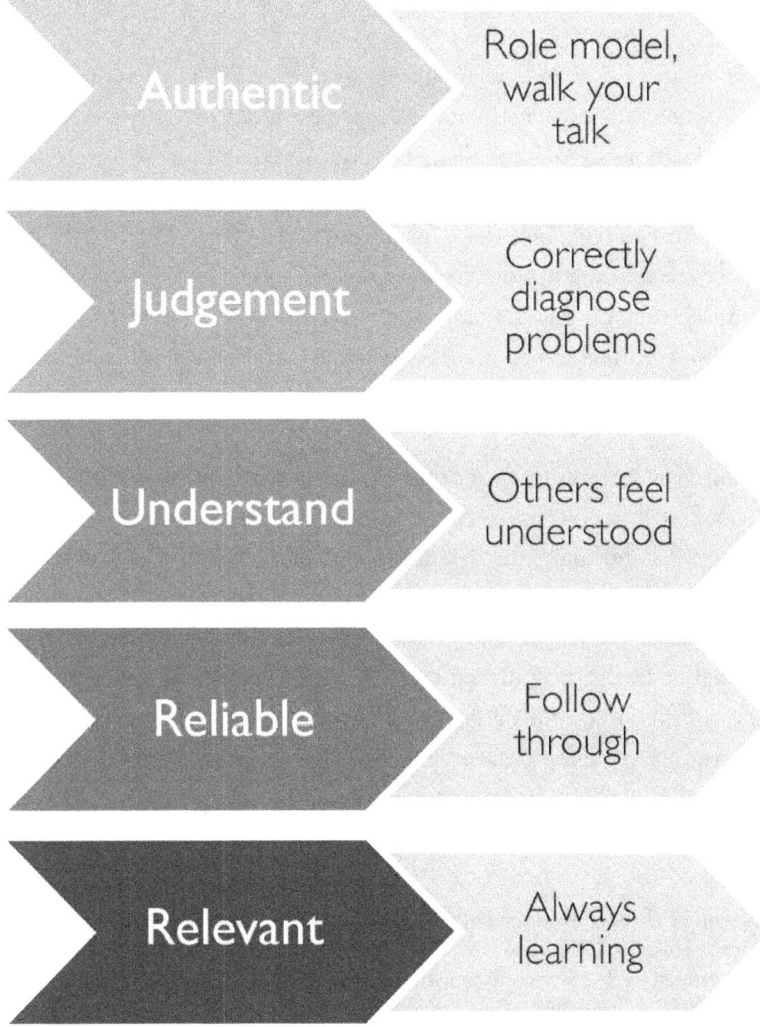

Figure 11–2: Core Characteristics of a Trusted Advisor

622 Adapted from Joseph Folkman. "Seven Steps to Becoming a Trusted Advisor in Your Organization." *Forbes.* June 16, 2022. https://www.forbes.com/sites/joefolkman/2022/06/16/7–steps–to–becoming–a–trusted–advisor–in–your–organization/

Even in consultation with your trusted advisors, as a business owner, you will likely need to make challenging choices without all the pertinent points of information in hand. As often as not, you will navigate the fog of uncertainty,[623] making the best decision you can with the information you have and then working hard to make your decision the right one. Your staff or management team should make routine decisions. Your leadership team can make the 90–10, 80–20, 70–30, or 60–40 decisions. If you are hiring top talent, they will want real authority to make real decisions. Your job is to get out of the way and watch them succeed.[624]

However, for those rare times when the 45–55 or even 49–51 decisions need to be made, a thoughtful use of your ownership authority is best utilized. Only the most challenging and uncertain decisions should bubble up to your plate. In those rare instances, the type of advice you seek will be different, depending on the situation you find yourself in. Garvin and Margolis stratify advice into these four types:[625]

- Discrete: exploring options for a single decision
- Counsel: providing guidance on how to approach a complex situation
- Coaching: enhancing skills, self–awareness, and self–management
- Mentoring: providing guidance and protection to aid career success

As the business grows, the complexity of the moving parts increases. Sometimes, only the owner has enough perspective across the entire organization to understand the interrelations of the moving parts and make the best tradeoff decisions given the problem at hand, the anticipated effects of the decision on the various parts of the organization, and the authority to make the decision and then make it "stick."

In my experience, the most difficult decisions involve balancing the needs of the organization, the opinions of senior leadership when they disagree as to a course of action, the financial constraints, the risks to the organization, guardrails of core values on the decision, and the explanation of the decision to staff and perhaps the public.

---

623 François Michelin, interviewed by Ivan Leval̇ and Yves Messarovitch, *And Why Not? The Human Person at the Heart of Business.* Translated by Mark Sebanc. (Lexington Books, 2003), 61.

624 The inability to delegate decisional authority to trusted leaders is one of core reasons business owners' plateau in size or decline over time. High control business owners often become their own worst enemy and they sabotage themselves as their business grows because they cannot bring themselves to delegate true authority, so they route most decisions through themselves. When they do this, top talent leaves to work for better employers. Over time, the owner is left with mediocre talent and then complains that no one is competent enough to step up and lead. When I bump into high control owners in my consulting business, I give them my feedback and then watch them walk away. Not only do high control owners have difficulty delegating authority, but they have equal difficulty hearing that they are the core cause of the problems in their business.

625 David A Garvin and Joshua D. Margolis, "The Art of Giving and Receiving Advice." *Harvard Business Review.* January–February, 2015. https://hbr.org/2015/01/the–art–of–giving–and–receiving–advice

As your business grows, the scope of your role as the owner narrows. More complex decisions will be placed on your desk. Do not make these decisions swiftly. Let the world spin a few times, talk with your trusted advisors, meet your senior leaders, and fully hear them out. Take time to pray through the decision to hear from God. Then, make the best decision possible. And, as I said before, after you have made your decision, work hard to make it the right one.

Conventional wisdom has much good to say about receiving advice and how to filter advice to arrive at a good decision. But again, conventional wisdom is godless in that it does not account for a transcendent God who speaks to us and to whom we can listen and follow. CBOs need the mind of Christ.

BIBLICAL WISDOM ABOUT ADVICE

The Scriptures have much to say about giving and receiving advice. Let us learn together as we look at this important topic.

Receiving Advice and Becoming Wise

Solomon connected the act of receiving advice with becoming or being wise. Those who do not receive advice are said to be fools. Here are several passages from his wisdom literature that make this connection:

> The way of a fool is right in his own eyes, but a wise man listens to advice. (Proverbs 12:15 ESV)

> The simple believes everything, but the prudent gives thought to his steps. One who is wise is cautious and turns away from evil, but a fool is reckless and careless. (Proverbs 14:15–16 ESV)

> Where there is strife, there is pride, but wisdom is found in those who take advice. (Proverbs 13:10 NIV)

> Listen to advice and accept instruction, that you may gain wisdom in the future. (Proverbs 19:20 ESV)

> Whoever walks with the wise becomes wise, but the companion of fools will suffer harm. (Proverbs 13:20 ESV)

> Better was a poor and wise youth than an old and foolish king who no longer knew how to take advice. (Ecclesiastes 4:13 NIV)

In the wisdom literature, an explicit connection is made between taking advice and being wise. Yet many Christians who own businesses are reluctant to take advice from anyone. Sometimes, their ego keeps them from asking for help[626] even though help is available.[627] Sometimes, they do not want to incur the expense of advice from a trusted advisor. Others see taking advice as a sign of weakness even though it would grow their business.[628] The "fake it 'til you make it" mentality leads business owners to keep up appearances when their business starts to fail.[629] Some continue to shun advice even when the danger signs of bankruptcy are apparent for all to see.[630]

Asking for help should be a sign of *strength*,[631] which is why the Bible portrays those who do not ask for advice as fools:

> The fear of the Lord is the beginning of knowledge; fools despise wisdom and instruction. (Proverbs 1:7 ESV)

> How long, O simple ones, will you love being simple? How long will scoffers delight in their scoffing and fools hate knowledge? (Proverbs 1:22 ESV)

> O simple ones, learn prudence; O fools, learn sense. (Proverbs 8:5 ESV)

> The wise of heart will receive commandments, but a babbling fool will come to ruin. Whoever walks in integrity walks securely, but he who makes his ways crooked will be found out. Whoever winks the eye causes trouble, and a babbling fool will come to ruin. The mouth of the righteous is a fountain of life, but the mouth of the wicked conceals violence. Hatred

---

626 Jacqueline Whitmore, "Get Your Ego Out of the Way and Ask for Help When You Need It." *Entrepreneur.* May 15, 2015. https://www.entrepreneur.com/growing-a-business/get-your-ego-out-of-the-way-and-ask-for-help-when-you-need/246157

627 Leslie Barber, "The Help You Need Is There for the Asking." *Entrepreneur.* February 27, 2015. https://www.entrepreneur.com/growing-a-business/the-help-you-need-is-there-for-the-asking/243221

628 Sujan Patel, "How Asking for Help Can Lead to Business Growth." *Forbes.* December 26, 2014. https://www.forbes.com/sites/sujanpatel/2014/12/26/how-asking-for-help-can-lead-to-business-growth/

629 Bill English, "The Emotional Price Business Owners Pay When Their Business Is Failing." *Bible and Business.* September 19, 2020. https://www.bibleandbusiness.com/2020/09/19/the-emotional-price-business-owners-pay-when-their-business-is-failing/

630 Bill English, "Twelve Warning Signs Your Business Is Headed for Disaster." *Bible and Business.* September 19, 2020. https://www.bibleandbusiness.com/2020/09/19/twelve-warning-signs-your-business-is-headed-for-disaster/

631 James Caan, "Small Business Owners Should Not Be Afraid to Ask for Advice." *The Guardian*, July 9, 2014. https://www.theguardian.com/small-business-network/2014/jul/09/small-business-advice-james-caan

stirs up strife, but love covers all offenses. On the lips of him who has understanding, wisdom is found, but a rod is for the back of him who lacks sense. The wise lay up knowledge, but the mouth of a fool brings ruin near. (Proverbs 10:8–14 ESV)

A fool despises his father's instruction, but whoever heeds reproof is prudent, (Proverbs 15:5 ESV)

Do not speak in the hearing of a fool, for he will despise the good sense of your words. (Proverbs 12:9 ESV)

The macro lesson is that if you want to be a wise and discerning steward of that which God has entrusted to you, then you need to submit yourself to the advice of others. God doesn't tolerate foolish stewards.

Advice that you should take seriously has specific characteristics listed in James 3:13–18 (NASB):

Who among you is wise and understanding? Let him show by his good behavior his deeds in the gentleness of wisdom. But if you have bitter jealousy and selfish ambition in your heart, do not be arrogant and so lie against the truth. This wisdom is not that which comes down from above, but is earthly, natural, demonic. For where jealousy and selfish ambition exist, there is disorder and every evil thing. But the wisdom from above is first pure, then peaceable, gentle, reasonable, full of mercy and good fruits, unwavering, without hypocrisy. And the seed whose fruit is righteousness is sown in peace by those who make peace.

When receiving advice, look for these qualities in the advice and the attitude of the advice–giver:
- Purity
- Peaceable
- Gentle
- Reasonable
- Merciful
- Unwavering
- Consistent

Advice that does not have these characteristics should be considered suspect as not coming from God, but from the unseen forces who oppose God.

Notice also that James mentions selfish ambition in this passage. He associates selfish ambition with jealousy, disorder, and "every evil thing." Echoing what I wrote earlier, it is poor advice to move forward in business *just because it makes sense to do so.*

An Example of Accepting Bad Advice

Let us consider the story of Absalom's rebellion against David. Absalom attempts to take the throne from his father, David, after four years of planning and building his coalition (2 Samuel 16:15–17:23).[632] Central to this story are two advisors, Ahithophel and Hushai.

Ahithophel, a Gilonite, was one of David's advisors whose advice was highly regarded (16:23). After years of service to David, Ahithophel turned against David by supporting Absalom. When David learned of Ahithophel's betrayal, he asked God to confuse the advice that Ahithophel would give to Absalom (15:31).

Hushai the Archite was loyal to David but pretended to be loyal to Absalom and faux–pledged his allegiance to Absalom in his presence. Absalom knew of Hushai's close friendship with David, so he was naturally suspicious. But his pride would not let him hear the ambiguities in Hushai's statement that his loyalty was with "the one that the Lord, the people, and all the men of Israel have chosen." (2 Samuel 16:18 CSB).[633] Indeed, Hushai was loyal to God's anointed—David—and would work to sabotage Absalom's plan. The success of Absalom's rebellion would depend on how he responded to the conflicting counsel he would receive from Ahithophel and Hushai.[634]

Upon entering Jerusalem after David fled to the Jordan River, Absalom asked Ahithophel what he should do next (16:20). While it may have been customary in the ANE for a king of a new dynasty to take the harem of the previous monarch,[635] it was undoubtedly sin to have sex with the wives and concubines of one's father (Leviticus 18:7–8), most of who were part of larger political alliances[636] that the new king may or may not endorse.

Ahithophel's advice was as ruthless[637] as it was dehumanizing.[638] Absalom followed through and engaged in public sex with David's wives and concubines, an act that he

---

632   I'll recommend you have your Bible open to 2 Samuel 16:15–17:23 while reading this section.

633   Mary J. Evans, *The Message of Samuel: Personalities, Potential, Politics and Power.* Edited by Alec Motyer and Derek Tidball. The Bible Speaks Today. (Inter–Varsity Press, 2004), 241.

634   Robert J. Vannoy, *Cornerstone Biblical Commentary: 1–2 Samuel.* Vol. 4. (Tyndale House, 2009), 369.

635   Lloyd Llewellyn–Jones, "Bathsheba and Beyond Harem Politics in the Ancient Near East." In: *Powerful Women in the Ancient World: Perception and (Self)Presentation.* Proceedings of the 8th Melammu Workshop, Kassel, January 30 – February 1, 2019, Melammu Workshops and Monographs, 4. (Zaphon, August, 2021), 148.

636   Lucas B. Freire, "Suzerains and Vassals: Patterns of Hierarchy in Ancient Near Eastern Diplomacy." 56th International Studies Association Annual Convention, New Orleans, February 18–21, 2015.

637   Joyce Baldwin, *1 and 2 Samuel: An Introduction and Commentary.* Vol. 8. Tyndale Old Testament Commentaries. (InterVarsity Press, 1988), 282–83.

638   Evans. Message of Samuel, 242.

thought would solidify his power as the new king. Certainly, this act fulfilled Nathan's prophecy (12:11–12) against David, but the act also made Absalom odious to David and all right-minded people in Jerusalem.[639]

Next, Ahithophel advises Absalom to attack David with overwhelming military force (17:1–4). But Hushai counters that Ahithophel's advice does not account for David's experience and fierceness in battle. Twelve thousand men will not be enough. He recommends gathering the entire nation of Israel as Absalom leads the nation into battle to kill David and his men. Absalom accepts Hushai's advice and rejects Ahithophel's advice.

As Hushai builds Absalom's ego,[640] Absalom does not understand that Hushai's advice is designed to protect David.[641] The writer tells us that God was behind Absalom's acceptance of Hushai's advice to bring disaster to Absalom. God may appear silent here, but he is working on David's behalf.[642] We should be encouraged by the writer's aside at this point in the story. This decision by Absalom was the turning point in the story and the "change in the situation was the work of God himself, who had heard the prayer of the king in his profound humiliation."[643]

Moving on with the story (17:15ff), Hushai goes behind Absalom's back and informs the priests Zadock and Abiathar of the advice Ahithopel gave to Absalom and what he, Hushai, advised. So he entrusted to Zadock and Abiathar the task of getting this intelligence to David with a recommendation of what David should do to protect himself. In a *James Bond*–style story, David is informed of Absalom's plans. So David escapes and thwarts Absalom's plans to kill him.

Ahithophel realizes his end is at hand. Because Absalom forfeited the advantage of surprise, the seasoned strategist Ahithophel knew that David would regain control and face death for treason. He accepts his situation and calmly puts his affairs in order, then kills himself.[644]

The battle ensues in the forest of Ephraim between David's forces (numbered in the thousands) and Absalom's forces (well over 20,000 (18:7)). Absalom runs into some of David's men and, in retreat, gets his head (hair) caught in the branches of an oak tree. Joab and his armor-bearers kill Absalom and throw his body into a large pit.

When comparing the characteristics of Ahithophel's advice with James 3:17–18, we can discern that his advice was not Godly. Table 11–1 surfaces the problems with Ahithophel's advice.

---

639 Baldwin, *1 and 2 Samuel*, 283.
640 Vannoy, *1–2 Samuel*, 370.
641 Baldwin, *1 and 2 Samuel*, 284.
642 Vannoy, *1–2 Samuel*, 371.
643 Gerhard von Rad, "The Beginnings of Historical Writing in Ancient Israel." In: *the Problem of the Hexateuch and Other Essays*. (Oliver & Boyd, 1966), 200.
644 Baldwin, *1 and 2 Samuel*, 285.

Table 11–1: Comparison of Godly Advice vs. Ahithophel's Advice to Absalom

Characteristic	Ahithophel's Advice
Pure	Pride: Placed A. in the position of getting the credit if David's life was terminated[645]
Peaceable	Murder is hardly promoting a state of well–being and happiness.
Gentle	Murder is hardly 'gentle' or 'kind'
Reasonable	Trying to kill God's anointed is unreasonable.
Full of Mercy	Murder shows no mercy toward the actions of the one being murdered.
Full of Good Fruits	The results of a murder do not honor Yahweh.
Unwavering	The word means not to cause divisions, to be impartial. In this story, the murder of David would polarize the nation of Israel.
Without Hypocrisy	Ahithophel's advice to murder David is utterly inconsistent with his religious beliefs in Yahweh and his commitment to follow the law, which forbids murder.

God answers David's prayer and confuses the perceptions of Absalom and his other advisors of the differing advice given to them between Ahithophel and Hushai. It is not that Absalom did not *hear* good advice; he did not *perceive* it as such. *Living in sin will create confusion in the sinner's mind* (Deuteronomy 28:20), *and sound advice can be confused with bad advice.* One of the reasons a CBO needs to live righteously is that a CBO can better discern between good and bad advice when one's mind is not confused by sin.

Absalom was living under the sin of pride, so God opposed him (James 4:6). God always opposes the proud. In this instance, He did so through his advisors. God frustrated the advice-giving process such that the very course of action everyone thought most appropriate turned out to be the one that cost them their lives. They were signing their death warrant and did not know it.

Sin and Confusion in Accepting Advice

We see this same dynamic—God confusing the counsel of the advisors—playing out in 1 Kings 22.5–28 when God consults with his divine council to figure out the best way to

---

645 Vannoy, *1–2 Samuel*, 370.

get rid of Ahab. A lying spirit is placed into the mouths of his advisors, and their advice—which seems wise and good—ends up costing Ahab his life. Again, one advisor gave Ahab good advice, but Ahab did not perceive it to be that way, so he muzzled the one advisor giving him good advice and heeded the bad advice of another counselor. Ahab, the king of Israel, followed lousy advice and was killed by a random arrow shot into the air—an improbable thing to occur. It is so unlikely that the writer makes the connection that it was God who sovereignly killed him.

In the Ahab story, we see God purposefully using an evil spirit to confuse the advice of Ahab's advisors. God had already decided it was time for Ahab to go. The only question was *how* Ahab was going to die. And God chose to allow an evil spirit to devise the plan that would kill him.[646] God knew that Ahab would listen to bad advice and thus knew that the plan would work.

This story teaches us that just because the advice we receive is compelling and logical does not mean it is the correct course of action. So, learning to discern good advice from bad advice is one of the characteristics of a mature, Godly leader. Therefore, learning to hear the voice of God and letting the Holy Spirit inform your discernment makes considerable sense.

An Example of Accepting Good Advice

The story of Jethro advising Moses in Exodus 8:1–27 is an excellent example of accepting good advice.[647] In this story, Jethro, Zipporah (Moses' wife), and Moses' two sons come from Midian to visit him at Sinai (1–4).

Upon arrival, Moses recounts to Jethro all that God has done to extract Israel from Egypt, all the hardships they had faced in the wilderness, and how the Lord delivered them (5–8).

The next day, Moses sat down and judged the complaints of the Israelites. He used the occasions to judge disputes as a way to teach the people about God's statutes and laws (15). Some cases were decided as a point of law. However, in those complex cases where sufficient evidence was lacking, the matter was handled "prophetically," meaning that Moses brought the situation before God.[648]

Jethro suggests that if Moses does not change his ways, he will wear out because judging all the people was too heavy for one man (17–18). So Jethro advised Moses to set up a

---

646 God's use of evil spirits in the Old Testament to accomplish his will occurs at least two dozen times. While God's use of evil for his purposes may present some difficult theological problems, it seems best to me to affirm what the Scriptures affirm. God can use evil for his purposes without doing evil himself.

647 I will recommend that you have your Bible open to Exodus 18:1–27 when you read this section.

648 Victor H. Matthews, Mark W. Chavalas, and John H. Walton, *The IVP Bible Background Commentary: Old Testament.* Electronic ed. (InterVarsity Press, 2000), np.

hierarchy of judges who have certain positive qualities and who can hear the less complex cases. Only the most difficult cases should come to Moses (19–23).

As a longtime priest of an established people, Jethro had experienced this problem and knew how to solve it. Moses needed to learn to delegate authority and share the burdens of these people. Jethro helped him realize a better way.[649] Moses accepted the excellent advice of Jethro and implemented the judging system Jethro suggested. The paradox that a Mideanite priest initiated the instantiation of the primitive roots of the Jewish legal system is not lost on Jewish scholars.[650]

MENTORING, DISCIPLESHIP, AND ADVICE

Mentoring and discipleship are two sides of the same coin. In a mentoring relationship, a disciple is learning, and a mentor helps the disciple mature in some way.[651]

Jethro's advice to Moses can be viewed as an example of mentoring and discipleship. Later, Moses would mentor his successor, Joshua (Deuteronomy 31:1–8).[652] Another example of mentoring and discipleship is in Elijah and Elisha's relationship. I want to focus on the story in 2 Kings 2:1–14.[653] The macro lesson of this story is that even when unsettling leadership changes occur within God's people, Yahweh raises new leaders who can continue God's work in and through his people.[654] In addition, I derive several more lessons from this story.

First, notice how Elijah, the mentor, kept progressing toward his final goal. The best mentors are active, continuing to do God's work until the day when they are taken to be with him. Christians who engage in mentoring have not "arrived," as if they have no more to do or learn. This idea of always learning, growing, and becoming is visceral to being a disciple of Christ and an effective mentor.

Second, Elisha was intent on carrying on Elijah's work, who kept giving Elisha opportunities to stop and stay behind as he traveled toward Jordan and beyond. One gets the feeling that Elijah's commands to "stay here" were more permissive than prohibitive[655]

---

649 Eugene Carpenter, *Exodus*, vol. 1, Evangelical Exegetical Commentary (Lexham Press, 2016), 618.

650 Naham Sarna, *Exodus*. The JPS Torah Commentary. (The Jewish Publication Society, 1991), 100. See also George Bush. *Notes, Critical and Practical, on the Book of Exodus*. Vol. 1. (Boston: Henry A. Young & Co., 1841), 230.

651 June Hunt, *Biblical Counseling Keys on Mentoring: How to Shepherd the Sheep*. (Hope For The Heart, 2008) 1.

652 Ken Davis, "Mentoring Church Planters." *Journal of Ministry and Theology*, 2010. 14(2):26.

653 Please read 2 Kings 2:1–14 in your Bible before continuing in this chapter.

654 Dale Ralph Davis, "The Kingdom of God in Transition: Interpreting 2 Kings 2." *Westminster Theological Journal*, 1984. 46(2): 394–395.

655 Richard D. Patterson and Hermann J. Austel, "1, 2 Kings." In *The Expositor's Bible Commentary: 1 & 2 Kings, 1 & 2 Chronicles, Ezra, Nehemiah, Esther, Job*, edited by Frank E. Gaebelein, Vol. 4. (Zondervan, 1988), 174.

and may have been a test of Elisha's faithfulness, which was answered by his refusal to leave Elijah.[656]

Elisha understands that Elijah is leaving him soon. Elisha's request for a "double–portion" makes sense, especially in light of Deuteronomy 21:17. His request was not that he would exceed Elijah, as has often been preached, but rather that "he should receive the eldest son's share according to the law (Deut. 21:17). Such a son had the responsibility to carry on the father's name and work."[657] Elisha wanted the status of the principal successor to Elijah.[658] A maturing disciple often wishes to be the one to carry on the work of his mentor, and Elisha is no different in this regard.

Last, Elijah—the mentor—knew his limitations. He did not have the power or right to give the gift of the Spirit to Elisha or anyone else.[659] Seeing Elijah's translation would indicate to Elisha that God had chosen him to carry the ministry forward in the power of the Spirit. Mentors know their limitations and understand when God alone must provide for their disciples, which indicates the mentor's work is finished. Some things can only be given by God and cannot be manufactured, no matter how much human effort is applied. The things of the Spirit can only come from God.

Building a Panel of Trusted Advisors

Every Christian business owner should have a group of trusted advisors on whom the owner relies for wisdom and advice. These advisors can take several different functions, which I will outline now.

Intercessors

Intercessors can run spiritual interference as they pray for you and your business. Having a group of intercessors is not the same as outsourcing your responsibility to pray for yourself, your family, your company, or your employees. But it is a way to add power and protection in the spiritual realm, often needed when moving forward for God. You might find that sometimes there are two to three months between communications, and other times, perhaps two to three days. But as you inform them and as they pray, God moves in you and through your business.

---

656   Donald Wiseman, *1 and 2 Kings: An Introduction and Commentary*. Vol. 9. Tyndale Old Testament Commentaries. (InterVarsity Press, 1993), 207.

657   Wiseman, *1 and 2 Kings*, 208.

658   Victor Harold Matthews, Mark W. Chavalas, and John H. Walton, *The IVP Bible Background Commentary: Old Testament*. Electronic ed. (InterVarsity Press, 2000), np.

659   Patterson, *1, 2 Kings*, 176.

Advisory Council

The Scriptures clarify that advisors are needed in efforts such as waging war. Counsel is also praised in the Bible. I believe privately held businesses should seek to establish an advisory council that meets twice to thrice yearly. This council is compensated, and members are available between meetings for specific questions. The council gives you a safe place to bounce ideas around, a group with whom to pray, and a set of trusted friends whose advice is trustworthy. Solomon wrote:

> Wounds from a friend can be trusted, but an enemy multiplies kisses. (Proverbs 27:6 NIV)

Even though the counsel may hurt at times, if it comes from trusted friends, you will know their counsel comes from a heart of love for you. You are more apt to accept it. Look for Christian business leaders with a proven track record of successfully running a business.

In addition, be sure that some of your council members are *not* good friends. Otherwise, your time together may devolve into a social engagement. Choose advisors who understand your vision and know how to question your choices.[660] If you only choose good friends as advisors, you will likely not do as well in your business.

Consider more than token compensation for your members. Adequate payment will help you and your members take your meetings seriously. If you do not have "skin in the game," you will likely not listen to them, and they will likely not continue helping you.

Now, be ready—if you get a group of talented, intelligent, and honest people in the same room and ask for constructive ways to improve your business and your performance, you will get what you asked for. So, be prepared that their insights and challenges may be more about your person and work than your business model or financial condition. Be ready to take some arrows. Remember Proverbs 27:6.

Trusted Professionals

You should seriously develop strong relationships with the following set of business advisors:
- Banker. Do not wait until you need money to develop a banking relationship. Get that line of credit when you do not need it. And be sure to share all of your information with your banker. If you do not show respect and loyalty to your banker during the good times, do not expect her to be there for you during the bad times.

---

660 Forbes Expert Panel Council Post. "Top Tips to Keep in Mind When Seeking The Right Advisor For Your Business." Forbes.com, August 11, 2021. https://www.forbes.com/councils/theyec/2021/08/11/top-tips-to-keep-in-mind-when-seeking-the-right-advisor-for-your-business/

- Lawyer. A good law firm is worth their weight in gold and will save you more than you can imagine. Good lawyers are hard to find, but you will wonder how you got along without them once you find one.
- Accountant. Beyond preparing your tax returns, they can assist you with reviews and audits if you are preparing to sell your business. If you have a new business, they can assist you in setting up your chart of accounts and developing a 13–week cash flow forecast. Be sure to introduce them to your controller and CFO. An annual audit with a view toward theft is a great control and protection for you and your financial team.
- Financial planner. As you grow your business, take some profit each year and invest wisely. A competent financial advisor can help you make wise investments and assist you with a 401K plan and a financial wellness program for your employees.
- Human resources. Whether you contract with a third–party firm or hire an HR professional in–house, you will need a competent HR attorney to advise you on employee matters. Roughly half of all lawsuits that small–business owners face relate to employment issues. It is wise to lower your risk of judgment by taking HR compliance issues seriously.
- Personal advisor or coach. The most successful business owners often have a personal coach to help them avoid their derailers and emphasize their strengths in their ownership role. An executive coach is an investment in yourself, which is an excellent use of your resources.

SUMMARY

In this chapter on receiving advice, I have suggested that Godly advice has the following characteristics:

- Pure
- Peaceable
- Gentle
- Reasonable
- Merciful
- Unwavering

I have also suggested that living in sin will create internal confusion, leading to accepting and rejecting lousy advice. I have also counseled you to build a panel of trusted advisors and humble yourself enough to hear their Godly counsel.

Receiving advice is part of the planning process. Every business owner plans for the future. So, let's learn what the Bible says about making and executing plans.

CHAPTER 12

PLANNING

It is impossible to be successful in business without proper planning, so a chapter is dedicated to this topic. Your plans often reflect your persona, what you value, and where you sense God is leading you. Plans should be held with an open hand, since God may change your plans after you have committed to them (Acts 16). The Bible has much to say about planning and making plans, so let us now focus on this crucial issue.

CONVENTIONAL WISDOM ON PLANNING

Strategy is a word that is used over and over in business every day. People act as if everyone understands what a strategy is, but this is not true. Depending on one's viewpoint, a strategy may be a plan[661] or a description of how the parts of an organization work together.[662] Evans says a "strategy is how a company achieves its goals by allocating its scarce resources to gain a sustainable competitive advantage."[663]

661   Susan H. Gebelein, Davd G. Lee, Kristie J. Nelson–Neuhaus, & E.B Sloan, *The Successful Executive's Handbook: Development Suggestions for Today's Executives*. (Personnel Decisions International, 1999), 89.

662   Robert S. Kaplan and David P. Norton, *The Strategy Focused Organization*. (Harvard Business School Press, 2001), 161–165.

663   Vaughan Evans, *Developing a Business Strategy: How to Use Strategic Planning to Start Up or Grow Your Business*. (Pearson Education Unlimited, 2013), 13.

Strategic planning was called "long–term planning" before it matured into a discipline that most large organizations embraced.[664] Today, strategic planning is "inextricably interwoven into the entire fabric of management; it is not something separate and distinct from the process of management."[665] Day–to–day operational management depends on strategic planning: the more transparent a strategic plan is, the more successful operational management can become.

Too much emphasis on strategic planning will likely result in an organization becoming a compulsive firm in which every move is carefully planned. An obsession with control reflects the fear of uncertainty, and planning can be seen as a way to seek control over anything that might surprise the organization.[666] Proper planning must consider known risks in the future and forecast changes in the organization and its environment while setting and developing action plans to achieve those objectives.

The conventional wisdom for strategic planning would suggest these elements be included in the plan:

- Leads and supports operational management
- Articulates goals for the organization
- Articulates the general action plans to achieve those goals
- Forecasts organization, market, and environment changes
- Must be balanced with an acceptance of a certain level of risk

Mission plans set out the goals to achieve within a one–year time frame. Mission plan elements are the same as strategic plan elements; the focus is only on a shorter period, and the short–term goals support achieving the long–term goals.

Creating strategic and mission plans may be more important than the plans themselves.[667] The macro value of the planning process is found in the questions that must be considered and the assumptions that need to be challenged. Time spent on planning activities related to a company's strategy and mission often keeps a forward-focused vision for the future.[668]

Conventional wisdom has much good to say about the planning process. But the Bible has even more to say because the Scriptures assume one's covenant with God is ambient in planning.

---

664 George A. Steiner, *Strategic Planning*. (Free Press, 1979), vii.

665 Steiner, Strategic Planning, 3.

666 Henry Mintzberg, "The Pitfalls of Strategic Planning." *California Management Review*. 1993. 36(1): 32.

667 Shane Jackson, "Why Your Business–Planning Process Is More Important than the Plan Itself." Januar 6, 2022. Forbes.com. https://www.forbes.com/councils/forbesbusinesscouncil/2022/01/06/why–your–business–planning–process–is–more–important–than–the–plan–itself/

668 Catherine Cote, "What is Strategic Planning Important?" October 6, 2020. *Harvard Business Review*.

BIBLICAL WISDOM AND PLANNING

At the core of Biblical wisdom for our planning efforts is the notion that our plans are both 'changeable' and 'interruptible' by God at any moment. When a CBO submits his plans to God, he recognizes that God can redirect his plans, resources, and goals anytime he desires to do so (Proverbs 16:3). Paul is a good example of God redirecting his plans and how we should respond when the Spirit changes our plans swiftly (Acts 16:6–10 CSB):

> [6] They went through the region of Phrygia and Galatia and were prevented by the Holy Spirit from speaking the message in Asia. [7] When they came to Mysia, they tried to go into Bithynia, but the Spirit of Jesus did not allow them. [8] So, bypassing Mysia, they came down to Troas. [9] During the night a vision appeared to Paul: A Macedonian man was standing and pleading with him, "Cross over to Macedonia and help us!" [10] After he had seen the vision, we immediately made efforts to set out for Macedonia, concluding that God had called us to evangelize them.

In these short verses, the Holy Spirit changes the plans of Paul and his team three times. How the Holy Spirit did his preventative work is a matter of speculation for us. But we know that through a vision, God gave them clear direction on where he wanted them to visit next.[669] We can discern that as God changed their plans, he did so through 'double guidance:' prohibition and restraint with permission and constraint.[670] Like Paul, we must be sensitive and obedient to the spirit's direct guidance. Sometimes, we must listen to the "still small voice" like Elijah (1 Kings 19:12) in understanding and obeying God's will and plans.[671]

Sensitivity is a two–way street. God's directive voice is quiet and sensitive to our obedience, too. We rarely think of the Spirit being sensitive to us, but he is. R.T. Kendall wrote:

> The *sensitivity of the Holy Spirit* refers to how sensitive he is when he is grieved ... If we can tune in to the sensitivity of the Spirit, we learn what grieves him, how to avoid grieving him, and how we must adjust to him if we want his intimate company. [But we also must be sensitive] *to* the Spirit. We must be tuned in to his active will or voice. If we develop a

---

669 John R. W. Stott, *The Message of Acts: The Spirit, the Church & the World.* The Bible Speaks Today. (InterVarsity Press, 1994), 260–61.

670 Arthur Pierson, *The Acts of the Holy Spirit.* (New York, Chicago, Toronto: Fleming H. Revell, 1895), 120–22.

671 Grant R. Osborne, *Acts: Verse by Verse.* Osborne New Testament Commentaries. (Lexham Press, 2019), 293–94.

sensitivity to the Spirit, we will hear him when he speaks and thus avoid quenching the Spirit.[672] [emphasis his]

When the Spirit is grieved (Ephesians 4:30), he withdraws. His is *quenched*.[673] He does not cut off from us and end his relationship with us, but he withdraws much like a spouse whom the other spouse has hurt withdraws to another room in the house. He leaves *quickly*. And he leaves *quietly*. When we disobey, The Spirit is grieved and unable to be what he *could be* in and through us.

Mature Christians sense when they have grieved the Spirit. They can feel his withdrawal. They are sensitive *to* the Spirit's presence, which means sensitivity to the Spirit's ways, direction, guidance, and, yes, changing our plans. *Our sensitivity to the Spirit alerts us to his leading and leaving. Without a tender sensitivity to the Spirit, we will miss his quiet voice when he speaks with us and his quiet leaving when our disobedience grieves him.*

Our sensitivity to the Spirit is often quenched because of the "cares of this world" and the "deceitfulness of wealth" (Matthew 13:18-23). The word becomes unfruitful because it is sown among the thorns. The thorns are a word-picture for the word of God not being able to take root in a Christian's heart and mind because he pays too much attention to the "cares of this world" and is deceived by the allure of wealth. "Cares of this world" include achievements, thrills, pursuing financial success, appearances, and reputation—chasing the "good life" that assumes you can have all of God and the good that the world offers. The cares of this world offer us nothing but a ruse. The word is choked out, the Spirit is quenched, and we wonder why we do not draw close to God, cannot overcome sin, or hear God's voice. We wonder why we lack sensitivity to the Spirit. We miss the truth that God will not compete with our affections. We must empty ourselves of the cares of this world so he can fill us with his Spirit. We will never be sensitive to the Spirit when we love the things of this world (1 John 2:15).

Paul is an excellent example for us. Paul is portrayed as being in touch with the Spirit well enough to understand the Spirit's leading and submissive and obedient to the Spirit's direction. Paul is an excellent example of how CBOs should engage in planning and the sensitivity a CBO should have toward the Spirit's ongoing direction while implementing those plans.

---

672   R.T. Kendall, *The Sensitivity of the Spirit*. (Charisma House, 2002), 25–26.

673   "It may be concluded that quenching the Holy Spirit is to suppress, stifle, or otherwise obstruct the ministry of the Spirit to the individual. In a word it is saying, "No," and replacing the will of the Spirit with the will of the individual." John F. Walvoord, "Contemporary Issues in the Doctrine of the Holy Spirit: Part III: New Morality." *Bibliotheca Sacra* 1973. 519(130):215.

Biblical Passages on Planning

The Bible does not give moral or pragmatic instructions about developing a plan. Instead, the Bible is concerned with the planner's intentions and asserts that humanity cannot thwart God's plans. At a minimum, we can learn several macro lessons about ourselves and our plans, even from a cursory reading of the Scriptures. I will do a brief review of these lessons now.

One's morality is revealed by the plans one makes. Proverbs 14:22 (NIV) says,

> Do not those who plot evil go astray? But those who plan what is good find love and faithfulness.

One's moral behavior is usually the result of many plans executed over a sustained period.[674] The planners of evil are contrasted with the planners of good. The former go astray (presumably from God's laws and his loving kindness), whereas the latter are met with God's reliable kindness.[675] A CBO should consider the outcome of his plans as one way to check his moral intentions.

God's plans will always succeed and endure. Psalm 33:10–11 (NIV) says,

> [10] The Lord foils the plans of the nations; he thwarts the purposes of the peoples. [11] But the plans of the Lord stand firm forever, the purposes of his heart through all generations.

Purposes and plans are intertwined. If you want to know a person's purpose, look at the plans he makes and executes. If his plans conflict with God's agenda, they will fail, indicating that he is not walking with God.[676] A CBO should make plans that do not conflict with God's plans. God's plans will endure, and when a CBO makes a plan that conflicts with God's plan, the CBO should plan to fail.

One of God's blessings for the righteous is that God ensures that the plans of the righteous succeed. In Psalm 20, David receives a list of blessings from his people as they wish him Godspeed before he heads into battle.[677] One of these blessings wished on David is

---

674 Allen P. Ross, "Proverbs." In *The Expositor's Bible Commentary: Psalms, Proverbs, Ecclesiastes, Song of Songs*, edited by Frank E. Gaebelein, Vol. 5. (Zondervan, 1991), 988.

675 Bruce Waltke, *The Book of Proverbs, Chapters 1–15*. The New International Commentary on the Old Testament. (Eerdmans Publishing, 2004), 600–01.

676 Willem A. VanGemeren, "Psalms." In *The Expositor's Bible Commentary: Psalms, Proverbs, Ecclesiastes, Song of Songs*, edited by Frank E. Gaebelein, Vol. 5. (Zondervan, 1991), 279.

677 Derek Kidner, *Psalms 1–72: an introduction and commentary*. (InterVarsity Press, 1973), 118.

that God would ensure his plans succeed (Psalm 20:4 NIV): "May he give you the desire of your heart and make all your plans succeed."

When God blesses his people, he ensures the plans of his people succeed more often and at a higher quality than would normally be expected. In some ways, a blessing partially mitigates the effects of sin and depravity in our world. Deuteronomy 28:2–6 (CSB) is one of several passages where we draw these conclusions:

> [2] All these blessings will come and overtake you, because you obey the Lord your God: [3] You will be blessed in the city and blessed in the country. [4] Your descendants will be blessed, and your land's produce, and the offspring of your livestock, including the young of your herds and the newborn of your flocks. [5] Your basket and kneading bowl will be blessed. [6] You will be blessed when you come in and blessed when you go out.

The conditions for God's blessing always start with covenant loyalty and obedience. The 'coming and going' refer to the breadth of God's blessing extending to all of life for the righteous (Deuteronomy 6:7).[678] Through obedience, the righteous find happiness and fulfillment.[679]

Comparing wicked and righteous plans

The Bible describes the plans of the wicked in stark terms. For example, the plans of the wicked come from hearts that hold fast to evil purposes, deceit, and injustice (Psalm 64:5–6). The wicked plan evil in their hearts and stir up conflict persistently (Psalm 140:2). The wicked stray from the ways of God (Proverbs 14:22) and self–exalt in arrogance (Proverbs 30:32). The wicked who devise plans are described as stubborn, rebellious (Jeremiah 18:12), and compounding their sin (Isaiah 30:1). Evil plans lead to coveting and oppression (Micah 2:1–2) as well as deceit and lying (Matthew 28:12–13). In addition, evil plans lead to quarrels, dissension, slander, evil suspicions and constant friction (1 Timothy 6:4–5). Because God protects the righteous, the plans of the evil will not succeed (Psalm 21:11).

By contrast, the plans of the righteous are described as just (Proverbs 12:5), loving and faithful (Proverbs 14:22), and lead to abundance (Proverbs 21:5). The plans of the righteous are peaceful and lead to joy (Proverbs 12:20). The righteous trust the Lord, acknowledge God in planning for the future and understand that God will make the righteous' plans

---

678 Eugene H. Merrill, "Deuteronomy." In *Cornerstone Biblical Commentary: Leviticus, Numbers, Deuteronomy*, edited by Philip W. Comfort, Vol. 2. (Tyndale House, 1996), 626.

679 Tremper Longman, III, ed. *Deuteronomy Thru Ruth*. Vol. 2. Layman's Bible Commentary. (Barbour Publishing, 2009), 78.

"straight" (Proverbs 3:5–6). The righteous "count the cost" of a plan before implementation and are not impulsive or hasty with plan development or evaluation (Luke 14:28–30).

A CBO understands that God sustains his plans if they have been created under his direction. Consider Proverbs 16:1–4 (LEB):

> [1] To mortals *belong* the plans of the heart, but from Yahweh *comes* the answer of the tongue. 2 All the ways of a man *are* pure in his own eyes, but Yahweh weighs the spirit. 3 Commit your work to Yahweh, and your plans will be established. 4 All Yahweh has made *is* for his purpose, and even the wicked for the day of trouble.

A CBO should commit his plans to the Lord to become part of God's larger plans.[680] Only God can accurately assess the motives that cause our plans. Our opinions of ourselves are often naive and therefore should be evaluated by God, not us.[681]

There is an unbroken connection between our motives and the results of our plans. The thrust of vss. 3–4 is that we can create our plans with great prudence, yet those plans must be committed[682] to God and approved by him if those plans—the results—are to endure.[683] "Trusting in Yahweh is more important than prudence,"[684] though we cannot jettison prudence as if it is unimportant. One gets the notion that God looks at our motives and plans and decides whether or not to incorporate them into his permanent agenda. If God does this, the results are positively solidified.

As presented in the Bible, planning (as a concept) is mostly concerned with:
- Trust in God
- The motivations of the planner
- The righteousness of the planner
- Submission to God's authority, plans, and direction

Figure 12–1 illustrates the contrast between plan development from a conventional wisdom perspective and plan development from a Biblical wisdom perspective. It is not that conventional wisdom is wrong; it is incomplete for a Christian business owner. The planning elements in conventional wisdom should be incorporated as prudent steps in developing

---

680 Bruce Waltke, *The Book of Proverbs, Chapters 15–31*. The New International Commentary on the Old Testament. (Eerdmans, 2005), 11.

681 Allen P. Ross, "Proverbs." In *The Expositor's Bible Commentary: Psalms, Proverbs, Ecclesiastes, Song of Songs*, edited by Frank E. Gaebelein, Vol. 5. (Zondervan, 1991), 1002.

682 "committed": roll one's troubles onto another or away from oneself, i.e., entrust wholly (TWOT)

683 Richard J. Clifford, *Proverbs: A Commentary*. First edition. (Westminster John Knox Press, 1999), 156.

684 Duane A. Garrett, *Proverbs, Ecclesiastes, Song of Songs*, vol. 14, The New American Commentary (Broadman & Holman, 1993), 156.

plans. Still, the higher aspects of trust, faith, and motivation must be overlayed in the planning process. Figure 12–1 illustrates this discussion.

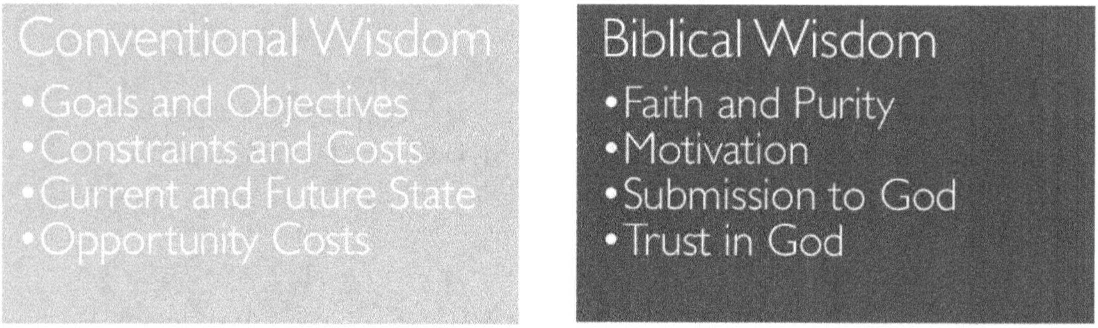

Conventional Wisdom
- Goals and Objectives
- Constraints and Costs
- Current and Future State
- Opportunity Costs

Biblical Wisdom
- Faith and Purity
- Motivation
- Submission to God
- Trust in God

Figure 12–1: Conventional and Biblical wisdom compared in plan development process.

SUMMARY

The CBO should learn the following lessons when it comes to one's planning process and implementing those plans:

- Plans can be made and implemented, but the follower of God will bear in mind that God can change the plans at any time
- An ongoing sensitivity and obedience to the Spirit's direction is needed for God's ongoing activities
- When God gives direction, CBOs immediately follow; there is no attempt to negotiate with God
- God's direction may not be the next logical step from man's viewpoint

In the next chapter, we'll learn what the Bible says about Governance, Risk, and Compliance (GRC). GRC is (or should be) an important topic to business owners, so let's turn the page and keep going.

CHAPTER 13

GOVERNANCE, RISK, AND COMPLIANCE

Governance, risk, and compliance are usually grouped because these foci are uniquely the domain of business ownership and are interrelated. Compliance with industry standards and government regulations cannot be ignored in our litigious society. Liability risk is reduced when one complies with regulations. Many day-to-day problems in business are related to governance, risk, and compliance.

In this chapter, I will suggest that the Divine Council is a model for us to follow in our governance efforts and that there are moral constraints on our governance models. I will also contend that risk mitigation is more about obedience to God's commands than anything else. In addition, I will argue that compliance with laws and regulations is part of giving to "Caesar what is Caesar's." I will discuss the theoretical notion that God can "take a risk" in the sense that we use that phrase, and I'll discuss a theology of civil disobedience. Finally, because assuming a risk always means one might be injured, the possibility of an injury may create worry and anxiety inside a business owner. I will argue that assuming risk, when directed by God, is the safest place an owner can be and that worry should not be a part of a CBO's persona.

IN MY EXPERIENCE, when one individual wholly owns a business, it will lack proper governance because traditional governance is often viewed as an unnecessary annoyance. The conventional governance roles of shareholders, board members, corporate officers, and employees are wrapped up into a single individual, so holding paper-based meetings to build a corporate record book often seems unnecessary.

However, as their business grows, a lack of adequate governance will dampen their success and open the owner to having his corporate veil pierced as a defendant in a legal proceeding.[685] Smart owners know how to leverage governance as a growth tool rather than viewing it as limiting their autonomy. Mediocre owners do not do governance well, leaving a lot of opportunity and profit on the table and exposure to liability should they engage in unethical or illegal practices.

Governance is managing an organization based on specific rules and values with accountability to another individual, group, or entity.[686] Governance is an allocation of power among the board, management, and shareholders[687] that results in a system of checks and balances meant to prevent abuse by executives entrusted with running the company on behalf of the shareholders and board of directors.[688] Governance decisions have deep tentacles in an organization and usually require legal, ethical, and social considerations.[689]

---

685 "Piercing the corporate veil" refers to a legal situation where a court holds the owners or shareholders of a corporation personally liable for the company's debts, essentially disregarding the separate legal entity of the corporation, because there was a lack of distinction between the company and its owners, often due to fraudulent or improper actions by the owners; meaning their personal assets can be used to pay off company debts. See Cornell Law School, "Piercing the Corporate Veil." n.d., law.cornell.edu. https://www.law.cornell.edu/wex/piercing_the_corporate_veil. See also Johnston Allison Hord, "Piercing the Corporate Veil: How to Avoid Personal Liability." July 30, 2024, jahlaw.com. https://www.jahlaw.com/piercing-the-corporate-veil-how-to-avoid-personal-liability-news-and-events/

686 Leading Governance, "What is governance and why is it important?" leadinggovernance.com, accessed 11/18/2023. https://www.leadinggovernance.com/blog/what–is–governance/

687 Robert Steinberg, *Governance, Risk Management, and Compliance.* (John Wiley & Sons, 2011), 1.

688 David Larker and Brian Tayan, *Corporate Governance Matters: A Closer Look at Organizational Choices and Their Consequences.* (FT Press, 2011), 1.

689 John Colley, Jacqueline Doyle, George Logan, and Wallace Stettinius, *Corporate Governance.* (McGraw–Hill, 2003), x.

CONVENTIONAL WISDOM AND GOVERNANCE

It is generally accepted that there are five core areas of corporate governance. These governance areas assume a publically traded company with a diverse matrix of shareholders, a healthy board, and corporate officers who manage the business's day–to–day activities on behalf of the shareholders:

- Effectiveness of the Board
- Compensation and Remunerations
- Risk and Crisis Management
- Relationships with Stakeholders
- Ethics and Transparency

Board members are elected to represent the interests of the owners who cannot represent themselves, and corporate officers are charged with running the business in the best interest of the owners who cannot run the business themselves. Mitigating conflicts of interest[690] that give rise to agency costs[691] is a vital governance effort in publicly traded companies and larger privately held companies.

Interestingly, Colley suggests that businesses privately held by an individual cannot have conflicts of interest by the owners.[692] Colley et al. assert that the owner's self–interest is identical to the business's best interests because the business and the owner are the same. So, when the individual owner acts in his self–interest, there is no conflict of interest between the business and the owner.

The position of Colley et al. is a godless position that does not account for the presence of God or his ownership of the business. When a CBO operates out of Biblical wisdom instead of conventional wisdom, the CBO acts in the best interests of God, setting aside his self–interests. Conflicts of interest may arise, but they are primarily conflicts within the CBO's persona (cf James 4:1). Conforming one's will to God's will is the solution to a conflict of interest in God's system of governance. Figure 13–1 illustrates the difference in governance viewpoints between today's conventional wisdom and Biblical wisdom in single–owner businesses.

---

690 A "conflict of interest" occurs when an individual becomes unreliable because of a conflict between the personal interests of that individual and the professional duties or responsibilities that individual holds in the organization. (Troy Segal, "What is a Conflict of Interest?" July 30, 2024. Investopedia.com. https://www.investopedia.com/terms/c/conflict–of–interest.asp.)

691 An "agency cost" occurs when the interests of an executive manager conflict with the interests of the company's shareholders. (James Chen, "What are Agency Costs?" March 28, 2001. Investopedia.com. https://www.investopedia.com/terms/a/agencycosts.asp

692 Colley, Corporate Governance, 13–14.

Conventional Wisdom	Biblical Wisdom
Single Owner	Single Owner
No conflict of interest	Conflicts of interest
Accountable to Self	Accountable to God
Self-governed	God-governed

Figure 13–1: The difference in governance between conventional and Biblical wisdom.

BIBLICAL WISDOM AND GOVERNANCE

The way we think of corporate governance today is unique to the time in which we live. The concepts of corporate governance are not taught in Scripture, but they are illustrated. For example, God governs this universe (cf Proverbs 8:14–16, Isaiah 9:6–7) through his divine council.[693] We can learn how God governs through his divine council—which is a council comprised of Yahweh and other gods or supernatural beings through which God governs the universe[694]—and then contrast God's governance with conventional corporate governance to gain a starting point from the Scriptures of how a CBO should govern his business.

Governance and the Divine Council

A council or assembly of gods is common in the religious literature of Mesopotamia, Ugarit, Canaan, and Phoenicia. These councils are a standard part of the organization of

693 Michael Heiser, *The Unseen Realm*. (Lexham Press, 2015), 34–35.
694 Faithlife, "Divine Assembly." In *Logos Bible Study Factbook*. (Faithlife, September 12, 2024). https://ref.ly/logos4/Factbook?id=ref%3abk.%25divineAssembly.

the divine realm. Decisions made by a council are binding on all the member gods, who are subject to the pantheon's decisions.[695]

The Bible says that God has a council of divine beings who carry out his decisions. It is referred to as God's assembly, council, or court. A primary difference between the ANE's and Biblical councils is that Yahweh is not one among equals in the council. He is not bound by any pantheon's decision(s). Instead, he is the incomparably great God who rules over the council and the universe. *The divine council does not moderate God's ultimate and incomparable greatness.*

There are a number of references to God's incomparable greatness and authority in the Scriptures. For examples, after Moses and Israel crossed the Reed Sea and God gave them victory over the Pharoah and the gods of Egypt, Moses cried (Exodus 15:11 NIV):

> Who among the gods is like you, Lord? Who is like you— majestic in holiness, awesome in glory, working wonders?

Moses asked a rhetorical question since no gods in Egypt or anywhere else could compare to Yahweh. "He is incomparable! He is indescribable! He is incomprehensible!"[696]

A.W. Tozer lamented what he called "the loss of the concept of majesty" in the minds of men:

> The church has surrendered her once lofty concept of god and has substituted for it one so low, so ignoble, as to be utterly unworthy of thinking, worshiping men … with out loss of the sense of majesty has come the further loss of religious awe and consciousness of the divine Presence. … no religion has ever been greater than its idea of God. Always the most revealing thing about the church is her idea of God, just as her most significant message is what she says about him or leaves unsaid, for her silence is often more elequent [sic] than her speech.[697]

Gaining a more mature—some would say "deeper"—concept of God's greatness will transform many other areas of our faith.

---

695 Mullen, E. Theodore, Jr., "Divine Assembly." In *The Anchor Yale Bible Dictionary*, edited by David Noel Freedman. (Doubleday, 1992).

696 Kenneth R. Cooper, "How Immeasurable Is God? A Vision of the Greatness of God in Isaiah 40:9–20 Examined," *Journal of Dispensational Theology.* 2009. 40(13): 45.

697 A.W. Tozer, The Knowledge of the Holy: The Attributes of God: Their Meaning in the Christian Life. (Harper & Row, 1961), 6–10.

Isaiah 40:12-31

While writing this chapter, I reread this passage from Isaiah, which jumped out from the page to me. While this passage is somewhat long, Isaiah 40:12–31 (LEB) should be read and re-read. I encourage you to slow down and let its' words transform your mind and soul:

^{12} Who has measured *the* waters in the hollow of his hand and marked off *the* heavens with *a* span, comprehended the dust of the earth in *a* third of a measure and weighed out *the* mountains in the scales, and *the* hills in a balance? ^{13} Who has measured up the spirit of Yahweh or informed him *as* his counselor? ^{14} With whom has he consulted, that he enlightened him and taught him *the* path of justice, and taught him knowledge, and made *the* way of understanding known to him? ^{15} Look! *The* nations *are* like a drop from a bucket, and they are counted like dust of *the* balances! Look! He weighs *the* islands like a thin covering. ^{16} And Lebanon *is* not enough to light a fire, and its animals not enough for a burnt offering. ^{17} All the nations *are* like nothing before him; they are counted by him as nothing and emptiness. ^{18} And to whom will you liken God? And to what likeness will you compare him? ^{19} A craftsman pours out the idol, and goldsmith overlays it with gold, and *he* smelts chains of silver. ^{20} The one who is *too* impoverished *for* a gift chooses wood *that* will not rot; he seeks a skillful artisan for himself to set up an image *that* will not be knocked over. ^{21} Have you not known? Have you not heard? Has it not been told to you from *the* beginning? Have you not understood *from* the foundation of the earth? ^{22} *He is* the one who sits above^{698} the circle^{699} of the earth, and its inhabitants *are* like grasshoppers; the one who stretches out *the* heavens like a veil and spreads them out like *a* tent to live *in,* ^{23} the one who brings princes to nothing; he makes rulers of *the* earth like nothing. ^{24} Indeed, hardly are they planted; indeed, hardly *are they* sown; indeed, hardly has their shoot taken root in the earth when he blows on them and they wither, and *the* tempest carries them like stubble. ^{25} "And to whom

---

698 Sits above, LEB, NASB, ESV; enthroned above , CSB; sits enthroned, NIV.

699 The horizon is understood as a vaulted sky. (Faithlife. "Horizon <=> Circle." In Logos Bible Study Bible Sense Lexicon. (Faithlife, September 12, 2024.) https://ref.ly/logos4/Senses?KeyId=ws.horizon.n.01.) From חוּג, (used only 3x in the OT), vault, horizon (BDB), mark out a boundary line between two vast endless areas as a figurative extension of a circle being without end (DBL).

you will compare me, and am I equal?" says *the* holy one. [26] Lift your eyes up *on* high, and see! Who created these? The one who brings out their host by number. He calls all them by name. Because *he is* great of power and mighty of power, not one is missing. [27] Why do you say, Jacob, and you speak, Israel, "My way is hidden from Yahweh, and my judgment is passed over by my God?" [28] Have you not known, or have you not heard? Yahweh *is* the God of eternity, *the* creator *of* the ends of the earth! He is not faint, and he does not grow weary! There is no searching his understanding. [29] *He* gives power to the weary, and he increases power for the powerless. [30] Even young people will be faint and grow weary, and *the* young will stumble, exhausted. [31] But those who wait for Yahweh shall renew *their* strength. They shall go up *with* wings like eagles; they shall run and not grow weary; they shall walk and not be faint.

Look at the ways that God's incomparable greatness is described in this passage:

- While man is confined to the earth, God sits far above it.[700]
- He who measures creation cannot be measured by creation. [701]
- God is able to do what is humanly impossible. [702]
- The power of all nations on earth *combined* are nothing compared to the power of Yahweh.[703]
- The world does not revolve around the nations and their interests. The world revolves around God and his agenda.[704]

---

700 Larry Pechawer, *Poetry and Prophecy*. Vol. 3. Standard Reference Library: Old Testament. (Standard Publishing, 2008), 136.

701 "God alone has measured the waters in the hollow of His hand, but He Himself is unmeasurable. He who has measured the creation cannot be measured by the creation. (Edward Young, *The Book of Isaiah, Chapters 40–66*. Vol. 3. (Eerdmans, 1972), 44.)

702 "These questions point not only to God's ability to do what is humanly impossible, but also to his unfathomable greatness and power." (Gary Smith, *Isaiah 40–66*. Vol. 15B. The New American Commentary. (Broadman & Holman Publishers, 2009), 109.) Also, consider Oswalt's comment: "If we cannot even take the measure of the physical world, how can we take the measure of God?" (John Oswalt, *The Book of Isaiah, Chapters 40–66*. The New International Commentary on the Old Testament. (Eerdmans, 1998), 90.)

703 "Compared to the greatness of God, all the power of earthly nations is next to nothing—a drop of water or a speck of dust." (Faithlife Study Bible. (Lexham Press, 2016), Isaiah 40:15.

704 "As a sovereign divine spirit being, God simply dwells in a different plane of reality. One of the implications of God's transcendent incomparability is that the world does not actually revolve around the great nations of the earth and is not determined by personal wishes, human accomplishments, or national goals. What goes on in this world is actually centered on God and his plans. Therefore, in reality these nations have no power." (Smith, *Isaiah 40–66*, 112–13.)

- God cannot be represented by that which he created and is inherently inferior to him.[705]
- God's power is incomparably greater than any political or military power on this earth.[706]
- God created the gods.[707]
- The restoration of God's people is grounded in God's nature.[708]
- God notices injustice and takes action to protect his people.[709]
- God gives us the strength to endure trials and suffering.[710]

Let us learn to see God high and lifted up, sitting on his throne, able to do anything he desires, complete in his perfections, unmoved by any outside force, incomprehensible yet knowable, and taking an unending interest in his creation (you and me) as he strengthens and preserves us to reign with him in eternity!

Several passages describe the divine council and are presented here for our learning. Surprisingly, this council is expressly taught and illustrated in the Bible and yet is so rarely taught in our churches and seminaries.[711]

God has taken his place in the divine council; in the midst of the gods he holds judgment (Psalm 82:1 ESV)

I said, "You are gods, sons of the Most High, all of you; nevertheless, like men you shall die, and fall like any prince. (Psalm 82:6–7 ESV)

---

705 "Men make the idol, but Israel's God made humanity (Gen 1–2)." (Smith, *Isaiah 40–66*, 115.)

706 "No king on earth is too firmly established to be blown away by the breath of God." (Pechawer, *Poetry and Prophecy*, 136.)

707 "The religions of the ancient Near East believed the stars were gods. Judah's religion asserted that God created the stars. The fact that he knew them by name indicates that they were his creation and they were protected by his power." (Tremper Longman, III, "Isaiah." In *CSB Study Bible: Notes*, edited by Edwin A. Blum and Trevin Wax. (Holman Bible Publishers, 2017), 1099.

708 Willem A. VanGemeren, "Isaiah." In *Evangelical Commentary on the Bible*, 3:471–514. Baker Reference Library. (Baker Books, 1995), 499.

709 "Nothing has or ever will be hidden from God, and no issue of justice has or ever will be overlooked by God." (Smith, *Isaiah 40–66*, 121.)

710 Pechawer, Poetry and Prophecy, 138.

711 To learn more, see Leland Ryken, Jim Wilhoit, Tremper Longman, Colin Duriez, Douglas Penney, and Daniel G. Reid. *Dictionary of Biblical Imagery*. (InterVarsity Press, 2000), 50–54, and Mullen, E. Theodore, Jr. "Divine Assembly." In *The Anchor Yale Bible Dictionary*, edited by David Noel Freedman. (Doubleday, 1992), v2, 214–17.

[6] One day the sons of God came to present themselves before the Lord, and Satan also came with them. [7] The Lord asked Satan, "Where have you come from?" "From roaming through the earth," Satan answered Him, "and walking around on it." [8] Then the Lord said to Satan, "Have you considered My servant Job? No one else on earth is like him, a man of perfect integrity, who fears God and turns away from evil." [9] Satan answered the Lord, "Does Job fear God for nothing? [10] Haven't You placed a hedge around him, his household, and everything he owns? You have blessed the work of his hands, and his possessions have increased in the land. [11] But stretch out Your hand and strike everything he owns, and he will surely curse You to Your face." [12] "Very well," the Lord told Satan, "everything he owns is in your power. However, you must not lay a hand on Job himself." So Satan left the Lord's presence. (Job 1:6–12 CSB)

[5] The heavens will praise Your wonders, O Lord; Your faithfulness also in the assembly of the holy ones. [6] For who in the skies is comparable to the Lord? Who among the sons of the mighty is like the Lord, [7] A God greatly feared in the council of the holy ones, And awesome above all those who are around Him? [8] O Lord God of hosts, who is like You, O mighty Lord? Your faithfulness also surrounds You. (Psalm 89:5–8 NASB)

8 When the Most High apportioned *the* nations, at his dividing *up* of the sons of humankind, he fixed the boundaries of *the* peoples, according to the number of the sons of God. 9 For Yahweh's portion *was* his people, Jacob the share of his inheritance. (Deuteronomy 32:8–9 LEB)

This council is made of spiritual beings that are less than God but greater than us. These passages do not make sense if they refer to men or idols—these *gods* are real. For purposes unknown to us, God chooses to administrate his rule of the cosmos through other divine beings, some of whom are in rebellion against Him. Psalm 82:6 refers to them as "sons of the Most High" (cf Job 1:6; 2:1). In Job 38:7, we are told they were with God before he created the earth and humanity.

In his council, these beings are decision–makers and participate in God's rule, yet God is incomparably greater than these beings, and they carry out his plans and agenda. While God works with his council, he is alone in his attributes and perfections. God is above these council members in every way. God is so completely *other* that he is incomprehensible to us unless He condescends to us as he discloses himself to us. Even though God rules

241

through his divine council, he is clearly incomparable and far above any spiritual being (which he created) in his council.

1 Kings 22:13–22 (CSB) is a good example of how God rules through his council:

> ^{13} The messenger who went to call Micaiah instructed him, "Look, the words of the prophets are unanimously favorable for the king. So let your words be like theirs, and speak favorably." ^{14} But Micaiah said, "As the Lord lives, I will say whatever the Lord says to me." ^{15} So he went to the king, and the king asked him, "Micaiah, should we go to Ramoth–gilead for war, or should we refrain?" Micaiah told him, "March up and succeed. Yahweh will hand it over to the king." ^{16} But the king said to him, "How many times must I make you swear not to tell me anything but the truth in the name of Yahweh?" ^{17} So Micaiah said: I saw all Israel scattered on the hills like sheep without a shepherd. And the Lord said, "They have no master; let everyone return home in peace." ^{18} So the king of Israel said to Jehoshaphat, "Didn't I tell you he never prophesies good about me, but only disaster?" ^{19} Then Micaiah said, "Therefore, hear the word of the Lord: I saw the Lord sitting on His throne, and the whole heavenly host was standing by Him at His right hand and at His left hand. ^{20} And the Lord said, 'Who will entice Ahab to march up and fall at Ramoth–gilead?' So one was saying this and another was saying that. ^{21} "Then a spirit came forward, stood before the Lord, and said, 'I will entice him.' ^{22} "The Lord asked him, 'How?' "He said, 'I will go and become a lying spirit in the mouth of all his prophets.' "Then He said, 'You will certainly entice him and prevail. Go and do that.'

God had decided it was time for Ahab to die, but did not decree the means of *how* Ahab would die. The council debated the manner of death for Ahab until one spiritual being came forward and offered a solution that God liked.[712] The spirit would be a lying spirit in the mouths of the prophets and Ahab would follow bad advice, leading to his death.

We see a similar situation in which God decides the outcome—the end result—and then involves his council in how to accomplish his decision in Daniel 4:13–17, 24 (CSB):

> ^{13} "As I was lying in my bed, I also saw in the visions of my mind an observer, a holy one, ^{n} coming down from heaven. ^{14} He called out loudly: Cut down the tree and chop off its branches; strip off its leaves

---

712 Michael Heiser, *The Unseen Realm: Recovering a Supernatural Worldview of the Bible.* (Lexham Press, 2015), 51. See also Michael Heiser. *Divine Council Intro.* Accessed 09/14/2024. 21:40. https://youtu.be/pKPid4i4SmI?si=TGoAc08IerXDfD5l

and scatter its fruit. Let the animals flee from under it, and the birds from its branches. [15] But leave the stump with its roots in the ground, and with a and of iron and bronze around it, in the tender grass of the field. Let him be drenched with dew from the sky and share the plants of the earth with the animals. [16] Let his mind be changed from that of a man, and let him be given the mind of an animal for seven periods of time. [17] This word is by decree of the observers; the matter is a command from the holy ones. This is so the living will know that the Most High is ruler over the kingdom of men. He gives it to anyone He wants and sets the lowliest of men over it … [24] This is the interpretation, Your Majesty, and this is the sentence of the Most High that has been passed against my lord the king.

The sentence—the decision to punish Nebuchanezzar—came directly from God, but *how* this punishment was carried out was a decision of the watchers. Heiser is spot on when he writes:

The takeaway is that God rules over the heavenly realm and the earthly realm with the genuine assistance of his imager–representatives. He decrees and they carry out his commands. These points are clear. What is perhaps less clear is that the way God's will is carried out and accomplished is open—imagers can make free decisions to accomplish God's will. God decrees the ends, but the means can (and apparently are at times) left up to the imagers.[713]

Learning from the Divine Council for Corporate Governance

Christian business owners can learn how to better govern their businesses by examining how God manages his divine council.

God makes a decision and sets the result in stone. God modeled this well in these two stories. I will paraphrase here: "It is time for Ahab to go!" or "Nebuchadnezzar must be punished." As owners, we should articulate the result in clear, measurable, discreet terms. It is better to say, "I want 1,000 widgets manufactured next month," instead of, "Make sure you manufacture as many widgets as possible next month." The former is better, more transparent, discreet, and more measurable.

---

713 Heiser, *Unseen Realm*, 54–55.

If your vision, mission, and decision–making processes (governance) are full of unclear or unmeasurable directives, your company will be confused about what you want. *When employees are confused and cannot gain clarity from you, they will work in good faith to "figure it out" on their own, supplying the clarity they need as best they can from what they know and can deduce to do their job. Their efforts will often conflict with other employees who have reached different conclusions. In addition, their efforts may work at cross purposes to what you wanted but did not articulate well, and you will likely blame them instead of yourself.*

Nothing can replace clarity and a well-articulated vision and mission. Nothing. If you are unclear in your decisions and the direction you want to go, do whatever it takes to become clear. Go to the library and read some books, take some classes, talk to other owners, hire a consultant, but work until you have clarity. Your employees will thank you, and you will better steward God's entrustment to you.

Involve and listen to your team to develop **how** to achieve your goals. Presumably, you have hired top talent, and once you have clarity on your vision and mission, it is time to step back and let your team shine. Heavily involve them in developing the plans to achieve your vision and mission. *Listen* to them. Let them offer ideas. Let them offer competing ideas. Let them work together to develop the best plans for your vision and mission. In doing so, they will implicitly take ownership of the plans, which is a good thing for you, the business owner. They will execute better on that which they own.

After the plans are developed and approved, stand back and watch them execute **their** plans. If you micromanage everything from plan development to execution, *you will mess it all up, and you will have more problems than if you let people accomplish your goals and objectives using their plans.*

Governance and Morality

Biblical governance is concerned with morality and discernment. Because of our sin, we have difficulty, if not an inherent inability, understanding God's moral governance of the world.[714] Consider 1 Kings 3:9 (NIV), where Solomon asked God for wisdom as he began to reign:

> [9] So give your servant a discerning heart to govern your people and to distinguish between right and wrong. For who is able to govern this great people of yours?

---

714 Robert V. McCabe, "The Message of Ecclesiastes." *Detroit Baptist Seminary Journal Volume 1,* 1996. 1:105.

At the heart of governing is the ability to discern right from wrong. But the source of morality must be God, not ourselves. Some advocate a moral law that obliges others to respect one's moral governance of oneself.[715] But elevating oneself to be the supreme authority in one's life is the essence of idolatry, and God will not tolerate that. Only God can be the true source of moral law for this universe.[716]

Governance and Conflicts

In Matthew 12, Christ teaches that persistent, unresolved conflicts at the governance layer of an organization will ensure the organization will fail and likely dissolve (Matthew 12:25b–26 NASB):

> Any kingdom divided against itself is laid waste; and any city or house divided against itself will not stand. [26] If Satan casts out Satan, he is divided against himself; how then will his kingdom stand?

When unresolved conflicts persist at the leadership level of an organization, different parts of the organization will likely work at cross purposes, permeating the governance conflict throughout the organization. That organization will be ineffective and eventually fail in its mission.

The shareholders and board members must agree regarding vision, mission, and core values at the governance layer. The organization's ongoing operations will flounder under the conflict to the extent that these groups do not agree.

In a traditional governance model, the shareholders hold the ultimate power and decide who will be on the board. They can determine the organization's core values, vision, and mission if they choose to do so. However, in a privately held business, these functions are wrapped up in the owner's role. They only need to be federated with others as the company grows, and you, the owner, reach a point where you're a bottleneck, which is to say that you cannot manage good governance by yourself.

CBOs reflect God's governing character by emphasizing right and wrong and ensuring justice is dispensed impartially. In business, dispensing impartial justice means holding everyone to the same standards and disciplining them accordingly. The standards to which I am referring are one's policies and processes. Uniform enforcement of policies and processes is equivalent to governing with justice within one's business context. By doing so, you will reduce conflict in your organization. Figure 13–2 summarizes our discussions.

---

715 Alberto Mingardi and Istituto Bruno Leoni, "A Sphere around the Person: Antonio Rosmini on Property." *Journal of Markets & Morality* (Spring and Fall 2004). 7(1):73.

716 Jim Newheiser. *Opening up Proverbs*. Opening Up Commentary. (Day One Publications, 2008), 28.

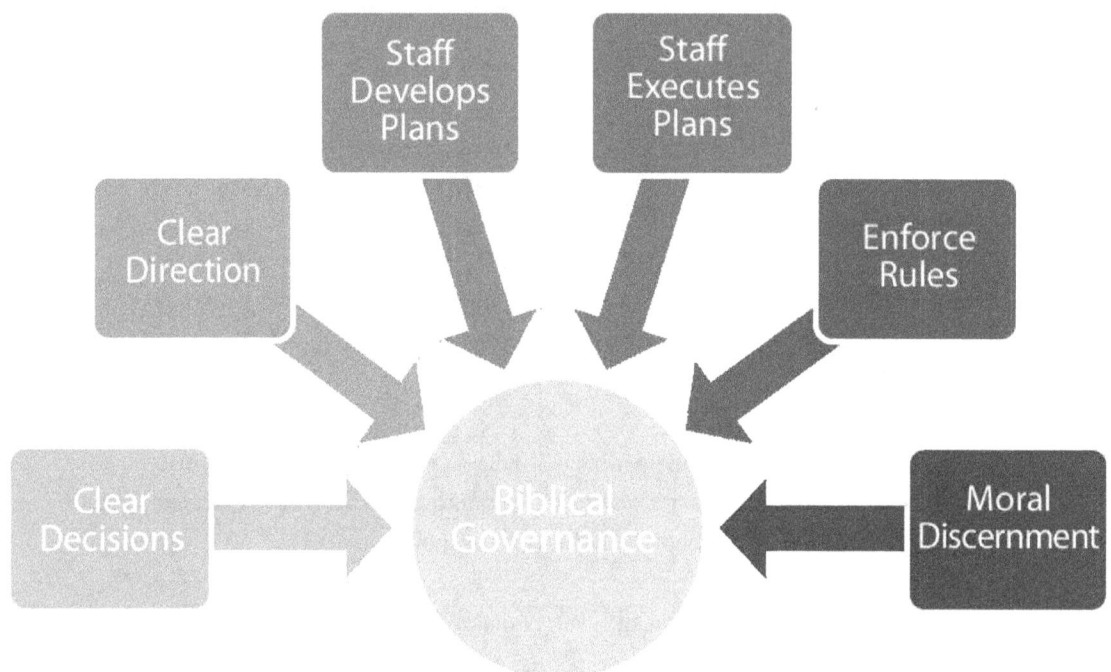

Figure 13–2: Biblical wisdom view of governance

CONVENTIONAL WISDOM ON RISK

The definition of risk varies from source to source. Steinberg defines risk as "uncertainty surrounding a potential event: "It is the possibility that something will happen—that is, an event will occur—with a negative outcome."[717] Lupton describes risk as "deviation from the norm, misfortune, and frightening events. This concept assumes human responsibility and that 'something can be done' to prevent misfortune."[718] Stern and Fineberg define risk as "a concept used to give meaning to things, forces, or circumstances that pose danger [*sic*] to people or to what they value."[719] Whereas Steinberg focuses on uncertainty with a negative outcome, Lupton describes risk as abnormality with a negative outcome. Stern and Fineberg focus on the concept of danger with an implicit nod to injury should the

---

717 Richard M. Steinberg, *Governance, Risk Management, and Compliance.* (John Wiley & Sons, 2011), 75.

718 Deborah Lupton, *Risk.* (2nd Ed.) (Routledge, 2013), 3.

719 P.C. Stern and H.V. Fineberg (Eds.), Glossary Term: "Risk." In: *Understanding Risk: Informing Decisions in a Democratic Society.* (National Academy Press, 1996), 214.

danger materialize. Note that all three assume a negative result emitting from a danger materializing.

Known as the Probability and Impact Matrix, a potential risk is assessed along two axes: the likelihood that the danger will become a reality and inflict an injury on one's business and the measure of severity (impact) one will experience if the danger comes to pass. Figure 13–3 is a simple example of implementing a Probability and Impact Matrix. Note that the higher the likelihood of the risk materializing and the higher the impact of injury of that risk on the individual or the organization, the further one moves toward the upper–right part of the matrix, where the severity assessments are "medium" or "high." Many variations of this theme are available on the market today, a few of which are rather complex.

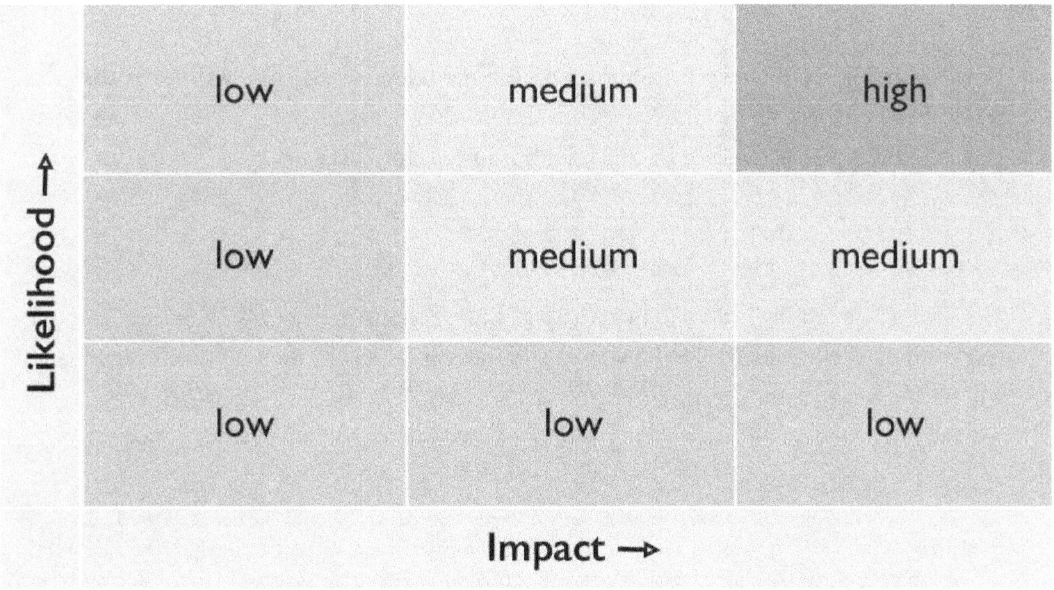

Likelihood →			
	low	medium	high
	low	medium	medium
	low	low	low
		Impact →	

Figure 13–3: Probability and Impact Matrix[720]

Assessing risk is only one side of the equation; mitigating risk is the other. Mitigating risk is one of the core tasks of a business owner. Lutkevich suggests that "risk mitigation is a strategy to prepare for and lessen the effects of threats faced by a company."[721] Risk mitiga-

720 PM Companion, "Probability and Impact Matrix." Accessed 11/21/2003, projectmanagement-companion.com. https://projectmanagementcompanion.com/probability–and–impact–matrix/

721 Ben Lutkevich, "What is Risk Mitigation? Accessed 10/13/2023, techtarget.com. https://www.techtarget.com/searchdisasterrecovery/definition/risk–mitigation

tion is usually carried out through a series of actions, such as performing a risk assessment, developing a risk mitigation plan, and implementing that plan.

Strategies for mitigating risk include risk sharing,[722] risk transfer,[723] risk avoidance,[724] or risk reduction.[725] Conventional wisdom in business is to use risk mitigation strategies, such as purchasing adequate insurance coverage (risk sharing) and engaging in an ongoing risk management effort that assesses potential risks and reduces the opportunity for any single threat to injure the company. These methods are helpful to any business owner. Still, these methods are godless in that they do not assume there is a God who owns all that exists and can act as a refuge against danger (Psalm 9:9, 11:1,16:1,18:2). For the CBO, I recommend embracing conventional wisdom with adequate risk sharing, risk transfer, risk avoidance, or risk reduction. However, I further suggest that the CBO's ultimate source of security comes from God, not from man's risk avoidance methods, products, and services.

BIBLICAL WISDOM ABOUT RISK

In this section, I will attempt to outline a Biblical view of risk. We will learn that the Biblical view of risk starts and stops with God's sovereignty over life's events. Let's learn what the Bible says about risk in this brief but important overview.

Righteous Living Leads to Security

Those who listen to the Lord will live with a feeling of security. They will be at ease, without fear of disaster. Proverbs 1:33 (ESV) says, "Whoever listens to me will dwell secure and will be at ease, without dread of disaster." Moreover, Proverbs 3:25–26 (CSB) says:

---

722 Risk sharing is defined as transferring the effects of a danger, should the danger materialize, to a third party. When a risk is shared, a portion of the effects of the danger are shouldered by the organization and the other portion(s) are shouldered by third–parties. (Study.com, s.a., "Risk Sharing Strategies & Overview: What is the Purpose of Risk Sharing?" Accessed 12/04/2023, study.com. https://study.com/buy/academy/lesson/risk–sharing–definition–strategies–examples.html

723 Risk transfer is defined as outsourcing the effects of a danger to one or more third–parties. These third–parties assume the liabilities of the transferring organization. When a risk is transferred, none of the effects of the danger are shouldered by the organization. (CFI Team, s.a., "Risk Transfer." Accessed 12/4/2023, cfi.com. https://corporatefinanceinstitute.com/resources/career–map/sell–side/risk–management/risk–transfer/)

724 Risk avoidance is the complete elimination of an exposure to risk that poses a potential loss. (The Investopedia Team, "Risk Avoidance vs. Risk Reduction: What's the Difference?" Accessed 12/04/2023, Investopedia.com. https://www.investopedia.com/ask/answers/040315/what–difference–between–risk–avoidance–and–risk–reduction.asp.

725 Risk reduction is defined as reducing the probability of a risk occurrence to the point where an organization is willing to shoulder the risk without involving a third–party. (Study.com, s.a., "What is Risk Avoidance and Risk Mitigation?" Accessed 12/04/2023, study.com. https://study.com/buy/academy/lesson/risk–avoidance–vs–risk–mitigation.html)

[25] Don't fear sudden danger or the ruin of the wicked when it comes, [26] for the Lord will be your confidence and will keep your foot from a snare.

Those who follow the ways of Biblical wisdom will not be "haunted by the specter of sudden reversal and the trouble that comes from sinful actions."[726] Christians live with an ease the wicked do not have because they have genuine security.[727] Even if a sudden "disaster" comes to them, they know that God is in control, and they rest in his sovereignty. "Nothing—absolutely nothing—comes to us except from the Father's hand."[728]

The Willingness to Give One's Life Away is Sometimes Associated with "Risk" in the Bible.

Consider Judges 5:18 (NIV): "The people of Zebulun risked their very lives; so did Naphtali on the terraced fields." The Hebrew word for "risked" means to lose all functions necessary to sustain life.[729] The people "risked their very lives." The ESV translates this phrase as "risked their lives to the death" (ESV), and the NASB translates this phrase as "despised their lives *even* to death."

In both the Old and New Testaments, in those passages where the translators found the English word "risk" to be a suitable translation for the Greek or Hebrew, the word represented a giving away of one's life in pursuing that which advantaged God. Table 13–1 outlines the danger(s) that existed and what the cost would have been had the danger materialized.

Table 13–1: Events and dangers in biblical passages translated as risk

Citation	Event	Danger	God's Advantage
Judges 5:18	Israel revolted against Jabin, King of Canaan, in a battle to control the Canaanite territory.	Losing their lives in battle	Israel would follow God, not a king of Canaan
Judges 9:17	Fighting against Midian	Loss of life	Israel would follow God, not Midian kings

726 Richard J. Clifford, *Proverbs: A Commentary*, First edition, The Old Testament Library (Westminster John Knox Press, 1999), 43.

727 Duane A. Garrett, *Proverbs, Ecclesiastes, Song of Songs*. Vol. 14. The New American Commentary. (Broadman & Holman, 1993), 73.

728 Roger Ellsworth, "The Sovereignty of God and Pastoral Ministry," *The Founders Journal*. 2003. Winter, 51: 19.

729 Faithlife, "To Die." *Logos Bible Study Bible Sense Lexicon*. (Faithlife, March 6, 2025.) https://ref.ly/logos4/Senses?KeyId=ws.die.v.01.

Citation	Event	Danger	God's Advantage
Genesis 37:20–24	Being sold into slavery	Loss of identity Loss of control Loss of family Loss of life	God used this event to create a reason for Jacob and his family to go to Egypt, so God could grow his people into a nation
Exodus 1:22	Bearing a baby boy	Throwing baby son into the Nile— loss of life	God's man to rescue Israel from Egyptian slavery is born in such a way as to ensure Moses would be raised in an environment that prepared Moses for God's call on Moses' life.
Psalm 51:13	Sin against God	Being thrown away from God's presence	God's plan to live with humanity advantages God
Acts 15:24–26	Sharing the Gospel	Losing their lives	God's gospel is spread
Romans 16:3–4	Unknown	Losing their lives	God's gospel is spread
Philippians 2:25–30	Service to another when gravely ill	Losing his life	God's gospel is spread

God Calls Some to Engage Significant Risk for Significant Ministry.

I define "significant ministry" as doing what God has asked one to do when the success of the ministry is entirely dependent on God acting outside expected, normal patterns and practices. Numerous examples of this principle are illustrated in the lives of biblical forefathers.

Let's start with the story of Noah. God is greatly disturbed by the evil that exists on the earth, so God decides to start over with humanity by sending a flood to rid the earth of all humans, save eight (Genesis 6:11–22). Luke remarks that humankind did not see God's judgment through a flood coming because they were "eating, drinking, marrying and being given in marriage up to the day Noah entered the ark" (Luke 17:26 NIV). Noah demonstrated great faith in building the ark (Hebrews 11:7), and God showed great patience with the sins of humanity (1 Peter 3:20).

What God asked Noah to do was preposterous based on human reasoning. Yet Noah obeyed. The significant ministry Noah accomplished was preaching about God before the flood (2 Peter 2:5) and then entering the ark without any hint of rain or flood, thus saving a remnant of humanity as God purged the earth of rebellious humans.

A second example is Gideon's defeat of the Midianites, found in Judges 7:1–25. By obeying God's commands and taking a significant human risk, Gideon took a fighting force of men from 30,000+ to 300 and then watched God cause the Midians to turn on themselves. By human standards, 300 men should not be able to defeat a well–resourced and large army like the Midianites. It must have been difficult to see the first tranche of 22,000 men heading home, leaving only 10,000. Then it must have been even more unnerving for the remaining 300 men when Gideon sent home 9700 of the 10,000 men. The maturity of faith in God required to follow through with these decisions was significant. The significant ministry that God accomplished through Gideon was setting Israel free from Midian oppression and giving the nation forty years of rest (Judges 8:28) as Israel followed the Lord.

A third example of engaging in significant ministry that required significant risk is Elijah's contest with the prophets of Ba'al in 1 Kings 18:16–45. In this story, Elijah competes with 450 prophets of Ba'al, eventually calling down fire from heaven that consumes the altar and its contents. The prophets are killed, and God is proven to be the one true God. Elijah's faith in setting up this contest and believing that God would be faithful is impressive.

One of the ways a CBO mitigates the dangerous effects of a risk is to have a deep faith that God, in his role as sovereign, will act according to his character. God is faithful within his covenant relationship with us, his stewards. Knowing that God handles the outcomes and that he will be covenantally faithful gives us great peace and confidence that whatever happens, we are following the safest path that can be followed.

There were times in the Bible when God asked people to take on immense risks with the command to "be strong and courageous" (or some variation on that theme) coupled with the promise of God's presence as these individuals obeyed his direction. Deuteronomy 31:1–8 is a prime example. Moses passed the leadership baton to Joshua, reminding him to be "strong and courageous." (New leadership positions often have much risk associated with them.) A second example is God encouraging Joshua to be strong and courageous in Joshua 1:1–9 after Moses has died and Joshua is readying Israel to enter Canaan. And a third example is Christ giving us his commission to evangelize and disciple the world in Matthew 28:18–20.

In the first two examples, the risk is assumed when the Jordan River is crossed and Israel battles the nations within Canaan to take their land. In the third example, the risk is persecution and martyrdom when the gospel of Christ is shared to the ends of the world. No matter how outsized the risk, his presence and courage will be greater when the risk is assumed under the direction of Yahweh. *As Christian business owners, when we assume risk under the direction of the Holy Spirit, we can be assured that God's presence, strength, and courage will go with us as we endeavor to be obedient, win the lost to Christ, disciple young believers, and be salt and light for Christ in the marketplace.*

As we look more closely at a Biblical view of risk in the next section, the following points will emerge as true:

- God is impassible and immutable (Malachi 3:6, James 1:17, Psalm 33:11, Isaiah 46:9–11, Numbers 23:19), so God is not affected by suffering, dangers, risks, and so forth (John 16:33), to which Biblical stewards are subject in this life.
- Stewardship success is defined as being faithful to God.
- God handles the outcomes of a situation, course of action, or decision when a steward faithfully obeys God's call on the steward's life.
- Part of a steward's faithfulness to God includes the willingness to accept significant risk when directed by God.
- The safest place an owner can be is following God's will. The owner is safe even if the owner is martyred by following God's will.
- Biblical stewards always advantage God, even if it means disadvantaging themselves.
- God asks his followers to be "strong and courageous" in the face of dangers that he has called them to live in.
- God promises his presence to those who assume dangerous risks when called to do so by God.
- The greatest risk anyone can assume is not to fear "the one who can destroy both soul and body in Hell" (Mark 10:28 NIV).

The next sections will discuss the points just enumerated.

Can God "Take a Risk"?

This question goes to the heart of two closely related characteristics of God: impassibility and immutability.[730] Impassibility is generally defined as a denial of God's subjection to "passibility," which includes A) the capacity to be acted upon from without, B) the capacity for changing emotions from within, and C) liability to the feelings of pleasure and pain caused by the action of another being.[731] The immutability of God means that God is incapable of change, "either in duration of life, or in nature, character, will, or happiness.

---

730 Paul Helm, "The Impossibility of Divine Passibility." In *The Power and Weakness of God: Impassibility and Orthodoxy.* Nigel, M. de S. Cameron (Ed.) (Rutherford House Books, 1990), 120.

731 Frank L. Cross and Elizabeth A. Livingstone (Eds), *The Oxford dictionary of the Christian Church.* 3rd ed. rev. (Oxford University Press, 2005), 828.

252

In none of these, nor any other respect, is there any possibility of change."[732] God is impassible because "God's being cannot be changed or harmed by anything outside himself."[733]

In a strict sense, some deduce that emotions represent a change in God or that an emotional response to man's sufferings or pleasures would represent a change in God, which a strict view of impassibility would not allow. But just as God's logic is higher than man's logic, so God's emotions are higher than man's. God's emotions are divine, not human.[734] In a way that humanity cannot understand, God can experience emotions yet not change in any material sense.

Calvin[735] and Clement of Alexandria[736] believed in *divine condescension*, which is the notion that anthropomorphic descriptions of God having emotions are an accommodation to our human limitations so that God could disclose himself to humanity. In a sense, all of God's revelation is divine condescension.

God's immutability is not affected by God having real, not merely accommodating, emotions. His essence does not change even though he has changing emotions or decisions. God remains impassible.

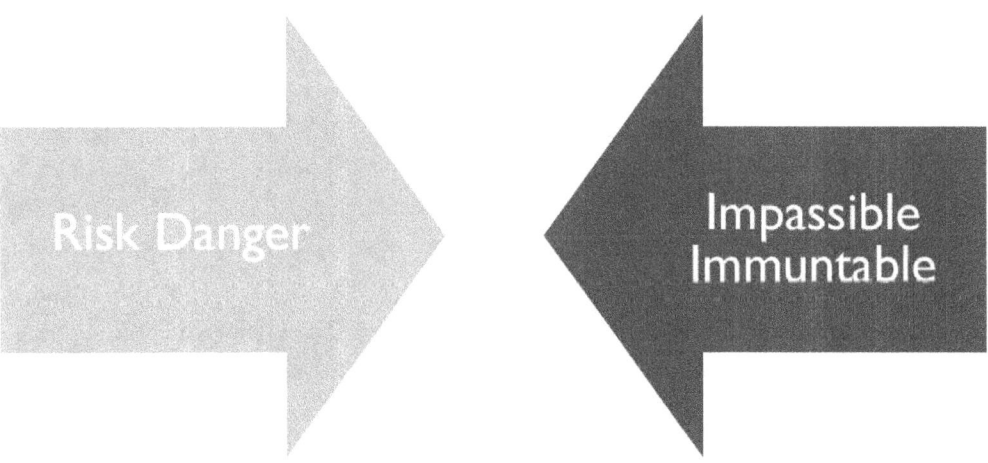

Figure 13–4: God's impassibility and immutability stop harmful danger from affecting God.

We should say that while God is not affected by people's sufferings, it does not mean he has no emotion at all. For example, God rejoices (Isaiah 62:5), can be grieved (Psalm 78:40),

---

732 James P. Boyce, *Abstract of Systematic Theology*. (Logos Bible Software, 2010), 73.

733 Wayne Grudem, *Systematic Theology, Second Edition*. (Zondervan Academic, 2020), 195.

734 Amos W. Oei, "The Impassible God Who 'Cried.'" *Themelios*, 41(2):238–47.

735 John Calvin & John Allen, *Institutes of the Christian religion*. (Hezekiah Howe; Philip H. Nicklin, 1816), 128.

736 George L. Prestige, *God in Patristic Thoughts*. (Wipf and Stock, 1964), 8.

pours out his wrath on his enemies (Exodus 32.10), and loves with everlasting love (Isaiah 54:8, Psalm 103:17). God becomes angry (Exodus 32:10–14, Jonah 3:10) and sometimes turns from fierce anger (Deuteronomy 13:17, Jeremiah 18:8). His emotions—even when they change in response to different situations, do not change his being, perfections, purposes, and promises.[737]

The answer to the question posed at the start of this section is grounded in God's impassibility and immutability. God cannot assume risk because any materialized danger posed by a risk cannot affect God (impassibility) or change God (immutability). In addition, God may have emotions concerning the threat and its effects on those involved, but emotions do not constitute a material change in God's character. Figure 13–4 graphically depicts this answer.

It is also God's impassibility and immutability that gives credit to Christ's claim that he has overcome the world:

> I have told you these things, so that in me you may have peace. In this world you will have trouble. But take heart! I have overcome the world. (John 16:33 NIV).

The only way that Christ could make this statement and make it stick is if A) his claim to be fully God was true and B) Christ carried in his humanity the characteristics of impassibility and immutability. If the world's troubles cannot injure God or change his being, perfections, purposes, and promises, then God does overcome the world, even though he exists in human form.

When assuming risk as directed by God, CBOs rely on these characteristics to provide a firm foundation upon which to count on God for the outcomes, even if the outcomes require supernatural intervention. Knowing about God's attributes is not merely an academic exercise for the academics. Instead, the CBO *actively relies on God's character, promises, purposes, and plans, who cannot be changed or affected by world events but operates within them.*

Definition of Success

In the preface of this book, I wrote that success is defined as faithfulness to God and perseverance in obedience because that is how success is described in the Bible. In the Bible, success is *never* determined in monetary terms for disciples of Jesus Christ.

Hence, Biblical stewards measure themselves covenantally, which is to say that CBOs measure themselves against their faithfulness to the commands of God. CBOs do not compare themselves to worldly business or popular church standards. Biblical stewardship

---

737 Louis Berkhof, *Systematic Theology.* (Eerdmans, 1938), 58.

is singularly focused on God's approval as the only measure of success. We do not compare ourselves to others. We have an audience of one.

Consider how Paul describes this echo chamber of success (2 Corinthians 10:12, 18 NIV):

> We do not dare to classify or compare ourselves with some who commend themselves. When they measure themselves by themselves and compare themselves with themselves, they are not wise ... For it is not the one who commends himself who is approved, but the one whom the Lord commends.

Some who commend themselves will say, "Compare your success with my success, and then do what I did." For example, if an owner turned $500 into $50M, that owner will be lauded as the standard for success. Those who have been "successful" will try to capitalize on their success by selling books, training materials, conference registrations, subscriptions—whatever—claiming that they "hold *the* secret to success" and "for $XXX, I will teach you my secret." They are commending themselves and measuring themselves by themselves. *This happens as much in Christian ministries as it does in business.*

Being on the receiving end of self-commendation can be difficult. It is easy to feel inferior or "less than" those who are so "successful." "Self–commendation robs those who practice it of any objective standard of judgment, and thus of any means of understanding themselves or their environment."[738]

Reframing success in Biblical terms should eliminate these distinctions and feelings of inferiority. Avoiding self-commendation is also a wise choice for a CBO. Extending this further, CBOs do not compare themselves to other CBOs. We do not measure our success by the "success" of another CBO because our standards of success are different than that of conventional wisdom. We are content with what God has entrusted to us. Our only realistic measure of success is God's approval. This means that we work to hear the accolades of one—God. And as long as God is pleased with us, then the applause of millions of men should not matter to us. We are content to hear, "Well done, good and faithful servant." (Matthew 25:21).

Success is rewarded in heaven more than on earth

Those who receive rich rewards in heaven "overcome" the temptations of this world by remaining faithful to God through difficult circumstances. Consider the seven endings of the warnings to the seven churches in Revelation as support of the rewards given to those who are faithful (all quotations are from NIV):

---

738 C. K. Barrett, *The Second Epistle to the Corinthians*, Black's New Testament Commentary (Continuum, 1973), 262.

- Revelation 2:7: "To the one who is victorious, I will give the right to eat from the tree of life, which is in the paradise of God."
- Revelation 2:11: "The one who is victorious will not be hurt at all by the second death."
- Revelation 2:17: "To the one who is victorious, I will give some of the hidden manna. I will also give that person a white stone with a new name written on it, known only to the one who receives it."
- Revelation 2:26–28: "^{26} To the one who is victorious and does my will to the end, I will give authority over the nations—^{27} that one 'will rule them with an iron scepter and will dash them to pieces like pottery' ^{z}—just as I have received authority from my Father. ^{28} I will also give that one the morning star."
- Revelation 3:5: "^{5} The one who is victorious will, like them, be dressed in white. I will never blot out the name of that person from the book of life, but will acknowledge that name before my Father and his angels."
- Revelation 3:12: "The one who is victorious I will make a pillar in the temple of my God. Never again will they leave it. I will write on them the name of my God and the name of the city of my God, the new Jerusalem, which is coming down out of heaven from my God; and I will also write on them my new name."
- Revelation 3:21: "^{21} To the one who is victorious, I will give the right to sit with me on my throne, just as I was victorious and sat down with my Father on his throne."

In all of these promises, rewards are in response to the believer's faithfulness *until the end*. Faithfulness on earth is rewarded in heaven. A true believer's hope is not based on material success. A believer's hope is based on the promises of God and God's faithfulness to admit us into heaven (God's presence) because we were faithful to God within our covenant relationship with him while on earth.

Whereas conventional wisdom has a godless view of risk assessment (i.e., there is no God to whom accountability is due), the Bible strongly connects our assumption of risk with our faithfulness to God. When God directs us to assume a risk, then success becomes assuming that risk. Success is defined as doing what God has asked us to do.

> If anyone would come after me, let him deny himself and take up his
> cross daily and follow me" (Luke 9:23 ESV).

Biblical success is built on a self–denial that culminates in faithfulness to God. Self–denial cannot be accomplished without a conscious effort to disadvantage oneself in some form or fashion.

256

A condemned criminal was forced to carry one bar of his cross to the place where he was going to be executed.[739] Carrying one's cross is the ultimate form of self–denial. Let us recall that denying oneself may include assuming a real risk with real danger in which God may ask us to participate in the sufferings of Christ (Philippians 3:10).[740]

As noted, risk means danger is in the picture and could materialize, causing injury to the business owner. However, following Christ "is the safe behavior (even if it leads to business failure or even martyrdom) and not following Jesus (more specifically the Holy Spirit) is the risky behavior."[741]

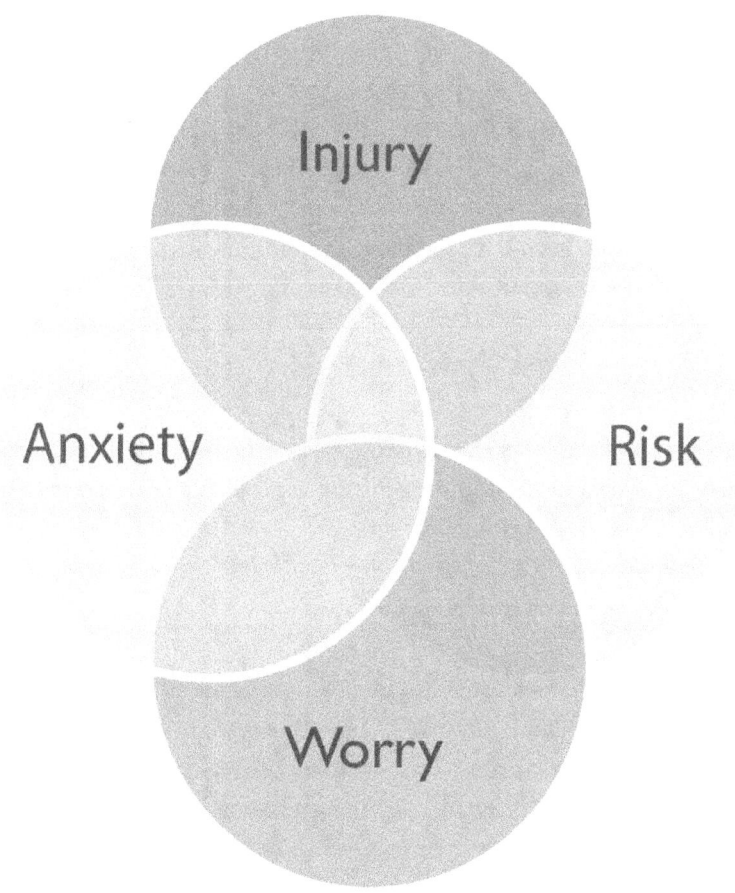

Figure 13–5: Illustration of how injury, risk, worry, and anxiety are related

---

739   Walter Liefeld. "Luke." In *The Expositor's Bible Commentary: Matthew, Mark, Luke*, edited by Frank E. Gaebelein, Vol. 8. (Zondervan Publishing House, 1984), 923–24.

740   Grant Osborne. *Luke: Verse by Verse*. Edited by Jeffrey Reimer, Elliot Ritzema, and Danielle Thevenaz, Awa Sarah. Osborne New Testament Commentaries. (Lexham Press, 2018), 252.

741   Dr. Rolf Engwall, Private email. 2023. Email on file.

The real danger—the highest risk—in life is choosing to reject God or living out a life that demonstrates a rejection of God because sin was repeatedly chosen, creating a pattern in life that was never changed or healed (Matthew 5:29–30). Consider also Matthew 10:28 (ESV)

> Do not be afraid of those who kill the body but cannot kill the soul. Rather, be afraid of the One who can destroy both soul and body in hell.

The highest danger—the highest risk in life—is not getting into heaven.

Hence, there are temporal risks for which risk mitigation strategies can be helpful. But there are eternal risks about which the Scriptures are far more concerned than temporal risks. Common risk mitigation strategies do not work against eternal risks. The way a business owner (or any person) mitigates the risk of not being with God in heaven is to enter into a covenant with God and then obey him (the safest course of action) even when following God involves significant earthly risk. The highest risk—the most reckless path—is to disobey God, even if disobedience is indicated as the correct course of action by common risk mitigation strategies.

Anxiety, Worry, and Risk

I thought it best to include this section on anxiety, worry, and risk because nearly all anxiety and worry is connected to an impending danger due to a danger becoming a reality. Figure 13–5 illustrates these relationships:

Conventional Wisdom about Anxiety

Common among business owners is anxiety, which includes feelings of despondency, powerlessness, uncertainty, and sadness.[742] Often, the uncertainties of owning a business can lead to chronic stress and anxiety. Pressure to succeed and the fear of failure frequently drive anxiety and worry for business owners, along with financial pressure and concerns.[743] Some business owners live with such deep insecurities that they quietly feel incompetent to own and run a business.[744] Moreover, being a business owner is negatively correlated

---

742 Faithlife, "Anxiety." In *Logos Bible Study Factbook*. (Faithlife, November 3, 2024.) https://ref.ly/logos4/Factbook?id=ref%3abk.%25anxiety.

743 Michelle Knight, "The Silent Struggle: Depression, Anxiety Among Male Business Owners." June 6, 2024, ihealthservices.org. https://ihealthservices.org/depression/the–silent–struggle–depression–anxiety–among–male–business–owners/

744 Deanna DeBara, "Small Business, Big Stress: How to Support Your Mental Health as a Small Business Owner." May 10, 2023, freshbooks.com. https://www.freshbooks.com/blog/small–business–mental–health

with good mental health, despite the glamorization of ownership in our society.[745] 62% of business owners report being depressed at least once a week, and half report that their mental health is negatively affected by owning a business.[746]

Conventional wisdom suggests that these feelings and pressures can be managed by developing a support system, delegating what you cannot do well, letting go of what you cannot control, and meditating to calm down.[747] Others would suggest mindfulness as a method of managing anxiety and worry. Mindfulness is described as an essential human ability to be fully present and aware of our surroundings but not overly reactive or overwhelmed by events outside of us. Mindfulness uses meditation to calm our inner selves as we listen to our bodies and emotions and stay present "in the moment."[748]

Looking at anxiety and worry from a systems viewpoint, it is important to remember that Christian business owners are members of at least three different relational systems: family, church, and business. Because the emotional processes are nearly identical in all three systems, unresolved issues in one system can produce symptoms in the other two, load balancing anxiety and worry across systems that did not originate the dysfunction.[749] Taking a nonanxious presence in one system will improve functioning in the other two, resulting in improved relationships across all systems.[750] Paying attention to your emotions and learning to be comfortable with uncomfortable emotions can help you gain a nonanxious presence.[751]

I have found it helpful to hold part of myself in reserve and learn to observe myself during a difficult situation that may be emotionally charged or filled with anxiety and worry. But this is not a way to achieve peace. It is simply a way to keep my emotions somewhat in check during anxious moments.

Conventional wisdom readily acknowledges the common experience of anxiety and worry for business owners, and it may have some helpful tips to manage anxiety a bit better. But it offers little if a person wants genuine peace amid the storm, or genuine rest under high stress.

---

745   Matt Lurie, "Let's Get Real About Mental Health and Owning a Business." Accessed 11–03–2024, ruby.com. https://www.ruby.com/blog/getting–real–mental–health–owning–a–business/

746   Robert Manolson, "What it's like to Live with Anxiety and Depression as a Small–Business Owner." Accessed 11–03–2024, careerwise.cerica.ca. https://careerwise.ceric.ca/2023/06/26/what–its–like–to–live–with–anxiety–and–depression–as–a–small–business–owner/

747   Anne Shaw, "How Small Business Owners can Lower Their Anxiety and Stress." August 15, 2022, sba.thehartford.com. https://sba.thehartford.com/business–management/small–biz–owner/lower–anxiety–and–stress/

748   Mindful.org, "Getting Started with Mindfulness." Mindful.org, Accessed 11/18/2024. https://www.mindful.org/meditation/mindfulness–getting–started/

749   Edwin Friedman, *Generation to Generation: Family Process in Church and Synagogue*. (Guilford Press, 1985), 1.

750   Friedman, *Generation to Generation*, 209–10.

751   A good read for building better relationships comes from Bob Leinberger, *The Relational Map: A Practical Guide to Improving all Your Relationships*. (Self–Published, 2003).

Biblical Wisdom about Anxiety

Two (among many) passages discuss worry and anxiety in the Scriptures. We will look at Philippians 4 and Matthew 6. Here are the passages, both in the ESV:

> 4 Rejoice in the Lord always; again I will say, rejoice. 5 Let your reasonableness be known to everyone. The Lord is at hand; 6 do not be anxious about anything, but in everything by prayer and supplication with thanksgiving let your requests be made known to God. 7 And the peace of God, which surpasses all understanding, will guard your hearts and your minds in Christ Jesus. (Philippians 4:4–7)

> 25 "Therefore I tell you, do not be anxious about your life, what you will eat or what you will drink, nor about your body, what you will put on. Is not life more than food, and the body more than clothing? 26 Look at the birds of the air: they neither sow nor reap nor gather into barns, and yet your heavenly Father feeds them. Are you not of more value than they? 27 And which of you by being anxious can add a single hour to his span of life? 28 And why are you anxious about clothing? Consider the lilies of the field, how they grow: they neither toil nor spin, 29 yet I tell you, even Solomon in all his glory was not arrayed like one of these. 30 But if God so clothes the grass of the field, which today is alive and tomorrow is thrown into the oven, will he not much more clothe you, O you of little faith? 31 Therefore do not be anxious, saying, 'What shall we eat?' or 'What shall we drink?' or 'What shall we wear?' 32 For the Gentiles seek after all these things, and your heavenly Father knows that you need them all. 33 But seek first the kingdom of God and his righteousness, and all these things will be added to you. 34 "Therefore do not be anxious about tomorrow, for tomorrow will be anxious for itself. Sufficient for the day is its own trouble. (Matthew 6:25–34)

The common threads across both passages are as follows. First, we are commanded not to be anxious. In Philippians, the defining phrase is "about anything," we are not to be anxious about *anything*. In Matthew, the phrase "about your life" is further defined as what we will eat, drink, or wear. Both phrases are all-encompassing. Yet, it's pretty tough to turn off anxiety for some.

Second, we must take on God's perspective of our situation. In Philippians, we are instructed to do several things:

- Rejoice always
- Pray with thanksgiving
- Give God our specific requests

Behind these requests is the assumption that we leave the problem or danger with God once we ask, *trusting his promises to protect and provide*. We do not ask God and then worry if he will come through for us. We do not listen to voices of doubt or distractions that pull us away from God. Instead, we rejoice in our present circumstances because we have trust and hope that God will take what is meant for evil in our lives and turn it into good (Romans 8:1). We worship God because he is worthy of our worship regardless of our circumstances. We focus our trust on the majesty and character of God instead of the potential injury we might experience due to a future danger.

In the Matthew passage, we are instructed to consider the futility of worry. Learning how God takes care of his creation informs how he will care for us. Hence, a third point is that we are reminded that we are far more valuable than animals and that our worry does nothing to change the future. We cannot worry enough to add even one hour to our lifespan. Instead, we are instructed to seek God's kingdom and righteousness and trust that God will meet our needs.

Worry usually has a godless outlook on the future, focusing on the potential injury that a future danger might impose on us. By *godless*, I mean our worry does not incorporate God's eternal, loving, and caring viewpoint. Taking on God's perspective of our situation means focusing on the eternal (God's kingdom), not the temporal (food and clothing). It means acknowledging the potential injury resulting from a future danger and trusting in God's promises of provision and protection.

Hence, to reiterate, the way out of a life of worry is to:
- Rejoice in your present circumstances
- Pray with thanksgiving
- Give specific requests to God
- We infuse our viewpoints with God's viewpoint
- We focus on the eternal, not the temporary

James 5:8 (CSB) encourages this last point: "You also must be patient. Strengthen your hearts, because the Lord's coming is near." To strengthen our hearts means to gain courage for the situation through trust in God.[752] When we follow Philippians 4 and Matthew 6, we will find our hearts strengthened through a courage that only comes from a visceral trust in God.

---

752 Darian R. Lockett and Craig A. Evans, "James." In *John's Gospel, Hebrews–Revelation*, edited by Craig A. Evans and Craig A. Bubeck, First Edition. The Bible Knowledge Background Commentary. (David C Cook, 2005), 285.

Fourth, behind these two passages, the sovereignty of God is assumed and must exist for these other three points to have meaning. The sovereignty of God means that God is absolutely in control of everything and has all authority over all creation. God's divine purpose will always be accomplished, and all he ordains will come to pass.[753] The sovereignty of God is important to resolving anxiety and worry because risks, uncertainties, and dangers in life *are always under his control.*

So, as we face uncertainties, such as divorce, employment termination, physical illness, financial hardship, untrue accusations, reputational damage, etc., we can know that God is in the future, managing that situation on our behalf. He may call us to suffer while he resolves the problem in his own time. But whether we suffer or not, we can be confident that we will experience his love and support. We are not to worry or become anxious.

Nevertheless, suffering for Christ is part of the walk of a Christian: "For it has been granted to you on behalf of Christ not only to believe in him, but also to suffer for him" (Philippians 1:29 NIV). By being a Christian, we are *called* to suffer for Him. Suffering is part and parcel of being a Christian. The prosperity gospel views suffering as a temporary failure. Christ views suffering as identifying with him so we can be like him (Philippians 2:1–11). Yet, even though we suffer, we understand that under God's caring sovereignty, we need not be anxious about future dangers we may face.

CONVENTIONAL WISDOM ABOUT COMPLIANCE

Compliance is the adherence to laws and regulations that legislatures, agencies, and the courts promulgate. In the United States, there are a bewildering number of compliance regulations with which business owners must comply. Many business licenses, permits, or certificates require unique compliance activities. Most companies implement compliance programs that include written policies and procedures, content standards, training, auditing, monitoring, discipline, and corrective action.[754] The less compliant a company is with any set of laws or regulations, the more risk (danger) there is for the owner to be civilly or criminally charged. In certain situations, some fines and penalties can be severe.

Conventional wisdom would assert a primarily legal responsibility to the business owner for a compliance program. Interestingly enough, in my consulting business, I find that a small percentage of owners accept the risk of non-compliance fines and penalties because the ongoing compliance costs are too high for them to absorb.

---

753 Thom S. Rainer, The Book of Church Growth: History, Theology, and Principles (B&H Academic, 1993), 98.

754 Will Kenton. "Compliance Program: Definition, Purpose, and How to Create One." July 9 2022. Investopedia.com. https://www.investopedia.com/terms/c/compliance–program.asp

Conventional wisdom believes that transparency, auditing, and reporting are three key elements that curb unethical and illegal behavior in business.[755] The conventional wisdom approach to compliance in business is godless, recognizing only one set of laws to which adherence must be given. Conventional wisdom does not consider that there might be a God who has laws that he expects owners to obey. The CBO seeks to comply with earthly laws and regulations except when those laws and regulations conflict with God's laws as expressed in the Scriptures. There is much to learn from conventional wisdom regarding compliance, but there is even more to learn from Biblical wisdom.

BIBLICAL WISDOM ABOUT COMPLIANCE

The Bible states that Christians are to obey government laws. In Romans 13:1–2, Paul tells Christians that governing authorities have been established by God. In the Bible, resisting legitimate government authority is equated to resisting God's authority because all legitimate human authority is derived from God's authority.[756] These authorities are instituted to do good and execute justice on those who resist legitimate laws. Bruner reminds us that "respect for government is an important form of respect for God."[757]

Similarly, Peter (1 Peter 2:13–14) requires submission to governmental authorities and notes that obedience to legitimate government authorities is God's will. However, in verse 17, Peter reminds Christians that Christians have a higher allegiance to God. While Christians are to "honor" the king, Christians "fear" God. Peter's reminder agrees with a passage referenced earlier in this paper (Mark 10:28) in which Christians are told not to fear the one who can kill our physical bodies but to fear the one who can destroy both our physical bodies and our souls In Hell.

Submission to authority is not unusual for Christians. In addition to submitting to governing authorities, Christians submit to their spiritual leaders (1 Corinthians 16:16), to one another (Ephesians 5:21), and employees to employers (Titus 2:9). Christian prophets submit to each other (1 Corinthians 14:32) and wives submit to their husbands (Colossians 3:18).[758] In our role as business owners, we might be "in charge" in a human sense, but we submit to God because of our covenant relationship with him. In addition, we submit to each other and our spiritual leaders. *There is no personal or professional role a CBO can assume where the CBO is not in submission to God or another Christian. Hence, an attitude*

---

755   James Weber & David Wasieleski, "Corporate Ethics and Compliance Programs: A Report, Analysis and Critique." *Journal of Business Ethics.* 112(4):609–626.

756   John Stott and Sandy Larsen, *Reading Romans with John Stott: With Questions for Groups or Individuals.* Vol. 1 & 2. (InterVarsity Press, 2016), 73.

757   Frederick Dale Bruner, *Matthew, Volume 2. The Churchbook Matthew 13–28.* (Word Publishing, 1990), 784.

758   Douglas J. Moo, *The Epistle to the Romans.* The New International Commentary on the New Testament. (Eerdmans Publishing, 1996), 797.

of submission should be the most prominent characteristic in our personal and professional relationships.

Give to Caesar what is Caesar's

Consider Mark 12:14–17 (LEB):

> [14] And *when they* came, they said to him, "Teacher, we know that you are truthful and you do not care what anyone thinks, because you do not regard the opinion of people, but teach the way of God in truth. Is it permitted to pay taxes to Caesar or not? Should we pay or should we not pay?" [15] But *because he* knew their hypocrisy, he said to them, "Why are you testing me? Bring me a denarius so that I can look at *it*!" [16] So they brought *one*. And he said to them, "Whose image and inscription *is* this?" And they said to him, "Caesar's." [17] And Jesus said to them, "Give to Caesar the things of Caesar, and to God the things of God!"

The first part of Christ's command does not limit the State in how arduous it can become in taxation, regulation, monitoring, and intrusive acts. While the state is not free to do as it chooses, the first part of Christ's command is highly general. There may be much a state does with which a CBO may disagree, but disagreement, by itself, is not a sufficient theological basis for disobedience or a charge of illegitimacy.

If the first half of Christ's directive is to respect the state, the latter half is a command of ultimate allegiance to God and a reminder to the state of its limitations before God: "As Caesar's coins bear Caesar's image and belong to Caesar, so God's humanity bears God's image and belongs to God."[759]

When Christians give to the state that which belongs to the state and to God that which belongs to God, the Christian is essentially satisfying debts in both realms. We have no inherent conflict when we fully obey Christ's command.[760]

Extremes are forbidden in our relationship with the state. Balances must be maintained. Hatred for the state and its laws is as much a sin as excessive patriotism. Jesus' command makes the state penultimate but meaningful still. As Christian business owners, we are commanded to give to the state what rightly belongs to the state. If taxes are due, taxes are to be paid. If honor is due, honor is to be given. If respect is due, respect is to be given. But we give eternal things to God: ultimate allegiance, obedience, love, and sacrifice.

---

759 Bruner, *Matthew*, 784.
760 Henry B. Swete, *The Gospel According to Mark*. (New York: MacMillian, 1898), 260.

Paying Taxes and Fees to the Government

Taxes are compulsory payments to the government to finance government operations and services.[761] The responsibility to pay one's tax to the government is unambiguous in the Scriptures. There is no moral wiggle room on this issue. A CBO cannot use government sin, such as authorizing abortions, as a reason to not pay one's tax. The Biblical command to pay one's tax is explicit. To obey God is to pay one's tax, regardless of the difficulty incurred in paying that tax or how unfair one might find the tax to be:

> 6 For because of this you also pay taxes, for *the authorities* are servants of God, busily engaged in this very *thing.* 7 Pay to everyone *what is* owed: *pay* taxes to whom taxes *are due*; *pay* customs duties to whom customs duties *are due*; *pay* respect to whom respect *is due*; *pay* honor to whom honor *is due.* (Romans 13:6–7 LEB)

and

> 17 Therefore tell us what you think. Is it permitted to pay taxes to Caesar or not?" 18 But *because he* knew their maliciousness, Jesus said, "Hypocrites! Why are you testing me? 19 Show me the coin for the tax!" So they brought him a denarius. 20 And he said to them, "Whose image and inscription *is* this?" 21 They said to him, "Caesar's." Then he said to them, "Therefore give to Caesar the things of Caesar, and to God the things of God!" (Matthew 22:17–21 LEB)

Jesus recognized the legitimate role of civil government and endorsed its right to collect taxes.[762] Taxation of nearly every commodity was common during Roman times, and those who refused to pay their taxes faced physical violence from the government.[763] The Roman historian Tacitus conceded that the total tax burden was way too high for the Jews, but

---

761 Faithlife, "Taxation." In: *Logos Bible Study Factbook.* (Faithlife, September 4, 2024.) https://ref.ly/logos4/Factbook?id=ref%3abk.%25taxation.

762 Richard Horsley, Jesus and the Spiral of Violence: Popular Jewish Resistance in Roman Palestine. (Harper & Row, 1987), 310.

763 William Simmons, "Taxation." In *The Lexham Bible Dictionary*, edited by John D. Barry, et al., (Lexham Press, 2016), np.

little was done by Rome to relieve their burden.[764]

Jews hated the Romans and they had deep contempt for fellow Jews who became tax collectors for Rome. These individuals were regarded as traitors to the Jewish people and equal to Gentile sinners (Luke 7:34, 15:1, 18:11–13; Matthew 18:17).[765] Taxation was an intensely explosive issue, equated by some with slavery.[766] Hence, the appeal to assert one's liberty through rebellion against the State was lived out by a minority of Jews, sometimes known as zealots.

Into this culture, Jesus was born. He would later be described as a friend of "tax collectors and sinners" (Matthew 9:10–11; Mark 2:15; Luke 7:34)—the very people whom Jews hated. Christ taught that a repentant tax collector was justified before God and the tax collectors who heeded his teachings were more righteous than the religious elders in Israel (Matthew 21:31–32; Luke 18:10–13).[767]

The Scriptures are silent on the amount, frequency, and method governments engage to generate revenues for their work. However, experience teaches us that throughout history, governments have always put themselves ahead of those they govern, and this will not change. The government's first interest is itself and its survival. Whatever the government needs from the populace to survive and accomplish its goals, the government will do.

A Christian business owner is not released to sin through non-payment of taxes because the owner believes the tax to be onerous and unfair or because the monies are used to fund immoral activities. God does not give us such permissions in the Bible. We are not allowed to make these types of tradeoff decisions.

Instead, we give Caesar what we owe him, but we give God the (much) greater value of our hearts and affections. We are on this earth for such a short time. If the government impoverishes us through onerous taxation, Christians comply because their ultimate allegiance is to God, not the state.

By the same token, we give Caesar transparency when Ceasar requires it. Transparency is closely connected to honesty, both in concept and in deed. While privacy concerns can

---

764 Simmons, *Taxation*, np.

765 A.M. Okorie, "The Characterization of the Tax Collectors in the Gospel of Luke." *Currents in Theology and Mission,* 1995, 27–32.

766 Flavius Josephus and William Whiston, *The Works of Josephus: Complete and Unabridged.* (Hendrickson, 1987), 476.

767 Simmons, *Taxation*, np.

moderate honesty in certain situations, they cannot and should not supersede Ceasar's requirement for transparency unless such transparency requires us to sin.

MinistryWatch[768] reports that an increasing number of ministries are applying for and gaining church status[769] under United States law to protect their religious liberties. The annual filing of form 990 coupled with additional state laws, seems to some to require *too much* transparency:

> Both California and New York were increasingly asking for more information on our donors on schedule B of the 990. [W]e wanted to avail ourselves of our legal right to protect ourselves from those who might target us because of those deeply–held convictions.[770]

Focus on the Family is not alone. The *Billy Graham Evangelistic Association* (BGEA) and the *Evangelical Council for Financial Accountability* (ECFA) have filed for church designation. Some ministries who gain this designation continue to file form 990, but they have the option to not do so in any given year. The ECFA completes form 990 and publishes it on their website, but they do not file it with the IRS.

The moral issue here is less the filing of Form 990 and more the assertion that they are a church when, clearly, they are not. There is a legal perspective that can be argued, perhaps compellingly, that they can be classified as churches under the law. But there is a moral issue that must be considered too. Is it acceptable *to God* to claim before Caesar that one's organization is something other than what it is? When required by Ceasar, transparency should be given, even if it is detrimental to the organization and its donors. At some point, these ministries claiming church status cross the line into lying, which God will not honor.

As Christian business owners, let us stop complaining about taxes and transparency rules. Instead, let us pay our taxes on time and provide transparency where it is required— all without complaining.

Civil Disobedience

Sometimes, earthly kingdoms conflict with God's laws because these kingdoms know no limitation to the state's authority. They usurp God's authority by demanding for their own that which belongs to God. When these kingdoms come into conflict, the laws of God's

---

768 https://www.ministrywatch.com

769 https://www.irs.gov/instructions/i990#en_US_2023_publink11283jd0e846

770 Bob Stephens, Spokesperson for *Focus on the Family*, interview with Kim Roberts, "Growing Number of Christian Ministries Seek IRS Designation as 'Church' or 'Association of Churches': The designation removes the requirement to file a Form 900." July 1, 2024. Ministrywatch.com. https://ministrywatch.com/growing–number–of–christian–ministries–seek–irs–designation–as–church–or–association–of–churches/

kingdom take precedence for the believer's obedience and allegiance. This is the essence of Christ's command to give what belongs to God to God. Bruner is correct in observing that

> The state tends to totalism … the state becomes demonic in the measure that it almost invariably asks for itself 'the things of God,' such as total commitment, unconditional obedience, or absolute allegiance.[771]

When forced, a Biblical steward may need to disobey a state law to obey God's commands. Purposely disobeying state laws is usually called *civil disobedience*.

There are several examples in Scripture of proper civil disobedience. For example, when the ruling authorities threatened Peter and John to stop telling others about Christ, they clearly (and swiftly) concluded that disobeying God was not an option (Acts 5:27–29 NIV). The state does not own a person's soul and should not exercise decisional authority over a person's ability to choose their eternal destiny:

> [27] The apostles were brought in and made to appear before the Sanhedrin to be questioned by the high priest. [28] "We gave you strict orders not to teach in this name," he said. "Yet you have filled Jerusalem with your teaching and are determined to make us guilty of this man's blood." [29] Peter and the other apostles replied: "We must obey God rather than human beings!"

Other examples of obeying unjust laws[772] include Hananiah, Mishael, and Azariah not bowing down to the statue in Daniel 3 or Daniel's continued daily ritual of prayer to God when the king ordered that everyone pray to him only for thirty days (Daniel 6).

> The teaching of all of Scripture, when rightly understood, is that God tells his people to be subject to governing authorities, but that we have no obligation to obey when the government commands us to sin (that is, disobey something that God commands us in Scripture).[773]

Puah and Shiphrah illustrate proper civil disobedience in Exodus 1:15–22 by not killing baby Hebrew boys after having been commanded to do so by the Pharaoh of Egypt. While the nationality of these midwives is debated,[774] what is clear is that these women "feared God" and that healthy fear created within their personas a "bravery in choosing God

---

771 Bruner, *Matthew*, 784–85.
772 An "unjust law" is a law that conflicts with one or more laws of God.
773 Wayne Grudem, *Christian Ethics: An Introduction to Moral Reasoning.* (Crossway, 2018), 189.
774 Eugene Carpenter, *Exodus.* (Lexham Press, 2016), 102.

rather than obeying Pharaoh."[775] These midwives did not kill the Hebrew male babies because they chose to obey God's laws rather than man's laws. Pharaoh demanded that which belongs to God—absolute obedience and authority of the population and to give and take life. Pharoah ventured outside the boundaries that God has for earthly kings, and he ultimately paid a heavy price for his usurpation of God's authority.

Compliance has to do with obeying laws and regulations. CBOs comply with laws and regulations as much as possible, in good faith. CBOs do not engage in civil disobedience simply because a law or regulation may be onerous or one with which the owner strongly disagrees.

But when those laws and regulations conflict with God's laws, the CBO must obey God's laws rather than man's. It is better to obey in the present realm and create rewards for oneself in heaven (Matthew 6:19–24) than forgo eternal rewards for temporary relief. Obeying God's laws will require an eternal perspective on present events and a deep awareness of one's covenant relationship with God. Figure 13–6 illustrates this hierarchy of laws and allegiances for a Christian steward.

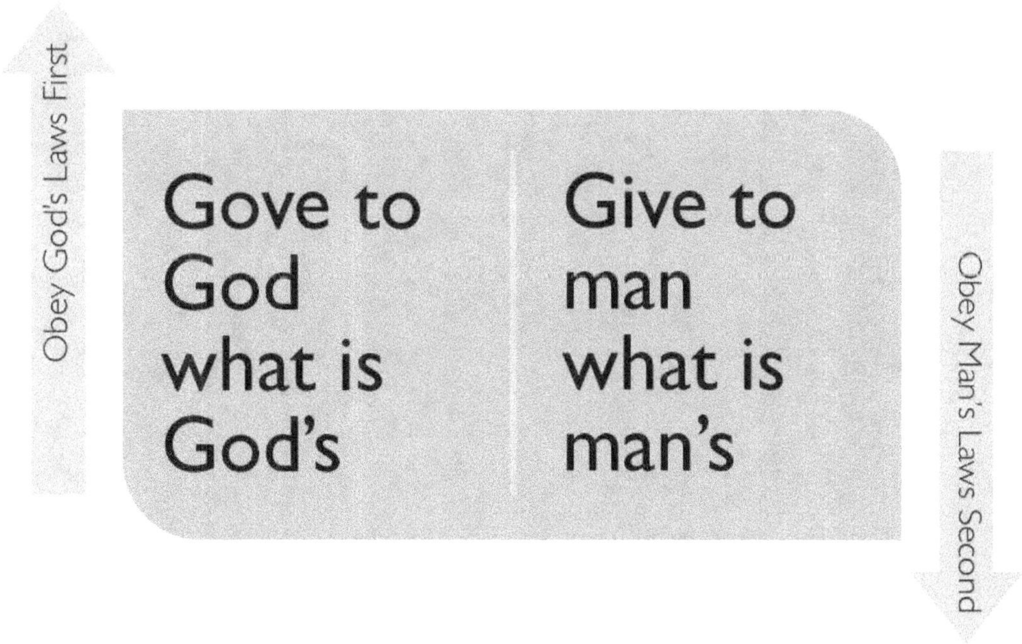

Obey God's Laws First

Gove to God what is God's

Give to man what is man's

Obey Man's Laws Second

Figure 13–6: God's Laws Over Man's Laws

775 Douglas Stuart. *Exodus*. (Broadman & Holman Publishers, 2006), 74.

Summary

Many day–to–day business problems are related to governance problems. In this chapter, I have argued that the Divine Council is a model for CBOs to follow by making clear decisions and then involving one's staff in the development and execution of those plans that will achieve the desired results. In addition, at the heart of Biblical governance is the ability to discern between right and wrong. Moreover, Biblical governance will require facing conflicts at the owner and leadership layers to align the organization's values, mission, strategy, and purposes.

I have suggested that risk mitigation is more about obedience to God's commands than anything else. In addition, I have argued that compliance with laws and regulations is part of giving to "Caesar what is Caesar's," even when compliance creates additional costs and efforts on our part. I asked the question, "Can God take a risk?" and concluded that due to his impassibility and immutability, God is unable to "take a risk" because God is not subject to dangers and injuries from outside forces. As a result, I have indicated that when God leads a CBO to assume a risk, then God shoulder's the outcomes with the CBO. Moreover, the safest place a CBO can be is in obedience to God, even if God asks the CBO to assume a significant risk. The most reckless place a CBO can be is living outside of God's will, in disobedience to what the CBO knows God has called the CBO to do.

In the next chapter, we'll turn our attention to Christian ethics and provide a realistic model for CBOs to use when faced with ethically–based decisions.

CHAPTER 14

LEGAL AND ETHICAL CONSIDERATIONS

Many decisions we make as Christian business owners are not plainly right or wrong. Add to this reality that we live in a litigious society where lawyers dominate the landscape and drive many decisions to avoid legal battles. What does the Bible say about our involvement in legal disputes? What is the basis for our ethical decisions? These questions and other difficulties are what I will discuss in this chapter.

I will offer my thoughts on when and who a Christian can sue and when a CBO must, by default, accept unfair and unjust suffering. I will also provide my model for Christian ethics, which is grounded in the two greatest commands: love God with every fiber of your being and love your neighbor as yourself.

CONVENTIONAL WISDOM ON LEGAL CONSIDERATIONS

We Americans like to sue each other. 13% of small business owners have been sued by a customer, employee, or vendor.[776] Over 100 million lawsuits are filed annually in the United States State courts.[777] Paying attention to the legal aspects of one's business is necessary and represents good stewardship.

Most business owners avoid lawsuits as much as possible because of the loss of time and focus on operating their business, the expense involved, and the expended emotional energy that can be debilitating personally and professionally.[778] Avoiding lawsuits is best accomplished by engaging a good lawyer early and often. Over the years, I have learned that proper engagement of a good attorney for non–litigious work is one of the best ways to reduce overall costs in a business. For example, engaging an attorney when a contract is being negotiated is less costly than after it is executed and a problem is discovered in the fine print.[779]

Conventional wisdom is highly concerned with protecting one's business from exposure to a costly judgment should one be sued. Biblical wisdom will share the same concern. Conventional wisdom's efforts to protect one's business from a lawsuit and the injury of a judgment are sound and should be implemented by a CBO:[780]

- Obtain business and professional liability insurance.
- Know the laws and regulations and follow them as much as possible.
- Protect intellectual property.
- Have written contracts that legal counsel reviews.
- Separate personal and business finances.
- Keep accurate financial and compliance records.

From a litigation viewpoint, conventional wisdom will indicate different desiderative outcomes. For example, if one is the plaintiff (the party initiating the lawsuit), then conventional

---

776 Hunter Hoffman. "Hiscox Study: Many Small Business Owners Cite Government Regulation as Major Obstacle to Their Business' Success and Growth." May 19, 2014. Hiscox.com. https://www.hiscox.com/newsroom/press/many–small–business–owners–cite–government–regulation–as–major–obstacle–to–their–business–success–and–growth.

777 Bagla Law. "Small Business Lawsuits: What are My Chances of Getting Sued?"April 3, 2019. Baglalaw.com. https://baglalaw.com/small–business–lawsuits–what–are–my–chances–of–getting–sued/

778 Bob Briner. Business Basics from the Bible: More Ancient Wisdom for Modern Business. (Zondervan, 1996), 73.

779 MacMain Leinhauser, 2020. *When Should Small Businesses Engage an Attorney?* July 9, 2020. Macmainlaw.com. https://www.macmainlaw.com/2020/07/09/small–businesses–attorney/

780 Cueto Law. "How to Protect Your Business from Lawsuit (6 Avoidance Tips)." nd. Cuetolawgroup.com. https://cuetolawgroup.com/how–to–protect–your–business–from–lawsuit/

wisdom says the goal of a civil lawsuit is to be made whole for any damages suffered.[781] Being "made whole" may include monetary recovery and preventing or allowing certain acts.[782] If one is a defendant in a lawsuit, conventional wisdom says that the best outcome is for the judge to dismiss the case.[783] But if a trial ensues, the best outcome for a defendant is to avoid a guilty verdict and not be ordered to pay any associated penalties.[784]

Conventional wisdom does not mind reconciliation as a conflict resolution tactic as long as one's legal goals can be attained or, at a minimum, one's legal position is protected. Conventional wisdom may prefer reconciliation efforts, but only to the extent that reconciliation supports the legal goals of the owner.

Reconciliation is not a moral concept for conventional wisdom. Reconciliation is just a tactic. However, for the CBO, reconciliation has moral and eternal considerations, so reconciliation goes beyond a legal settlement and hopes to restore a harmonious relationship between the conflicted parties. Whereas a settlement is legal, reconciliation is personal.[785]

BIBLICAL WISDOM ON LEGAL CONSIDERATIONS

The Scriptures do not discuss legal matters, *per se,* but they have much to teach about a Christian's conduct and involvement in legal disputes. God does not like Christians using pagan courts to resolve conflicts and prefers reconciliation and suffering over a win–at–all–costs mentality.

Biblical wisdom about being a defendant

When being sued, Matthew 5:23–26 (CSB) gives the CBO clear direction:

> [23] So if you are offering your gift on the altar, and there you remember that your brother has something against you, [24] leave your gift there in front of the altar. First go and be reconciled with your brother, and then come and offer your gift. [25] Reach a settlement quickly with your adversary while you're on the way with him, or your adversary will hand

---

781 Christy Bieber. "Civil Lawsuit Guide (2024)." May 15, 2023. Forbes.com. https://www.forbes.com/advisor/legal/personal–injury/civil–lawsuit/

782 Hopkins Roden. "The Civil Lawsuit Process: From Start to Finish." December 26, 2019. Hopkinsroden.com. https://www.hopkinsroden.com/news–and–resources/posts/2019/december/the–civil–lawsuit–process–from–start–to–finish/

783 Content Team. "Dismissal." May 22, 2015. Legaldictionary.net. https://legaldictionary.net/dismissal/

784 GlespyNorson. "When to Settle (And Not to Settle) a Lawsuit." September 7, 2020. Westerlaw.org. https://westerlaw.org/when–to–settle–and–not–to–settle–a–lawsuit/

785 Shawn Manaher. "Settlement vs. Reconciliation: Deciding Between Similar Terms." nd. Thecontentauthority.com. https://thecontentauthority.com/blog/settlement–vs–reconciliation

you over to the judge, the judge to the officer, and you will be thrown into prison. ^{26} I assure you: You will never get out of there until you have paid the last penny!

The comparison of anger and its outcomes to being liable to judgment before a council, hell of fire, or a court indicates that a relationship breakdown with a state of hostility has ensued.[786] The need for reconciliation is all–important; hence, "come to terms quickly with your accuser" is the command when being sued. The Biblical steward must attempt reconciliation when sued and do so quickly, as much as it is in the steward's power to achieve peace (Romans 12:18).

Matthew 5:38–41 (CSB) builds on Matthew 5:21–25 and describes generosity by taking a "one–down" position as a way to reconcile with a legal adversary:

^{38} "You have heard that it was said, An eye for an eye and a tooth for a tooth. ⁹ ^{39} But I tell you, don't resist an evildoer. On the contrary, if anyone slaps you on your right cheek, turn the other to him also. ^{40} As for the one who wants to sue you and take away your shirt, let him have your coat as well. ^{41} And if anyone forces you to go one mile, go with him two. ^{42} Give to the one who asks you, and don't turn away from the one who wants to borrow from you.

Likewise, Romans 12:14 and 17 (ESV) says,

^{14} Bless those who persecute you; bless and do not curse them … ^{17} Repay no one evil for evil, but give thought to do what is honorable in the sight of all.

Christian business owners are commanded to be generous and non-retaliatory against those who have harmed us—even if there is a clear path to winning in court. Allen writes,

The question is [*sic*] here contemplated from the point of view of the individual wronged, not from that of social justice. So far from seeking to injure his oppressor by calling in the aid of the law to inflict penalties upon him, the Christian disciple should quietly submit to wrong.[787]

---

786   John Nolland, *The Gospel of Matthew: a Commentary on the Greek text.* (Eerdmans; Paternoster Press, 2005), 233–34.

787   Willoughby C. Allen, *A critical and exegetical commentary on the gospel according to St. Matthew.* (C. Scribner's Sons, 1907), 54.

As we'll see, what appears to be a blanket command in Matthew 5:38–41 and Romans 12:14–17 is moderated by other passages.

First, other Scripture passages illustrate Christians escaping from legal and personal danger. For example, David avoided the violence that Saul tried to commit against him when he dodged the spear Saul threw at him in an attempt to kill him (1 Samuel 19:10). David did not turn the other cheek. He did not return the spear to Saul and offer to stand still a second time while Saul tried to kill him.

Other examples include Paul eluding capture by King Aretas (2 Corinthians 11:32–33), Jesus escaping an angry crowd (Luke 4:29–30), and Jesus hiding in the temple to escape hostile Jews (John 8:59, 10:39). Many in the ancient church left Jerusalem once great persecution broke out against the followers of Jesus Christ (Acts 8:1–3). Escaping danger is a form of self–defense and would violate Matthew 5:38–41 if a broad, passive non-resistance was the core teaching of that passage.

Second, there are clear examples of Christians defending themselves in legal and quasi-legal proceedings. When Peter and John were accused of wrongdoing by the Jewish Sanhedrin, they defended themselves (Acts 4:5–22). Later, all the apostles were arrested and defended themselves before the Sanhedrin (Acts 5:27–42). Stephen offered his defense before being killed for his faith in Acts 7. Paul defended himself before the city authorities in Philippi (Acts 16:37), the Roman tribune in Jerusalem (Acts 21:27–39), a hostile mob in Jerusalem (Acts 22:1–21), before the Jewish Sanhedrin (Acts 23:1–10), the Roman governor Felix (Acts 24:10–21), the Roman governor Festus (Acts 25:8–12) and King Agrippa (Acts 26:1–29). In all these situations, if passive non-resistance was the only law of God, none of the apostles would have defended themselves. Yet they defended themselves. The apostles did not consider Christ's words in Matthew 5 to be a blanket prohibition against self–defense. Their practice of self–defense teaches the Biblical steward that a right of self–defense is given to us by God and that we can (not must) exercise that right when appropriate.[788]

In Matthew 5:38–41, Jesus rejects personal vengeance and does not teach a broad, passive non–resistance to injury or harm.[789] Murray agrees:

> We are not to suppose that he is including passive non–resistance under all circumstances of attack upon our persons or property and that when injured or insulted, we are to invite more.[790]

---

788 Mark D. Liederbach & Evan Lenow, *Ethics as Worship: The Pursuit of Moral Discipleship*. (P&R Publishing, 2021), 465–84. See also Francis Schaeffer. *The Complete Works of Francis A. Schaeffer: a Christian Worldview*. (Crossway Books, 1982), v5, 475–92.

789 William D. Davies & Dale C. Allison, Jr., *A Critical and Exegetical Commentary on the Gospel according to Saint Matthew*. (T&T Clark., 2004), 540. See also Frederick Dale Bruner, *Matthew, Volume 1 The Christbook Matthew 1–12*. (Word Publishing, 1987), 208–11. See also Craig Blomberg, *Matthew*. (Broadman & Holman Publishers, 1992), 113.

790 John Murray, *Principles of Conduct: Aspects of Biblical Ethics*. (Eerdmans, 1957), 175.

It would be a misinterpretation of these passages to assert that the Scriptures prohibit defending oneself in a legal proceeding.[791] To sum up, if reconciliation cannot be achieved with the one suing you, you can offer a robust defense through a settlement process or arguments in court.

Biblical wisdom about being a plaintiff

The Scriptures do not speak to the role of a plaintiff. Still, the Scriptures teach about the heart attitudes that often accompany the act of suing, such as vengeance, a need for justice, and forgiveness's role in the process. The Scriptures also address how to gain freedom when justice cannot or should not be pursued.

Keeping Matthew 5:38–41 and Romans 12:14–17 in mind, when considering initiating a lawsuit against another entity, let's remember to include these two questions as we seek to be obedient to God's commands:
- Is it best for the Kingdom of God?
- Is it best for righteousness?

At first blush, it appears that it would be a rare case in which we could answer these questions in the affirmative and still initiate a lawsuit. An example would be suing the state over abortion laws that allow the killing of unborn babies. But in most cases, the core question becomes this: If or when should a Christian use the earthly court system to find justice? I sense the answer is "rarely."

Conventional wisdom may suggest that gaining justice is a supreme pursuit of life. At first blush, there is Biblical support for pursuing justice above all else. Consider Deuteronomy 16:18–20 (ESV):

> [18] You shall appoint judges and officers in all your towns that the Lord your God is giving you, according to your tribes, and they shall judge the people with righteous judgment. [19] You shall not pervert justice. You shall not show partiality, and you shall not accept a bribe, for a bribe blinds the eyes of the wise and subverts the cause of the righteous. [20] Justice, and only justice, you shall follow, that you may live and inherit the land that the Lord your God is giving you.

But upon closer inspection, our attention is directed to the notions that justice is perverted when partiality ("pay regard to") is shown to one party vs. the other or when bribes are taken because bribes "encourage people to do the very things just forbidden."[792] Therefore, impartiality is paramount when justice is dispensed because impartiality is the only way

---

791 Wayne Grudem, Christian Ethics: An Introduction to Moral Reasoning. (Crossway, 2018), 552–55.
792 Eugene H. Merrill, *Deuteronomy*. (Broadman & Holman, 1994), 258.

true justice can be administered. But pursuing justice more than God is not taught in this passage or anywhere else in Scripture.

God's System of Justice

God's system of justice starts with God's sovereignty. Hence, *God gets to define what fair is because He is God.* We have no business questioning if God is fair, whether He is just, or to whom He shows forgiveness or judgment. God is fair.

In Romans 9:6–21, we find Paul making this same assertion—that God, in his sovereignty, should not be questioned even though his decisions might be considered unfair by us (take a moment and read Romans 9:6–21). We can see that even though God's hardening of some for his purposes might be "unfair" from our perspective, we are not to question God's decisions and ways precisely because we are *humans,* and he is *God.* He is incomparably *greater* than us. He is so much *other* than us that had he not accommodated our limited brains, he could not have disclosed himself to us. If God chooses to harden some for his glory, who are we to question him?

In the same way, God's forgiveness is also fair or just, as the apostle John notes in 1 John 1:8–9 (NIV):

> If we claim to be without sin, we deceive ourselves and the truth is not in us. If we confess our sins, he is faithful and just and will forgive us our sins and purify us from all unrighteousness.

God's point is that if we confess our sins, it is fair for him to forgive our sins and cleanse us from all unrighteousness. Why would he need to say that? Well, not only to remind us of the glorious truth that our sins can be totally and wholly forgiven but also to remind us that what Jesus endured on our behalf was *unfair to him* so that God could save us.

Even though God directed Christ to endure the cross, and Christ did so voluntarily, what man did to God was entirely unjust—completely unfair. That is why we are reminded that when God forgives our sins, his act is "just" or "fair" because Christ bore the penalty for our sins and endured the full wrath of God for our sins. In God's system of justice, the penalty for our sins has been paid by Christ Himself.

When you are on the positive end of an unfairness, it will not bother you nearly as much as if you are on the negative end. Since Christ was on the negative end of the cross, and we are on the positive end, it is easy for us to forget just how unfair God's forgiveness is *to Jesus*.

Hence, we can describe God's system of fairness —God's system of justice—as *substitutionary*, not *individualistic*. Christ voluntarily substituted himself for us and took God's wrath that would have been fairly applied to us for our sins. This is an unfamiliar system of justice to us because, by contrast, we have an individual system of justice in America.

For example, when a person commits a crime, that person must pay for his crime. If it is a speeding ticket, a check is written by the one who was speeding, and the matter is settled. If it is murder, then the one who committed the murder will spend years—perhaps a lifetime—in prison for his action(s). The courts will not allow someone else to serve out the murderer's sentence. The individual who commits the crime pays individually for his crime. Even if he confesses his crime in court and asks for forgiveness, the court will likely sentence him because *someone must pay the penalty for the crime*. Without payment for the crime, there is no justice. If a court were never to impose a sentence after the criminal is found guilty, that would be a miscarriage of justice.

Forgiveness, confession, and justice are intertwined in God's substitutionary system. If a person commits murder and does not accept Christ as Savior and Lord, then that person will pay for his crime in hell because he did not receive the forgiveness Christ offers. However, if a person commits murder, then confesses his sin to God and accepts Christ as the Savior and Lord of his life, the payment for his murder is transferred to Christ, who bore all of God's wrath on the cross for all of man's sin. So God's justice is satisfied, and that person can spend eternity with God, never having to pay the penalty for his murderous act.[793]

---

793 This does get to the notion of limited atonement, one of several pillars of John Calvin's theology. I do reject the notion of limited atonement, that Christ died only for the sin of those who are chosen by God. By the same token, I also reject universalism, the notion that since Christ died for all sin for all time, that all will eventually be saved by God and brought into Heaven. I think both errors are based on a faulty logic of pressing various texts to say more than they really do.

This is not fair, you say. You are right! It is unfair that any of us "get off the hook" for our sins. But this is God's system of justice. It is substitutionary, not individualistic.

Only God, who is sovereign over all, can create a substitutionary system of justice and have the sovereignty to declare what is and isn't fair.

Leave Vengeance to God

Vengeance is harming another person in return for an injury or offense that one has suffered due to the action or inaction of the other person.[794] Vengeance is not the administration of justice; vengeance is an act committed outside of the justice system and usually is an illegal act in and of itself. Christian business owners—as tough as it can be sometimes—leave vengeance to God. Romans 12:19–21 (LEB) says,

> [19] Do not take revenge yourselves, dear friends, but give place to *God's* wrath, for it is written, "Vengeance *is* mine, I will repay," says the Lord. [20] But "if your enemy is hungry, feed him; if he is thirsty, give him *something* to drink; for *by* doing this, you will heap up coals of fire upon his head." [21] Do not be overcome by evil, but overcome evil with good.

Paul cites Deuteronomy 32:35, in which Moses reminds Israel that at the right time, God will avenge those who have harmed God and his people. Merrill suggests that much of God's vengeance is enacted through "natural" or human means,[795] even when God uses an evil agent who will one day be punished to carry out God's vengeance (Isaiah 10:5–14; Ezekiel 25:12–15).

The Deuteronomy passage is based on the law given to Israel. Leviticus 19:18 (NIV) says,

> Do not seek revenge or bear a grudge against anyone among your people, but love your neighbor as yourself. I am the Lord.

---

794 Faithlife. "Vengeance." In *Logos Bible Study Factbook*. (Faithlife, September 22, 2024.) https://ref.ly/logos4/Factbook?id=ref%3abk.%25vengeance.

795 Merrill, *Deuteronomy*, 422.

"Bearing a grudge"[796] affirms a correlation between the inner man's thoughts and emotions and the expression of those emotions through action (Leviticus 19:18, Matthew 5:21–25, 38–41, Luke 6:44–45). When a person maintains anger toward another, nothing good can come from that situation. While a Christian cannot control the actions of another person, any Christian can control inner emotions and thoughts through the transforming power of the Holy Spirit. When one has been wronged, letting go of one's anger will involve agreeing to live with the hurt and pain the other has caused without taking action to obtain justice. This is precisely the definition of forgiveness.

Consider the Opportunity Costs Before Suing

Earthly justice means that the law is applied without prejudice against those who have violated the law: violators receive just punishment for wrongful actions. Forgiveness means the injured person acknowledges one's injury because another has violated a law, standard, or contract. But besides acknowledging the violation, forgiveness also accepts the hurt and pain the other has caused and gives up the right to hurt the other party in return or see justice in another way. Forgiveness does not require a just punishment for the party who created the injury and violated the law.[797] Forgiveness leaves to God the responsibility to create justice in his own time and method.

Even though an injured party may gain justice through the court system as a plaintiff, Christians in business understand that earthly justice is rarely enough to restore wholeness. A CBO may gain legal justice using the court system, but the Scriptures are more interested in relational restoration. We are on this earth for such a short time that focusing on bringing others to God is the more considerable opportunity when compared to winning in court. One may win in court, but the opportunity cost of losing a relationship with one who does not know God may outweigh the value of winning.

Justice is Never Enough

Family members in family businesses suing each other is not uncommon. In the last couple of years, I've encountered several situations in which family members sued each other for various reasons.

---

796   The Hebrew word nāṭar means *to keep guard, reserve or maintain*, hence, in this context, *to hang onto one's anger.* (TWOT)

797   Faithlife, "Forgiveness." In *Logos Bible Study Factbook.* (Faithlife, September 23, 2024). https://ref.ly/logos4/Factbook?id=ref%3abk.%25forgiveness.

For example, in Newton, PA, Nina Kaplan was successfully sued by her father and is now required to pay $2.13 million because of poor business results and suspicions about embezzlement. Her business was forced to close. A sign on the door read, in part, "My own father suing me. There are no words for this."[798] In 2018, Patrick Yu sued his father, Bong Yu, for stewarding their family business to benefit the Yu family, but at Patrick's personal expense, creating a breach of the fiduciary duty owed to him by his family members who serve as officers in their family business. Hence, Patrick is seeking dissolution of the family business.[799]

In a public, embarrassing action in the Twin Cities, Kim Lund was awarded $45.2 million for her shares in the Lunds & Byerly corporation.[800] She had sought $80 million. At this time, it appears their family dispute is headed to the Minnesota Supreme Court. The judge in this case, Hennepin County Chief Judge Ivy Bernhardson quoted the Bible at the end of their trial: "But I tell you that anyone who is angry with a brother or sister will be subject to judgment". She said to both parties, "Family life is too intimate to be preserved by the spirit of justice. It can be sustained by a spirit of love that goes beyond justice … while they are only words, there are profound thoughts behind these words. I wish the parties peace."

In the last few years, I've seen a sister and brother divide and cut off over $34,000 in a $1.1 million business. I have seen four siblings force their fifth sibling—their sister—out of their family business, driving a wedge within the family that will never be removed. I have seen a sister and her husband cut off from their siblings because a $200,000 loan was not repaid when the $16 million business failed. I have seen another brother and sister nearly cut off from each other because of persistent conflict about capital expenditures in the $300,000 – $500,000 range in a $4 million business. I have learned about two brothers who are 50–50 owners in their business and now communicate only through their lawyers.

798 Kara Seymour, "Newtown's BLC Beauty Closes After Family Dispute." September 1, 2017. Patch. com. https://patch.com/pennsylvania/newtown–pa/newtowns–blc–beauty–closes–after–family–dispute

799 Justia. "Matter of Yu v Bong Yu." Accessed 11/23/2024. Law.justia.com. https://law.justia.com/cases/new–york/other–courts/2018/2018–ny–slip–op–32009–u.html

800 Mike Hughlett, "Kim Lund asks Minnesota Supreme Court to Uphold $45M Ruling." February 27, 2019. Startribune.com. https://www.startribune.com/kim–lund–asks–minnesota–supreme–court–to–uphold–45m–ruling/506443862

In all these cases, several things were true:

- Retaining money and power was more important than preserving family relationships.
- The need for justice and "I am right" eclipsed the need to forgive.
- The lawyers made enormous amounts of money.
- Everyone agreed that injured family relationships were the most significant loss.
- Nieces, nephews, and grandchildren bore the full brunt of the adult's conflicts.

Justice means that the law is applied without prejudice against those who have violated it: violators receive just punishment for their wrongful actions. Forgiveness means I acknowledge you have violated the law while accepting the hurt and pain you have caused me. But here is the catch: I give up the right to hurt you. I do not require a just punishment for your wrongful actions.

Forgiveness is tough stuff. It's not for the faint of heart. While it doesn't continue to accept abusive, illegal, or violating behavior, it also gives up the right to find equitable outcomes where the offended party is made whole.

Forgiveness is born in love and grown in the soil of maturity. Finding people who cannot forgive in business (or life) demonstrates that their hurt is so deep that it has driven their love for the offender away. Revenge is the natural outcome for those who cannot forgive.

Forgiveness is always a choice. It is not an emotion. Although forgiveness usually does not lead to reconciliation or restoration, it does release the forgiver from the bondage of hate and bitterness that often hinders one's success and thriving life.

For family businesses to survive and families to thrive together, forgiveness must be present and exercised regularly. At times, members must give up the right to be right. At those exact times, justice must be subordinated to love.

In our hyper-individualistic culture, where money and individual rights are sacred and worshipped as such, the message of forgiveness and love can be counter-cultural. But without those two gifts that family members give each other, family businesses will likely fail, and the family will be generationally injured.

Forgive Before Suing

There will be times when a CBO needs to exercise forgiveness. In addition to leaving vengeance to God, Christians forgive others for two reasons. First, Christians forgive others to continue to receive forgiveness from God. Christ said (Matthew 6:14 NIV),

> [14] For if you forgive other people when they sin against you, your heavenly Father will also forgive you. [15] But if you do not forgive others their sins, your Father will not forgive your sins.

Luke records this sentiment more succinctly in Luke 6:37 (NIV): "Forgive, and you will be forgiven." Christians forgive "just as Christ forgave you." (Ephesians 4:32 NIV). When another injures a CBO, the owner's first reaction should be to forgive so that the owner can continue to receive forgiveness from God.

Second, Christians forgive others so that their "land" can be healed and give them rest in the future. When an owner (or any Christian) forgives those who have caused injury, God promises to hear the owner's prayers, forgive the owner's sin, and heal the owner's land:

> If my people, who are called by my name, will humble themselves and pray and seek my face and turn from their wicked ways, then I will hear from heaven, and I will forgive their sin and will heal their land. (2 Chronicles 7:14 ESV).

One way we can be "wicked" is not to forgive those who have wronged us (Matthew 6:12–13). But when we forgive another who has injured us, God will forgive our sin and heal our land.

Healing the land is part of God's restoration from sin. This promise is based partly on Leviticus 26:41, Jeremiah 30:17, and 33:6–7. In Ephesians 6:1–4, the reward for obedience that pleases the Lord is "living long in the land," as promised in Exodus 20:12, the only positive command with a positive promise in the Decalogue. A land at rest coupled with rest from one's enemies is part of God's covenant with David in 2 Samuel 7:8–11.

Part of God's promise to heal one's land is to bring rest between his people and their enemies. I believe such rest extends to the businesses God has entrusted to his stewards. When we forgive those who wronged us, we can expect God's blessings of rest and restoration personally and in our business.

Lawsuits Between Christians

Lawsuits are being filed at an increasing rate in the United States by Christians against Christians for defamation, discrimination, sexual abuse, and divorce.[801] These suits may represent situations that have actual injury and injustice, but many of these suits violate Paul's commands in 1 Corinthians 6:1–8 (ESV) which says:

> "[1] When one of you has a grievance against another, does he dare go to law before the unrighteous instead of the saints? [2] Or do you not know that the saints will judge the world? And if the world is to be judged by you, are you incompetent to try trivial cases? [3] Do you not know that we are to judge angels? How much more, then, matters pertaining to this life! [4] So if you have such cases, why do you lay them before those who have no standing in the church? [5] I say this to your shame. Can it be that there is no one among you wise enough to settle a dispute between the brothers, [6] but brother goes to law against brother, and that before unbelievers? [7] To have lawsuits at all with one another is already a defeat for you. Why not rather suffer wrong? Why not rather be defrauded? [8] But you yourselves wrong and defraud—even your own brothers!"

Paul assumes that Christians will have disputes. The problem is not the existence of conflicts but taking them to public court.[802] These disputes should be settled before church leadership, not in front of unbelievers in the court system. If Christians utilize the court system, the kingdom of God is disadvantaged, and both sides—regardless of who is right or wrong—have already lost in God's eyes. "The believers were looking for a victory in court, but Paul informs them that the very presence of lawsuits signals a stunning defeat and reversal."[803] Forgiveness has not been exercised, and a loss of focus on advancing God's

---

801 Kim Roberts, "Christians Suing Each Other: An Analysis." May 24, 2022. Ministrywatch.com. https://ministrywatch.com/christians-suing-each-other-an-analysis/

802 Roy Ciampa & Brian Rosner, *The First Letter to the Corinthians*. (Eerdmans, 2010), 234.

803 Thomas R. Schreiner, *1 Corinthians: An Introduction and Commentary*. Schnabel, E.J. (Ed.). (InterVarsity Press, 2018), 120.

kingdom has been experienced while Christ's reputation is tarnished. God is disadvantaged when Christians air their dirty laundry by suing each other in public court.

Recalling that all of life for the Christian is preparatory for reigning with Christ in eternity, Paul's main point in verses 2–3 is that judging ordinary matters among fellow Christians should not be a problem for those destined for the high calling of judging much greater things.[804] Moreover, when wronged by another believer, a Christian should voluntarily opt to suffer when wronged (Matthew 5:40, Luke 6:29) rather than go to public court and plead their case (vs. 7).[805]

Reconciliation Using the Matthew 18 Process

The ideal way that disputes among Christians should be managed is given to Christians in Matthew 18:15–17 (CSB):

> [15] "If your brother sins against you, go and rebuke him in private. If he listens to you, you have won your brother. [16] But if he won't listen, take one or two more with you, so that by the testimony of two or three witnesses every fact may be established. [17] If he pays no attention to them, tell the church. But if he doesn't pay attention even to the church, let him be like an unbeliever and a tax collector to you.

The directives of this passage do not include annoying or frustrating behavior; instead, they include sinful behavior. The brother has sinned and is presumably not repentant.[806] So, the one offended goes to his brother in private. A private conversation allows honest dialogue to lead to (hopefully) reconciliation. Airing the problems publicly causes the other party to become defensive and withdrawn and can create a desire to counter-attack.[807]

If the first step fails, try involving at least one or two other people and go to the brother again. Involving one or two others creates witnesses, which fulfills the command of Deuteronomy 19:15. In this step, privacy and restoration remain the two core goals.

If step two fails, then the matter goes before the church. As a pragmatic way of engaging in this step, I believe it is best to go confidentially before the church elders and see if elder involvement can achieve reconciliation. Privacy can be maintained, though the circle has widened from two or three to ten or twelve. I conclude that going before the elders of a church is equivalent to "telling it to the church" (vs. 17). If the entire church body is to

---

804   Charles K. Barrett, *The First Epistle to the Corinthians*. (Continuum, 1968), 136–37.

805   Ciampa, *Corinthians*, 236.

806   John Nolland, *The Gospel of Matthew: a commentary on the Greek text*. (Eerdmans; Paternoster Press, 2005), 745.

807   Dan Doriani. "Forgiveness: Jesus' Plan For Healing And Reconciliation In The Church (Matthew 18:15–35)." *Southern Baptist Journal of Theology*. 2009. 13(3):23–34.

be informed of the situation (step 3), that communication should come from the elders or pastors rather than from the wronged brother. Of course, if the unrepentant believer is put out of the church (step 4), then that is a public matter that the church is responsible for managing.

Common litigation scenarios CBOs may face

There are several common scenarios that a CBO may face where Matthew 18 or 1 Corinthians 6 will apply. I will share my thoughts on these scenarios.

Contractor

If a CBO is contracting with a fellow believer in Christ, and conflict occurs, the Matthew 18 process should be followed. The Matthew 18 process is the Biblical, God-honoring way to manage small and large disputes between Christians. It is the only governing process a CBO should follow when disagreeing with another Christian. The 1 Corinthians 6 passage prohibits suing another Christian in a public court of law.

What if both believers attend different churches in various parts of the country or the world? Whose church leadership should be involved? The process of Matthew 18 becomes more difficult to follow when the believers in the dispute attend different churches. In steps 3 and 4, Paul assumed both parties were members of the same body of believers. Coordination between elder boards and pastors will likely be needed to follow the Matthew process fully. In today's toxic legal climate, it may be difficult for churches to coordinate due to fear of being sued.[808] But such fear should not stop pastors and elder boards from collaborating to fulfill their ordained duties.

Christian Ownership

Is suing a business owned by a Christian equivalent to suing a brother in the Lord, thus violating the 1 Corinthians 6 Passage? I will filter this question through the three basic business structures: sole proprietor, partnership, and corporation.

---

808   One example of this phenomena is the Southern Baptist convention (sbc.net). Fear of being sued and losing in court kept the Southern Baptists silent for nearly twenty years while they protected roughly 700 known sexual abusers working in their churches. The SBC leadership made a conscious tradeoff decision to protect their reputations and bank accounts at the expense of young people being sexually abused. (Terry Gross, "How the Southern Baptist Convention Covered Up its Widespread Sexual Abuse Scandal." June 2, 2022. Npr.org. https://www.npr.org/2022/06/02/1102621352/how–the–southern–baptist–convention–covered–up–its–widespread–sexual–abuse–scand).

Sole Proprietor

In a sole proprietor business formation, the ownership of the business and the business itself are the same. The business is not a separate legal entity. Suing a company formed as a sole proprietor is the same as suing an individual. If both parties are Christians, then the Matthew 18 process should be followed, and lawsuits should be avoided.

Partnership

In the formation of a partnership, the ownership of the business is shared by the partnership members. The partnership is not a separate entity apart from the partners. Suing a partnership is equivalent to suing each partner severally and equally because no separate legal entity can be sued.

I recognize that suing a partnership with 300 partners where the number of Christian partners is likely not many is considerably different from suing a two-person partnership where both partners are Christians. I believe that the more numerous the number of partners in a partnership, coupled with the relative number of Christians in the partnership (if discernable), Matthew 18 applies more or less. For example, if a lawsuit is contemplated against a partnership with five partners, three of whom are Christians, I believe that a Christian suing that partnership would be a sin. But if the partnership has 300 partners with just a few Christians, the "directness" of suing a brother is diluted by the sheer number of unbelievers in the partnership. In my view, suing a larger partnership, such as an accounting firm or a law firm, would not violate 1 Corinthians 6 and Matthew 18 would not apply.

Corporation

In the Corporate business formation, the corporation's ownership is shared by the shareholders. A corporation's "personal–ness" relative to its ownership can vary widely between corporations, based on the number of shareholders. Many business owners are incorporated and own 100% of the corporate shares, so when the corporation is sued, the owner is likely to personalize the lawsuit, even though the lawsuit names the corporation as the defendant and not the owner individually.

Burkett suggests a one-size-fits-all approach that allows any corporation to be sued by a Christian. Burkett reasons that a corporation is a separate entity, and since Paul took action against his own government (cf Acts 16—a separate entity), it is appropriate to sue a corporation.[809] Burkett's reasoning is unconvincing when he equates asserting legal rights under current law (which Paul did in Acts 16) with suing a corporation (which Paul did

---

809 Crown Team, "Should a Christian Sue a Company?" February 26, 2012. Crown.org. https://www.crown.org/all–resources/should–a–christian–sue–a–company/

not do). Suing a government and suing a corporation are entirely different actions. Burkett also neglects the interpersonal dynamic of one Christian suing another in situations where the corporate ownership is only or mostly Christian.

Sande suggests that in conflict resolution, the principle to apply is to "keep the circle of people involved in a conflict as small as possible for as long as possible."[810] The principle that I advocate builds on Sande's insight and suggests to a CBO that the more "personal" any Christian shareholders will experience a lawsuit, the more likely it is that a lawsuit should not be filed. For example, if a Christian is suing a large corporation with thousands of shareholders, surely that is a different scenario than a Christian suing a corporation that another Christian solely owns. Christian shareholders in the former will not experience the lawsuit as "personal" nearly as much as the latter.

From where I sit, there is no one–size–fits–all answer, but the following principles seem to be wise to me (these principles can be applied to a Partnership as well):

The more numerous the shareholder list is for a corporation, the more likely a Christian can sue that corporation. For example, if there are six shareholders in the corporation, that is a different scenario than if there are six thousand shareholders.

Suppose some shareholders are Christians, and this is known to the brother who has been offended. How likely is it that defending the suit or having a judgment placed against the corporation will damage the Christian brother? The more likely a lawsuit would damage one's Christian brother, the more likely it is that a lawsuit would violate 1 Corinthians 6.

If some shareholders are Christians in a smaller group of shareholders, can the offended brother contact them and speak with them, *ala* Matthew 18? They may not have been personally responsible or involved in the offense, but perhaps they could have some influence on the resolution.

If some shareholders are Christians, how much control or influence did they have in the corporation's offensive behavior? The less power or influence these Christians had or could have had, the more likely a Christian can sue the corporation.

The offended CBO should seek God's direction and the counsel of trusted advisors before filing suit in public court. If God's name would be tarnished through a lawsuit in public court or if the four questions offered earlier cannot be answered in the affirmative, I believe that the offended brother should choose to be offended and suffer instead of seeking justice. This choice is an example of disadvantaging oneself so that the kingdom of God can be advantaged.

What if the one who has wronged the CBO claims to be a Christian, but there is little or no evidence of genuine transformation, can one conclude this person is not a Christian and sue? In theory, a Christian is allowed to sue anyone who is not a Christian because the only court of justice available to those who do not believe in Christ is an earthly court.

---

810   Ken Sande, *The Peacemaker: A Biblical Guide to Resolving Personal Conflict.* (Baker Books, 2004), 186.

However, even though Christ told believers that another person's heart can be known by the fruit of the other's actions (Matthew 7:15–20), only God can know what is truly in that person's heart (Luke 16:15, Acts 15:18, 1 Thessalonians 2:4, 1 Samuel 16:7). The conflict of interest in deciding to sue another who claims to be a believer but does not bear Christian fruit is enough for me to advise a CBO to refrain from suing in this scenario.

Is Binding Arbitration or Mediation equivalent to suing or being sued? I believe neither binding arbitration nor mediation is equivalent to suing another person or entity. Arbitration is a form of dispute resolution where both parties voluntarily choose arbitrators to act as neutral decision–makers. The conflict and resolution are kept private.[811] Mediation differs from arbitration in that the mediator is a facilitator who helps the conflicted parties arrive at an agreement that both can support. The mediator is not a decision–maker because both parties agree to a resolution they create.[812]

The public nature of a court proceeding is one of two characteristics that Paul wrote against in 1 Corinthians 6, the other being subject to a judge who is not a believer. Neither of these elements is true in mediation, so a CBO can use mediation without violating Paul's commands in 1 Corinthians 6.

In arbitration, however, the element of a final decision–maker apart from the conflicted parties is present. So, if both conflicted parties choose a fellow believer as the arbiter, then a CBO can use arbitration without violating the commands of 1 Corinthians 6. But if an unbelieving arbiter is selected, I suggest that submitting to that arbiter's decision is equivalent to having the conflict decided before unbelievers, so a CBO cannot use an unbelieving arbiter.

CONVENTIONAL WISDOM ON ETHICS

There are myriad books and courses on business ethics, yet a set of standards to which most business professionals adhere is elusive. To examine the various systems of ethics is pointless because what one finds "ethical," another will find "unethical." Even the definition of "ethic" will vary widely, as we will see.

Aristotle held that the highest ethic was the attainment of happiness, though he admitted that happiness would be disagreed upon by those living in society. For example, happiness would be defined as becoming rich if one was poor or becoming healthy if one was ill.[813]

---

811 Trey Hendershot. "What is the Difference Between Arbitration and Litigation?" March 24, 2021. Hchlawyers.com. https://www.hchlawyers.com/blog/2021/march/what–is–the–difference–between–arbitration–and–l/

812 Jacob Imm, "Mediation vs. Arbitration." July 28, 2021. Northcentralcollege.edu. https://www.northcentralcollege.edu/news/2021/07/28/mediation–vs–arbitration

813 Aristotle. *Nicomachean Ethics*. Translated by Robert C. Bartlett and Susan D. Collins. (University of Chicago Press, 2011), 5.

As part of his ethical system, Aristotle there were eleven moral virtues that one should attain in life:

- Courage
- Moderation
- Liberality
- Magnificence
- Greatness of Sour
- Ambition
- Gentleness
- Friendliness
- Truthfulness
- Wittiness
- Justice

It is out of these virtues that ethical actions are taken. If one lacks these virtues, one is less likely to behave as correct reason indicates.[814]

While Aristotle's ethics may be laudable, they are godless. I believe the Scriptures offer a much better foundation and framework for ethics in business.

BIBLICAL WISDOM ON ETHICS

When the Scriptures are silent on a decision or topic, ethical values inform our decisions and judgments. Values help us judge right from wrong, good from evil, and moral from immoral.[815] This section will offer you, the Christian business owner, a foundation for ethical decision–making.

Every system of ethics must have an ultimate basis of right and wrong, ethical and unethical.[816] The Christian faith, grounded in the Holy Bible, is the best basis for making moral and immoral judgments and discerning right from wrong.

Finding a starting point for Christian ethics

The Christian community has differences in the starting point for Christian ethics. For example, Hill has offered a starting point for Christian ethics based on three divine characteristics that are repeatedly emphasized in the Bible:[817]

---

814 Aristotle, *Nicomachean Ethics*, Book 3, Chapter 6 thru Book 5, Chapter 11.
815 Robert Dailey, *Organizational Behaviour*. Edinburgh Business School: Heriot–Watt University. (Study Guide OB–05, 2013), 10.
816 Stephen Mott, *Biblical Ethics and Social Change*. (Oxford University Press, 1982), 23.
817 Alec Hill, *Just Business: Christian Ethics for the Marketplace*. (IVP Academic, 2018), 7.

- God is holy
- God is just
- God is loving

Hill offers little reason for these selections to the exclusion of other topics other than the repeated emphasis on them in Scripture. Based on his assumptions, his starting point seems too arbitrary.

Mott begins his system of Christian ethics in God's grace,[818] whereas Geisler grounds Christian ethics in the written revelation of God—an "ethic of divine command."[819] Mott and Geisler's starting points appear so broad (grace or the entire Bible) that the starting point itself becomes diluted, meaning there is no specific starting point.

Stapleford starts with two broad areas: Christian theology and the nature of God.[820] I appreciate his observation that "we should be able to determine some elements of Christian ethics from the nature of God, as revealed in Scripture. Even when the Bible does not prescribe specific behavior, we can still model our lives after the God it describes"[821], but, like Hill, Stapleford's starting point feels too hazy to be an adequate starting point for Christians working in business.

I have concluded that Christ indirectly answers the question of a starting point for Christian ethics in Mark 12:28–31 (NIV):

> One of the teachers of the law came and heard them debating. Noticing that Jesus had given them a good answer, he asked him, "Of all the commandments, which is the most important?" "The most important one," answered Jesus, "is this: 'Hear, O Israel: The Lord our God, the Lord is one. Love the Lord your God with all your heart and with all your soul and with all your mind and with all your strength.' The second is this: 'Love your neighbor as yourself.'

Christ is recorded as being even more succinct in Matthew 7:12 (NIV):

> So in everything, do to others what you would have them do to you, for this sums up the Law and the Prophets.

Paul said it this way in Galatians 6:2 (NIV):

> Carry each other's burdens, and in this way you will fulfill the law of Christ.

---

818 Mott, *Biblical Ethics*, 23–25.
819 Norman Geisler, *Options in Contemporary Christian Ethics*. (Baker, 1981), 25.
820 John Stapleford, *Bulls, Bears and Golden Calves: Applying Christian Ethics in Economics*. (IVP Academic, 2009), 21.
821 Stapleford, *Bulls*, 23.

It appears that the answer to the question of a starting point for ethics in the Scriptures are the two great commands—to love the Lord God with all one's heart, soul, mind, and strength (Deuteronomy 6:5) and to love one's neighbor as oneself (Leviticus 19:18b). These two commands are the most comprehensive in Scripture. All other commands "hang on" these two commands (Matthew 22:40). Hence, boiled down to common English, the starting point for Christian ethics should be:

- Is it loving toward God?
- Is it loving toward men?

Bringing in the Decalogue (commonly known as the Ten Commandments),[822] these two questions can be expanded in more detail but not in scope. The first four of the ten commandments are "vertical" ("love the Lord your God") and are balanced by the final six "horizontal commands" ("love your neighbor"). Thus, the Ten Commandments can be considered a commentary on the two great commands. These Ten Commandments were given by God to Moses and by Moses to the Israelites in Exodus 20.1–17.[823] Table 14–1 outlines these commands.

Table 14–1: The Ten Commandments with Topic Domain Assignments

Reference	Command	Topic Domain	Vertical/ Horizontal
Exodus 20:3	"You shall have no other gods before me."	Preeminence of God	Vertical
Exodus 20:4	"You shall not make for yourself an image."	Loyalty to God	Vertical
Exodus 20:7	"You shall not misuse the name of the Lord your God."	Honoring God	Vertical
Exodus 20:8	"Remember the Sabbath day by keeping it holy."	Worshipping God	Vertical

822 Raymond F. Collins, "Ten Commandments." In *The Anchor Yale Bible Dictionary*. Edited by D.N. Freedman. (Doubleday, 1992), v6, 383.

823 Jewish scholars believe that these commands or "ten words" (Exodus 34:28), are universal to all societies since they were given in the wilderness and not within any national boundaries (Nahum M. Sarna, *Exodus*. The JPS Torah Commentary. (Jewish Publication Society, 1991), 109.) In Roman Catholic tradition, the first and second command are combined into one command with the tenth command being divided into the ninth and tenth command. Protestants usually bifurcate verses 3 and 4 into two commands and keep verse 17 as a single command.

Reference	Command	Topic Domain	Vertical/Horizontal
Exodus 20:12	"Honour your father and your mother."	Honoring authority	Horizontal
Exodus 20:13	"You shall not murder."	Valuing human life	Horizontal
Exodus 20:14	"You shall not commit adultery."	Valuing purity in relationships	Horizontal
Exodus 20:15	"You shall not steal."	Respecting Private Property	Horizontal
Exodus 20:16	"You shall not give false testimony."	Truthfulness in speech	Horizontal
Exodus 20:17	"You shall not covet."	Contentment	Horizontal

These commands are all given in the second person singular—"You (singular) shall not." Yet, these commands are spoken to all of Israel. The singular "you" gives them greater personal impact.[824] Hence, I will suggest the primary starting point for Christian ethics be the two commands about loving God and loving one's fellow man, followed by a secondary filter of the Decalogue for more difficult ethical decisions should the first two commands be inconclusive. Figure 14–1 offers a visual representation of this discussion.

Common Types of Ethical Decisions Business Owners Face

Ethical situations are not created equal. We may face different ethical scenarios as business owners. It is helpful to know the type of decision facing us:[825]

Moral temptation: the owner can benefit or avoid loss. Moral temptations require moral willpower.

Stand up for ethics: the owner will suffer if the correct ethical decision is made. Standing up for ethics requires moral courage.

---

824 Noel D. Osborn & Howard Hatton, *A Handbook on Exodus.* (United Bible Societies, 1999), 471.

825 Mark S. Schwartz, *Business Ethics: An Ethical Decision–Making Approach.* (Wiley Blackwell, 2017), 234–35.

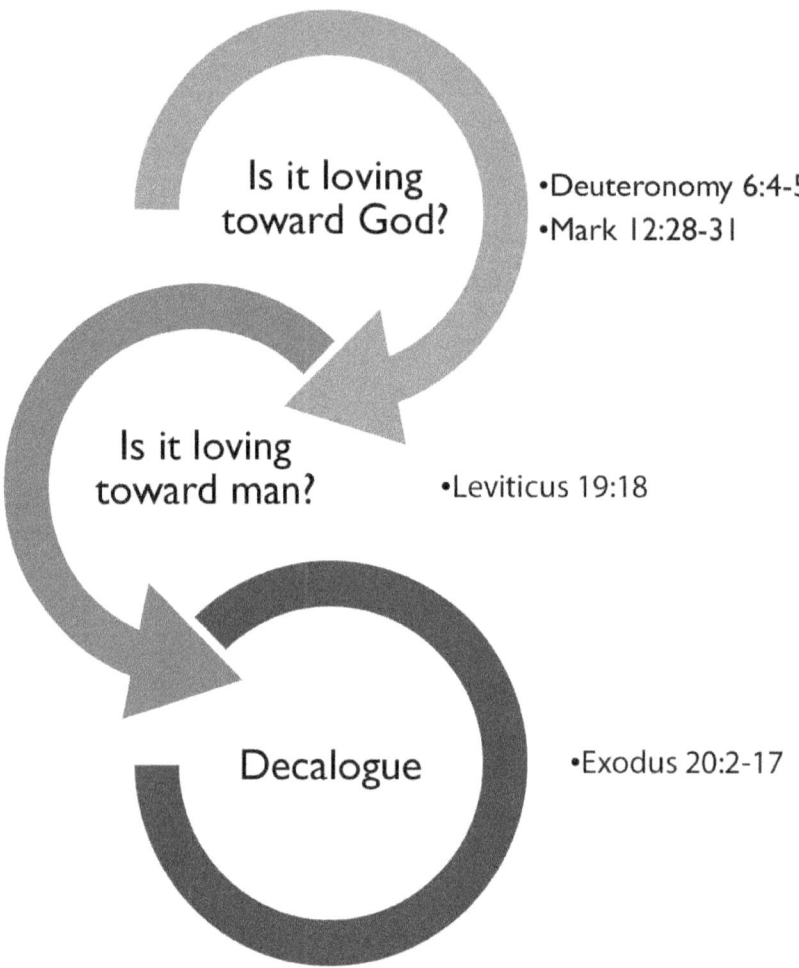

Figure 14–1: Visual representation of Christian ethics's starting point and secondary filter.

Ethical trade-offs: some will benefit while others suffer. Trade-off decisions require moral competence.

Common Ethical Violations

Applying the starting points for Christian ethics to common ethical decisions that a business owner faces could consume several books. The point of this section is to be illustrative rather than comprehensive. Several ethical situations will be presented inside the following framework:

- Brief description of the problem
- Type of ethical situation

- Filter the details through the two great commands and the Ten Commandments
- Correct ethical decision

Overworking your staff to save on payroll expenses

Description of the Problem: Some owners naturally work sixty or seventy hours weekly. They enjoy their work, and they cannot imagine doing anything else. These owners willingly miss family, church, or community events to do emails, read contracts, meet with customers, or assess a new vendor. These owners have few friends outside of work relationships and take family relationships for granted. Social plans are rarely made, and when such plans exist, these owners often uncommit at the last minute because of a "fire" or "pressing issue" at work.

These owners save on payroll costs by expecting employees to work as hard as the owner. Selfless dedication is the unwritten expectation for all company employees. These owners

> Routinely overload their subordinates, contact them outside of business hours, and make last–minute requests for additional work. To satisfy those demands, employees arrive early, stay late, pull all-nighters, work weekends, and remain tied to their electronic devices 24/7. And those who are unable—or unwilling—to respond typically get penalized. By operating in this way, owners pressure employees to become what sociologists have called ideal workers: people totally dedicated to their jobs and always on call. The phenomenon is widespread in professional and managerial settings … In such places, any suggestion of meaningful outside interests and commitments can signal a lack of fitness for the job."[826]

When owners drive their employees to the point of the employee having little work-life balance coupled with an expectation of complete allegiance, then the owner has A) asked for some of what belongs to God (i.e., the employee's primary allegiance) and B) is receiving the productivity of more than one employee from one employee. This payroll cost savings benefits the owner at the expense of the employee.

Type: This ethical decision is a Moral Temptation and Ethical Trade-off.

Filter: Demanding sixty or seventy hours per week of work from an employee week after week is stealing from that employee by robbing the employee of personal time. In an indirect sense, it is also stealing from someone who could have been employed to perform the current employee's overload work. The owner's demands are an unloving act toward

---

826 Erin Reid and Lakshmi Ramarajan, "Managing the High–Intensity Workplace." In *HBR's 10 Must Reads for New Managers.* (Harvard Business Review Press, 2017), 41.

295

the employee, and it is a form of coveting what another person has to wrongfully make it your own and use it for your purposes: personal time.

An owner who creates a high–intensity workplace and demands full allegiance to the owner's whims supplants the role of Yahweh in the employee's life, which is a form of creating a god (the owner) before God. Finally, when the owner drives employees this hard, the owner's drive betrays a lack of contentment of what God has already given her and a lack of dependence on God to supply her needs. As a result, she fails to fulfill her stewardship role before God.

Correct Decision: The correct ethical decision is for the owner to hire enough staff to (reasonably) distribute the workload across enough positions to create a healthy work-life balance for each employee. The owner should cease being the organizing principle in the employee's life and encourage primary allegiance to God rather than the owner and the business. The owner must learn to be content with lower profits and higher payroll costs.

Right-sizing your company to save it from bankruptcy

Description of the Problem: Nearly every company must be right-sized at some point in its lifecycle. No business ever has sustained growth. There are always downturns that owners face.

Owners get caught in a downward spiral when they believe revenue growth is the answer to a sustained deficit. Rather than right-sizing the business and getting to profitability quickly by lowering payroll and other expenses, the owner attempts to sell more, build more, and create more to generate more revenue. The problem with this approach is that owners often are more optimistic than events would warrant. The owner often underestimates the time required to break even and the amount of cash that will be burned while getting to break even. More importantly, the owner underestimates the stress this process causes and the significant impact that even minor setbacks can have on his efforts to reach profitability.

Most owners do not implement a proper right-sizing plan because the plan usually requires profoundly emotional decisions. Most owners care deeply about their employees and do not want to see their employees suffer. The ethical dilemma appears when an owner concludes he needs to lay off a group of employees who have worked hard and given good work product, but instead of receiving a bonus, the employee receives a termination notice.

However, after working in several turnaround situations, I have learned that the real ethical dilemma is not doing what needs to be done to keep the business profitable. Suppose a business has fifty employees. If laying off five of those employees, along with other cost reductions, saves the other 45 jobs, returns the business to profitability, and enables the owner to hire more people in the future, then the real ethical dilemma is sacrificing all fifty jobs through bankruptcy because the owner could not make an emotionally difficult decision.

Type: This ethical decision is an Ethical Trade–off

Filter: The ethical trade-off is that either a few suffer through layoffs or all suffer through bankruptcy. For a business owner, loving one's fellow man will sometimes mean ending the employment of one or more employees when the business needs to be right-sized. Paradoxically, it is unloving to the other 45 employees if an owner does not do what is necessary to reach profitability again. It is also unloving to the firm's customers, vendors, and other stakeholders. Moreover, it is unloving to the community not to run a profitable business that can sustain itself for the foreseeable future. Among other elements, communities need profitable companies that provide predictable employment, stable influence, and quality products and services that enable the community to flourish.

For those laid off from employment, it is good to remember that God has something good for them in this experience, too. The owner can trust God's sovereignty and know that God will supply their need in such a way as to bring glory to himself while maturing their faith in him. Moreover, research has shown that many laid off start their own business within twelve months. For example, one survey reported that out of 4,000 laid-off tech workers, 1,007 started their own businesses.[827]

Regarding the Ten Commandments, when an owner keeps up a façad that it is reasonable to believe the business can grow out of the sustained devolution, he is not being honest with himself or his employees. This violates, in a sense, the command not to give false testimony.

Correct decision: When right–sizing a business is needed, reducing expenses to be under expected revenues is ethical. This will often mean reducing payroll expenses through lay-offs or position eliminations.

Generating Fake Online Reviews to Boost Sales

Description of the problem: Word–of–mouth advertising has always been considered the best because it costs nothing and is one of the most trusted forms of marketing.[828]

In this scenario, the owner hires a firm to write positive but fake reviews of the owner's products or services. Whether the fake reviews are generated by AI or through real people does not materially affect this ethical decision. Roughly 90% of all internet users consult online reviews before making a purchase,[829] and fake reviews can lead them astray about the actual quality of a product or service.

---

827 Bernhard Schroeder, "Layoffs are Fueling a New Wave of Entrepreneurs. Here's How You Can Join Them." April 3, 2023. Forbes.com. https://www.forbes.com/sites/bernhardschroeder/2023/04/03/layoffs–are–fueling–a–new–wave–of–entrepreneurs–heres–how–you–can–join–them/?sh=476fb54468af

828 Jon Tan, "Why Word–of–Mouth is the BEST Marketing Tool You Have." April 29, 2015. Referralcandy.com. https://www.referralcandy.com/blog/word–of–mouth–marketing–strategy

829 Diana Kaeming, "Online Reviews Statistics to Know in 2022." December 14, 2023. Qualtrics.com. https://www.qualtrics.com/blog/online–review–stats/

Fake reviews come in several packages:[830]
- Vendors that sell both positive and negative reviews
- Business owners who generate fake reviews through fake profiles they created for themselves
- Employees who are asked to write reviews on the owner's products or services that they would otherwise not write
- Ex–Ex-employees writing negative reviews as retaliation for being terminated or laid off
- Customers lying or exaggerating to ensure they receive a refund
- Family and friends write several positive reviews in a short period (known as "Review Cluster") that are not followed by other reviews for a sustained period.

Type of situation: This is a moral temptation.

Filter: When business owners use fake reviews to build a reputation for a product not based on a broad range of consumer experiences, they lie to potential new customers and steal from the consumer by creating a false narrative that helps the consumer justify purchasing her products or services. Lying and stealing are not loving actions toward others or God. Moreover, the owner does not steward the products and services God has entrusted to her well when she creates a false narrative in the marketplace.

Correct ethical decision: The owner should engage more closely with his customers and ask them to write online reviews of his products or services. The owner should resist the temptation to generate fake reviews.

Compromising Product Quality

Description of the Problem: Product quality refers to the product's manufacturing and marketing. If the marketing suggests that the product is of average quality, then the consumer can expect an average quality in manufacturing the product and the price paid for the product. But, an ethical decision will present itself when there is a mismatch between marketing, manufacturing, and pricing. An obvious example is when a product is marketed as a high–end product manufactured with only the highest grade of ingredients or raw materials, but lesser quality ingredients or materials are used to produce the product, yet a high–end price is charged for the product.

Type: This situation is a moral temptation for the owner.

Filter: An owner can increase gross margins on each product by presenting the product as "top–quality," which justifies a "top price," but is manufactured with lower quality, lower priced materials, thus creating a wider gross margin because less quality materials

---

830   Greg Sterling, "Fake Reviews Problem is Much Worse Than People Know." April 22, 2020. Searchengineland. com. https://searchengineland.com/fake–reviews–problem–is–much–worse–than–people–know-333331

generally cost less. The ethical problem lies not in manufacturing a product using less quality materials. The ethical problem is in marketing's presentation of the product to the customers that it is manufactured with only the finest ingredients or materials.

Compromising product quality while marketing the product as high–quality with a high–quality price is not an example of "loving your neighbor as yourself." Would an owner be delighted to overpay for an average product or service? The answer is "no." Compromising product quality without full disclosure is also a form of lying (You shall not give false testimony) and dishonors the customer (Honor your father and mother).

Correct ethical decision. A Christian business owner should work hard to ensure consistency between the quality level of manufacturing, marketing, and pricing.

Uninforming Your Banker(s) and Financial Advisors

Description of the Problem: I have known more than a few business owners—including Christians—who have carefully curated the information that flowed to their bankers and accountants. These owners doctor the financials they send to their banker and then send a different set of financials to their accountant at tax time. They go into their accounting package and reclassify transactions to make themselves look better (more profitable, hence, more creditworthy) to their banker. Then, they reclassify many transactions again to create losses or minimize profits to lower their taxable income. Their accountant sees one set of financials, and their banker is given a different set.

In addition, it is not uncommon for these owners to have two banking relationships who do not know about each other. I have seen owners apply for a line of credit at one bank with one set of financials and simultaneously apply for another at the other with the same set of financials. Since neither bank knows about the existence of the other bank, they both approve a line of credit in similar amounts. The owner thinks he has "gamed the system" to his advantage. Both banks think they are the senior secured creditor with this owner, and the owner signs loan agreements indicating as much. The owner expends much energy to ensure neither bank knows about the other and then hides certain transactions from his accountant to ensure he pays the smallest amount in taxes possible.

In essence, only the owner knows his business's entire financial picture. Suppose a vendor needs financials from the owner to approve credit. In that case, the owner will likely reclassify transactions repeatedly until he can ensure his vendors find him creditworthy.

In a Bernie Madoff–style setup where secrecy is paramount, these owners generally keep their books by hand or in different accounting systems. I had one owner I consulted with who laughed out loud when he was approved for two lines of credit on the same day. He commented on how stupid he thought his bankers were and how they would never catch him. That engagement only lasted three months, partly because he grew tired of me challenging his ethics.

Type: this is a moral temptation for the owner.

Filter: Clearly, what these owners are doing is outright lying to their bankers, their accountants, and the government. It is not loving toward God to represent him so poorly, nor is it loving to your fellow man (banker) to betray his trust and treat him disrespectfully. Lying in business always has the elements of betrayal and disrespect.

Correct ethical decision: The correct decision ensures that transactions are classified according to GAAP[831] and faithfully represent the full financial picture of your company to your bank and the government. Curating a false narrative of one's financial performance to impress a banker or pay less in taxes may be undetectable in the short-run, but God sees what you are doing and will not bless your deceit.

SUMMARY

Where the commands of Scripture are plainly given, the CBO can be confident that these commands are authoritative, clear, necessary, sufficient, inerrant and inspired. These commands are worthy of the owner's allegiance, attention, and devotion.

But in those situations where there is no clear biblical command, the owner can rely on the Spirit of God to actively instruct through the two commands to love God with all one's heart, soul, mind, and strength and to love others as oneself. If further clarification is needed, the Ten Commandments can be used as a secondary filter to assess the potential ethical decision.

As an owner matures in hearing the voice of God and becomes more and more sensitive to the Spirit's leading through the commands of Scripture, the owner will naturally become more dependent on God for life and sustenance. Such dependence is a good and proper outcome of a life lived in communion with God. This dependence helps prepare the owner to reign with God throughout eternity. In addition, the owner becomes more and more effective as a steward of what God has entrusted to the owner, advancing God's kingdom on this earth.

In the next chapter, I will examine what the Bible says about supply chain and vendor management.

---

831 Generally Accepted Accounting Principles. To learn more, visit the Financial Accounting Standards Board at https://fasb.org/standards.

CHAPTER 15

SUPPLY CHAIN AND VENDOR MANAGEMENT

Every business needs supplies to operate. Vendors are needed to supply a business with what it needs to achieve its mission and vision. Vendors supply everything from paperclips to insurance to software to professional services. Managing your vendors to achieve maximum value in your supply chain is vital to your success as a Christian business owner.

This chapter will discuss my views on worker exploitation and environmental stewardship. I will suggest that uncertainties in our supply chains should not create worry or anxiety but should give us ample opportunities to trust God fully.

SUPPLY CHAIN MANAGEMENT (SCM) is the "handling of the entire production flow of a good or service—starting from the raw components to delivering the final product to the consumer."[832] The concept of a supply chain usually refers to a manufacturing and distribution process. However, it can be loosely applied to a service business that does not manufacture goods or products.

---

832   IBM.com, "What is Supply Chain Management?" ibm.com. https://www.ibm.com/topics/supply-chain-management [Accessed 12/16/2023]

Vendor management is a discipline that enables an organization to "gain increased value from their vendors throughout the deal life cycle."[833] Vendor management is concerned with developing quality relationships that drive high value in performance so that the organization can achieve its objectives. Whereas supply chain management is process–focused,[834] vendor management is relationship-focused. A good supply chain process depends on healthy vendor relationships. As a former Forbes Council Member,[835] Petrik noted, "Business is powered by the relationships we develop."[836] Vendor relationships are just as meaningful as customer relationships."

Service businesses will be more concerned with vendor management because service businesses do not have a manufacturing process requiring supplies to create a finished product. However, service-based businesses must still order products such as office furniture or training and education to deliver quality customer service.

At first blush, one could be forgiven if one concluded that the Bible has little to say about supply chain and vendor management. However, upon further inspection, the Scriptures address several considerations that affect an owner's supply chain and vendor relationships, including worker safety, exploitation, environmental stewardship, fairness, and transparency.

Even a brief review of supply chains and vendor management literature will consume many pages. So, I will focus on those topics which will help us focus on the areas the Bible addresses.

FOREIGN CORRUPT PRACTICES ACT AND BRIBERY

I want to note the existence of the Foreign Corrupt Practices Act (FCPA). Under this American act,[837] it is unlawful for a United States person or company to offer, pay, or promise to pay money or anything of value to any foreign official to obtain or retain business. The act is intended to ensure that a given company can obtain no improper advantage when securing supplies from a foreign entity or nation.[838] Bribery is giving money or valuables to someone

833 Gartner, "Vendor Management." Gartner.com. https://www.gartner.com/en/information–technology/glossary/vendor–management [Accessed 12–16/2023].

834 Keely Croxton, Sebastian García-Dastugue, Douglas Lambert, & Dale Rogers, "The Supply Chain Management Processes." *The International Journal of Logistics Management*, 2001. 12(2):13–36.

835 https://councils.forbes.com/

836 Andrei Petrik, "Small Business is All About Relationships." November 22, 2021. Forbes.com. https://www.forbes.com/sites/forbesbusinesscouncil/2021/11/22/small–business–is–all–about–relationships/

837 Those who live in countries other than the United States may or may not have similar laws in their countries.

838 US Department of Justice. "Foreign Corrupt Practices Act." September 26, 2023. Justice.gov. https://www.justice.gov/criminal/criminal–fraud/foreign–corrupt–practices–act.

in authority in exchange for their use of authority for one's benefit.[839] Bribery removes objectivity and fairness in matters that should be handled objectively and fairly. Bribery constitutes a crime in the United States, and both parties can be criminally charged.[840]

In the Scriptures, bribery is described in despicable terms: "The wicked accepts a bribe in secret to pervert the ways of justice." (Proverbs 17:23 ESV). Bribery "blinds those who see" and "twists the words of the innocent" (Exodus 23:8 ESV):

> Any system that legitimizes bribery gives the rich an unfair advantage in persuading leaders and judges; the poor find it difficult to get a fair hearing. Innocent people who are poor can be condemned; guilty people who are rich can offer a sizable bribe and go free.[841]

A CBO should never be involved in accepting or offering a bribe. Conventional wisdom and Biblical teaching fully align on this point: bribery should be avoided and is never acceptable.

CONSIDERATIONS IN SUPPLY CHAIN MANAGEMENT

There are sourcing practices that are considered unethical and should be avoided. As business becomes more global, more interconnectivity with foreign actors is experienced, even for smaller businesses that are privately held. Supply chains are becoming increasingly global, placing additional responsibilities on us as Christian business owners to pay attention to procurement issues considering the commands of Scripture and vendor selection. This section will focus on Biblical teaching that supports a Christian view of these ethical issues.

Worker Exploitation

Worker exploitation occurs when one party takes unfair advantage of another through manipulation, coercion, or deception.[842] Worker exploitation always involves the employer's selfishness to misuse the inherent power imbalance between the employee and employer for the employer's advantage (Ephesians 6:5–9). Anytime a power imbalance is used to advantage the powerful while disadvantaging the weak, sin is committed.

---

839 David Witthoff, Andres Fuller, Jessica Parks, and Cory Taylor, "Bribery." In *The Lexham Cultural Ontology Glossary*. (Lexham Press, 2014).

840 Legal Information Institute. "Bribery." Law.cornell.edu. https://www.law.cornell.edu/wex/bribery. Accessed 09/25/2024.

841 Walter Elwell & Barry Beitzel. "Bribe, Bribery." In *Baker encyclopedia of the Bible*. Elwell, W.A. and Beitzel, B.J. (Eds.) (Baker Books, 1998), v1, 380.

842 Faithlife, "Exploitation." In *Logos Bible Study Factbook*. (Faithlife, September 25, 2024.) https://ref.ly/logos4/Factbook?id=ref%3abk.%25exploitation.

Paul assumes the inherent power imbalance between employers and employees in Ephesians 6:5–9 (CSB):

> [5] Slaves, obey your human masters with fear and trembling, in the sincerity of your heart, as to Christ. [6] Do not work only while being watched, in order to please men, but as slaves of Christ, do God's will from your heart. [7] Serve with a good attitude, as to the Lord and not to men, [8] knowing that whatever good each one does, slave or free, he will receive this back from the Lord. [9] And masters, treat your slaves the same way, without threatening them, because you know that both their Master and yours is in heaven, and there is no favoritism with Him.

The phrase "Stop your threatening" comes from the Greek, ἀνιέντες τὴν ἀπειλήν, literally, "refrain from inflicting harm." ἀπειλέω means "to declare that one will cause harm to someone, particularly if certain conditions are not met."[843] Such threats cannot occur unless an employer misuses his inherent power imbalance against the employee.[844] Threatening to harm one's employee in some way if the employee does not perform well violates Ephesians 6:9. A Christian business owner expresses his submission to Christ by treating his employees with respect.[845]

A CBO does not threaten the owner's employees because the employee and the owner have the same Master in heaven. God does not favor one over the other. Hodge affirms:

> In this world some men are masters and some are slaves. In the next, these distinctions will cease. There the question will be, not, Who is the master? and, Who the slave? but who has done the will of God?[846]

Workers can also be exploited through deficient compensation, not only verbal threats. As Christian business owners, we should bear in mind the inherent power imbalance between us and our employees and not allow them to negotiate an unfair or lower–than–market compensation package because they lack negotiating power. Instead, we should be "generously fair" with our employees and contractors. Proverbs 22:22–23 (NIV) says,

> [22] Do not exploit the poor because they are poor and do not crush the needy in court, [23] for the Lord will take up their case and will exact life for life.

---

843 LN, v1, 421.

844 Harold W. Hoehner, Philip W. Comfort, & Peter Davids, *Cornerstone Biblical Commentary: Ephesians, Philippians, Colossians, 1&2 Thessalonians, Philemon.* (Tyndale House, 2008), 125.

845 Steven M. Baugh, *Ephesians.* Evangelical Exegetical Commentary. (Lexham Press, 2015), 523.

846 Charles Hodge, *A Commentary on the Epistle to the Ephesians.* (New York: Robert Carter and Brothers., 1858), 357.

This first of thirty sayings from the sage in Proverbs 22:17—24:29 uses the example of the powerful using the court system to oppress the powerless for their purposes. The unwritten teaching behind this example is that followers of God with the power of business ownership are to be kind and fair to those in desperate situations instead of using the court system to exploit them. When we find someone in a hopeless situation—even if that desperation results from their sin—as Christian business owners, we should not advantage ourselves by taking advantage of the other's plight.

One example from the Old Testament of an employer exploiting an employee is the story of Jacob working for Laben to gain Rachel in marriage. In Genesis 30:15–30, Laban had agreed to give Rachel to Jacob after seven years of service. Having completed the required seven years, Jacob understandably asked to marry Rachel. Laban agreed and then deceived Jacob by giving him Leah, Rachel's older sister. I suspect Laban knew Jacob would work another seven years for Rachel, so he took advantage of Jacob's love for Rachel and extracted fourteen years of labor from Jacob to take advantage of himself. Desperate to marry Rachel, Jacob agreed to Laban's unfair terms.

We also see the powerful exploiting the powerless in the example of the rich man and Lazarus in Luke 16:19–31 or the fictional story of the rich man taking the poor man's ewe in Nathan's rebuke of David in 1 Samuel 12:1–4. The larger point is that those in a position of power are responsible for *not* using available power to advantage themselves while simultaneously disadvantaging the powerless. Power is an entrustment from God to be stewarded toward advantaging God and his agenda.

The Lord is the defender of those who are exploited (Psalm 140:12; 146:7; Job 36:15; Psalm 12:5; 14:6; 102:17; Deuteronomy 24; Exodus 22:21–27) and will do to the oppressor what the oppressor has done to the poor:

> God is not merely a formidable [opponent]… appearing before the unjust tribunal, on behalf of the wronged; he is not merely a judge sitting in a higher court of appeal; he is the executor of the universal laws of justice to which the judges as well as the arraigned of earth are alike amenable. When Jehovah "cheats or spoils", it is in vindication and not in violation of eternal justice and right."[847]

The opposite of exploitation is generosity. Deuteronomy 15:11 (NIV) says,

> There will always be poor people in the land. Therefore I command you to be openhanded toward your fellow Israelites who are poor and needy in your land.

847 John Lange, Philip Schaff, Otto Zöckler, & Charles Aiken, *A Commentary on the Holy Scriptures: Proverbs*. (Logos Bible Software, 2008), 197.

Merrill commented that

> the very attitude of stinginess is unbecoming to one who claims to be a servant of the Lord. Rather, one should give freely, not grudgingly, for this delights the Lord and prompts him to respond in like manner with blessing and prosperity.[848]

Some of our employees will be living paycheck–to–paycheck. Some will have experienced unexpected expenses such as auto repair or medical bills. Some may come to us from extended unemployment and be deeply in debt. Hence, we will always have opportunities to be generously fair with our employees, and we should be happy to do so.[849]

What I write about compensation and exploitation applies to non-profit organizations and churches as much as for-profit organizations. The Scriptures make no distinction between the two. I have concluded that our entire evangelical culture assumes a dysfunctional compensation structure for pastors and other full-time ministry employees. Churches often lack the resources to pay their pastors fairly, which is an obvious admission that our laity is not walking with God. If the laity were walking with God, they would be generous toward him, and our churches could pay pastors median salaries for the communities in which they live. Low compensation of pastors is a symptom of a larger problem: our congregations are lukewarm toward God.

For those rare churches that enjoy surplus cash, it is not enough to justify paying lower wages because of the salary ranges in area churches. Instead, the cost of living in one's community should be included in developing compensation ranges. A loaf of bread costs the same whether you are a business owner or a youth pastor. The cost is the same. Church boards should reorient their views on compensation to be generously fair and account for the sheer cost of living in a given area.

When church members rob God by not being generous toward him and not giving as they should to their local church and then they expect their pastors to live on compensation packages that they would never accept, they are sinning and living a life of hypocrisy. God will not honor their efforts, and they will stagnate in their relationship with God because they tolerate sin in their lives.

On the subject of worker exploitation, conventional wisdom and Biblical stewardship will agree: workers should not be exploited but should be treated fairly and generously.

---

848 Eugene H. Merrill, *Deuteronomy*. (Broadman & Holman Publishers, 1994), 245.
849 John A. Thompson, *Deuteronomy: An Introduction and Commentary*. (InterVarsity, 1974), 208.

Environmental Stewardship

Environmental stewardship concerns protecting and properly managing the earth and its natural resources. Most Christians will agree that God is the creator and owner of the world, and because God owns the earth, physical matter has inherent value and should be cared for accordingly.[850] Also, most Christians will agree that we should be better stewards of the physical environment.[851] Yet, where current environmentalism has become so strident as to create what approximates a religious "doctrine," Christians have not been shy about speaking the truth from Scripture,[852] rejecting the notion that the physical world should be worshipped.

Biblical stewards understand that the earth and its resources belong to God. God created the earth and claims ownership of it all (Job 41:11, Psalm 24:1, 89:11).[853] Because God owns the earth, he has the authority to entrust the care of the earth to humanity, which he has done:

> [28] And God blessed them, and God said to them, "Be fruitful and multiply, and fill the earth and subdue it, and rule over the fish of the sea and the birds of heaven, and over every animal that moves upon the earth." [29] And God said, "Look—I am giving to you every plant *that* bears seed which *is* on the face of the whole earth, and every kind of tree [that bears fruit]. They shall be yours as food." [30] And to every kind of animal of the earth and to every bird of heaven, and to everything that moves upon the earth in which *there is* life *I am giving* every green plant as food." And it was so. (Genesis 1:28–30 LEB)

Sometimes referred to as the "Covenant with Creation,"[854] a visceral aspect of the Covenant of Works was God's entrusting the physical world to humanity to "subdue" it. When focused on the management of the earth, Genesis 2:15–17 is a restatement of Genesis 1:28–30. Humankind is to "rule over" the animals and consider animals and plants as food. People are responsible for caring for the earth with the same diligence God used to create it. Hence, as Christian business owners, we take great care of the environment because it is another entrustment from God and belongs to him.

---

850 Benjamin B. Phillips, "Getting into Hot Water: Evangelicals and Global Warming." *Journal of Markets & Morality (Spring and Fall 2009)* 12, no. 1 & 2 (2009), 321.

851 Southern Baptist Convention, "Resolution on Environmental Stewardship. June 1, 1990. Sbc.net. https://www.sbc.net/resource–library/resolutions/resolution–on–environmental–stewardship/. See also

852 Phillips, *Hot Water*, 321.

853 Mark F. Rooker, *Leviticus*. (Broadman & Holman, 2000), 306.

854 Peter Gentry, & Stephen Wellum, *God's Kingdom through God's Covenants: A Concise Biblical Theology*. (Crossway, 2015), 211.

When this teaching about our stewardship responsibility to care for the physical earth is applied to selecting vendors and building a supply chain, the definition of the *right* vendor may change dramatically. For example, if we are sourcing products manufactured for resale to our customer base, to as reasonable an extent as possible, we need to evaluate the vendor's manufacturing process to ensure they are caring for the environment as well as reasonably possible. We may need to visit their facilities, watch their processes, assess how waste is managed, or evaluate the safety of their facilities for their workers.[855]

Implementing safety measures for workers and processes that better steward the earth's resources is costly. As Christian business owners, we may need to purposefully purchase *more expensive* products from vendors who invest in environmental care and worker safety and health. *When Christian business owners fail to properly assess their vendors for worker exploitation, safe working conditions, proper compensation and care for their employees, and ensuring the vendor cares for the environment, we (essentially) partner with the vendor in their sin when we purchase products from them. We cannot and should not support the abuse of people or the environment so that we can source products at a lower cost.*

WORRY AND PROVISION

Conventional wisdom says that supply chain uncertainty is a phenomenon nearly all businesses wrestle with and should be tightly managed to reduce risk and cost.[856] Sources of uncertainty include customer demand, demand amplification (inaccurate forecasts), manufacturing process, faulty information flow, and supply uncertainty. Overall, research suggests that there are 14 supply–chain uncertainty sources coalesced into three groups: A) internal organization uncertainty, B) internal supply–chain uncertainty, and C) external uncertainties. Research further suggests that 21 management approaches exist to reduce uncertainty from those 14 sources, including techniques such as making processes more lean, better vertical and internal integrations, selecting the right software system, implementing just–in–time production cycles to better align with customer demand, and developing multiple suppliers who can deliver quality resources, on–time.[857] While tight management of one's supply change can help ease both risk and worry, the conventional wisdom approach is godless.

855 These are just two of many articles one can find with simple internet searches on how workers are exploited in Asia in order to produce products for the West. Wareonwant, "Sweatshops in China." October 12, 2009, Waronwant.org. https://waronwant.org/news–analysis/sweatshops–china. See also CNN Business, "Report Slams Walmart for 'Exploitative' Conditions in Asia Factories." June 1, 2016. Money.cnn.com. https://money.cnn.com/2016/05/31/news/companies/walmart–gap–hm–garment–workers–asia/index.html

856 G. Tomas M. Hult, Christopher W. Craighead, & David J. Ketchen, "Risk uncertainty and supply chain decisions: a real options perspective." *Decision Sciences*, 2010. 41(3):435–458.

857 Eliot Simangunson, Linda Hendry & Mark Stevenson, "Supply–Chain Uncertainty: A Review and Theoretical Foundation for Future Research." *International Journal of Production Research*. 2012. 50(16):4493–4523.

As Christian business owners, we will utilize conventional wisdom methods in supply chain management to reduce risk and uncertainty. However, we will ultimately place our faith and trust in God's promised provision rather than our ability to manage the complex supply chain process. Relying on God's promises of provision brings freedom from worry, even in business.[858]

In addition, by relying on God for our supplies, we avoid the temptation to conclude that by management approaches alone, provision for what our business needs can be attained. There is the ever-present temptation to believe the lie that being well–supplied today means one is immune from provision gaps tomorrow. However, while being amply supplied today may temporarily ease one's worry, a CBO will find lasting peace by relying on God alone to supply the owner's needs rather than the owner's management approaches (Matthew 6:25–33).[859]

SUMMARY

In this brief chapter, I have demonstrated that bribery is a sin and that there is no situation in which a Christian business owner should be engaged in it. I have also shown that worker and environmental exploitation is sin. Both should be managed as God intends. CBOs should be generously fair with their employees. They should visit (if possible) the manufacturing plants of their vendors to ensure that they are not exploiting either their employees or the environment.

In the next chapter, we'll focus on truthfulness and marketing. There are ethical issues to consider, so let us move forward and see what God has for us.

---

858 Larry Richards. *Every promise in the Bible.* (Thomas Nelson, 1998), 237.

859 Tim Clinton & John Trent, *The Quick–Reference Guide to Marriage & Family Counseling.* (Baker Books, 2009), 210.

CHAPTER 16

MARKETING

Marketing produces the public face of your company. What you say and do in your marketing materials has both moral and business considerations. As Christian business owners, our greatest temptation to sin lies in what we allow our marketing collateral to say and what we allow our sales teams to say and do in their sales process.

This entire chapter will be devoted to demonstrating that we must be truthful in our marketing practices if we are going to claim we are Christian business owners. My claim is not profound or unique. But it has several tangential considerations which will be discussed.

AS A CHRISTIAN business owner, you must be serious about ethical marketing,[860] what is communicated, what is promised, and what is delivered. Some of your greatest temptations to sin as a Christian business owner will come through your marketing efforts.

---

860   I realize that to a certain extent, this chapter's discussions will not be strictly limited to marketing, but may bleed into a sales process. I'm using the term *marketing* to include a sales process where appropriate.

CONVENTIONAL WISDOM

Research suggests there are several common criticisms of marketing, which are summarized below.[861] These criticisms form part of the conventional wisdom picture about marketing and sales.

Marketing is Deceptive

The first criticism in conventional wisdom concerning marketing is that marketing is deceptive. Many believe that most marketing campaigns contain lies, do not disclose fully relevant information, and usually exaggerate the truth.[862] In most countries, stating something contrary to fact and persuading a customer to take action based on a misleading statement is illegal. On the other hand, puffery—which is praise for a product or service with subjective opinions, superlatives, or exaggerations that a reasonable person would not take seriously—is not illegal, but it can be unethical.[863] "World's best coffee" or "Number 1 pizza" are common examples of puff. Conventional wisdom advises that the more "specific the claim that is made, the more important it is for companies to have objective evidence that it [the claim] is true."[864]

Some in the marketing profession seem to have adopted a "ho-hum" attitude toward deception in marketing. Some research equates marketplace deception with persuasion.[865] While researchers can describe deceptive persuasion in marketing materials, they do so with seemingly little interest or concern about the morality of deceiving one's customers.

I was surprised to find scant discussions in the current literature that addressed how to overcome deceptive marketing practices. When I did find a discussion, most practitioners started with regulatory protections and then advised consumers on how to protect themselves. Little attention is given in the conventional wisdom to the marketer who needs to become more truthful and less "puffy" with his claims. In a moment of uncommon candor, Godin asserts nearly all marketers will lie, so he suggests we recast

---

861 Minette Drumwright, "Ethical Issues in Marketing, Advertising, and Sales." In *The Routledge Companion to Business Ethics.* Health, E., Kaldis, B, Marcoux, A. (Eds.) (Routledge Taylor & Francis Group, 2018), 508–15.

862 Patrick Murphy & Paul Bloom, "Ethical Issues in Social Marketing." In *Social Marketing: Promoting the Causes of Public and Nonprofit Agencies.* Fine, W. (Ed.) (Allyn and Bacon, 1992), 73.

863 Shaheen Hoosen, "What's the Difference Between Puffery and Misrepresentation?" March 25, 2019. Lwpath.com. https://lawpath.com.au/blog/whats–the–difference–between–puffery–and–misrepresentation

864 Jonathan Judge, "Mere Puffery vs False Advertising: Recent Trends." September 28, 2022. Afslaw. com. https://www.natlawreview.com/article/mere–puffery–vs–false–advertising–recent–trends

865 David Boush, Marian Friestad, & Peter Wright, *Deception in the Marketplace: The Psychology of Deceptive Persuasion and Consumer Self–Protection.* (Routledge, 2015) 11–12.

marketing as telling an authentic story, which he asserts is the ticket to overcoming deceptive marketing practices.[866]

It seems to me that we can sometimes overcomplicate things. So, let us do this: stop deceptive marketing practices by implementing truthful marketing practices. Just tell the truth, including the truth about trade-off decisions, risks, and giving enough information to ensure consumer autonomy. About thirty years ago, Smith proposed a "Consumer Sovereignty Test" comprised of three simple questions, which he postulated would overcome deception in marketing.[867] Thirty years later, I find his thinking helpful:

Consume Capability: Is the consumer vulnerable in ways that limit consumer autonomy in their decision–making?

Availability and Quality of Information: Do consumers have sufficient information to judge whether a purchase is right?

Rollback or Opportunity to Switch: After purchasing a product or service, if consumers want to move to a competitor for a similar product or service, does the consumer incur a substantial cost in doing so, or can the consumer move freely, with little cost to rollback the consumer's first purchase?

When companies are truthful in their marketing messages, they contribute to a level playing field with competitors. A short–term competitive advantage can be gained through embellishments in product or service quality or benefits. However, in the long run, the truth usually comes out, and customers typically punish companies that use deceptive marketing as these consumers move to purchase from other competitors.

Marketing is Unfair

The criticism of unfairness is closely related to the previous criticism of deception. What is meant by this criticism is that marketers often have more technical and use case information about their products and services than individual customers, which means an inherent knowledge and power imbalance exists between the customer and the company. I believe it is unethical to respond to this criticism by asserting caveat emptor.[868] Marketers should not be relieved from giving enough information to aid consumers in purchasing decisions. Conventional wisdom advises marketers to be honest about the downsides of their products or services—but only to a point. Conventional wisdom's sense of ethics is weak on this point. Marketers should call out trade-offs, risks, or uncertainties to enable consumers to

---

866 Seth Godin, *All Marketers Tell Stories: The Underground Classic that Explains How Marketing Really Works—and Why Authenticity is the Best Marketing of All.* (Penguin Group, 2009), 10–15.

867 Craig Smith, "Marketing Strategies for the Ethics Era." *Sloan Management Review.* 1995. 36(4): 85–97.

868 "The principle that the buyer alone is responsible for checking the quality and suitability of good before a purchase is made." (Dictionary.com). An alternative definition includes the concept of a warranty: "a principle in commerce: without a warranty the buyer takes the risk." (Merriam–Webster.com).

make independent, competent, and informed purchasing decisions. Unfortunately, most marketing collateral across nearly all industries does not call out the downsides of the offered products or services.

In online marketing, I have witnessed search engines like Google mark sponsored ads in the user interface. For example, if one were to search for the word "coffee" at Google (www.google.com), the chances are good that at the top of the first result page, sponsored ads will appear and will be called out with the word "Sponsored" in bold (without the quotation marks). Ads marked as sponsored are an example of Google considering fairness for consumers who expect the free results to be as unbiased as possible.[869]

Stealth marketing uses paid influencers to talk about and publically use the marketer's products or services without disclosing the paid relationship between the product manufacturer and the influencer. Those who follow these influencers are more open to (what is essentially) a peer group recommendation.[870] Some research concludes that stealth marketing is unethical because of the inherent deception in the non-disclosure of the paid relationship between the commercial sponsor and the influencer.[871] Moreover, research has found that stealth marketing "cynically exploits human good nature, which is wrong in itself."[872] Consumer autonomy is compromised by concealing the commercial nature of the influencer's relationship with the marketer.

Marketing is Manipulative

Close in concept to deception and unfairness is manipulation. Research points out that effective marketing is constructed to influence consumers' values and behaviors.[873] But when a customer is influenced to violate the customer's values, or when marketing's influence persuades customers to buy products detrimental to them (tobacco or junk food, for example) or to buy things these customers do not need (an expensive warranty plan or a luxurious car, for example), many would say this is unethical manipulation. I agree with that conclusion.

Customer vulnerabilities come to light in this criticism. If a marketing effort preys on a particular vulnerability that the customer may have, especially if the copy and images are

---

869 Barry Schwartz, "Can Searchers Tell the Difference Between Ads and Free Listings? Google Engineer Says 'Yes'." December 24, 2018. Searchengineland.com. https://searchengineland.com/can–searchers–tell–the–difference–between–ads–and–free–listings–google–engineer–says–yes–309798

870 Andrew Kaikati & Jack Kaikati, "Stealth Marketing: How to Reach Consumers Surreptitiously." *California Management Review.* 2004. 46(4):6–22.

871 Kelly Martin & Craig Smith, "Commercializing Social Interaction: The Ethics of Stealth Marketing." *Journal of Public Policy and Marketing.* 2008. 27(1):45–56.

872 Martin & Smith, Ethics of Stealth Marketing, 50.

873 Sara Dolnicar & Yolanda Jordaan, "A Market–Oriented Approach to Responsibly Managing Information Privacy Concerns in Direct Marketing." *Journal of Advertising.* 2007. 36(2):123–149.

designed to motivate the customer to change the customer's normal decision–making process substantively, then, more than likely, the marketing is manipulative to the customer.[874]

An inappropriate use of persuasion[875] also comes to light in this criticism. Discerning between persuasion and giving information is difficult. While persuasion generally appeals to emotions, information advertising—designed to provide factual information and objective details[876]—is focused on educating the consumer. This distinction is somewhat academic since persuasion usually includes data. Besides, information advertising usually has some emotional appeals embedded in its presentation.[877]

Most advertising contains both elements, and some would argue that some amount of persuasion is necessary to grab the consumer's attention, make them pay attention to the information, and help them change their behavior.[878] Yet, despite the fine lines between information and persuasion, a Christian business owner should be highly sensitive to inappropriate persuasion tactics, including myths encompassing a range of flawed arguments, from faulty reasoning to false–cause claims.[879] Table 16–1 outlines these myths that a Christian business owner should avoid and offers ways to more ethically present marketing messages.

Table 16–1: Persuasion myths and appropriate messaging

Myth Name	Definition	How a CBO mitigates this myth
Bandwagon	Suggests the behavior(s) presented in the advertising is universal	Honestly describe where the behavior starts and stops.
Authority	Uses a celebrity endorsement to bolster the appeal of a product and its quality	Use non–celebrity but real people endorsements.
Ad Hominem	Occurs when an ad campaign attacks a competitor rather than highlighting its benefits	Leave your competitor alone and focus on communicating the benefits of your products or services.

874 Shlomo Sher, "A Framework for Assessing Immorally Manipulative Marketing Tactics." *Journal of Business Ethics*. 2011. 102(1):97–118.

875 Persuasion: "Attempting to win others over to one's own point of view. It can be either positive, as with preaching the gospel, or it can spring from a malign intent to seduce people from the truth." (Faithlife. "Persuade." In *Logos Bible Study Factbook*. (Faithlife, September 26, 2024.) https://ref.ly/logos4/Factbook?id=ref%3abk.%25persuade.)

876 Ron Sela, "The Basics of Information Advertising." June 22, 2023, ronsela.com. https://www.ronsela.com/informative–advertising/

877 Harry Lees, "Persuasive vs Informative Advertising: What's the Difference?" May 7, 2021. Solutions.trustradius.com. https://solutions.trustradius.com/buyer–blog/persuasive–vs–informative–advertising/

878 Hannah Bartle, "Informative vs Persuasive Advertising." Accessed on 9/26/2024. Aburnadvertising.com. https://www.auburnadvertising.com/articles/98–informative–vs–persuasive–advertising

879 Mediatool.com, "Fallacies in Advertising: Navigating the Fine Line Between Persuasion and Deception." February 20, 2024. Mediatool.com. https://mediatool.com/blog/fallacies–in–advertising

Myth Name	Definition	How a CBO mitigates this myth
False Dilemma	Presents consumers with limited options, often forcing a choice between extremes when other choices are available	Present an honest range of options.
Slippery Slope	One choice will lead to highly adverse outcomes to create fear and manipulate consumer's emotions.	Present an honest range of options.
Hasty Generalization	Broad claims based on limited evidence that bolsters the product's quality	Claims should match the evidence presented. Do not embellish or exaggerate.
Post Hoc	Implies causation from correlation.	Claims should match the evidence presented. Do not embellish or exaggerate.
Straw Man	Misrepresent a competitor's product to make it easier to attack.	Be honest in all details. Do not embellish or exaggerate.
Red Herring	Distract the consumer from the main issue with irrelevant information.	Emphasize the important and de-emphasize the unimportant.
Emotional Appeal	Purposefully appeal to the consumer's emotions to bypass logical reasoning.	Emotional decisions usually do not turn out well. Appeal more to the mind than emotion.

Christian business owners are responsible for being honest in their advertising messages and not embellish or exaggerate. Companies who are careful to craft honest, believable marketing usually build such trust in the marketplace that they do better than others who exaggerate or motivate through fear.

There are several stories in the Bible of persuasion. I like Paul's attempt to persuade Agrippa in Acts 26. We can learn some lessons from how Paul managed himself and apply those lessons to our marketing efforts today. The chapter is too long to reproduce here, so I will ask that you take a moment to read Acts 26 and then continue reading at this point.

I first notice Paul's respect for Agrippa (Acts 26:2–3). Our marketing should respect all parties concerned, including our customers and competitors.

Second, Paul's defense is more of an apology for our Christian faith than a legal defense.[880] Good marketing not only informs and appropriately persuades, but it also

880 Grant Osborne, *Acts: Verse by Verse*. Osborne New Testament Commentaries. (Lexham Press, 2019), 443.

316

defends by making truthful claims that cannot be disputed. Generally, the more honest we can be about our products and services, including the deficiencies and trade–offs, the more the market will trust and purchase from us, even if initial sales are lower than desired.

Third, Paul reacted kindly to Festus' negative and sarcastic reaction (Acts 26:24), who asserted that Paul lacked common sense.[881] Sometimes, our integrity and character will be called into question by some in the marketplace. Our best marketing will respond with direct kindness, giving genuine and reasonable responses. Avoiding our emotions to strike back, our claims must be supported by facts.[882]

Fourth, our marketing should make a direct "ask." Paul gives Agrippa the opportunity to believe in Christ before everyone who was listening (Acts 26:27–29). Paul is courageous and direct. Our marketing should be the same.

Fifth, our marketing should be patient. When Agrippa evades Paul's question about his own beliefs, Paul responds by saying (Acts 26:29) in effect, "However difficult it may be or however long it may take, I will be persistent in persuading you, Agrippa, to become a Christian." Paul was ready to go the extra mile with Agrippa if Agrippa was ready to take that path with him. Our marketing should have a patient, long–term view of its efficacy.

Last, Paul gave truthful information about Christ and his situation. He did not embellish but used those facts to support his effort to persuade Agrippa. Our marketing messages should be truthful and support the "ask" in the marketing copy.

Marketing is an Invasion of Privacy

The International Association of Privacy Professionals (IAPP)[883] defines privacy as "the right to be let alone, or freedom from interference or intrusion." If this definition is used, most marketing is inherently invasive, especially considering that behavioral and technical advances have given marketers more and more abilities to collect a wide range of individual data, often used to present individualized advertisements to us. Even though some messages may be highly customized based on a niche group's demographics, marketing messages are still considered invasive.

Some believe the government is the greater threat to our privacy,[884] while others assert that many tech companies, such as *Amazon* or *Google*, know so much about us individually that they likely know more about most people than the individuals know about

---

881 Ben Witherington, III, *The Acts of the Apostles: A Socio–Rhetorical Commentary*. (Eerdmans Publishing, 1998) 749.

882 Osborne, *Acts*, 453.

883 https://iapp.org/

884 Jim Harper, "Why Government is the Greater Threat to Privacy." November 2, 2012. Ipi.org. https://www.ipi.org/ipi_issues/detail/why–government–is–the–greater–threat–to–privacy

themselves.[885] Companies often complete their customer profiles by purchasing customer data from other companies.

Because all this data is digital and everywhere we go on the internet leaves a digital footprint,[886] we need to remember that

> The very essence of our daily online existence—our political opinions, prejudices, religious beliefs, sexual tastes and personal quirks—are all becoming part of an immense, organic media soup that is congealing into a permanent public record. What is different about the digital archiving phenomenon is that our beliefs, habits, and indiscretions are being preserved for anyone to see.[887]

At the heart of this criticism are the questions of who owns an individual's purchasing and general behavioral data and who should control access to that data.[888] I agree that the concept of privacy must include an individual's right to control one's personal information, how it is collected, who can access it, how it is used, and whether it can be bought or sold to other third parties.[889]

Individual privacy is not taught as a moral concept in the Bible but is assumed in several places. For example, in Matthew 18, where a conflict resolution process is laid out, privacy of the problem and protecting the brother's reputation is ambient to that teaching.[890] Going public with details is not advised until the offending brother has met privately with the one offended (Matthew 18:15), then met a second time with the offended brother and a witness (Matthew 18:16).

Privacy is assumed in several proverbs. For example, gossip can separate close friends (Proverbs 16:28). The essence of gossip is to make public that which was meant to be private (Proverbs 11:13). A gossip betrays confidences (Proverbs 20:19), which means that the betrayed person's privacy has been exploited for the personal gain of the gossiper.[891]

---

885 Nicholas Thompson, "When Tech Knows You Better than You Know Yourself." October 4, 2018. Wired.com. https://www.wired.com/story/artificial-intelligence-yuval-noah-harari-tristan-harris/

886 Social forgetting is important, but we are losing that phenomenon in this world due to the digital remembering of everything. To learn more about the healthiness of forgetting, see Jean-FranDois Blanchette and Deborah G. Johnson, "Data Retention and the Panoptic Society: The Social Benefits of Forgetfulness. *The Information Society,* 18(1):33–45. See also Victor Mayer-Schönberger, *Delete: The Virtue of Forgetting in the Digital Age.* (Princeton University Press, 2009.)

887 J.D. Lasica, "The Net Never Forgets." November 25, 1998, Salon.com. https://www.salon.com/1998/11/25/feature_253/

888 Kord Davis, *The Ethics of Big Data.* (O'Reilly Media, 2012), 3.

889 Alexei M. Marcoux, "Much Ado About Price Discrimination." *Journal of Markets & Morality (Spring and Fall 2006)* 9, no. 1 & 2 (2006).

890 Timothy C. Seal, "Church Discipline: Recovering the Lost Treasure." *Theology for Ministry: Issues in Church Polity* 1 (2006): 89–102.

891 Tim Clinton and Diane Langberg, *The Quick-Reference Guide to Counseling Women.* (Baker Books, 2011), 153.

Private sin is to be dealt with privately,[892] yet Paul instructs us to bear one another's burdens (Galatians 6:1–2) and to confess our sins to one another (James 5:16), recalling that God does not despise a broken and contrite heart (Psalm 51:17).

In church history, privacy has been assumed for certain situations. For example, Augustine discussed the nature of God's omniscience and human privacy. In his "Confessions," he reflected on his inner life and the transparency of his soul before God. He understood that God knows all, yet he treated his inner life as private.[893]

The concept of privacy and the right to privacy are American constructs to which Christian business owners must pay attention. In our marketing efforts, we should be careful to treat confidential information that our customers and society would claim to be private. To do less than this is to give opportunity to others to call into question our faith and our commitment to God, not to mention our professionalism.

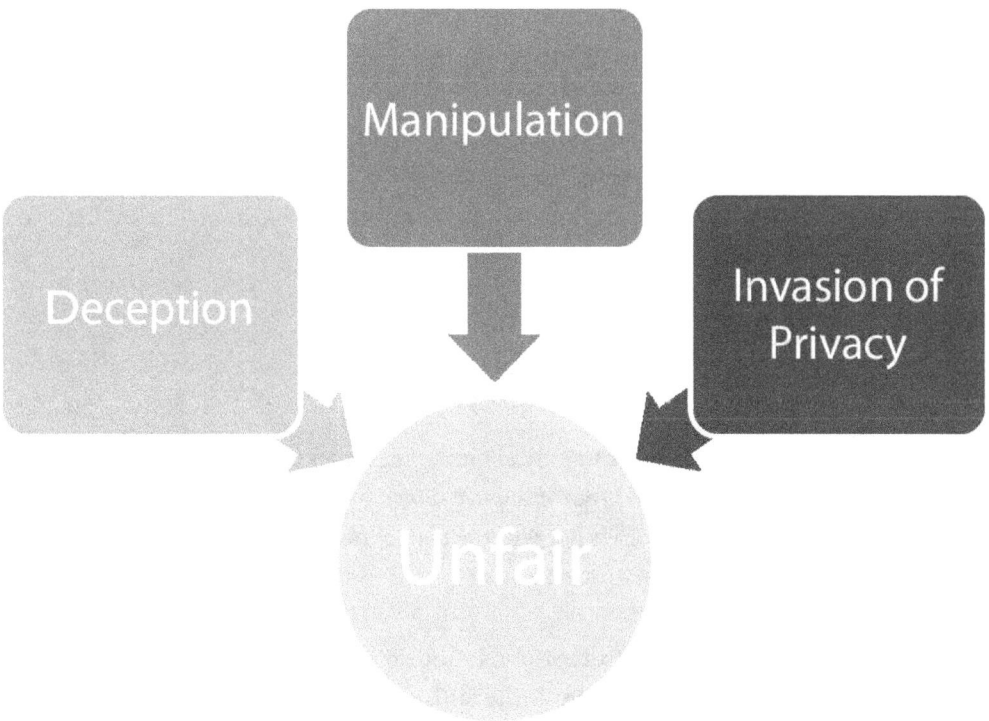

Figure 16–1: Unfairness at the Core of Marketing Criticisms

892 Ed Glasscock, "Forgiveness and Cleansing according to 1 John 1:9." *Bibliotheca Sacra* 2009. 166(662): 222.

893 Augustine of Hippo, *Confessions*. Edited by Roy Joseph Deferrari. Translated by Vernon J. Bourke. Vol. 21. The Fathers of the Church. (The Catholic University of America Press, 1953), 421–22, Book 13, Chapter 14.

Discussion of Marketing Criticisms

These four criticisms of marketing—deceptive, unfair, manipulative, and invasion of privacy–revolve around a lack of fairness in how the marketer treats the consumer. For example, it is perplexing how a marketer could be deceptive without being unfair. It is difficult to discern how a marketer could invade a consumer's privacy without being unfair, and it is problematic to assert that a marketing campaign could manipulate customer vulnerabilities without being unfair to that customer. Figure 16–1 illustrates how these deceptions relate and how engaging in one type of deception likely means a marketer is also engaging in other kinds of deception.

So why does problematic, unethical marketing continue to plague our experiences? Fassin offers several reasons:[894]

- Greed and the pursuit of profit
- Desire to win and beat one's competition
- Fear of failure and loss of respect and status
- Changing norms as society develops: materialism and a pre-occupation with money and wealth
- Globalized economy and a concentration of political power
- Short–term financial considerations
- The inefficiencies of the legal system due to the cost and likelihood of real litigation being quite low
- Reward and evaluation system of stakeholders
- Profit and power motive
- Law has replaced ethics

Of the ten reasons Fassin offers for unethical marketing, at least six are concerned directly with profit and money. The other four influence how a business owner views or manages power and money. The desire for wealth is at the core of unethical behavior. Paul wrote in 1 Timothy 6:10 (NIV):

> For the love of money is a root of all kinds of evil. Some people, eager for money, have wandered from the faith and pierced themselves with many griefs.

Unethical behaviors can often be tied to money and the desire for wealth or power. When one's desire for wealth and power persists, one will wander from one's faith in God. That

---

894 Yves Fassin, "The Reasons Behind Non–Ethical Behaviour in Business and Entrepreneurship." *Journal of Business Ethics*. 2005. 60(3):265–279.

person will live a life of one painful experience after another, all the while seeking that which cannot satisfy, sacrificing all to acquire wealth or power.

BIBLICAL WISDOM

As I wrote earlier in this chapter, most ethical problems with marketing could be resolved by simply telling the truth. I will elaborate on this point in this section.

Speech and Truth-Telling

To be truthful means to convey that which is reliable or factual.[895] A CBO must recognize that marketing copy is a form of speech. The CBO must take an interest in the words that appear in sales and marketing collateral. Ultimately, what is written or spoken in your marketing collateral reflects who you are as a person and a Christian. I would advise every CBO to equate their marketing copy with their verbal speech from an ethical and moral perspective.

Speech has great power. What is said, when it is said, is highly important. Once words leave our mouths, they cannot be taken back. Similarly, those words cannot be taken back once marketing copy is posted online or consumed by anyone outside our office. Proverbs 18:20–21 (NIV) says,

> [20] From the fruit of their mouth a person's stomach is filled; with the harvest of their lips they are satisfied. [21] The tongue has the power of life and death, and those who love it will eat its fruit.

We should remain cognizant that our speech can be life–giving or life–taking (demoralizing). The care we take in the quality of our speech will directly impact whether we are "filled" or "satisfied."[896] For example, as a short exercise, think back to when your speech left you satisfied with yourself or dissatisfied (and perhaps horrified) with yourself. Perhaps you can still experience the "filled" or "empty" feelings you felt after those words left your mouth. What we say to others and how we say it can satisfy or dissatisfy us. This passage focuses on us, the speaker, and how our speech impacts us.[897]

---

895 Faithlife, "Truth." In *Logos Bible Study Factbook*. (Faithlife, September 27, 2024.) https://ref.ly/logos4/Factbook?id=ref%3abk.%25truth.

896 Derek Kidner, *Proverbs: An Introduction and Commentary*. (InterVarsity Press, 1964), 123.

897 Stephen J. Lennox, *Proverbs: a Bible commentary in the Wesleyan tradition*. (Wesleyan Publishing House, 1998), 186.

Intensities of Speech

Language has degrees of intensity that should be considered. Exaggeration, which is enlarging the truth,[898] often uses words that are of higher intensity than the raw truth of the situation would warrant. For example, assume I had a friend in an automobile accident but walked away unharmed. This event could be described as an:

- Mishap
- Accident
- Wreck
- Disaster
- Tragedy
- Catastrophe

That list of words becomes increasingly intense. My friend walked away from the automobile accident unharmed, so it likely would be an exaggeration to describe the accident as a disaster, tragedy, or catastrophe. It would more likely be described as an accident or a wreck. Perhaps a modifier to accident, such as "serious accident" might be used. Modifiers would be appropriate to help describe the type of accident.

Marketing copy should consider degrees of intensity in language and only use superlatives when warranted. Our culture uses the most intense superlatives often. When children grow up hearing extreme superlatives to describe minimal efforts, we create a situation where true compliments cannot be given for outstanding behavior or accomplishments. The descriptors and language of compliments should fit the effort and achievement. Here is what I wrote in another book:[899]

> When it comes to compliments, we should strive for measured, accurate, honest, and genuine compliments. Compliments should be given only when deserved and not delivered too quickly. A well–timed, well–articulated praise can be immensely encouraging and, sometimes life–changing. Don't waste your compliments, but don't be stingy with them either.

Marketing copy should strive for measured, accurate, honest, and genuine words.

---

898 Merriam–Webster. "Exaggerate." Accessed 2/11/2024. Merriam–webster.com. https://www.merriam–webster.com/dictionary/exaggerate.

899 Bill English, *Biblical Wisdom for Business Leaders: Thirty Sayings from Proverbs*. (Bible and Business, 2022), 62.

Slow to Speak

CBOs should be slow to speak (James 1:19), and perhaps less marketing is better than more marketing.

> When words are many, transgression is not lacking, but whoever restrains his lips is prudent. (Proverbs 10:19 ESV).

The sage in Proverbs understands that the more that is said, the more likely it is that sin is present. We should apply this principle to marketing, learning to say more by saying less. Christian business owners should not be quick to push out new marketing copy, but instead, should be a bit slower than usual, being circumspect about their public claims and comments.

Seriousness of Speech

Ecclesiastes 5:1–7 (LEB) says this:

> ¹ Guard your steps when you go to the house of God; draw near to listen *rather* than to offer a sacrifice of fools, for they do not know that they are doing evil. 2 Do not be rash with your mouth, and do not let your heart be quick to utter a word before God. for God is in heaven, and you *are* on earth; therefore, let your words be few. 3 For a dream comes with many cares, and the voice of a fool with many words. 4 When you make a vow to God, do not delay in fulfilling it, for he takes no pleasure in fools. Fulfill what you vow! 5 It is better that you not vow than that you vow and not fulfill it. 6 Do not let your mouth lead your flesh into sin, and do not tell the messenger that it *was* a mistake. Why anger God at your words, so that he destroys the work of your hands? 7 For with many dreams *come* vanities and numerous words. Therefore, fear God!

This Ecclesiastes passage warns against a casual attitude toward God, evidenced by a casual attitude toward speech that treats lightly that which is holy (Matthew 7:21, 23:16, 1 Corinthians 11:27).[900] Fools offer insincere sacrifices, which they attempt to pass off as "mistakes" or unwitting sin.[901] Biblical stewards should never be found discussing the things of God in a casual or joking way, even in marketing collateral.

---

900 Derek Kidner. *The Message of Ecclesiastes: A Time to Mourn, and a Time to Dance.* Motyer, J.A. and Tidball, D. (Eds.) (InterVarsity Press, 1984), 53.

901 Gordon D. Fee and Robert L. Hubbard Jr., eds., *The Eerdmans Companion to the Bible.* (Eerdmans Publishing, 2011), 366–67.

Levels of Speech

In terms of moral purity, there are three levels of speech, either illustrated or taught in the Scriptures. Figure 16–2 graphically depicts these three levels.

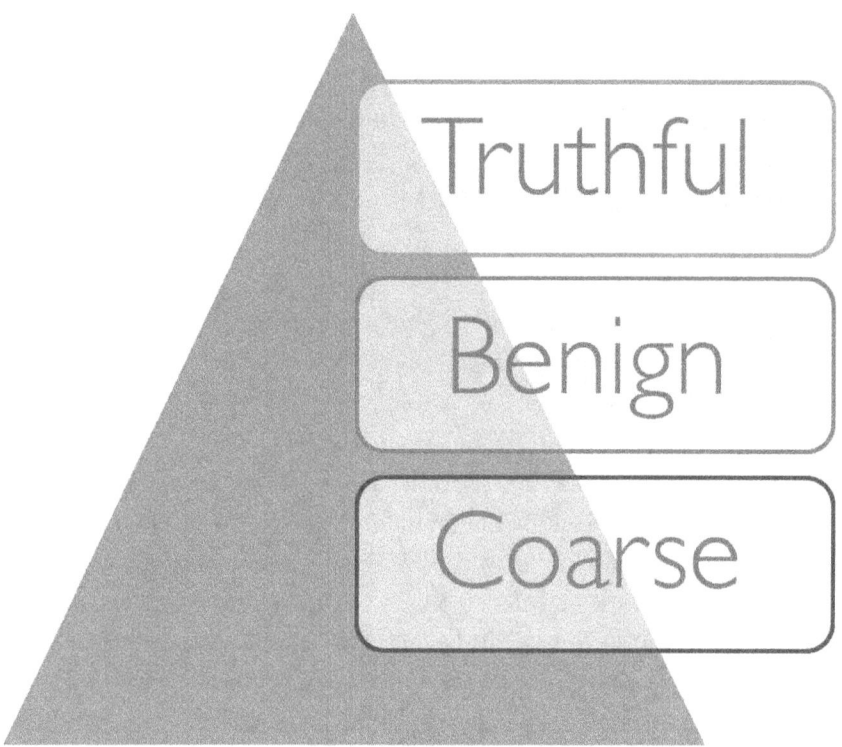

Figure 16–2: Three Levels of Speech

Coarse Language

Ephesians 5:4 (ESV) says this:

> Let there be no filthiness nor foolish talk nor crude joking, which are out
> place, but instead, let there be thanksgiving.

"Filthiness" translates αἰσχρότης, an hapax legomena (a word that occurs only once in a corpus),[902] meaning "behavior that flouts social and moral standards, shamefulness,

---

902 Faithlife, "Hapax Legomena." In *Logos Bible Study Factbook*. (faithlife, September 27, 2024.) https://ref.ly/logos4/Factbook?id=ref%3abk.%25hapaxLegomena.

obscenity."[903] "Foolish talk" translates μωρολογίαν, another hapax legomena, meaning "foolish or silly talk."[904] "Crude joking" translates εὐτραπελία, a third hapax legomena, meaning "coarse jesting involving vulgar expressions and indecent content—vulgar speech, indecent talk."[905] Behavior that flouts social and moral standards—stupid or rash conversation—vulgar expressions and indecent content—these types of speech (Ephesians 4:29) are "out of place" for the Christian business owner in all situations, including marketing, because "they are not worthy of the calling with which believers were called."[906] This prohibition applies even to marketing copy intended to reach an edgy, young crowd.

New Believer Uses Crude and Coarse Language in Evangelism

I know of a young believer in the Lord who has lived a difficult life battling addictions to drugs and alcohol.

This young man is talented. He works in the music industry and is drawn to gangster rap. He performs his music and works with other artists on their music. He spends much time in studios nationwide, recording and collaborating on music.

He has a heart for the Lord and wants to see others come to Christ. But given his audience, if he does not use coarse, crude, and vulgar language, he has concluded that those he tries to reach will not listen to him. His social media posts are filled with language he would never use at church. He claims the difference is the two different environments, hence, two different speech styles.

After confronting him for the second time about his speech, he said nothing, got up, and left right before our church service was going to start. We have not seen him since. He has unfriended me and several others on social media, cutting off from us because we insisted he follow the Scripture about God's commands in speech.

---

903 BDAG, 29.
904 BDAG, 663.
905 LN, 392.
906 William Hendriksen. *Exposition of Ephesians*. (Baker Books, 1968), 229.

What comes out of our mouths reflects what is in our hearts. Coarse, crude, or vulgar language nearly always contains an element of rebellion. If your marketing attempts to reach a rebellious crowd, think seriously about what you are trying to do. Using rebellion to reach the rebellious for Christ is likely not how to present him to those far from him.

Course speech includes cursing, which is wishing condemnation or God's judgment on a person.[907] We are to bless others instead of cursing them (Romans 12:4). James (3:8–10) reminds us that blessings and curses should not come from the same mouth. These Biblical passages remove any support for a CBO to use coarse language in sales and marketing materials, even if such language would reach a particular demographic better than non-course language.

Common Speech

Common speech is needed to conduct life's affairs but has little moral consequence. For example, setting an appointment with the mechanic to repair a car, teaching another how to use a computer program, or merely relaying facts of an event are examples of common speech. Common speech can inform, instruct, or merely relay facts.

The Scriptures do not instruct us about common speech *per se*, though there are many illustrations. Genesis 4:19 (ESV) is an example of common speech:

> [19] Lamech married two women, one named Adah and the other Zillah. [20] Adah gave birth to Jabal; he was the father of those who live in tents and raise livestock. [21] his brother's name was Jubal; he was the father of all who play stringed instruments and pipes. [22] Zillah also had a son, Tubal–Cain, who forged all kinds of tools out of bronze and iron. Tubal–Cain's sister was Naamah.

In this passage, the writer is relaying facts. This type of speech could become a moral issue if the facts are misrepresented. However, as long as benign speech is truthful, it has little moral consequence and can be classified as common speech.

---

907 Grudem, *Ethics*, 293.

Truthful Speech

The reliability of a CBO's word should be transparent and persistent:

> [12] But above all, my brothers, do not swear, either by heaven or by earth or by any other oath, but let your "yes" be yes and your "no" be no, so that you may not fall under condemnation. (James 5:12 ESV).

In Biblical times, oaths were used to confirm the truthfulness of one's word, bind individuals in contracts, or confirm God's intent to act according to God's words. The breaking of an oath would incur curses (Genesis 21:23–24, Joshua 6:26). Because the Old Testament characters operated under covenants instead of contracts, God "served as a guarantor of an individual's oath."[908] God's involvement was why breaking an oath was virtually unthinkable.[909]

A Biblical steward's speech should be truthful, even if such speech harms the steward's financial position or persona. How a person responds to the truth—how an individual manages the truth—why the truth came to be—all can be a problem. But the raw truth of the facts of the situation is never the problem. A CBO's speech should be reliable, full of grace, and truthful. As I've said before, marketing and sales copy is an extension of our speech because that copy is under our control. Truthfulness takes precedence over persuasion if one must be chosen from the two.

SUMMARY

In this chapter, I have suggested that the words we use in our marketing materials equate to those we speak to others. I reviewed the main criticisms of marketing in the conventional wisdom literature. I have also reviewed some admonishments in the Scripture for those who engage in course, foolish, or coarse language. I have suggested it is better to say more by saying less. I have reviewed how we must be accurate in the intensities of our speech and the seriousness of being slow to speak.

In the next chapter, we'll focus on the areas of human resources to which the Scriptures speak. I'll see you in the next chapter.

---

908   Jacob Cerone, "Oath." In *The Lexham Bible Dictionary*. Barry, J. D. (Ed.) (Lexham Press, 2016.)
909   Yves Ziegler, *Promises to Keep: The Oath in Biblical Narrative*. (Koninklijke Brill, 2008), 47–48.

CHAPTER 17

HUMAN RESOURCES

How we operate as Christian business owners in human resources (HR) will directly affect our ability to image God's character to our employees. Ambient to this section is the truth that all employees are both created in God's image and alienated by sin from him (Colossians 1:21). In addition, God gives different people unique abilities to accomplish different tasks (Romans 12:6–8; 1 Corinthians 12:1–11), and this truth is no less true in a business setting than in a ministry setting. God loves every employee equally and desires that each one enter into a covenant relationship with him (2 Peter 3:9). We understand that employee management must consider what God may do or is doing in the life of an employee and account for God's activities that may or may not align with the mission, purpose, and direction of the business which God has entrusted to us.[910]

In this chapter, I will consider what the Scriptures say to us as Christian business owners about two core areas of human resources: recruiting and orientation and performance reviews. I will suggest that we refrain from hiring fools. I will offer ideas on how to hire and fire well. I will also derive several principles for performance reviews from the Scriptures.

910   David J. Hoover, "Biblical Principles Applied to Human Resources." In *Biblical Principles & Business: The Practice*. Chewing, R.C. (Ed.) (NavPress, 1990), 146–60.

I am keenly aware that other areas of human resources are not discussed, such as benefits, training, and employee engagement, to name a few. I address only those topics in human resources, which I believe the Scriptures speak into.

GOD ASKS US as Christian business owners to partner (in a sense) with him in furthering the professional, personal, and spiritual development of an employee's persona. This truth enables us to view the development of an employee from eternal and immediate perspectives. Organizationally speaking, HR is the department through which we will most often bless our employees and invest in their professional growth, fulfilling one of the five purposes of business.

RECRUITING AND ORIENTATION

Recruiting is the process of finding and hiring new employees.[911] Orientation is introducing new employees to your company and work environment.[912] Conventional wisdom bifurcates orientation from onboarding.[913] In orientation, the new employee is
- Given an overview of the company's mission, values, and goals
- Introduced to coworkers
- Asked to complete new hire paperwork

In onboarding, the new employee is
- Introduced to the job duties and the day–to–day activities
- Given the tools and technologies needed to be successful
- Introduced to their specific role

Onboarding may consume several weeks or even months of employment

Conventional wisdom suggests that as part of a new employee's introduction to the company, their first-day agenda should be shared with them in advance, a welcome packet should be provided, and they should not be overwhelmed with too much, too fast.[914]

---

911   Merriam Webster, "Recruit". Accessed 09/28/2024. Merriam–webster.com. https://www.merriam–webster.com/dictionary/recruit

912   Collins Dictionary, "Orientation." Accessed 09/28/2024. Collinsdictionary.com. https://www.collinsdictionary.com/us/dictionary/english/orientation

913   4 Corner Resources, "How to Use Employee Orientation to Set New Hires Up for Success." August 21, 2024. 4cornerresources.com. https://www.4cornerresources.com/blog/how–to–use–employee–orientation–to–set–new–hires–up–for–success/

914   Anna Baluch, "New Hire Orientation Checklist & Best Practices (2024)." April 29, 2024. Forbes.com. https://www.forbes.com/advisor/business/new–hire–orientation/

Most employers have been taught to hire "top talent," generally defined as someone who consistently delivers quality results, has integrity, and takes the initiative because they are self–motivated.[915] Some are moving away from the notion of top talent to one of "right talent." The former may have negative effects in the long term[916] , whereas the latter keeps the focus where it is needed: character and skill, which deliver the results the company needs from that position.

One of the greatest challenges we will face as business owners is hiring the right person for the right job. If you have been hiring for over a year, you will likely admit—as I have acknowledged many times—that you have made some wrong hires. I like the notion of "hire character, train skill." While following that standard has proven helpful, it has not protected me entirely from hiring the wrong person for an open position.

Biblical Wisdom on Hiring Well

The Scriptures do not directly teach how a business owner can hire well. While hiring is illustrated in the Bible, the hiring process itself is not discussed directly. The Scriptures suggest that the business owner hire top talent if such talent is available. In Proverbs 22:29 (NIV), the sage asks and answers his own question:

> Do you see someone skilled in their work? They will serve before kings;
> they will not serve before officials of low rank.

This passage shows top talent associated with the best employers (kings). It stands to reason that the best employers will hire the most skilled. However, as I mentioned in the leadership chapter, we often confuse genuine leadership skills and top talent skills with traits of personality deficiencies that, at first, look similar, but have negative long-term effects.

Psychopathy, Sociopathy, APD, and NPD

Many people are confused about the differences among psychopathy, sociopathy, antisocial personality disorder and narcissistic personality disorder. Although the terms are frequently treated as interchangeable—by the general public and professionals alike—they refer to related but not identical conditions.

---

915   Kelly Keefe, "The 8 Defining Qualities of Top Talent." January 31, 2012. Yourerc.com. https://yourerc.com/blog/the–8–defining–properties–of–top–talent/

916   Lisa Toppin, "It's Time to Rethink the Use of the Term 'Top Talent'." November 28, 2023. Forbes.com. https://www.forbes.com/councils/forbeshumanresourcescouncil/2023/11/28/its–time–to–rethink–the–use–of–the–term–top–talent/

Psychopathy is a personality disorder [that] describes [people who] without a conscience. They are incapable of empathy, guilt, or loyalty to anyone but themselves.

Sociopathy is not a formal psychiatric condition. It refers to patterns of attitudes and behaviors considered antisocial and criminal by society but are seen as normal or necessary by the subculture or social environment in which they developed. Sociopaths may have a well-developed conscience and a normal capacity for empathy, guilt, and loyalty, but their sense of right and wrong is based on the norms and expectations of their subculture or group. Many criminals might be described as sociopaths.

Antisocial personality disorder (APD) is a broad diagnostic category found in the American Psychiatric Association's Diagnostic and Statistical Manual of Mental Disorders, 4th edition (DSM-IV). Antisocial and criminal behaviors play a major role in its definition and, in this sense, APD is similar to sociopathy. Some of those with APD are psychopaths, but many are not. The difference between psychopathy and antisocial personality disorder is that the former includes personality traits such as lack of empathy, grandiosity, and shallow emotion that are not necessary for a diagnosis of APD. APD is three or four times more common than psychopathy in the general population and in prisons. The prevalence of those we would describe as sociopathic is unknown but likely is considerably higher than that of APD.[917]

APD is characterized by the disregard and violation of other's rights, including actions such as nonconformity to social standards, repeated lying, impulsivity, irritability and aggression, disregard for the safety of themselves or others, irresponsibility, and a lack of remorse for the negative effect their actions have on others.

Narcissistic Personality Disorder (NPD) is characterized by a grandiose view of oneself. They have an intense need to be admired and lack empathy for others' plights. They are preoccupied with fantasies of unlimited success, power, brilliance, beauty or ideal love. They believe they are special and

---

917   The entire sidebar is a quote from Paul Babiak and Robert D. Hare, *Snakes in Suits: When Psychopaths Go to Work* (HarperCollins, Kindle Edition), 18-19.

unique, concluding that most cannot genuinely understand them. They will have unreasonable expectations of favorable treatment by others and are often envious of others who they perceive are getting the admiration and applause they deserve. Many would say these people are arrogant and haughty.[918]

The Christian business owner community has its fair share of owners who fit one or more of these descriptions. Unfortunately, so does the pastor and non-profit leadership groups. Executive coaching is one way to help these individuals heal, but in all likelihood, God will need to take them through deep waters before they can jettison their personality deficiencies.

Many people who are top talent have considerable raw talents given by God. Yet many never achieve what could be achieved given the talents and intellect God gave them. These individuals lack persistence in becoming competent at their trade, alliance–building skills, and developing an integrated character.[919] They lack the necessary character traits to achieve all their brains and talents, which indicates they could achieve. Laziness and distractions toward the unimportant are two reasons these talented individuals never achieve their desired levels of success. They often implode when given more responsibility than they can realistically manage because their characters are not ready.

One of the lessons of the Mars Hill debacle[920] is that it is unwise to give a platform that outsizes a person's character and maturity even though their talents and charisma may indicate they are ready.[921] Charisma is often confused with competence by hiring managers. Immature characters often succeed in business and life by replacing competence with charm and dissimulation.[922]

The number of leaders whose character deficiencies led to devastating failure and injury of others in business and ministry is nearly uncountable. You can find compilations of

---

918   American Psychiatric Association, *Diagnostic and Statistical Manual of Mental Disorders*, 5th Edition, Rvised, DSM-TR-5, 2022. 760.

919   Henry Cloud, *Integrity: The Courage to Meet the Demands of Reality*. (HarperCollins, 2006), 3–11.

920   Mike Cosper, "The Rise and Fall of Mars Hill." Accessed 09/28/2024. Christianitytoday.com. https://www.christianitytoday.com/podcasts/the–rise–and–fall–of–mars–hill/

921   Mike Cosper, "Who Killed Mars Hill?" Accessed 09/28/2024. Christianitytoday.com. https://www.christianitytoday.com/wp–content/uploads/2021/06/22903.pdf, page 16.

922   Paul Babiak and Robert Hare, *Snakes in Suits: When Psychopaths Go to Work*. (HarperCollins, 2006), 124.

these stories in business from publishers like *Forbes*[923] and the *Wall Street Journal*[924] and in ministry from publishers like *Ministry Watch*[925] and *The Roys Report*.[926]

In most situations involving breach of trust, scandal, ethical failure, or moral failure, there were several common factors:

- A charismatic leader who could turn on charm when needed.
- Private sin flourished through a lack of genuine accountability.
- Weak governance boards.
- Weak accountability to standards and morals.
- Success results that were difficult to ignore.

Nearly all of these individuals could fool multiple boards, constituents, and (in many cases) donors. But in the end, their private sin and broken characters overtook their carefully choreographed public personas. They revealed an immaturity and lack of an integrated personality that was not ready for the platform they had been given.

As a lesson for us all, when interviewing candidates for a potential role in your company, beyond asking about competencies and skills, ask the underlying competency questions that will help you flesh out any character deficiencies. Here are some sample questions:

Impressions:

- How does this candidate come across?
- How serious is the candidate about his or her career and this job?
- Is he or she likable?
- Is he or she bright?
- Did the candidate prepare for this interview?
- Is the candidate being forthright with information?

Underlying competency questions:

- Does this person communicate well in a somewhat stressful face–to–face conversation?
- Does the candidate stay focused on the question asked or ramble along?
- Did the candidate exhibit good judgment in the career moves he or she made?

---

923 Frans Wiwanto, "Major Scandales Driving the Rise of Modern Compliance." February 3, 2021. Forbest.com. https://www.forbes.com/councils/forbesfinancecouncil/2021/02/03/major–scandals–driving–the–rise–of–modern–compliance/

924 Wall Street Journal, "Risk & Compliance Journal." Accessed 09/28/2024. Wsj.com. https://www.wsj.com/news/types/risk–compliance–journal

925 Ministry Watch, "Investigations." Accessed 09/28/2024. Ministrywatch.com. https://ministry-watch.com/investigations/

926 Roys Report, "Investigations." Accessed 09/14/2024. Julieroys.com https://julieroys.com/investigations/

- Did the candidate grow in his or her job and take on more responsibilities over time or merely do the same thing repeatedly?
- Did the candidate demonstrate leadership, integrity, effective communication, teamwork, and persuasion skills?[927]

If a person's presentation is too good to be true, it probably is. In your hiring processes, it takes time and hard work to ask the questions that determine a person's personality deficiencies. However, the larger the platform an open position holds in your organization, the more critical your responsibility to God and yourself is to take the time necessary to drill into those areas of character and maturity to ensure you are not captivated by their charisma and fooled by their charm. You must ensure they are ready for the platform that may be handed to them.

Hiring Fools

Proverbs 16:6–10 (CSB) teaches that hiring a fool is a bad idea and usually leads to unwanted outcomes. Hence, we should choose who we hire carefully:

> [6] The one who sends a message by a fool's hand cuts off his own feet and drinks violence. [7] A proverb in the mouth of a fool is like lame legs that hang limp. [8] Giving honor to a fool is like binding a stone in a sling. [9] A proverb in the mouth of a fool is like a stick with thorns, brandished by the hand of a drunkard. [10] The one who hires a fool or who hires those passing by is like an archer who wounds everyone.

> More Info: You'll find an appreciable overlap between the descriptions of a fool in this section and the characteristics of those discussed in the previous sidebar on psychopaths, sociopaths, APD, and NPD.

While scholars acknowledge that the Hebrew text is difficult to translate in verse 10,[928] the main point of verse 10 seems to be that one should not commit important tasks to fools.[929] Hiring a fool is similar to an archer who shoots without aiming; hence, check references carefully and have a thorough interview and vetting process.[930]

---

927   Questions taken from Babiak, *Snakes in Suits*, 218.

928   Duane A. Garrett, *Proverbs, Ecclesiastes, Song of Songs.* (Broadman & Holman, 1993), 213. See also Stephen J. Lennox, *Proverbs: a Bible commentary in the Wesleyan tradition.* (Wesleyan Publishing House, 1998), 272.

929   Garrett, *Proverbs*, 213.

930   Lennox, *Proverbs*, 272.

The chiastic structure of verses 6–10 in Proverbs 26 equates the folly of giving important business decisions to a fool.[931] Here is the chiastic structure:[932]

A: Sending a message by the hand of a fool (vs 6)
B: A proverb in a fool's mouth (vs 7)
C: Honoring a fool (vs 8)
B1: A proverb in a fool's mouth (vs 9)
A1: Hiring a fool (vs. 10)

Both hiring and messaging in business are important functions not normally delegated to entry-level employees. The sage reminds us that important business functions should be delegated to those competent in skill with a mature character to perform those functions.

Ecclesiastes 10:5–6 (ESV) speaks directly about hiring and placing fools in leadership positions:

> There is an evil I have seen under the sun, the sort of error that arises from a ruler. Fools are put in many high positions while the rich occupy the low ones.

In this passage, St. Jerome took the word "rich" to mean "rich in speech and wisdom" and "rich in good works."[933] The sage describes social chaos in which incompetent, unprepared people assume leadership roles and those prepared for leadership are placed in servant roles.[934] The Proverbs 26 and Ecclesiastes 10 passages teach that hiring (or promoting) a fool or a person unprepared for leadership for a position in management or influence in one's business is an "evil" and an "error."

Characteristics of a Fool

So, what are the characteristics of a fool?[935] Proverbs has much to say about this and describes fools as those who

• Despise wisdom and discipline, 1:7
• Hate knowledge, 1:22
• Are complacent, 2:32
• Spread slander, 10:18

---

931 Bruce K. Waltke, *The Book of Proverbs, Chapters 15–31*. (Eerdmans, 2005), 350.

932 Garrett, *Proverbs*, 213.

933 St. Jerome, *St. Jerome: Commentary on Ecclesiastes*. Edited and translated by Richard J. Goodrich and David J. D. Miller. Vol. 66. Ancient Christian Writers. (The Newman Press, 2012), 112.

934 August H. Konkel and Tremper Longman III, *Cornerstone Biblical Commentary, Vol 6: Job, Ecclesiastes, and Song of Songs*. (Tyndale House Publishers, 2006), 315.

935 This discussion on fools is taken largely from English, 2021:308–310.

- Lack of judgment, 10:21
- Do not listen to advice, 12:15
- Quickly show their annoyance, 12:16
- Mock at making amends for sin, 14:9
- Hotheaded and reckless, 14:16
- Full of talk, but they do not work hard, 14:23
- Do not accept advice, 17:10
- Love to give their opinions, 18:2
- Quick to quarrel, 20:3
- See danger, but they do not change course, 27:12

While there are more verses than these about fools in the Scriptures, this list gives us a starting point for candidate characteristics that should not be hired in one's business.

Table 17–1 lists each characteristic of a fool from Proverbs and legal questions that can be asked during the interview process to discern the presence and intensity of each characteristic. Naturally, all individuals exhibit foolish characteristics at one time or another. However, the more persistently a wider range of characteristics is present, the more likely the owner is interviewing a fool and should demur from further discussions with that candidate.

Table 17–1: Characteristics of a Fool and Interview Questions

Characteristic	Potential Screening Question
Despise wisdom; hate knowledge; do not listen to advice	Who do you go to for mentoring? Who has been a mentor to you in the last ten years? What books have you read for professional development in the last five years? What are the guiding principles for your career development?
Despise discipline	Tell me about the last person you worked for. What did you like and not like about your last manager?
Complacency	Are you satisfied with your career development at this stage of your life? What would you want to accomplish professionally while you're here?
Spread slander	Tell me about the last co-worker you worked with that you did not get along with—what were they like and how did you handle yourself?

Characteristic	Potential Screening Question
Lack of judgment	Give them an ethical scenario and ask them how they would handle it. Run a background and credit check—how they handle money will indicate strongly what kind of judgment they have.
Quickly show their annoyance.	What kind of people annoy you?
Do not make amends for something they have done wrong	Ask them to describe the last business mistake they made and what they did to correct it.
Big talk, small work	Give them thirty minutes to complete a work task as an interview question. Can they do what they claim on their résumé?
Love to give their opinions	Ask them about a hot-button issue and see if they proffer their opinions strongly.
See danger coming, but do not change course to avoid the danger	Ask them to describe the last three business decisions they made. Listen for the risk/reward elements and discern accordingly.

Fools, as described in the Bible, should be avoided when hiring. Weeding out fools during the hiring process is essential. Yet, no matter how hard we try, we occasionally make bad hiring decisions. When a termination is in order, it is important to know what the Bible says about firing well.

Biblical Wisdom on Firing Well

Firing an employee is a difficult thing to do. The aftermath can be just as difficult.

Pritchett believes that if an owner has already considered ending a person's employment, the time is past due to fire the employee.[936] Most business owners avoid terminations because they are unsure whether an ending is necessary or if the situation is "fixable." Also, many fear a termination confrontation, dislike hurting another person, and do not possess the skills and words needed to perform a proper employment termination.[937] Employment terminations can happen due to poor performance, downsizing, selling or buying a business, lack of the person's fit with the culture or values, and illegal or unethical behavior.

---

936 Bob Pritchett, *Fire Someone Today And Other Surprising Tactics for Making Your Business a Success.* (Thomas Nelson, 2006), 3–4.

937 Henry Cloud, *Necessary Endings.* (HarperCollins, 2010), 9.

While there is no painless way to fire an employee, conventional wisdom advises that the termination process first frame the situation truthfully, then ensure the termination process is as fair as possible, then follow up well by (perhaps) paying for outplacement counseling, offering a severance package, or offering an alternative job at the company to which the employee can apply.[938] In addition, firing well starts by hiring well in the sense that setting expectations during the hiring and onboarding process will help set the stage for firing well if the employee does not perform as needed. Regular communication and coaching are essential: no one should ever be surprised at being terminated.[939] Documentation on the employee's performance must be clear and up–to–date. Also, how the employees' duties will be re-assigned to others needs to be planned out in advance. Owners are highly advised not to fire impulsively but to do so with forethought and planning without elongating the process too much.[940]

The Scriptures have little say about terminating an employee's employment. I do not equate Scripture passages about throwing out a worthless servant into darkness, where there is immense pain (Matthew 8:5–13; 13:36–43; 22:–14) as analogous to employment terminations. These warning passages are salvific and should not be equated or analogized with employment terminations.

Hence, it is unsurprising that I could not find any source material from a Biblical perspective on terminating employment. I am not alone. Not one verse was quoted or referenced in the section of Burkett's book, *Biblical Principles for Firing*.[941] Moreover, Pritchett, who once owned the Logos company[942] that manufactures the Logos software that was extensively utilized to write this book, placed the chapter on firing an employee at the beginning of his book. Again, even though it appears Pritchett is a person of faith, no Biblical passages were quoted or referenced in the chapter on firing an employee.[943]

Ambiently, all the commands of Scripture that teach how a follower of God is to treat another person still apply during a termination proceeding. For example, a CBO loves his employee, even if that employee has turned against her and caused her harm (Matthew 5:43–48). We should not use coarse language (Ephesians 5:4) or display anger (James 1:19–20). In humility, we should continue to look out for the interests of the one who is being terminated (Philippians 2:4). We should not gossip (Romans 1:29–30) and should

---

938 Ben Hardy, "The 3 Fs of Firing: How to Let People Go 'Well'." July 31, 2024. Forbes.com. https://www.forbes.com/sites/lbsbusinessstrategyreview/2024/01/31/the–3–fs–of–firinghow–to–let–people–go–well/?sh=67a21f301a82

939 William Vanderbloemen, "What I've Learned About How to Fire People Well." April 27, 2017. Forbes.com. https://www.forbes.com/sites/williamvanderbloemen/2017/04/27/firing–people–well/?sh=3bb2cc603d77

940 Lyndsy McDonald, "The Definitive Guide to Firing Well." June 16, 2023. Castle–hr.com. https://castle–hr.com/blog/firing–well–guide/

941 Larry Burkett, *Business by the Book*. (Thomas Nelson, 1998), 128–29.

942 https://www.logos.com

943 Pritchett, *Fire Someone*, 1–11.

never model a love for money and wealth (Hebrews 13:5). Literally, we are to imitate Christ, even during a termination process (Ephesians 5:1).

If we terminate an employee in anger, we sin. If we gossip negatively about an employee, we sin. If we do not account for the loss of income our employee will experience (when reasonably possible), and we know that a termination will leave them financially destitute, and we do nothing about their plight, we sin. Even during a difficult termination, where the employee is not taking personal responsibility for the employee's underperformance and is blaming the manager or us, such immature or sinful behavior does not allow us to sin against our employee or God.

Firing well means we embrace conventional wisdom where possible but extend that wisdom by self-management in a way congruent with God's character. We adhere to the standards God has set for any Christian to obey regarding interpersonal relationships. In addition to embracing conventional wisdom about performing terminations, we behave in ways that will please God.

PERFORMANCE REVIEWS

Feedback on the quality and helpfulness of one's work is essential to employees remaining engaged and motivated. Like growing from childhood to teen years to being an adult, where a sense of growing and maturing helps one build an integrated personality,[944] so employees need a sense of growing professionally as they mature. Consistent, constructive feedback is essential to a person's professional growth.[945]

Conventional Wisdom on Performance Reviews

An increasing number of professionals believe the traditional annual performance review model is broken and outdated. Garr asserts that traditional performance reviews alienate employees and cost employers too much money in terms of both lack of employee engagement and managerial time.[946] She further comments that compensation increases should be decoupled from more frequent coaching exercises in which employee skills are built, confidence is increased, and processes are simplified.

---

944 David Elkind, All Grown Up and No Place to Go: Teenagers in Crisis. (Perseus, 1998), 111–34.

945 Manuel London & James W. Smither, "Feedback Orientation, Feedback Culture, and the Longitudinal Performance Management Process." *Human Resource Management Review*. 2002. (12)1:81–100.

946 Stacia Garr, "Performance Management is Broken: Replace "rank and yank" with coaching and development." March 5, 2014. Deloitte.com. https://www2.deloitte.com/us/en/insights/focus/human–capital–trends/2014/hc–trends–2014–performance–management.html

Laurinavicius agrees with Garr. Laurinavicius advises the business owner to advise, not admonish, one's direct reports and that feedback should help the employee practice the right actions and give the employee a sense of recognition for work that was performed.[947]

Christian business owners should embrace the conventional wisdom Garr and Laurinavicius offer. However, we should also learn to think Biblically about performance reviews and add particular Biblical emphases to our review process.

Biblical Wisdom on Performance Reviews

There are examples of performance reviews in the Scriptures, where someone's work product was evaluated. These examples are presented in Table 17–2.

Table 17–2: Examples of Performance Reviews in the Bible (not exhaustive)

Passage	Parties Involved	Occasion	Outcome	General Focus
Genesis 1–2	God	Creation of the world and universe	God evaluates God's work as "good."	Quality of Work
Genesis 4	Cain, Abel, God	Cain's offering to God is not a "first fruit," hence, unacceptable to God; out of jealousy, Cain kills Abel.	God disregards Cain's offering; God removes Cain's productive abilities; God assigns Cain to be a wanderer for life.	Faithfulness and obedience
Genesis 41	Pharoah, Cupbearer, Joseph	Pharoah's troubling dreams predict seven years of plenty and seven years of famine.	Joseph correctly interprets Pharoah's dreams and is named Egypt's Prime Minister.	Quality of work
Leviticus 10	Nadab, Abihu, God	Unauthorized offer of fire to God	God kills Nadab and Abihu	Faithfulness and obedience

947 Tomas Laurinavicius, "Performance Review Template & Examples (2024)." April 30, 2024. Forbes.com. https://www.forbes.com/advisor/business/performance–review/

Passage	Parties Involved	Occasion	Outcome	General Focus
Numbers 13	Moses, the spies, God	Gathered military intelligence about Canaan; gave mixed reports to Moses	God caused forty years of wandering while those who rebelled against God died	Trust in God's character
Numbers 20	Moses, Israel, God	Moses strikes the rock instead of speaking to it at Meribah	God forbids Moses to enter the promised land	Faithfulness and obedience
1 Samuel 15	God, Saul	Saul makes an unlawful sacrifice, engages in a rash vow, turns from God, engages in divination.	God tears the kingdom from Saul's family and gives it to another (Jesse's family)	Faithfulness and obedience
Daniel 2	Daniel, Nebuchadnezzar, God	Interpretation of Nebuchadnezzar's dreams	Daniel is promoted and given gifts; Daniel's friends are promoted	Quality of Work
Matthew 20	Master and hired laborers	Work in the master's vineyard for pay	All were paid the same, even though some worked less than others.	Quality of work; the generosity of the owner
Matthew 23	Scribes, Pharisees, teachers of the law	Preach heavy burdens, but do not practice what is preached	Called hypocrites seven times; Christ gives them seven woes	Faithfulness and obedience
Matthew 25; Luke 19	Master, three servants	Talents are entrusted to the servants: two produce more talents; one does not.	The servants who produced more talents were given more of the master's presence and were entrusted with more; the one who did not produce another talent was fired and called "worthless."	Faithfulness and obedience

Passage	Parties Involved	Occasion	Outcome	General Focus
Matthew 25	God, Christ, all nations of the earth, all people	Separated into two groups	Those who imitated the character of God are invited into God's eternal presence; those who did not are sent away from God's presence eternally.	Faithfulness and obedience
Luke 12	The wise manager, master, household servants	Parable	If the manager gives them food at the proper time, then the master will bless the manager and provide the manager with much more to manage; if the manager mistreats the master's servants, the master will find the manager unfaithful and will give the manager a severe beating.	Faithfulness and obedience
Revelation 2:1–7	Church in Ephesus	God's review of this church	To the one who overcomes, God will allow eating from the Tree of Life in heaven.	Faithfulness and obedience
Revelation 2:8–11	Church in Smyrna	God's review of this church	To the one who overcomes, God will ensure the second death does not injure those individuals.	Faithfulness and obedience
Revelation 2:12–17	Church in Pergamum	God's review of this church	To the one who overcomes, God will give hidden manna, a white stone with a new name written on the stone known only to the recipient.	Faithfulness and obedience
Revelation 2:18–26	Church in Thyatira	God's review of this church	God will give authority to rule the nations and the morning star to the one who overcomes.	Faithfulness and obedience

Passage	Parties Involved	Occasion	Outcome	General Focus
Revelation 3:1–6	Church in Sardis	God's review of this church	To the one who overcomes, God will cloth that person in white garments, never remove that individual's name from the Book of Life, and confess that individual's name before God the Father and God's angels.	Faithfulness and obedience
Revelation 3:7–13	Church in Philadelphia	God's review of this church	To the one who overcomes, God will make this individual a pillar in God's temple; the individual's name will be written on the new Jerusalem.	Faithfulness and obedience
Revelation 3:14–22	Church of Laodicea	God's review of this church	To the one who overcomes, God will grant that individual the right to sit on Christ's throne.	

As seen in Table 17–2, faithfulness and obedience to God are often criteria against which one's conduct is evaluated. Much is promised to those who "overcome"[948] life's temptations not to abandon following God. We can learn from Table 17–2 that we should value general faithfulness and work quality over achieving individual job description duties. Another learning is that if we model the character of God in our business, we will place a higher value on the qualities of faithfulness and adherence to culture and directives over meeting the letter of the law of one's job description.

SUMMARY

In this chapter, I have suggested that we need to hire top talent and avoid hiring fools. In addition, in our performance review processes, we should emphasize faithfulness and obedience as success factors for our employees.

---

948 νικάω, "to win in the face of obstacles" (BDAG, 673); "prevail, triumph, be victorious" (DBL, 3771).

In the next chapter, I dive into the difficult subject of partnerships. I will discuss what makes a great partner and what makes a lousy partner. There is much to learn, so let's keep going.

CHAPTER 18

PARTNERSHIPS

In this chapter, I will assert there are character qualities that can be readily discerned that make another person(s) a great partner. I will equally argue that there are character deficiencies that can be readily discerned that make another person a lousy partner. Before you enter a partnership, consider the content presented in this chapter. Following my advice may save you years of heartache and pain.

I will readily admit that this chapter is more "Bill than Bible." Consider the advice given in this chapter as coming from one who has spent over thirty–five years starting and growing businesses in at least four different industry verticals.

PARTNERSHIPS ARE THE simplest structure for two or more people to own a business together. In American law, there are two types of partnerships: Limited partnership (LP) and Limited Liability Partnership (LLP).[949] A limited partnership must be owned by two or more parties, one of which is the general partner and has unlimited liability for debts. The limited partners have liability only up to the amount of their

---

949   Small Business Administration. *Choose a Business Structure*. Accessed 08/05/2023. Sba.gov. https://www.sba.gov/business–guide/launch–your–business/choose–business–structure

investment.[950] Limited liability partnerships ensure every partner has a limited personal liability for the partnership's debts.[951]

Partnerships can benefit businesses with multiple owners and professional groups (like attorneys). Partnerships are created through a legal contract outlining each partner's responsibilities.[952]

It is best to form a partnership with someone living in a covenant relationship with God. But many partnerships are not clean, two-person entities where both know and are committed to the Lord. For example, consider an attorney joining a law firm with over 600 lawyers, 200 of whom are partners. Or consider an accountant joining an accounting firm with thirty partners and 200 accountants. Being a partner in either of these situations is substantively different from being a partner with one or two others in an automobile repair shop or a manufacturing plant.

So, to what extent should Christians demur from partnering with those who are not Christians? Let's look at the answer to this question more closely.

BEING UNEQUALLY YOKED

Some Christians hold to a bumper–sticker theology that is black and white: Christians should not be partners in business with unbelievers. Some will assert that 2 Corinthians 6:14–15 (LEB) prevents Christians from going into business with other Christians:

> 14 Do not become unevenly yoked with unbelievers, for what participation *is there between* righteousness and lawlessness? Or what fellowship *does* light *have* with darkness? 15 And what agreement *does* Christ *have* with Beliar? Or what share *does* a believer *have* with an unbeliever?

Those who assert a simple theology of separation lack appreciation for nuance, as found in this passage.

The phrase "unequally yoked"[953] means to avoid becoming mismatched with someone through forming an intimate relationship or a close association that is imbalanced.[954] Paul

---

950   Evan Tarver. "Limited Partnership (LP): What It Is, Pros and Cons, How to Form One." June 25, 2024. Investopedia.com. https://www.investopedia.com/terms/l/limitedpartnership.asp

951   Andrew Beattie. "Limited Liability Partnership (LLP): Meaning and Features." August 20, 2024. Investopedia.com. https://www.investopedia.com/articles/investing/090214/limited–liability–partnership–llp–basics.asp

952   Leonard, *6 types*, n.p.

953   ἑτεροζυγοῦντες from ἑτεροζυγέω, *mismated, not belonging together* (BDAG).

954   Pragmatically, I find the meaning of this word implies a high degree of difficulty in exiting the relationship, too.

combines two words into a hapax legomenon[955] to communicate a nuance. This verb is difficult to render. Garland translates the Greek verb "other yoked."[956] Dr. Harris writes:

The verb ἑτεροζυγέω is not found elsewhere in biblical Greek nor in Greek literature before the Christian era. The verb means "pull the yoke [ζυγός] in a different [ἕτερος] direction than one's fellow," and figuratively, "make a mismatched covenant" or "mismate." In alluding to Leviticus 19:19 and Deuteronomy 22:10 by the use of the verb ἑτεροζυγέω, Paul is saying that just as the yoking together of animals of two disparate species to form a team will cause an incongruous mismatch where members are pulling in different directions, so close attachments and intimate association between believers and unbelievers will produce an ill-matched union and total dissonance.[957]

How far or tightly one applies this passage to business partnerships is a matter of conscious. But clearly, there must be a balance in how a Christian interacts with and owns businesses with others who hold different theological beliefs or no beliefs. Garland's comments are helpful at this point:

> Pagan values and practices surrounded the Corinthian Christians. Just because the Spirit has sealed them does not mean they can be careless about their relationships and associations with the world. Paul's clarification in 1 Corinthians 5:9–10 makes it clear, however, that Paul is not asking believers to shun pagans altogether. He assumes that they will shop in the market (1 Corinthians 10:25) and encourages them to go to dinner at a pagan's home if they are invited and disposed to go (1 Corinthians 10:26). But he does want to form their spiritual identity so that they are distinguished from the pagan society surrounding them and will realign their values accordingly. Christians hold values dear that others reject. They must not allow themselves to be hitched to the same yoke as those whose beliefs are hostile to the Christian faith. Therefore, Paul pleads with them to withdraw from these unholy alliances.[958]

Garland says that isolating oneself from those who do not know Christ is not expected or pragmatic. We cannot live our lives interacting with only those who believe the way we do. We must go about living with those who believe differently than we do. Applying this principle to business ownership and partnerships will require maturity.

---

955 A word used only once in a corpus

956 David E. Garland, *2 Corinthians*. (Broadman & Holman, 1999), 331.

957 Murray J. Harris, *The Second Epistle to the Corinthians: a commentary on the Greek text*. (Eerdmans Publishing, Paternoster Press, 2005), 498–99.

958 Garland, *2 Corinthians*, 332.

Hence, requiring a business partner to have similar theological beliefs may be preferred, but it is unnecessary to enjoy a healthy partnership. Those with theological differences might still make successful business partners because they may hold to similar values and have the character qualities to be great partners.

Forming a business partnership is different from forming a new church or marriage. Instead, only a new business relationship is being formed. If planned properly, the partnership will have legal ways to exit without unnecessary personal harm. So, whether the entrepreneur is forming a

- Partnership with one or more in a new venture,
- Adding one or more partner(s) in an existing venture,
- Joining as a new partner in an existing venture with one or more existing partner(s),
- Entering into a long–term agreement with a customer or vendor who, in effect, acts as a business partner,

it does not appear wise to say, "If the other partners are not Christians, you cannot join that partnership." I will suggest a continuum be considered: the fewer partners involved in the partnership, the more important the alignment of values and perhaps theological beliefs will be. The more numerous the partners are, the less important it will be for others to hold to a Christian's theological beliefs, though value alignment will still be necessary. So, others being Christians with a similar faith in God is preferred but not required by Scripture.

Partnership relationships are contractual, not covenantal. This reality is due mainly to the time-limited nature of the relationship and the legal contract all partners should sign to create their professional relationship. There will be covenantal flavors to the legal relationship in that each partner has a duty of loyalty to the other partners. However, I think it would be a mistake to say that a business partnership is covenantal, similar to our relationship with God.

OBVIOUS WARNING SIGNS

Christians in business should consider several warning signs when considering joining an existing partnership or forming a new partnership. These warning signs represent temptations to sin:

- If the partnership is producing a product or service, that is sinful.
- If the partnership will cause one to sin.
- A partnership that makes it difficult to be faithful to God or makes it easy to break one's covenant with God.
- A partnership that would keep one from pursuing one's stewardship responsibilities or place limits on fulfilling God's call.

- A partnership that funds activities inconsistent with biblical values.
- Partners who demand the business become the most important priority in one's life.

CBOs should know these and other similar elements before joining a partnership. CBOs should thoroughly investigate the partnership agreement with the partners before entering the partnership. A core question for a Christian to consider before joining a partnership could be phrased this way: "Can your allegiance to God remain intact in the proposed partnership?"

Pragmatically, the answer to this question means:

- A written, legally binding agreement with a clear and fair process is needed to exit the partnership.
- Having partners and an agreement that will not hinder the Christian's covenant with God or keep the Christian from fulfilling the Christian's stewardship responsibilities.
- Ensuring the products and services enable customers and their communities to flourish without worrying about sin.

It is best to recognize that the nature and culture of partnerships change over time because people change as people grow older. The character and persona of one's partners today will probably be different in the coming years, so the partnership agreement should have a way to gracefully exit with minimal damage to the exiting partner or the partnership itself.

This instruction accounts for all partnerships ending, some voluntarily, some involuntarily, and some through natural attrition. Exiting a partnership is not an implicit admission that the partnership or the individual partner has failed. However, if other partners move in an incompatible direction, then there is a need for one or more partners to enjoy the protection of an agreement that provides a legal way out of the partnership. So, at the outset, the partnership should not be created if there is resistance to entering a coherent, well–discussed, and well–written partner agreement that includes a clear exit process.

OTHER PERSONAL CHARACTERISTICS OF A POTENTIAL PARTNER A CHRISTIAN SHOULD CONSIDER BEFORE ENTERING A PARTNERSHIP

The personal character qualities of one's partner are immensely important. I have developed the following discussion of personal qualities through observation and experience. Christians entering a new business partnership should consider this discussion.

Character

The first quality to consider is commonly termed "character." In the Bible, "character" usually describes a person's moral and ethical features.[959] In Christian theology, the twin theologies of original integrity (also termed original righteousness) and original sin directly impact understanding and assessing a person's character.

The first thing to look for is if your potential partner has suffered and matured due to his or her experience. Consider Romans 5:3–5 (CSB):

> We rejoice in our afflictions, because we know that affliction produces endurance, ⁴endurance produces proven character, and proven character produces hope.

Godly character does not come naturally to us. Instead, when Adam sinned (Genesis 3:1–7), his sin resulted in losing his original integrity. Original integrity is defined as perfect conformity to the law of God by man as he was first created.[960] Adam's sin fundamentally changed his character in that his morality and ethics became depraved and inherently corrupted (Psalm 51:5, 58:3).[961]

Adam affected us all through his sin. Romans 5:12 (NIV) says this:

> Therefore, just as sin entered the world through one man, and death through sin, and in this way death came to all people, because all sinned.

Adam's loss of original righteousness was passed on to mankind through heredity at birth and negatively affected humanity's nature.[962] As a result, every person has a depraved character at birth. But God has made a path to redeem and heal humanity's depraved nature. Romans 5:17–18 (LEB) says,

> ¹⁷For if by the trespass of the one *man*, death reigned through the one *man*, much more will those who receive the abundance of grace and of the gift of righteousness reign in life through the one, Jesus Christ. 18 Consequently therefore, as through one trespass *came* condemnation to all people, so also through one righteous deed *came* justification of life to all people.

---

959 Faithlife, "Character," In *Logos Bible Study Factbook*. Accessed 08/13/2023. https://ref.ly/logos4/Factbook?ref=bk.%25character

960 Alan Cairns, *Dictionary of Theological Terms*. (Ambassador Emerald International, 2002), 317.

961 Milton S. Terry, *Biblical Dogmatics: An Exposition of the Principal Doctrines of the Holy Scriptures*. (Eaton & Mains; Jennings & Graham, 1907), 84.

962 Milton Valentine, *Christian Theology & 2*. (Lutheran Publication Society, 1906), 420–421.

The contrast between Adam and Christ is clear in these verses (and in the larger section of Romans 5:12–21). Paul stresses the superiority of grace to sin and Christ to Adam. The "abundance of grace" means that grace more than undoes the depraving effects of sin and is something that is undeserved by humanity ("free gift").[963]

Applying this discussion to business partnerships is important. Partners with a depraved character that the Holy Spirit has not regenerated will present more difficulties in relations and work habits than those who have been regenerated. While I have previously argued that other partners are not required by Scripture to be Christians for a Christian to enter a partnership, this brief discussion on the depravity of our characters adds emphasis to the notion of partnerships not lasting long or performing well if the grace of God has not undone the effects of sin in the partners' characters. So, as I suggested earlier, while Scripture does not require that one's partners are Christians, it is highly recommended that this be the case.

In addition, when assessing the character of a potential partner, one should look for an individual who has completed a class or two in what is commonly termed "the school of hard knocks." Good character is produced by endurance, which is produced through suffering:

> We rejoice in our sufferings, knowing that suffering produces endurance, and endurance produces character, and character produces hope, and hope does not put us to shame. (Romans 3:5 ESV).

By discussing their past business and personal experiences and observing their character and work product in the present, the CBO can learn the substance of another's character, both faults and strengths. The Christian should look for whether the other's character has matured through difficult experiences or whether the other's experiences have produced negative results, such as bitterness, cynicism, fear, or some other immaturity.

The core of another's character will often reveal itself only when stressful situations occur. Undeveloped or immature characters can wreak havoc on the partnership when stressful times come to the partnership. While these individuals may be highly talented and be good to work with 95% of the time, when a partner's dark side appears during stressful times, their 5% negative words and actions can outweigh the 95% positive work product and interactions.

Hence, a person considering joining an existing partnership or contemplating forming a new one should assess the potential partner's character over time and observe the partner(s) under stress. The quality and maturity of another's character can not be assessed until sufficient time has been consumed focusing on the other's character. This

---

963   Charles K. Barrett, *The Epistle to the Romans*. Rev Ed. (Continuum, 1991), 108.

exploratory relationship work is essential to building a healthy partnership. Nothing can replace the test of time as business professionals consider taking on a partner or forming a new partnership.

Communication

Communication is a second consideration for the CBO. What is in view here is not only the partner's ability to communicate a message well but also the content of the message because the content of the message reveals what is in the other's heart.

Three Scriptural passages come to mind when discussing communication. One is Ephesians 4:29 (NIV):

> Do not let any unwholesome talk come out of your mouths, but only what is helpful for building others up according to their needs, that it may benefit those who listen.

To have a good partnership, it is best if the partners keep their speech clean and encouraging. Clean speech is usually more difficult than coarse speech because the former requires a broader command of linguistics and more self–control. In addition, offering encouraging words is typically helpful in building unity and strength in relationships. Businesses benefit when communication is encouraging instead of being discouraging or uncivil.

Incivility, which is rude, unsociable, or impolite speech,[964] can cause significant damage to a partnership. Consider these realities of the effects of incivility in a business:[965]

- 53% of employees surveyed lost work time worrying about an uncivil incident and future interactions with the offender.
- 28% lost work time trying to avoid the offender.
- 37% reported a weakened sense of commitment to their organization.
- 22% reduced their efforts at work.
- 10% decreased the time they spent at work.
- 46% thought about changing jobs.
- 12% changed jobs.

A person should consider the effects of incivility on business and employment relationships before joining a partnership where one or more partners can be uncivil or rude in their

---

964 Dictionary.com, "Incivility." Accessed 08/17/2023. https://www.dictionary.com/browse/incivility
965 Christine Pearson and Christine Porath, *The Cost of Bad Behavior: How Incivility is Damaging Your Business.* (New York: Penguin Group, 2009), 31.

business interactions. Having worked with uncivilized types, I can attest that life is too short and no job is worth that much hassle.[966]

A second passage is Colossians 4:6 (LEB):

> Let your speech always *be* with grace, seasoned with salt, so that *you* may know how it is necessary for you to answer each one.

The "salt" is the power of Christ's grace, banishing all impurity of motive and all uncleanness of allusion, and at the same time, giving the pleasant savor of sound and nourishing "food for thought."[967] When compared to Ephesians 4:29, the focus of Colossians 4:6 is one of mature speech where the message itself is appropriate to the situation.[968]

Finally, Matthew 12:34 (CSB) reveals much about communication:

> Brood of vipers! How can you speak good things when you are evil? For the mouth speaks from the overflow of the heart.

Here, the emphasis is that the message reflects what is in the individual's heart who is speaking. A person does not become good from resolutions, such as "I shall be good."—but from being—that which is in a person's internal reservoirs: "Doing comes from being, fruit from roots, speech from hearts."[969] *If you want to know what is in another's heart—beliefs, values, emotions, conclusions, attitudes, and so forth—listen well to what that individual says and how they say it. The speech of any individual reflects what is in that person's heart.*

Compensation

Next on the list of qualities to look for is compensation, which is value given in payment for one's labor.[970] I am not simply referring to a salary or bonuses. The subject of compensation must include the joys of sharing in the profits and the risks of sharing in the losses.

---

966   At the age of fifteen, George Washington wrote down his rules for civility, published in a little–known set of papers later titled *George Washington's Rules of Civility*, (George Washington. *George Washington's Rules of* Civility. 1890. Moncure D. Conway, Ed. (digireads.com, 2004)). Washington had titled them *Rules of Civility and Decent Behavior in Company and Conversation.* Civility is important to showing respect and maintaining a certain decorum when work with others. Those that can't maintain civility injure themselves as well as others around them.

967   Handley Carr Glyn Moule, *The Epistle to the Colossians and to Philemon with Introduction and Notes.* The Cambridge Bible for Schools and Colleges. (Cambridge: Cambridge University Press, 1898), 136.

968   Erin K. Simpson and Frederick F. Bruce, *The Epistles to the Ephesians and the Colossians.* The New International Commentary on the Old and New Testament. (Wm. B. Eerdmans., 1957), 300–301.

969   Frederick Dale Bruner. *Matthew, Volume 1 The Christbook Matthew 1–12.* (Word, 1987), 464.

970   Faithlife, "Compensation," Accessed 08/18/2023. https://ref.ly/logos4/Factbook? ref=ws. Compensation.n.01.

A true partner is financially able and willing to shoulder the financial risk of the business, not just share in the company's profits.

It is unrealistic to think that a business will never experience a financial loss or need to be right–sized to be positioned for growth. "Every company—no matter how great—faces difficult times … They all have ups and downs."[971] In addition, business cycles happen—and they cannot be stopped or avoided by the business owner.[972] Every organism is born, lives for a while, and then dies. Every organization has a beginning and an end. In these life cycles, besides growth, there is always a downturn—when the organization constricts and, if not managed properly, will eventually die. During the downturn, the goal of management is to recognize the challenge in front of them and manage the organization into the next phase of growth. Their goal is to minimize the downturn but not avoid it. Instead, the downturn is captured as an opportunity to reset the organization for the next growth phase.[973]

When (not if) there is a downturn in the business, the chances are good that financial losses will occur if the partners do not properly right–size the business. When there is a loss, someone must pay for that loss. One of the undeniable truths of business is that *someone always pays for a loss*, especially when the company becomes bankrupt. Perhaps society bears the loss; maybe it is a bank or investors, but someone always pays for a loss.

The best partners can pay for a loss. Good partners can weather financial storms when (not if) the business has a downturn. If a partner can share in the risks, then the partner should share in the profits. The opposite is true: *if a person cannot or will not share in the risks, then that individual should not share in the profits and should not be a partner.*

Compatibility

In business partnerships, compatibility has to do with a co–existence that does not lead to constant friction or conflict. Compatibility speaks to the long–term governance aspect of a partnership. For a partnership, governance is as much about pre–deciding how future events will be managed as it is about completing day–to–day activities.

Pre–deciding future events via a partnership agreement is essential to the survival of the business and the partnership (if there are more than two partners) because compatibility between partners can change over time due to natural changes in individual partners. It is not uncommon for people to change as they age. A partner's interests, energy levels, needs, drive, and physical or intellectual capabilities can change. Sometimes, a partner stops working or disengages. An aging partner may not learn a new, essential technology.

---

971   Jim Collins, *Good to Great.* (HarperCollins, 2001), 213.

972   Todd Knoop, *Recessions and Depressions.* (Praeger Publishers, 2004), 15–20.

973   Ichaz Adizes, *Corporate Lifecycles: How and Why Corporations Grow and Die and What to do About it.* (Prentice Hall, 1988), 2–10.

Other life events can lead to incompatibility, such as illness, divorce, apathy, bankruptcy, or discontent.

Partnership agreements usually address at least these issues:
- Outside consulting activities and ventures.
- Sale of partnership interests.
- Confidentiality and non–compete agreements.
- Firm management.
- Allocation of net income and net losses.
- Compensation methods and allocations.
- Decision–making authorities.
- Ability to bind the partnership to legal commitments.
- Liquidation and Dissolution of Partnership.
- Triggering events, such as bankruptcy, felonies, and so forth.
- Ability to involuntarily terminate partner agreement.
- Leave of absence.
- Other elements that might arise based on the uniqueness of the partnership.

Partnerships can be an outstanding business structure if all parties are able and willing to abide by good governance, which helps to create compatibility between the partners. However, a partnership can be equally destructive to a business if there is a lack of compatibility because of poor governance. Be sure to enter partnerships with those who value good governance and a well–written partner agreement.

Competence

One last element to look for in a partner is competence, which is the ability to perform at a level that can achieve a goal or accomplish a task.[974] Each partner should be competent at what the partner does and have a right to expect the other partners to be competent too. Cloud writes:

People who become leaders, or really successful, tend to have three qualities. Number one, they have some set of competencies. In other words, they know their field, their industry, their discipline, or whatever. If you are Bill Gates, it helps to know something about the computer industry. If you are going to be a leading surgeon, you have to know what you are doing. In other words, you can only fake it for so long, boys. So, get yourself in the library or wherever and master your craft. Get good at what you do … You just have to get good at what you do, period. There are no shortcuts."[975]

974 Faithlife. "Ability," In *Logos Bible Study Factbook*. Accessed 08/18/23. https://ref.ly/logos4/Factbook?ref=bk.%25ability

975 Henry Cloud. *Integrity: The Courage to Meet the Demands of Reality*. (HarperCollins, 2006), 4–5.

Now, competence alone does not guarantee success in one's role as a partner. There are plenty of competent people who would make lousy partners. Therefore, the other partner characteristics need to be balanced with competence. Moreover, no matter the other's competence, if it can be outsourced to a third party, it may not be the proper skill set to look for in a new partner.

WHEN PARTNERSHIPS GO BAD

Over the years, I have observed that these six characteristics kill partnerships (and marriages, too). If a partnership has any single "A," it will introduce a difficulty that must be managed and resolved if possible. Two or more, and the partnership will die without intervention and substantive change. It does not matter which two characteristics are present. The partnership will die if two or more exist persistently.

Anger

It is difficult to work with angry partners. They shut down communication and cause others to walk on eggshells. They might be likable and competent when they are not angry, but their anger detracts from their effectiveness.

Anger can come from jealousy. We read in Genesis 4.2–7 (NIV):

Now Abel kept flocks, and Cain worked the soil. In the course of time Cain brought some of the fruits of the soil as an offering to the Lord. And Abel also brought an offering—fat portions from some of the firstborn of his flock. The Lord looked with favor on Abel and his offering, but on Cain and his offering he did not look with favor. So Cain was very angry, and his face was downcast. Then the Lord said to Cain, "Why are you angry? Why is your face downcast? If you do what is right, will you not be accepted? But if you do not do what is right, sin is crouching at your door; it desires to have you, but you must rule over it.

God accepted Abel's offering and not Cain's because Cain did not obey God. So, instead of admitting his sin, he became jealous of Abel, and his anger increased to the point where he killed him.

Anger can be a response to hearing the truth. Consider 2 Chronicles 16.7–10 (NIV):

At that time Hanani the seer came to Asa king of Judah and said to him. "Because you relied on the king of Aram and not on the Lord your God, the army of the king of Aram has escaped from your hand. Were not the Cushites and Libyans a mighty army with great numbers of chariots and horsemen? Yet when you relied on the Lord, he delivered them into your hand. For the eyes of the Lord range throughout the earth to strengthen those whose hearts are fully committed to him. You have done a foolish thing, and from now on you will be at war. Asa was angry with the seer because of this; he was so enraged that he put him in prison. At the same time Asa brutally oppressed some of the people.

Here we see Hanani giving a truthful message from God directly to Asa. Yet Asa responds with significant anger and puts Hanani in prison, then brutally oppresses his people.

Anytime a person responds to the truth with anger, you can count on this person being, at best, a difficult one with whom to work. *Angry people make horrible partners. There is not a more direct way to say it.* It would be best if you avoided them in business.

Moreover, if you partner with an angry person, get out as soon as possible. You will never really succeed in business with this type of person as your partner, and the stress of working with them is not worth it.

Anger can come from not getting your way. Entrepreneurs can look into the future and see what could be. For them, it is nearly as real as their present–day reality. But when others get in their way of achieving their dream, they can become frustrated and angry.

Finally, some use anger to manipulate others. They purposefully get angry to redirect, focus, or motivate a team. I find manipulation to be a form of lying and an admission that the one who uses anger as a management tool lacks more mature, sophisticated ways of leading a team to success. Using anger as a management tool should not be characteristic of a Christian in business.

The command to avoid angry people applies to one's decision about joining or remaining in a partnership. Proverbs 22:24–25 (LEB) says:

^{24} Do not befriend an owner of anger, and with a man of wrath you shall not associate; ^{25} lest you learn his way and become entangled in a snare to yourself.

Dr. Waltke sums up these two verses well:

Do not associate yourself with a hothead ... whose judgment is clouded by irrational thought and who loses all sense of proportion, acts impetuously, often in a terrifying way, and is incapable of measured utterance. The quick–tempered is like a bomb with a short fuse, ready to explode at any moment with devastating consequences ... The habits of the hothead are both infectious and lethal ... In addition to involving his companions in deep trouble, the hothead conforms them to his image. And so introduces the inevitable consequences of taking to oneself the underhanded dangers of that life–style. [There is] a trap [that] signifies lethal hidden danger. By associating with the hothead, one becomes fatally involved even before he becomes aware of it himself...The metaphor is ironic. One avoids traps to save one's life, not fetches them to kill one's self.^{976}

While it is common for us to get frustrated and perhaps occasionally angry in business, anger should not be characteristic of our lives or a management pattern.

---

976   Bruce K. Waltke, The Book of Proverbs, Chapters 15–31. (Wm. B. Eerdmans, 2005), 232.

Christian business owners and ministry leaders[977] should be slow to become angry (James 1:19). Why? Because our anger does not accomplish the good we think it will (James 1:20). If you want to see your employees' behavior permanently change for the better, getting mad at them will not help.

Apathy

James 4:17 (NIV) says:

> If anyone, then, knows the good they ought to do and doesn't do it, it is sin for them.

What James has in mind here is the situation in which you have the means to do good, an opportunity to do good, and a person who needs your act of goodness, so you are faced with a choice: should you help or not? James says that if we choose not to help, this is sin.

Not helping is called *apathy*. Apathy is a sin of omission. There can be medical or emotional causes for apathy, but the type I am talking about is more about a heart that does not care. Whether it is apathy toward God's plans for our lives or apathy toward others, the principle is the same: not caring about another's needs when you have the opportunity to help is a sin.

In a partnership, apathy is often seen as not wanting to be bothered. A partner may quietly withdraw, lessening his contribution to the firm. Others may observe that the partner does not have the same quality or intensity of care or concern he once had for the firm's products and services, customers, partners, vendors, etc.

You cannot manage or fix apathy in another person. All you can do is react to it. Once apathy solidifies, you must look for ways to end or exit the partnership. Just like servant–leadership does work when the other does not want to be led, apathetic partners cannot be motivated to change. They will become millstones around your neck.

An apathetic partner is one example of when a well–written partner agreement with good governance will help you manage the situation as well as possible.

---

977 I've known a number of ministry leaders who get angry quickly. Their anger dishonors God and damages his church. Some of the most angry managers I have observed are Senior Pastors of churches. They may not yell and scream, but they are curt, short, demeaning, discounting, or rude when they are challenged or do not get their way. All of those characteristics (and more) are forms of anger. They may be gifted communicators, but they can be as mean as a junkyard dog behind closed doors. As an example, watch this interview of Kenneth Copeland. Careful attention to his demeanor will reveal that he was very angry with the reporter's questions, but he covered up his anger quickly. (Inside Edition. "Full Interview: Preacher Kenneth Copeland Defends Lavish Lifestyle." 0:50/11:56. https://www.youtube.com/watch?v=9LtF34MrsfI)

Affairs

While a person's private life is his or her private life, sexual or emotional affairs can present, in some scenarios, tough situations that need to be addressed.

First, if a divorce is in process, the partner agreement should provide a process for protecting the other partners and the firm's assets to preclude the transfer of units or shares to the divorced spouse, who may or may not have any interest or ability to contribute to the partnership meaningfully. No one should be forced to be in a legal partnership with a divorced spouse.

A partner agreement may prescribe what to do when an affair is with a firm employee or someone employed elsewhere. The partners should have a process to follow that protects the partnership and the unoffending partners so that the business can continue.

Even if all the partners are Christ followers, do not think affairs cannot happen. Affairs can and do occur. Affairs reveal character defects that are likely damaging other parts of your firm. And if word gets out—which it likely will—it could seriously damage your company's reputation, not to mention expose your company to expensive liability.

Do not ignore the professional effects of personal affairs. Dealing with affairs is sticky and messy but must be dealt with decisively.

Abuse

Abuse is deliberately misusing one's power or privileges that injure others while enhancing your station. Verbally, abuse includes deliberately insulting other people.[978]

The Bible clearly warns against the abuse of others by those in power. Business owners, by definition, have ultimate power within their businesses. Abusing others by the misuse of your privileges as a business owner is sin.

The Bible warns against employers abusing employees (Ephesians 6:9, Leviticus 25:43, and Deuteronomy 24:14). The fact that there are warnings means this will be a temptation to sin for you as a business owner. In reality, your temptations as a *Christian* business owner might be more intense because the powers who oppose God will want to destroy you through your sin while dragging Christ's name through the mud.

Abuse of power exists in families (Ephesians 6:4, Colossians 3:21), churches (1 Peter 5:2–3, Ezekiel 34:2–7), foreign relations (Exodus 22:21, 23:9), rich over the poor (Exodus 22:22, Proverbs 22:22, Ezekiel 22:9), and general leadership activities (Matthew 20:25–27, Mark 10:42–44).

---

978 Faithlife, "Abuse." In *Logos Bible Study Factbook*. (Faithlife, August 25, 2024.) https://ref.ly/logos4/Factbook?id=ref%3abk.%25abuse.

Addictions

I won't say much here about the harmful effects addictions can have on your partnership other than to point out the obvious: one who is in bondage to addiction will likely not make a good partner. Their addiction will consume them and will make it extremely difficult for them to be a good partner. It is best to cut ties with a partner who has an addiction and move on.

An exception to my seemingly harsh recommendation is giving as much forgiveness, grace, and support to an addicted partner seeking treatment and freedom. While I favor cutting ties with a partner living in addiction for the health of the partnership itself, I also (highly) favor giving grace and forgiveness to a partner who is seeking wholeness and healing in Jesus Christ. Gaining freedom is not easy, is always messy, and is never a linear process. Giving grace and forgiveness to an addicted partner seeking treatment may improve the health of the partnership itself.

To the extent the addicted partner is putting in effort and time to find freedom, other partners may decide to walk with their addicted partner through the process.

Arrogance

The Bible has much to say about arrogance. Arrogance is one of the core characteristics of a wicked person. Arrogance is expressed in heart attitudes. Mark 7.21–22 says:

> What comes out of a person is what defiles them. For it is from within, out of a person's heart, that evil thoughts come—sexual immorality, theft, murder, adultery, greed, malice, deceit, lewdness, envy, slander, arrogance and folly. All these evils come from inside and defile a person." [979]

Arrogance is a problem of the heart. It is a belief in one's superiority or greater importance than others. Psalm 73.3–12 (NIV) says:

For I envied the arrogant when I saw the prosperity of the wicked. They have no struggles; their bodies are healthy and strong. They are free from common human burdens; they are not plagued by human ills. Therefore pride is their necklace; they clothe themselves with violence. From their callous hearts comes iniquity; their evil imaginations have no limits. They scoff, and speak with malice; with arrogance they threaten oppression. Their mouths lay claim to heaven, and their tongues take possession of the earth. Therefore their people turn to them and drink up waters in abundance. They say, "How would God know? Does

---

979 NIV Mark 7.20–23

the Most High know anything?" This is what the wicked are like— always free of care, they go on amassing wealth.

In human terms, these people described in Psalm 73 are strong. They look good. They are prosperous and seemingly have no struggles. However, their pride and superiority make them violent without limits to their evil. They oppress others and act as if God is stupid—if He even exists at all. And they are wealthy and hoard it.

But in God's economy, they are weak, lost, haters of God, and lovers of evil. They are "living the dream"—being "on top." God will one day bring them low, and they, too, like everyone else who has ever lived, will bow their knee to Jesus Christ and "acknowledge that Jesus Christ is Lord, to the glory of God the Father." (Philippians 2:10–11 NIV)

Arrogance is rebellion against God. Consider Nehemiah 9:16–17 (NIV):

Our ancestors became arrogant and stiff–necked, and they did not obey your commands. They refused to listen and failed to remember the miracles you performed among them. They became stiff–necked and in their rebellion appointed a leader in order to return to their slavery.

In addition, rebellion is equated to divination:

For rebellion is like the sin of divination, and arrogance like the evil of idolatry. Because you have rejected the word of the Lord, he has rejected you as king. (1 Samuel 15:23 NIV)

Arrogance is a rejection of God while setting up oneself as god—so it is idolatry too. It is all that God hates. And if you live your life in arrogance, remember that God will *always* oppose you (James 4.6).

Arrogant people are those with whom it is tough to work. They are rebellious and usually not team players. Often, they are exceptionally talented, crazy–smart people who bring interesting competencies to the table. However, they can make the mistake of thinking that if they are highly competent in a few areas, they must also be qualified in most other areas. So they become highly opinionated people about things they know little about. You'll find this combination of talent and opinion difficult for a partnership.

Arrogant people:
- Are difficult to coach.
- Have a strong need to be right all the time.
- Unwilling to be emotionally vulnerable.
- Have slippery ethics—the ends usually justify the means.
- Lack gratitude for what other people do for them.
- Often lack genuine concern for others.
- Often preoccupied with themselves.
- Often demeaning of others.

Arrogance is never helpful to a partnership. If you find a successful partner becoming increasingly arrogant, then know a time is coming when you'll be faced with a difficult decision to end or exit the partnership (1 Corinthians 1:28–31, Isaiah 2:17–18, 1 Samuel 15:23).

SUMMARY

In this chapter on partnerships, I have written more out of experience than the Scriptures. I have suggested there are key character traits to look for in others who will become your partner. I have also suggested that there are certain character traits to avoid—traits that kill good partnerships.

In the next chapter, we'll focus more closely on how we define ourselves in Christ. I'll suggest that ambient to Biblical stewardship is understanding our identity in Christ.

CHAPTER 19

FINISHING WELL

How we end our lives is vital for several reasons. First, the Bible repeatedly talks about being faithful until the end, and only then does it say we have "overcome." Second, finishing well means leaving behind a legacy of material and non-material goods that will bless our children and communities. Third, the quality of our life is judged by how we end, causing some to accept our example and others to reject how we lived.

In this chapter, I will argue for two core points. First, selling your business in exchange for cash is not prohibited in Scripture. Second, while we will slow down as we age, we must remain productive to the extent we can. The idea of retiring to a life of leisure and play is antithetical to stewardship in the Bible.

YOU WILL LEAVE your business someday. The question is not "if" but "how." There are only three ways an owner can leave his business: a sale, a liquidation, or death. The latter is not preferred since, usually, the untimely death of the owner swiftly devalues the business, and one's family is left with both the reality of grieving and the task of selling the business (if no one is available to run it).[980]

---

980 In some situations, the 2nd generation is ready to take the reigns of the business and move forward, but in most situations I have seen, they have not been ready or they never had interest in the business, so a "fire sale" ensued.

Liquidation—bankruptcy—is even more undesirable since the business becomes worthless, and there is nothing to sell. Exchanging the value of the business for something of other value, usually money, is the preferred method of leaving one's business. The Bible has some thoughts on this matter, so selling your business is the focus of the next section.

CONVENTIONAL WISDOM ON SELLING YOUR BUSINESS

This section is not intended to thoroughly review how to sell your business or when. But I will cover some aspects I have found important in my limited sell-side work and observing other sale processes.

You know you are ready to sell your business when you want to do something else, life events indicate you should sell, your industry is on a downhill slope, or you have lost your edge and passion for the business.[981] Also, entering a sale transaction is no cavalier task. There is a nearly universal agreement in the conventional wisdom literature that you must know why you are selling because your reasons are significant and personal, and will dictate the direction of the terms of the transaction.[982] The ideal time to start thinking about selling your company is when you start your business because some early decisions have long-term consequences that could enhance or detract from your sale.[983] But in reality, most owners do not consider selling until nearing retirement. Most do not understand that selling one's business is a six to twelve-month process, often with an additional three to nine-month pre-sales process to prepare the company for a sale.

When you sell, having a group of advisors in your corner is best. These advisors, if they are competent, will push you to the point of irritation several times, forcing you to produce and build documents that will be needed by the buyer and will present your business in the best light possible. Competent advisors know how due diligence works and will ask penetrating questions you may find ridiculous to answer. But your answers, in the long run, will help you sell your business because you will be prepared for the buyer's questions.

In addition, conventional wisdom would advise you to be sure you are financially ready, that you are likely to get the price you desire, that your operation is a turn-key operation in which the buyer does not purchase headaches and problems, that you are not fighting any legal or regulatory battles, that your business has a strong growth path, that your financial

---

981 Lien De Pau, "Why Sell My Business? 3 Reasons, 1 Hurdle, and a Way Forward. April 10, 2024. Forbes.com. https://www.forbes.com/sites/liendepau/2024/04/10/why-sell-your-biz-3-reasons-1-hurdle-and-a-way-forward/. See also Lien De Pau, "7 Signs It's Time to Sell Your Business: A Straight-Talk Guide." March 4, 2024, forbes.com. https://www.forbes.com/sites/liendepau/2024/03/04/7-signs-its-time-to-sell-your-business-a-straight-talk-guide/.

982 Kristin McKenna, "How to Sell Your Business: What to do Before, During, and After the Sale." May 4, 2021, forbes.com. https://www.forbes.com/sites/kristinmckenna/2021/05/04/how-to-sell-your-business-what-to-do-before-during-and-after-the-sale/.

983 Sara Friedman, "How to Sell Your Business and Make a Successful Exit." August 24, 2022. Blog. hubspot.com. https://blog.hubspot.com/sales/sell-your-business

records are in order and have been reviewed by a third party, and you have secured the appropriate advisors to help you through the process.[984]

In terms of finding the right advisors, start with your panel of trusted advisors, and then, if you need more help, talk with others who have sold their business, learn who they used, and why. Then interview those individuals whom your business associates and friends have recommended.

Selling Truths

Now, no matter who you are, there are some truths about selling that you need to understand. These truths are my own observations and are presented in no particular order.

Your business is not worth what you think it is worth. No matter what your business is worth, the buyer will think it is worth less. The corollary is also true: Your business is usually worth more than the buyer thinks. This tension between the buyer and the seller usually produces the fair market value for a business.

Great ideas have no inherent value. I could spend pages telling stories about entrepreneurs with great ideas but could not get them to market and make money. Until you can monetize an idea, it is pragmatically worthless.[985]

Buyers will respect your hard work, but they pay for results, not effort. If your hard work does not lead to profits, buyers may admire it, but they will buy based on their criteria and reasons. You may want them to reward you for your hard work, but that's not how the world works.

Buyers pay based on multiples of profit. This multiple is based on EBITDA.[986] Usually, buyers don't pay a multiple of top-line revenue. In some industries, buyers may pay based on the value of your assets if you are in an asset-heavy industry. Fewer may pay a multiple of gross margin. Even fewer people may not care about margin because they want something unique in your business (such as IP or a customer list) that they plan to "tuck into" their business to make their business more profitable. Those buyers tend to be strategic buyers who will buy based more on how your business can extend theirs. Financial buyers (usually private equity or family offices) will be primarily about the numbers. Having said all this, nearly all buyers usually want a strong EBITDA, regardless of the basis for their offer.

---

984 Dennis Coughlin, "Seven Essentials When Preparing to Sell Your Business." May 29, 2024. Kiplinger.com. https://www.kiplinger.com/business/sell–your–business–how–to–prepare. Most books and articles on preparing to sell your business will highlight these themes, though different authors may package and view these general themes in different ways.

985 To this end, you may want to read Constance Lutoff-Carroll, *From Innovation to Cash Flows: Value Creation by Structuring High Technology Alliances.* (Wiley, 2009).

986 Adam Hayes, "EBITDA: Definition, Calculation Formulas, History, and Criticisms." September 6, 2024, investopedia.com. https://www.investopedia.com/terms/e/ebitda.asp.

The value of your business is not what it could become. I have witnessed sellers want 8x or 10x of meager EBITDA because of "what this business could be." Buyers will not pay you for their efforts to grow your business after the transaction closes. Buyers pay for the present state of your business, not for your dreams of what could be in the future.

Without reliable financials aligning with the business's larger narrative, good buyers will walk away every time. As an example of walking away, for a business I operated in the past, we looked at a small "tuck-under" business with over $100,000 net profit on their income statement with $1M annual revenue. But when we looked at their customer data and sales transactions, we could only find ~$800,000 of revenue. Their sales data and income statement were "off" by $200,000 (for such a small business, this was a big number). The sellers and their representatives could not account for the difference, so their financial and sales data became worthless to us. We were unsure what the true numbers were.

But we were a strategic buyer, so incorporating their customers and services aligned so well with what we were doing that we decided to offer an earn-out-only purchase: the seller would get a percentage of the gross margins we could generate for two years with no guarantees and no money paid at closing.

The seller was offended because the seller's agent had told her she would get at least $4M for her business (do not ask me how that agent arrived at that number). Our offer would have likely given her something in the range of $100,000 (basically 1x of net income, assuming her numbers were accurate). But we were not about to put money down for a business whose financials and sales data did not align. When we pointed out the incongruence to the agent, he was (literally) speechless.

This story points to two things. First, the seller's advisor/representative was either lazy or incompetent (I don't say this lightly). He had created the expectation of $4M at closing (assuming 4x of top-line revenue), but had not done his due diligence on her business because he took her word that her numbers "tied out.". Had he done his homework, he would not have taken her to market without getting her numbers aligned to support the narrative of her business. Second, when you go to sell, all of your data needs to align, "tie out," balance, and make sense. If it does not, the value of your business will go down quickly. It is likely that most buyers will walk away mainly because they do not trust your numbers.[987]

The buyers need good agents, too. The best deals include competent advisors who have experience buying and selling businesses and understand how the due diligence process works.

Most sell-side advisors will not want you in the room when negotiating with the buyers. Their desire to not have you in the room is due to the emotional nature of selling your business. Your emotions will go up and down. These deals often have unexpected twists and turns that can emotionally pull you in myriad directions. It is best to trust your advisor to negotiate skillfully on your behalf and to stay out of the room.

987 Investing in a Quality of Earnings report, though costly, may be worth the expense. Talk with your accounting professional for more information.

You may be wealthy for one year. Due to how the American tax system works, the year you sell will likely see your income at an inflated level. You may be considered "rich" that year and will pay much more in federal and (perhaps) state taxes. Consult with your tax advisor at least a year before selling so that you can shift as much of the earnings to capital gains treatment instead of ordinary income.

The higher the purchase price, the more risk-averse buyers become. Angel investors will have a higher tolerance for risk than financial (private equity) or strategic (in the same or complementary industry) buyers. The reason buyers do so much due diligence is that they have a low tolerance for risk, so they dive into the details to ensure they are not spending money on a business that looks good on the surface but has underlying problems that will cost them more money to resolve after the sale.

You MUST have a firm idea of what God calls you to do after the sale. Conventional wisdom says that business owners must have something to "retire to," which is their way of saying that the owner must have a purpose to turn his attention toward after the transaction is completed. I have met more than a few owners who sold, only to "fail" at retirement. They could not relax and "take it easy," so they started another business. If you do not have something deeply purposeful to turn your attention to after your business sells, you are likely not ready to sell your business.

In family succession for a business, most 1st generation wait too long to pass their business to their children. I know of one owner who took a $20M business from his father and turned it into an $800M+ business, but he will not pass it on to his sons until he dies. His sons (he had no daughters) will be in their sixties or early seventies when he dies. This is selfish on his part. He should have transitioned his business to them ten years ago.

One of the pre-sale tasks is to separate personal and business expenses. Most business owners treat their business checking account as a slush fund for personal expenses. However, buyers will only want to see business-related financial data. So, backing out everyday personal expenses like auto leases, club memberships, and the like is essential before taking one's business to market. Backing out personal expenses will give the buyers a more accurate picture of the performance of your business.

BIBLICAL WISDOM ON SELLING YOUR BUSINESS

There is much in conventional wisdom to embrace when you are selling your business. And there is much to embrace if you are a family business implementing a succession plan for the next generation to take over both the management and the ownership of your business.

The Bible illustrates the sale of business assets, but does not directly teach on this topic. An illustration is Jacob purchasing some of the flock from Laben in Genesis

30:25–36. In this story, Jacob is finished working for Laban after fourteen years of service. He now wants to move on and establish his own family. In the story, Laban and Jacob strike a deal in which Jacob will continue to shepherd Laban's flocks but in return, he gets to take a portion of Laban's business by taking all of the spotted animals as his. Jacob negotiates a way to start his own business and use sweat equity to acquire the assets he needs to get started. Laban 'sold' some of his business in exchange for Jacob's continued labor.

In the NT, the exchange of something tangible for money is in the parable of the hidden treasure (Matthew 13:44) and the pearl of great value (Matthew 13:45–46 ESV). Here are the two parables:

> [44] "The kingdom of heaven is like treasure hidden in a field, which a man found and covered up. Then in his joy he goes and sells all that he has and buys that field. [45] "Again, the kingdom of heaven is like a merchant in search of fine pearls, [46] who, on finding one pearl of great value, went and sold all that he had and bought it."

In both parables, there is an exchange of an asset for money, which is exchanged again for another asset. In the parable of the hidden treasure, all that the man owns is sold to purchase a field. In the parable of the pearl of great value, all that the man owns is sold to purchase the pearl. What catches my attention for this discussion is that the fair exchange of an asset for money is not forbidden in Scripture. There is no indication that God disapproves of exchanging an asset for money. In addition, such an exchange is illustrated in Acts 4:34–37 (ESV):

> [34] There was not a needy person among them, for as many as were owners of lands or houses sold them and brought the proceeds of what was sold 35 and laid it at the apostles' feet, and it was distributed to each as any had need. 36 Thus Joseph, who was also called by the apostles Barnabas (which means son of encouragement), a Levite, a native of Cyprus, 37 sold a field that belonged to him and brought the money and laid it at the apostles' feet."

While an argument from silence, there is no indication that exchanging an asset for money is inherently wrong or sinful. Hence, a Christian business owner does not sin by exchanging the value of his business for cash or cash equivalents.

CONVENTIONAL WISDOM ON RETIREMENT

Retirement is often viewed as a single event in a person's life wherein that individual leaves paid employment to lead a tranquil and peaceful life.[988] Retirement in America is defined largely in negative terms, such as what people are *not* doing—e.g., not working for pay.[989] The rise of retirement—as a concept and an accepted practice—began in the 1880s. It occurred roughly simultaneously in Europe, Britain, and the United States. The rise of retirement was driven by two core factors: older people living longer and a deterioration in mental and physical capabilities while they were still alive.[990]

The conventional wisdom about the "success" (if one can use that term) of retirement is mixed. For some, retirement is a reward for working hard over several decades.[991] Yet others retire and continue to work. For example, many retirees start a new job (even if unpaid) or a new business after retirement. The average age of a new business owner in America is over fifty-five,[992] sometimes preceded by a layoff event in the person's life.[993] In addition, research estimates that 25% of retirees start new businesses, many using the skills and experiences gained during a corporate career.[994]

Retirement is associated with a decline in health. Research has found a positive correlation between retirement and the risk of being diagnosed with a new chronic condition that is cardiovascular or cancerous.[995] In addition, other research has found that those who retire and do not work experience a significant negative effect on cognitive functioning,[996] leaving these individuals at a greater risk for various types of dementia.[997]

---

988 H. Hodkinson, "Learning to work no longer: exploring 'retirement.'" *Journal of Workplace Learning.* 2010. (22)1/2:94–103.

989 Frank T. Denton & Byron G. Spencer, "What is Retirement? A Review and Assessment of Alternative Concepts and Measures." *Canadian Journal on Aging.* 2009. (28)1:63–76.

990 Dora L. Costa, The Evolution of Retirement: An American Economic History, 1880–1990. (University of Chicago Press, 1998), 6–31.

991 Patrick Skerrett, "Is Retirement Good for Health or Bad for it?" December 10, 2012, health.harvard. edu. https://www.health.harvard.edu/blog/is–retirement–good–for–health–or–bad–for–it–201212105625

992 US Chamber of Commerce, "Small Business Data Center." Accessed 10/01/2024. Uschamber. com. https://www.uschamber.com/small–business/small–business–data–center.

993 ClarifyCapital, "From Fired to Founder." October 23,2023, clarifycapital.com. https://clarifycapital. com/from–fired–to–founder.

994 John Timpane, "More Adults Over 50 Starting Their Own Businesses." November 15, 2019. Aarp. org. https://www.aarp.org/work/small–business/older–adults–becoming–entrepreneurs/.

995 Stefanie Behncke, "Does Retirement Trigger Ill Health?" *Health Economics,* 2012. (21)3:282–300.

996 Eric Bonsang & Stephane Adam, "Does Retirement Affect Cognitive Functioning?" *Journal of Health Economics.* 2012, (31)3:490–501.

997 Cella Wright, "Think Retirement is Smooth Sailing? A Look at its Potential Effects on the Brain." July 2, 2019, ideas.ted.com. https://ideas.ted.com/think–retirement–is–smooth–sailing–a–look–at–its–potential–effects–on–the–brain/.

Conventional wisdom recommends the following elements if one is going to retire happy:[998]

- Be a saver, not a spender, but do not be miserly
- Have interests that capture one's attention
- Have healthy, daily routines that help you take your health seriously
- Stay close to one's family
- Create a new identity that is not connected to work or career
- Stay connected to friends
- Be willing to get outside one's comfort zone
- Invest for income returns, not increase in portfolio size

BIBLICAL WISDOM ON RETIREMENT

If the word 'retirement' means to cease productive work and live one's life comfortably and easily, then 'retirement' is not a choice a Christian business owner can make without sinning. However, if 'retirement' means "to cease working for compensation," then it appears that a 'working retirement' can be lived out Biblically. The focus is on being productive—to the extent one can—until God calls one home. There is ample Biblical support for being productive in purposeful work, as much as one reasonably can, until death.

2 Thessalonians 3:10 (NIV) says, "The one who is unwilling to work shall not eat." Being productive is associated with supporting oneself (and others, presumably). Keener[999] believes this verse is also an instruction from Paul to the Thessalonian church (and other churches by extension) that a non–disabled person who refuses to work, because that person is lazy, should not be provided food through the church's care programs. Hendriksen agrees: "If he refuses to work, let him go hungry. That may teach him a lesson."[1000]

In Paul's teaching, no age limitation on work is mentioned. No matter how old a Christian becomes, that person should be productive, even if that individual is not earning an income from their productivity. One's capacity to work will deteriorate as one ages, so the expectation is that one works at the level one can, given one's age. 2 Thessalonians 3:10 precludes a Christian from living off the productivity and generosity of others when he can work and provide (or help provide) for himself. This passage does not preclude a Christian from living off savings from the individual's past productivity, but such a Christian should still engage in productive, meaningful work.

---

998 Bruce Horovitz, "10 Secrets of a Happy Retirement." December 9, 2021, aarp.org. https://www.aarp.org/retirement/planning–for–retirement/info–2021/happy–retirement–secrets.html.

999 Craig S. Keener, *The IVP Bible Background Commentary: New Testament* (InterVarsity Press, 1993), 2 Thessalonians 3:10, np.

1000 William Hendriksen and Simon J. Kistemaker, *Exposition of I–II Thessalonians*. Vol. 3. New Testament Commentary. (Baker Books, 1953–2001), 201–02.

Work and Retirement

Work is a gift from God that existed before sin entered the world (Genesis 2:8), and God worked to create the world (Genesis 2:2). We will work throughout eternity as we reign with Christ (Revelation 5:10). Work is not an activity to be avoided or resisted. Psalm 92:12–15 (NIV) indicates that Christians should be productive throughout their older years.

> [12] The righteous will flourish like a palm tree, they will grow like a cedar of Lebanon; [13] planted in the house of the Lord, they will flourish in the courts of our God. [14] They will still bear fruit in old age, they will stay fresh and green, [15] proclaiming, "The Lord is upright; he is my Rock, and there is no wickedness in him."

The Hebrew translated "bear fruit" means to sprout, to germinate, to increase.[1001] What is in view here is a freshness that can only come with age.[1002] In the Lord's favor, the righteous are sustained and productive even in old age. The elderly's health and vitality are attributed to living in God's presence.

The Scriptures contain examples of those who worked until they passed. For example, when God took Moses to Mount Nebo to die (Deuteronomy 32:48–52; 34:1–12), the writer noted that Moses' eyesight and physical strength were fully present. Moses could have worked many more years and was productive until his death. While the Mosaic law fixed the retirement age for Levites at age fifty (Number 8:25), retired priests continued to work mentoring younger priests. The New Testament accounts of Zechariah, the father of John the Baptist, the apostle Paul, and John all provide a basis for working until the end of life. Figure 19–1 illustrates the differences between conventional wisdom and Biblical wisdom regarding retirement.

1001 W. Gesenius, S.P. Tregelles, *Gesenius' Hebrew and Chaldee lexicon to the Old Testament Scriptures.* (Logos Bible Software, 2003) 157–58.

1002 Derek Kidner, *Psalms 73–150: An Introduction and Commentary.* Vol. 16. Tyndale Old Testament Commentaries. (InterVarsity Press, 1975), 369.

Figure 19–1: Summary of conventional wisdom and Biblical wisdom regarding retirement

SUMMARY

In this chapter, I have demonstrated that exchanging the ownership of your business for cash or other instruments is not sin. Also, I have demonstrated that a life of retirement to leisure and play should not be engaged by a CBO. Instead, we should be as reasonably product as possible until the day we pass to be with the Lord.

EPILOGUE

I HAVE SPENT ten years writing this content. In one sense, I'm glad I'm done. In another sense, I'm sad. Finishing this book is like saying goodbye to a good friend.

Moving forward, I want to call on Christian academicians hither and yon. Numerous areas need more research and thoughtful reflection. Some areas of potential integration have not even been broached in this book. I hope other academics and industry leaders will pick up on what I have done and extend it with their own thinking and research. I hope that one day, colleges and seminaries will always include an integrative class in their business and theological tracks similar to this book. And I hope that someday, the Christian community will have a shared, common understanding of what it means to be a Christian business owner from a theological perspective.

No ministry exists without business operations, and every business is a ministry. Both theology and business need each other. The siloed approaches in our colleges and seminaries have killed our abilities to live and think theologically before we live and think professionally, regardless of vocation or area of inquiry. Every Christian, regardless of vocation, should be a theologian first and a professional second.

Thank you for taking the time to read this book. I hope you allow God to transform who you are by reading this book. I know I have been transformed by writing it.

ACKNOWLEDGMENTS

WHERE TO START? I want to thank those who reviewed parts or the entire book to help make this a better product. These include Bruce Powers, Steve Douglas, Randy Somercik, Bill Turcotte, Rolf Engwall, Kathy English, David English, Andy Schwandt, Dr. Dale Hutchcraft, Dr. Paul Miantona, Fred Noble, and Rick Mattsen.

I want to thank my wife, Kathy, for enduring the ups and downs of entrepreneurship and the constant changes in income, financial security, and our future. It takes a special person to be married to someone like me. Kathy, you are a GREAT life partner. I also want to thank David and Anna—the two best children anyone could ever have—for following God and committing their lives wholly to the Lord.

Last and foremost, I want to thank Jesus Christ, who gave me the call, talent, and passion to author this content and without whom I would be lost forever.

Bill English, PhD
April 2025
Maple Grove, Minnesota

ERRATA

AS I DRAW to the end of writing this book, I feel a bit like Pilate: "What I have written, I have written." (John 19:22 ESV). But unlike the Scriptures—which are perfect and flawless in the original autographs—it is impossible to write and publish a book like this without some mistakes in it.

This book is the twentieth book I have authored or co-authored. Every book I have ever published has had something wrong with it. Of course, I don't know where the mistakes are, but sometimes readers are kind enough to let me know, and I can fix them before the next printing occurs.

So, if you find a mistake—a typo, a misspelling, an incorrect cross-reference, an awkward sentence, etc.—would you be so kind as to let me know? You can email me at bill@bibleandbusiness.com.

Thank you!

ABOUT BILL ENGLISH, PHD

BILL ENGLISH IS an experienced entrepreneur, author, speaker, and business advisor specializing in small–business ownership issues. Bill draws on his experience in leading companies to help business owners through difficult transitions and turnarounds.

Bill led a national training company for twelve years. He has also served as CEO for a $2M retail company, a $23M warehouse/distribution company, and a $25M healthcare company with 550 employees. He now works as an executive coach (onpathcoaching.com) for faith-based business owners who aspire to improve their performance as business owners.

Bill holds two master's degrees, one in divinity and the other in counseling psychology, both from Trinity Evangelical Divinity School. He has a PhD in Business Management from the International Business Relations Network (Berlin) in partnership with Kairos University (formerly North American Baptist Seminary) in Sioux Falls, SD. He holds two post-graduate certificates from Villanova University, one in strategic organizational leadership and the other in business process management, and a third post-graduate certificate in negotiations from the University of Notre Dame.

Bill is a Minnesota Licensed Psychologist (MA, LP) and holds a post-graduate certificate in Bowen Family Therapy from the Minnesota Institute of Family Dynamics. He is certified to use the Hogan Leadership Assessment tools and is a Myers–Briggs MBTI Certified Practitioner. Bill is also a Rule 114 Minnesota Qualified Neutral (inactive).

Bill has written fourteen technical books (Exchange and SharePoint) for publishers like Addison Wesley, Sybex, Osborne McGraw Hill, and Microsoft Press. Bill was named a Microsoft Most Valuable Professional for eleven years (SharePoint). Bill has appeared weekly on Faith Radio (myfaithradio.com) for over eleven years to discuss integrating faith and business ownership.

He is the publisher of Bible and Business (bibleandbusiness.com) and offers executive coaching services through OnPath Coaching (onpathcoaching.com).

He has been married to Kathy for over thirty years. They have two adult children, David and Anna, and live in Minneapolis, Minnesota, where he describes summer as the best eleven days of the year!

OTHER WORKS BY BILL ENGLISH

Biblical Wisdom for Business Leaders
Working for a Difficult Boss: Lessons from the Life of Daniel
The Transformative Power of Generosity Toward God

CONNECT THROUGH SOCIAL MEDIA

YOU CAN CONNECT with Bill through social media and other means:

Email: bill@bibleandbusiness.com

Twitter: @biblebusiness

Facebook: www.facebook.com/bibleandbusiness

Facebook discussions: www.facebook.com/groups/bibleandbusiness

Instagram: www.instagram.com/Biblebusiness

LinkedIn: www.linkedin.com/company/9189201

Website: www.bibleandbusiness.com

YouTube: www.youtube.com/channel/bibleandbusiness

Now to him who is able to keep you from stumbling and to present you blameless before the presence of his glory with great joy, to the only God, our Savior, through Jesus Christ our Lord, be glory, majesty, dominion, and authority, before all time and now and forever. Amen.

(Jude 24-25 ESV)

To God be the glory! Great things He hath done!